PRAISE FOR SIMON JOHNSON AND JAMES KWAK'S *13 BANKERS*

"The best explanation yet for how the smart guys on Wall Street led us to the brink of collapse. In the process, Johnson and Kwak demystify our financial system, stripping it down to expose the ruthless power grab that lies at its center."

—Elizabeth Warren, Professor of Law, Harvard Law School;
Chair, TARP Congressional Oversight Panel

"Too many discussions of the Great Recession present it as a purely economic phenomenon. . . . Simon Johnson was the first to point out that this was and is a crisis of political economy. His and James Kwak's analysis of the unholy intertwining of Washington and Wall Street—a cross between the gilded age and a banana republic—is essential reading."

—Niall Ferguson, Professor of History, Harvard University;
Professor, Harvard Business School;
and author of *The Ascent of Money*

"A disturbing and painstakingly researched account of how the banks wrenched control of government and society out of our hands—and what we can do to seize it back." —Bill Moyers

"Essential reading for anyone who wants to understand what comes next for the world economy. Dangerous and reckless elements of our financial sector have become too powerful and must be reined in. If this problem is not addressed, there is serious trouble in all our futures."

—Nouriel Roubini, Professor of Economics, Leonard N. Stern
School of Business, New York University;
Chairman of Roubini Global Economics

SIMON JOHNSON AND JAMES KWAK
13 BANKERS

Simon Johnson is Ronald A. Kurtz Professor of Entrepreneurship at MIT's Sloan School of Management and a senior fellow of the Peterson Institute for International Economics. He is coauthor, with James Kwak, of *The Baseline Scenario*, a leading economic blog, described by Paul Krugman as "a must-read" and by Bill Moyers as "one of the most informative news sites in the blogosphere."

James Kwak has had a successful business career as a consultant for McKinsey & Company and as a software entrepreneur. He is currently a student at Yale Law School.

baselinescenario.com

13
BANKERS

13
BANKERS

*The Wall Street Takeover
and the Next Financial Meltdown*

SIMON JOHNSON AND JAMES KWAK

*Vintage Books
A Division of Random House, Inc.
New York*

FIRST VINTAGE BOOKS EDITION, JANUARY 2011

Copyright © 2010, 2011 by Simon Johnson and James Kwak

The Library of Congress has cataloged the Pantheon edition as follows:
Johnson, Simon.
13 bankers : the Wall Street takeover and the next financial meltdown /
Simon Johnson and James Kwak.
p. cm.
Includes bibliographical references and index.
1. Banks and banking—United States.   2. Bank failures—United States.
3. Finance—United States.   4. Financial crises—United States.
I. Kwak, James.   II. Title.   III. Title: Thirteen bankers.
HG2491.J646 2010 332.10973—dc22
2010000168

Vintage ISBN: 978-0-307-47660-9

*Author photographs © Anthony Armand Placet (Johnson) and
courtesy of the author (Kwak)
Book design by M. Kristen Bearse*

www.vintagebooks.com

Printed in the United States of America
10   9   8   7

TO OUR FAMILIES

They were careless people, Tom and Daisy—they smashed up things and creatures and then retreated back into their money or their vast carelessness, or whatever it was that kept them together, and let other people clean up the mess they had made.

—F. Scott Fitzgerald, The Great Gatsby[1]

Contents

13
BANKERS

INTRODUCTION

13 Bankers

My administration is the only thing between you and the pitchforks.
—Barack Obama, March 27, 2009[1]

Friday, March 27, 2009, was a lovely day in Washington, D.C.—but
not for the global economy. The U.S. stock market had fallen 40 percent in just seven months, while the U.S. economy had lost 4.1 million
jobs.[2] Total world output was shrinking for the first time since World
War II.[3]

Despite three government bailouts, Citigroup stock was trading
below $3 per share, about 95 percent down from its peak; stock in
Bank of America, which had received two bailouts, had lost 85 percent
of its value. The public was furious at the recent news that American
International Group, which had been rescued by commitments of up
to $180 billion in taxpayer money, was paying $165 million in bonuses
to executives and traders at the division that had nearly caused the
company to collapse the previous September. The Obama administration's proposals to stop the bleeding, initially panned in February,
were still receiving a lukewarm response in the press and the markets.
Prominent economists were calling for certain major banks to be
taken over by the government and restructured. Wall Street's way of
life was under threat.

That Friday in March, thirteen bankers—the CEOs of thirteen of
the country's largest financial institutions—gathered at the White

House to meet with President Barack Obama.* "Help me help you," the president urged the group. Meeting with reporters later, they toed the party line. White House press secretary Robert Gibbs summarized the president's message: "Everybody has to pitch in. We're all in this together." "I'm of the feeling that we're all in this together," echoed Vikram Pandit, CEO of Citigroup. Wells Fargo CEO John Stumpf repeated the mantra: "The basic message is, we're all in this together."[5]

What did that mean, "we're all in this together"? It was clear that the thirteen bankers needed the government. Only massive government intervention, in the form of direct investments of taxpayer money, government guarantees for multiple markets, practically unlimited emergency lending by the Federal Reserve, and historically low interest rates, had prevented their banks from following Bear Stearns, Lehman Brothers, Merrill Lynch, Washington Mutual, and Wachovia into bankruptcy or acquisition in extremis. But why did the government need the bankers?

Any modern economy needs a financial system, not only to process payments, but also to transform savings in one part of the economy into productive investment in another part of the economy. However, the Obama administration had decided, like the George W. Bush and Bill Clinton administrations before it, that it needed *this* financial system—a system dominated by the thirteen bankers who came to the White House in March. Their banks used huge balance sheets to place bets in brand-new financial markets, stirring together complex derivatives with exotic mortgages in a toxic brew that ultimately poisoned the global economy. In the process, they grew so large that their potential failure threatened the stability of the entire system, giving them a unique degree of leverage over the government. Despite the central role of these banks in causing the financial crisis and the recession, Barack Obama and his advisers decided that these were the banks the country's economic prosperity depended on. And so they dug in to

---

* The CEOs and their banks were Ken Chenault, American Express; Ken Lewis, Bank of America; Robert Kelly, Bank of New York Mellon; Vikram Pandit, Citigroup; John Koskinen, Freddie Mac; Lloyd Blankfein, Goldman Sachs; Jamie Dimon, JPMorgan Chase; John Mack, Morgan Stanley; Rick Waddell, Northern Trust; James Rohr, PNC; Ronald Logue, State Street; Richard Davis, US Bank; and John Stumpf, Wells Fargo. There were also two representatives of industry organizations at the meeting.[4]

defend Wall Street against the popular anger that was sweeping the country—the "pitchforks" that Obama referred to in the March 27 meeting.[6]

To his credit, Obama was trying to take advantage of the Wall Street crisis to wring concessions from the bankers—notably, he wanted them to scale back the bonuses that enraged the public and to support his administration's plan to overhaul regulation of the financial system. But as the spring and summer wore on, it became increasingly clear that he had failed to win their cooperation. As the megabanks, led by JPMorgan Chase and Goldman Sachs, reported record or near-record profits (and matching bonus pools), the industry rolled out its heavy artillery to fight the relatively moderate reforms proposed by the administration, taking particular aim at the measures intended to protect unwary consumers from being blown up by expensive and risky mortgages, credit cards, and bank accounts. In September, when Obama gave a major speech at Federal Hall in New York asking Wall Street to support significant reforms, not a single CEO of a major bank bothered to show up.[7] If Wall Street was going to change, Obama would have to use (political) force.

Why did this happen? Why did even the near-collapse of the financial system, and its desperate rescue by two reluctant administrations, fail to give the government any real leverage over the major banks?

By March 2009, the Wall Street banks were not just any interest group. Over the past thirty years, they had become one of the wealthiest industries in the history of the American economy, and one of the most powerful political forces in Washington. Financial sector money poured into the campaign war chests of congressional representatives. Investment bankers and their allies assumed top positions in the White House and the Treasury Department. Most important, as banking became more complicated, more prestigious, and more lucrative, the *ideology* of Wall Street—that unfettered innovation and unregulated financial markets were good for America and the world— became the consensus position in Washington on both sides of the political aisle. Campaign contributions and the revolving door between the private sector and government service gave Wall Street banks influence in Washington, but their ultimate victory lay in shifting the conventional wisdom in their favor, to the point where their lobbyists' talking points seemed self-evident to congressmen and administration officials. Of course, when cracks appeared in the consensus, such as in the aftermath of the financial crisis, the banks could still roll out their conventional weaponry—campaign money and lobbyists; but because of their ideological power, many of their battles were won in advance.

The political influence of Wall Street helped create the laissez-faire environment in which the big banks became bigger and riskier, until by 2008 the threat of their failure could hold the rest of the economy hostage. That political influence also meant that when the government did rescue the financial system, it did so on terms that were favorable to the banks. What "we're all in this together" really meant was that the major banks were already entrenched at the heart of the political system, and the government had decided it needed the banks at least as much as the banks needed the government. So long as the political establishment remained captive to the idea that America needs big, sophisticated, risk-seeking, highly profitable banks, they had the upper hand in any negotiation. Politicians may come and go, but Goldman Sachs remains.

The Wall Street banks are the new American oligarchy—a group that gains political power because of its economic power, and then uses that political power for its own benefit. Runaway profits and bonuses in the financial sector were transmuted into political power through campaign contributions and the attraction of the revolving door. But those profits and bonuses also bolstered the credibility and influence of Wall Street; in an era of free market capitalism triumphant, an industry that was making so much money had to be good, and people who were making so much money had to know what they were talking about. Money and ideology were mutually reinforcing.

This is not the first time that a powerful economic elite has risen to political prominence. In the late nineteenth century, the giant industrial trusts—many of them financed by banker and industrialist J. P. Morgan—dominated the U.S. economy with the support of their allies in Washington, until President Theodore Roosevelt first used the antitrust laws to break them up. Even earlier, at the dawn of the republic, Thomas Jefferson warned against the political threat posed by the Bank of the United States.

In the United States, we like to think that oligarchies are a problem that other countries have. The term came into prominence with the consolidation of wealth and power by a handful of Russian business-men in the mid-1990s; it applies equally well to other emerging market countries where well-connected business leaders trade cash and political support for favors from the government. But the fact that our American oligarchy operates not by bribery or blackmail, but by the soft power of access and ideology, makes it no less powerful. We may have the most advanced political system in the world, but we also have its most advanced oligarchy.

In 1998, the United States was in the seventh year of an economic boom. Inflation was holding steady between 2 and 3 percent, kept down by the twin forces of technology and globalization. Alan Greenspan, probably the most respected economist in the world, thought the latest technology revolution would allow sustained economic growth with low inflation: "Computer and telecommunication based technologies are truly revolutionizing the way we produce goods and services. This has imparted a substantially increased degree of flexibility into the work-place, which in conjunction with just-in-time inventory strategies and increased availability of products from around the world, has kept costs in check through increased productivity."[8] Prospects for the American economy had rarely seemed better.

But Brooksley Born was worried.[9] She was head of the Commodity Futures Trading Commission (CFTC), the agency responsible for financial contracts known as derivatives. In particular, she was worried about the fast-growing, lightly regulated market for over-the-counter (OTC) derivatives—customized contracts in which two parties placed bets on the movement of prices for other assets, such as currencies, stocks, or bonds. Although Born's agency had jurisdiction over certain derivatives that were traded on exchanges, it was unclear if anyone had the authority to oversee the booming market for custom derivatives.

In 1998, derivatives were the hottest frontier of the financial ser-vices industry. Traders and salesmen would boast about "ripping the face off" their clients—structuring and selling complicated deals that clients did not understand but that generated huge profits for the bank

that was brokering the trade.[10] Even if the business might be bad for
their clients, the top Wall Street banks could not resist, because their
derivatives desks were generating ever-increasing shares of their profits while putting up little of the banks' own capital.* The global market
for custom derivatives had grown to over $70 trillion in face value (and
over $2.5 trillion in market value)† from almost nothing a decade
before.[11]

The derivatives industry had fought off the threat of regulation once
before. In 1994, major losses on derivatives trades made by Orange
County, California, and Procter & Gamble and other companies led to a
congressional investigation and numerous lawsuits. The suits uncovered, among other things, that derivatives salesmen were lying to clients,
and uncovered the iconic quote of the era, made by a Bankers Trust
employee: "Lure people into that calm and then just totally f—— 'em."[12]
Facing potential congressional legislation, the industry and its lobbying
group fought back, aided by its friends within the government. The
threat of regulation was averted, and the industry went back to inventing ever more complex derivatives to maintain its profit margins. By
1997, the derivatives business even had the protection of Greenspan,
who said: "[T]he need for U.S. government regulation of derivatives
instruments and markets should be carefully re-examined. The application of the Commodity Exchange Act to off-exchange transactions
between institutions seems wholly unnecessary—private market regulation appears to be achieving public policy objectives quite effectively
and efficiently."[13] In other words, the government should keep its hands
off the derivatives market, and society would benefit.

But Born was not convinced. She worried that lack of oversight

---

*Because the accounting treatment of derivatives was unclear, the amount of capital that
banks had to set aside for their derivatives positions was generally disproportionately low
compared to the amount of risk they were taking on. Because they could generate higher
profits with less capital, their "return on equity" was higher.

†Derivatives are essentially zero-sum transactions. The face value, or notional value, of a
derivative is the basis on which the value of the transaction is calculated. For example, in an
interest rate swap, the payments made by the two parties are calculated as interest rates (per-
centages) on the notional value; the amount of money that changes hands is much lower
than the notional value. The market value of a derivative contract is calculated by the Bank
for International Settlements as the current value of the contract to the party that is "in the
money"—in other words, the amount of money that would change hands in order to close
out the contract at this moment.

allowed the proliferation of fraud, and lack of transparency made it difficult to see what risks might be building in this metastasizing sector. She proposed to issue a "concept paper" that would raise the question of whether derivatives regulation should be strengthened. Even this step provoked furious opposition, not only from Wall Street but also from the economic heavyweights of the federal government—Greenspan, Treasury Secretary (and former Goldman Sachs chair) Robert Rubin, and Deputy Treasury Secretary Larry Summers. At one point, Summers placed a call to Born. As recalled by Michael Greenberger, one of Born's lieutenants, Summers said, "I have thirteen bankers in my office, and they say if you go forward with this you will cause the worst financial crisis since World War II."[14]

Ultimately, Summers, Rubin, Greenspan, and the financial industry won. Born issued the concept paper in May, which did not cause a financial crisis. But Congress responded in October by passing a moratorium prohibiting her agency from regulating custom derivatives.[15] In 1999, the President's Working Group on Financial Markets—including Summers, Greenspan, SEC chair Arthur Levitt, and new CFTC chair William Rainer—recommended that custom derivatives be exempted from federal regulation. This recommendation became part of the Commodity Futures Modernization Act, which President Clinton signed into law in December 2000.

We don't know which thirteen bankers were meeting with the deputy treasury secretary when he called Brooksley Born; nor do we know if it was actually twelve or fourteen bankers, or if they were in his office at the time, or if Summers was actually convinced by them—more likely he came to his own conclusions, which happened to agree with theirs. (Summers did not comment for the *Washington Post* story that reported the phone call.) Nor does it matter.

What we do know is that by 1998, when it came to questions of modern finance and financial regulation, Wall Street executives and lobbyists had many sympathetic ears in government, and important policymakers were inclined to follow their advice. Finance had become a complex, highly quantitative field that only the Wall Street bankers and their backers in academia (including multiple Nobel Prize winners) had mastered, and people who questioned them could be dismissed as ignorant Luddites. No conspiracy was necessary. Even Summers, a brilliant and notoriously skeptical academic economist (later to become treasury secretary and eventually President Obama's chief economic counselor), was won over by the siren song of financial innovation and deregulation. By 1998, it was part of the worldview of the Washington elite that what was good for Wall Street was good for America.

The aftermath is well known. Although Born's concept paper did not cause a financial crisis, the failure to regulate not only derivatives, but many other financial innovations, made possible a decade-long financial frenzy that ultimately created the worst financial crisis and deepest recession the world has endured since World War II.

Free from the threat of regulation, OTC derivatives grew to over $680 trillion in face value and over $20 trillion in market value by 2008. Credit default swaps, which were too rare to be measured in 1998, grew to over $50 trillion in face value and over $3 trillion in market value by 2008, contributing to the inflation of the housing bubble;[16] when that bubble burst, the collapse in the value of securities based on the housing market triggered the financial crisis. The U.S. economy contracted by 4 percent, financial institutions took over one trillion dollars of losses, and the United States and other governments bailed out their banking sectors with rescue packages worth either hundreds of billions or trillions of dollars, depending on how you count them.[17]

Brooksley Born was defeated by the new financial oligarchy, symbolized by the thirteen bank CEOs who gathered at the White House in March 2009 and the "thirteen bankers" who lobbied Larry Summers in 1998. The major banks gained the wealth and prestige necessary to enter the halls of power and sway the opinions of the political establishment, and then cashed in that influence for policies—of which derivatives nonregulation was only one example—that helped them double and redouble their wealth while bringing the economy to the edge of a cliff, from which it had to be pulled back with taxpayer money.

The choices the federal government made in rescuing the banking sector in 2008 and 2009 also have significant implications for American society and the global economy today. Not only did the government choose to rescue the financial system—a decision few would question—but it chose to do so by extending a blank check to the largest, most powerful banks in their moment of greatest need. The government chose *not* to impose conditions that could reform the industry or even to replace the management of large failed banks. It chose to stick with the bankers it had.

In the dark days of late 2008—when Lehman Brothers vanished, Merrill Lynch was acquired, AIG was taken over by the government, Washington Mutual and Wachovia collapsed, Goldman Sachs and Morgan Stanley fled for safety by morphing into "bank holding companies," and Citigroup and Bank of America teetered on the edge before being bailed out—the conventional wisdom was that the financial crisis spelled the end of an era of excessive risk-taking and fabulous profits. Instead, we can now see that the largest, most powerful banks came out of the crisis even larger and more powerful. When Wall Street was on its knees, Washington came to its rescue—not because of personal favors to a handful of powerful bankers, but because of a belief in a certain kind of financial sector so strong that not even the ugly revelations of the financial crisis could uproot it.

That belief was reinforced by the fact that, when the crisis hit, both the Bush and Obama administrations were largely manned by people who either came from Wall Street or had put in place the policies favored by Wall Street. Because of these long-term relationships between Wall Street and Washington, there was little serious consideration during the crisis of the possibility that a different kind of financial system might be possible—despite the exhortations of prominent economists such as Paul Krugman, Joseph Stiglitz, and many others. There was no serious attempt to break up the big banks or reform financial regulation while it was possible—when the banks were weak, at the height of the crisis. Reform was put off until after the most powerful banks had grown even bigger, returned to profitability, and regained their political clout. This strategy ran counter to the approach the U.S. Treasury Department had honed during emerging market financial crises in the 1990s, when leading officials urged crisis-stricken countries to address structural problems quickly and directly.

As we write this, Congress looks likely to adopt some type of banking reform, but it is unlikely to have much bite. The measures proposed by the Obama administration placed some new constraints on Wall Street, but left intact the preeminence and power of a handful of megabanks; and even these proposals faced opposition from the financial lobby on Capitol Hill. The reform bill will probably bring about some improvements, such as better protection for consumers against abusive practices by financial institutions. But the core problem—massive, powerful banks that are both "too big to fail" and powerful enough to tilt the political landscape in their favor—will remain as Wall Street returns to business as usual.

By all appearances, the major banks—at least the ones that survived intact—were the big winners of the financial crisis. JPMorgan Chase, Bank of America, and Wells Fargo bought up failing rivals to become even bigger. The largest banks increased their market shares in everything from issuing credit cards to issuing new stock for companies.[18] Goldman Sachs reported record profits and, through September 2009, had already set aside over $500,000 per employee for compensation.[19] Lloyd Blankfein, CEO of Goldman Sachs, was named Person of the Year by the *Financial Times*.[20]

The implications for America and the world are clear. Our big banks have only gotten bigger. In 1983, Citibank, America's largest bank, had $114 billion in assets, or 3.2 percent of U.S. gross domestic product (GDP, the most common measure of the size of an economy). By 2007, nine financial institutions were bigger relative to the U.S. economy than Citibank had been in 1983.[21] At the time of the White House meeting, Bank of America's assets were 16.4 percent of GDP, followed by JPMorgan Chase at 14.7 percent and Citigroup at 12.9 percent.[22] A vague expectation that the government would bail them out in a crisis has been transformed into a virtual certainty, lowering their funding costs relative to their smaller competitors. The incentive structures created by high leverage (shifting risk from shareholders and employees onto creditors and, ultimately, taxpayers) and huge one-sided bonuses (great in good years and good in bad years) have not changed. The basic, massive subsidy scheme remains unchanged: when times are good, the banks keep the upside as executive and trader compensation; when times are bad and potential crisis looms, the government picks up the bill.

If the basic conditions of the financial system are the same, then the outcome will be the same, even if the details differ. The conditions that created the financial crisis and global recession of 2007–2009 will bring about another crisis, sooner or later. Like the last crisis, the next one will cause millions of people to lose their jobs, houses, or educational opportunities; it will require a large transfer of wealth from taxpayers to the financial sector; and it will increase government debt, requiring higher taxes in the future. The effects of the next meltdown could be milder than the last one; but with a banking system that is even more highly concentrated and that has a rock-solid government guarantee in place, they could also be worse.

The alternative is to reform the financial system now, to put in place a modern analog to the banking regulations of the 1930s that protected the financial system well for over fifty years. A central pillar of this reform must be breaking up the megabanks that dominate our financial system and have the ability to hold our entire economy hostage. This is the challenge that faces the Obama administration today. It is not a question of finance or economics. It is ultimately a question of politics—whether the long march of Wall Street on Washington can be halted and reversed. Given the close financial, personal, and ideological ties between these two centers of power, that will not happen overnight.

We have been here before. The confrontation between concentrated financial power and democratically elected government is as old as the American republic. History shows that finance can be made safe again. But it will be quite a fight.

1

THOMAS JEFFERSON
AND THE FINANCIAL ARISTOCRACY

> Great corporations exist only because they are created and safe-
> guarded by our institutions; and it is therefore our right and our duty
> to see that they work in harmony with these institutions.
> —Theodore Roosevelt, State of the Union message,
> December 3, 1901[1]

Suspicion of large, powerful banks is as old as the United States, dating back at least to Thomas Jefferson—author of the Declaration of
Independence, secretary of state under President George Washington, third president of the United States, and staunch proponent of
individual liberty. Although Jefferson is one of the most revered
founders of the republic, according to conventional wisdom he was
not much of an economist.[2] Jefferson believed in an agrarian society
with decentralized institutions and limited political and economic
power. He was deeply suspicious of banks and criticized them in vitri-
olic terms, writing, "I sincerely believe, with you, that banking institutions are more dangerous than standing armies."[3] In a letter to James
Madison, Jefferson even suggested, quite seriously, that anyone who
cooperated with a federally chartered bank was guilty of treason and
should be executed.[4]

The United States, however, did not turn out to be a decentralized
agrarian society, in part because finance, commerce, and industry have
also had their supporters throughout American history. Jefferson was
opposed by Alexander Hamilton, Washington's secretary of the treasury, who favored a stronger federal government that actively supported economic development. In particular, Hamilton believed that

the government should ensure that sufficient credit was available to fund economic development and transform America into a prosperous, entrepreneurial country. This would require the introduction of modern forms of finance opposed by Jefferson. This tension between Jefferson and Hamilton has endured to the present day.

Hamilton favored a publicly chartered (though largely privately owned) bank modeled on the Bank of England, which would manage the federal government's money and provide an important source of credit to the government and the economy. Legislation to create the (First) Bank of the United States passed Congress easily in 1791. Jefferson lobbied hard for President Washington to veto it, however, arguing that the power to charter a bank was not expressly granted to Congress by the Constitution and therefore remained with the states under the Tenth Amendment ("The powers not delegated to the United States by the Constitution, nor prohibited by it to the States, are reserved to the States respectively, or to the people").* Washington went so far as to request that James Madison (principal author of the Constitution and the Bill of Rights) draft a veto, but he also allowed Hamilton the opportunity to respond.[5] Hamilton's fifteen-thousand-word memo, largely written at the last minute, convinced Washington that a federal bank was a "necessary and proper" application of Congress's power and responsibility to promote fiscal stability and regulate trade by supporting the broader commercial system.[6] The president signed the legislation without allowing Jefferson a rebuttal.[7]

After all the furor and rhetoric, the immediate historical aftermath was rather dull. The Bank of the United States functioned broadly as advertised by Hamilton, managing the government's incoming revenues and outgoing payments and facilitating payments across an otherwise small-scale and fragmented financial system.[8] It won over many supporters, although not Jefferson and Madison (at least at first), who formed the Democratic-Republican Party to oppose Hamilton's Federalist Party, in part because of the Bank of the United States.

When it came to the basic economic issues, Hamilton was right. Economic development in the early United States depended heavily

---

* The Tenth Amendment, part of the Bill of Rights, was technically not yet in force, but by the end of 1790 it had been ratified by nine states of the ten necessary.

on the creation of a well-functioning financial system, as shown by modern scholars such as Richard Sylla and Peter Rousseau.[9] The United States in the 1780s "lacked nearly all the elements of a modern financial system, [but] by the 1820s had a financial system that was innovative, large and perhaps the equal of any in the world."[10] This was due not only to the Bank of the United States, but also to other financial reforms implemented by Hamilton, such as his careful management of cash flows into and out of the Treasury while keeping money on deposit with "approved banks," as well as his highly influential reports to Congress on credit and manufacturing.[11] Hamilton successfully argued that the federal government should assume the debts incurred by the individual states during the American Revolution, thereby setting the valuable precedent that the United States would always pay its debts.[12] In Ron Chernow's words, "Hamilton did not create America's market economy so much as foster the culture and legal setting in which it flourished."[13] The result was a stable and relatively favorable environment for banking. The United States had only three banks in 1789, but twenty-eight banks were chartered in the 1790s and another seventy-three in the first decade of the 1800s.[14] Bank shareholders had limited liability, a real innovation at the time (in England before the 1850s, only the Bank of England had limited liability) that helped attract entrepreneurs and money.[15] By 1825, when the United States and the United Kingdom had roughly the same population (11.1 million and 12.9 million, respectively), the United States had nearly 2.5 times the amount of bank capital as the United Kingdom.[16]

The United States also rapidly developed a healthy equity market that was able to attract capital from around the world. Already by 1803, more than half of all U.S. securities were held by European investors.[17] By 1825, there were 232 listed securities in the United States (in New York, Philadelphia, Boston, Baltimore, and Charleston combined), approaching the 320 securities listed in England, and the level of equity market capitalization was similar in both countries. Many of the companies listed in American stock markets represented the leading sectors of the modern economy, including insurance, transportation, utilities, and manufacturing.[18] The abundance of both bank capital and equity financing meant that there was plenty of money available to invest in new and expanding businesses—initially concentrated in New England, but soon spreading to the rest of the country.[19]

A modern financial system became even more important with the spread of the Industrial Revolution early in the nineteenth century, which neither Jefferson nor even Hamilton foresaw. At the time of their debates, the Industrial Revolution was decidedly small-scale and largely confined to England. But the progressive application of technology to the production of goods would vastly raise the potential output of the American economy and permanently change its place in the world. Because industrialization required investments in new technology, it also required credit. Jefferson's small-scale farms may have represented a democratic political ideal (at least for those fortunate enough to own those farms and not be slaves working on them), but long-run prosperity required large-scale commerce and industry, both of which required banks. In retrospect, Jefferson's economic positions seem either cranky and uninformed or motivated by his distaste for the Northern commercial interests that he correctly predicted would benefit from a strong central government and eventually undermine Southern plantation (and slave) owners such as himself.[20]

But while Hamilton may have been right about the economics, that was not Jefferson's primary concern. His fear of large financial institutions had nothing to do with the efficient allocation of capital and everything to do with power. Jefferson correctly discerned that banks' crucial economic functions—mediating financial transactions and creating and managing the supply of credit—could give them both economic and political power. In the 1790s, Jefferson was particularly worried that the Bank of the United States could gain leverage over the federal government as its major creditor and payment agent, and could pick economic winners and losers through its decisions to grant or withhold credit. Over the past two hundred years, financial institutions and markets have only become more intertwined with the day-to-day functioning of the economy, to the point where large companies depend on the short-term credit they use to manage their cash flow as much as they depend on electricity. In Jefferson's eyes, the increasing importance of finance to society would only give banks even more power—power that could be used to benefit the bankers themselves, or in extreme cases could even threaten to undermine American democracy.

In matters of economic policy, we tend as a nation to lean toward Hamilton. As President Calvin Coolidge said in 1925, "[The American people] are profoundly concerned with producing, buying, selling, investing and prospering in the world."[21] And for most of American history, that has served us relatively well. The United States would not have the largest economy in the world without a financial sector that has, most of the time, funneled capital toward the investments in new technology and processes that are critical to long-term productivity growth.

However, our Hamiltonian inclinations—to seek out efficiency, to celebrate bigness, and to look favorably on anything that makes money—have been kept at least partially in check by the legacy of Jefferson. Although Jefferson lost the battle over the Bank of the United States (and his worst fears did not materialize), the cause of restraining concentrated economic or financial power was taken up by three of his most important successors. In the 1830s, Andrew Jackson's showdown with the Second Bank of the United States set back the development of a concentrated financial sector. At the beginning of the twentieth century, the crusade against the industrial trusts begun by Theodore Roosevelt ultimately left intact the powerful private banks symbolized by J.P. Morgan; but during the Great Depression of the 1930s, Franklin Delano Roosevelt was finally able to break up the largest banks and constrain their risky activities. While they did not achieve all of their aims, the Jeffersonian tradition represented by these presidents has served as a counterweight to Hamilton's influence, helping prevent a powerful and unfettered financial system from undermining broader prosperity. The American financial system has oscillated between concentration and fragmentation; but over the long term, it helped give us unrivaled prosperity without undermining our democratic system—at least not yet. Today, as we face the largest and most concentrated financial sector in our nation's history, Jefferson's legacy again demands our attention.

JEFFERSON'S REVENGE

Jefferson's fear of big banks was something close to an obsession for the seventh president of the United States, Andrew Jackson. "Old

Hickory," like Jefferson, favored the ideal of an agrarian republic and distrusted big-city bankers.[22] Just as important, he believed in presidential power, and he saw a major national bank as a rival that needed to be dealt with.

After its charter expired in 1811, legislation to recharter the Bank of the United States narrowly failed. However, the economic dislocation caused by the War of 1812 and the resulting chaos in the financial system convinced politicians of the need for a national bank. Congress passed legislation creating the Second Bank of the United States, which was signed by President James Madison, and the bank went into operation with a twenty-year charter in 1816.[23]

By the time Jackson was elected president in 1828, the Second Bank functioned as an "important administrative agency of the government"[24]—regulating the money supply, handling the day-to-day financial operations of the U.S. government, issuing bank notes, and providing credit for both federal authorities and private sector clients (including prominent politicians). Under the management of Nicholas Biddle, it supported the development of the American capital markets and helped coordinate a banking system that primarily operated at the state or local level.[25]

Jackson, however, opposed the Second Bank on both economic and political grounds. He hated paper money and believed only in the hardest of hard money—gold and silver. Paper money, he thought, allowed banks and bankers to distort the economy at the expense of common people. In addition, the Second Bank's monopoly over government finances gave Biddle and his friends power (and profits) that, he felt, rightfully belonged to the executive branch. The president was particularly enraged that Biddle used his economic power to curry favor with Congress, influencing elected representatives to support his aims; almost every prominent person supporting Biddle was also substantially in his debt (including some of the leading politicians of the day, such as Daniel Webster and Henry Clay).[26] As Jackson's secretary Nicholas Trist put it, echoing Jefferson, "Independently of its misdeeds, the mere *power*,—the bare existence of such a power—is a thing irreconcilable with the nature and spirit of our institutions."[27]

The "Bank War" began when Biddle and his ally, Henry Clay, attempted to renew the Second Bank's charter in 1832, four years before it expired, in part to create a political issue that Clay could use in his campaign to become president.[28] In order to gain support, Biddle directed the Bank to expand its lending in a bid for popularity.[29] Congress voted to renew the Bank's charter, but Jackson vetoed the renewal. His veto message mixed together a rebuke to the Supreme Court (which had finally resolved the Jefferson-Hamilton debate over the constitutionality of the Bank of the United States in favor of Hamilton), an attack on paper money ("Congress have established a mint to coin money. . . . The money so coined, with its value so regulated, and such foreign coins as Congress may adopt are the only currency known to the Constitution"), a defense of states' rights, and a swipe at the economic elites ("It is to be regretted that the rich and powerful too often bend the acts of government to their selfish purposes.")[30] In private, Jackson was more personal: "The Bank," he said to Martin Van Buren (his running mate in 1832), "is trying to kill me, *but I will kill it.*"[31] The veto held up when Jackson defeated Clay in the 1832 presidential election. Biddle did not go quietly, however. When Jackson began transferring the federal government's deposits out of the Second Bank to his favored "pet banks," the Second Bank demanded payment on bills issued by state banks and reduced its loans by over $5 million, contracting the money supply and causing interest rates to double to 12 percent. Biddle hoped, by damaging the economy, to stir up opposition to Jackson; in the process, he showed that Jackson had not been wrong to fear the power of a major bank to distort the economy for its own purposes.[32]

Eliminating the most efficient commercial bank in the United States was probably not a textbook example of sound macroeconomic management, especially according to today's textbook. Jackson's veto most likely slowed the development of an integrated payments and credit system such as those seen in more advanced parts of Europe.[33] Without a major national bank or a central bank with the ability to stabilize the financial system, the U.S. economy also suffered through severe business cycles through the rest of the nineteenth century.

However, the primary importance of the Bank War was not economic, but political.[34] Although Jackson's economic grounds for opposing a new charter may have been weak, the Second Bank's behavior showed the political danger presented by a powerful private bank. Biddle was able to bribe, cajole, or otherwise pressure congressmen into taking his side against the president. Not all of the Bank's supporters were in it for the money. But as the war raged, Daniel Webster wrote to Biddle, "I believe my retainer has not been renewed or *refreshed* as usual. If it be wished that my relation to the Bank should be continued, it may be well to send me the usual retainers."[35] More ominously, at least as interpreted by Jackson's supporters, Biddle had attempted to hold the economy hostage to his political ends, first expanding credit in order to gain political support and then withholding it (and triggering a recession) in order to punish Jackson.[36] This was exactly what Jefferson had feared.

Both Jefferson and Jackson saw a powerful bank as a corrupting influence that could undermine the proper functioning of a democratic government. While this was not a foregone conclusion—the First Bank had lost its bid for a renewed charter in part because of its political weakness[37]—the Bank War gave a hint of the way financial power could be misused for political ends. Jefferson and Jackson did not think the government could control finance; the idea of a modern, technocratic central bank lay beyond their imagination, far in the future. Instead, they feared that powerful, privately owned financial institutions would gain disproportionate influence over the government. Given the choice between the Second Bank and no national bank at all, Jackson chose the latter. As a result, central banking developed slowly and informally in the United States, especially when compared to Europe.[38] But even with this handicap, the U.S. economy continued to innovate and grow through the nineteenth century.

Most important, Jackson's victory ensured that a powerful private bank was not able to install itself in the corridors of political power and use its privileged position to extract profits for itself, inhibit competition, and hamper broader economic development. Perhaps the United States could in any case have avoided the fate suffered during the same period by Mexico or Brazil—where a small elite controlled a concentrated banking sector, with unfortunate economic results—and by many recent emerging markets.[39] Had Jackson lost the Bank War, it is possible that the Second Bank might have gradually evolved into a modern central bank without distorting the political system to its own advantage.[40] But this was not a risk that Jackson wanted to take, and his populist prejudices against financial elites (and his desire for increased presidential power) ensured that the American financial system would err on the side of fragmentation and decentralization. Although the resulting financial system was vulnerable to macroeconomic shocks, it was generally able to supply the capital needed by a growing business sector, and it did not soon generate a small elite with a dangerous amount of economic and political power.

THE MONEY TRUST

By the late nineteenth century, however, industrialization had created a powerful economic elite that held political power at all levels, with its supporters in substantial control of the Senate, the Republican Party, and the presidency. Seventy years after Jackson, it was time for another confrontation between an independent-minded president and concentrated economic power.

Despite its decentralized financial system, nineteenth-century America had turned out to be a great place to develop new ideas and make money. Americans were among the first to invent or commercialize many new technologies that arose after 1800, building companies based on innovations in agricultural implements, canals, telecommunications, steam power, railroads, chemicals, and other industries. By the end of the nineteenth century, American companies were at the forefront of almost all of the technology-intensive industries that were making it possible to produce more and better goods with fewer and cheaper inputs.[41] Finance played a constructive supporting role during this period, providing the crucial connection or "intermediation" between savers on the one hand and people with productive investment opportunities on the other hand.[42] Capital continued to flow into productive uses even after the demise of the Second Bank.[43]

The innovations that changed the economic landscape changed the political landscape as well. Social mobility and the lack of an entrenched aristocracy meant that newly successful companies and industries could gain political representation quickly, at least when compared to European societies. New money could make its way into politics, whether legally or illegally. By the late nineteenth century, the Senate had become known as the "Millionaires' Club"; buying political support with cash was considered by many to be just an extension of normal business practices.[44]

Railroad wealth was the most prominent late-nineteenth-century example of the entrance of new money into politics. In the three decades immediately following the Civil War, America was swept by a craze for building new railroads. Fortunes were made and lost and businesses built and destroyed, while long-distance travel became much faster and hauling freight became much cheaper than ever before. The railroad barons and their industrial allies acquired great political power, coming to dominate the Senate by the turn of the century. Two of their strongest allies, Senators Mark Hanna and Nelson Aldrich, were important power brokers in the Republican Party, which controlled the White House for all but eight years from 1869 to 1913 and had a Senate majority for all but two years from 1883 to 1913. Hanna managed William McKinley's successful 1896 presidential campaign and dominated the Republican Party machine into the Theodore Roosevelt years; Aldrich was one of the most powerful men in the Senate and largely dictated its positions on government regulation of industry and banking.[45]

Political representation for rising industrial interests is preferable to ossified social structures that restrict innovation and keep new people away from the levers of power.[46] Most of the European societies that had such restrictions struggled to keep up with the Industrial Revolution and fell behind their competitors. The United States also turned out much better than Latin American countries, such as Mexico, which started at roughly similar income levels but where elites controlled concentrated banking systems; in some cases a lack of effective corporate governance led to nepotism and insider transactions that took advantage of outside shareholders.[47]

At the same time, however, the openness of the American political system has always made it possible for the current business elite to use its political power to shift the economic playing field in its favor. Any growing and profitable sector can take this route, from railroads, steel, and automobiles to defense and energy. Each of these industries has used the argument that "what's good for (fill in the blank) is good for America" in order to obtain preferential tariffs, tax breaks, or subsidies.[48]

This was the case for the new industrial trusts that emerged late in the nineteenth century.* These massive agglomerations of economic power were brought on in part by the spread of railways, which created national markets for many goods, making possible economies of scale of previously unheard-of dimensions.[49] Consolidation was also a reaction to prolonged economic downturn and perceived overcapacity in some industries. But it stemmed as well from the old-fashioned instincts of successful industrialists, who realized that combining with their competitors (at least the ones they hadn't been able to wipe out) could give them an effective monopoly, and with it the power to increase prices and profits. The rise of the trusts was a momentous development in American economic history in its own right. But it was also important because it brought concentrated financial power back onto the economic stage.

Standard Oil was an early pioneer of the trusts, followed closely by imitators in other industries. According to historian Thomas McCraw, "in the period 1897–1904 . . . 4,227 American firms merged into 257 combinations. By 1904, some 318 trusts . . . were alleged to control two-fifths of the nation's manufacturing assets."[50] The rise of the trusts depended heavily on investment bankers, who provided the money needed to buy shares and rearrange shareholdings and also offered the social glue necessary to bring disparate industrial interests together. A handful of bankers led by J. P. Morgan played a central role in this rapid transformation of the business landscape, giving Morgan an economic importance unmatched by any financier since Biddle, if not the beginning of the republic.[51] Morgan's empire handled an extraordinary share of the money flowing into American industry—as high as 40 percent of total capital raised at the beginning of the twentieth century.[52] In a lightly regulated banking system, industrial concentration led naturally to financial concentration, and J. P. Morgan stepped forward to take the reins of the financial system.

---

*A trust was a form of legal organization used to combine multiple companies into a single business entity.

The 1896 election of McKinley as president was welcomed by large corporate interests that feared the alternative—populist crusader William Jennings Bryan. However, they would be less happy with his second-term vice president and successor (after McKinley's assassination in September 1901), Theodore Roosevelt, who adopted "trust-busting" as a signature policy and made improved supervision of large corporations a major theme of his 1901 State of the Union address.[53] (McKinley had begun investigating the trusts, but Roosevelt was the first president to take them on directly.) Roosevelt pushed through major legislation to tighten regulation of the railroads. More important, his Department of Justice pioneered the use of the Sherman Antitrust Act of 1890 to break up large trusts, first taking aim at the Northern Securities Company, a railroad combination engineered by J. P. Morgan among others.[54] In 1904, the Supreme Court agreed with the Roosevelt administration and dissolved Northern Securities as "an illegal combination in restraint of interstate commerce."[55]

The industrial-finance barons didn't understand why Roosevelt was so worked up; J. P. Morgan's response was "If we have done anything wrong, send your man to see my man, and they can fix it up."[56] But Roosevelt, following in the tradition of Jefferson and Jackson, opposed concentrated industrial power for political reasons; he believed that dominant private interests were bad for democracy and for economic prosperity.[57] In taking on the trusts, he sought not only to obtain greater economic benefits for consumers (the prevailing modern interpretation of antitrust law), but to safeguard democracy from monied elites and maintain an economic system that was open to new ideas and new businesses. In the process, he helped change the way Americans thought about big business. As Nobel Prize–winning economist George Stigler wrote, "A careful student of the history of economics would have searched long and hard on July 2 of 1890, the day the Sherman Act was signed by President [Benjamin] Harrison, for any economist who had ever recommended the policy of actively combatting collusion or monopolization in the economy at large."[58] After Roosevelt, however, the consensus view became that antitrust law should be used to break up monopolies and prevent abuses of market power.

The Roosevelt administration's successful prosecution of antitrust cases in the courts led to more cases brought under Presidents

William Howard Taft and Woodrow Wilson, including the court-ordered breakup of Standard Oil in 1911. However, these policies did little to disturb the concentration of money and power that had taken place in the financial sector in parallel with the rise of the industrial trusts. The wave of industrial concentration at the end of the nineteenth century was supposed to stabilize individual markets and cushion particular industries against overexpansion and price wars.[59] Instead, the interaction between large industrial trusts and their bankers created the backdrop for the worst financial crisis in American history to date, which brought concentrated banking power to the political forefront.

In October 1907, a routine (for the time) attempt to manipulate the price of stock in the United Copper Company by company insiders and their Wall Street banker went awry, triggering a run on banks perceived to be connected to the scheme.[60] The panic soon spread to the Knickerbocker Trust Company, one of the largest financial institutions in New York, and then to many other banks in the city. In order to raise cash quickly, banks were forced to sell whatever they could, pushing down asset prices across the board; stock prices also fell as banks cut back on loans to stockbrokers. This is a standard feature of any financial crisis.[61] Any bank has deposits that customers can withdraw immediately, while many of its loans (such as mortgages) cannot be called in on demand. As banks stop lending, borrowers are forced to liquidate assets in order to pay off their debts, reducing asset prices even further and creating more pressure on banks. In any banking system, a crisis can be rapidly magnified by this vicious cycle, sometimes called the "financial accelerator."[62]

This is the type of crisis that central banks are supposed to prevent; but thanks to Andrew Jackson's victory in the Bank War, the United States had not developed a central bank. Instead, J. P. Morgan—the man—stepped in to fill the gap. He and his team, led by Benjamin Strong, decided which banks should fail because they were irredeemably insolvent and which should be saved because they only needed some cash to get them through the panic; then they pressured other major financial institutions to join with Morgan in providing loans and deposits to threatened banks in order to ensure their survival. They were brutal in these choices, and their decisions were final. But despite J. P. Morgan's financial muscle, the private sector could not come up with sufficient funds. The only entity with enough ready money to stabilize the situation was the U.S. government, which deposited $25 million into New York banks to provide the liquidity needed to keep the financial system afloat.[63]

The Panic of 1907, which nearly brought the financial system crashing down, clearly demonstrated the risks the American economy was running with a highly concentrated industrial sector, a lightly regulated financial sector, and no central bank to backstop the financial system in a crisis. The major private banks might be able to reshape industries as they wished, but they could not be relied upon to stabilize the financial system in a crisis, especially with J. P. Morgan in his seventies. Something needed to be done. The stage was set for another political battle over the financial system.

On one side, Nelson Aldrich represented the viewpoint of the banking industry.[64] "No one can carefully study the experience of the other great commercial nations," he argued in an influential 1909 speech, "without being convinced that disastrous results of recurring financial crises have been successfully prevented by a proper organization of capital and by the adoption of wise methods of banking and of currency"—which, to him, meant a central bank that could act as a lender of last resort in a crisis.[65] Aldrich was chair of the National Monetary Commission, founded in the aftermath of the Panic of 1907, which recommended the creation of a central banking system largely controlled by the private sector bankers themselves. The details of the planned system were hammered out at a secret meeting of top politicians and financiers at Jekyll Island off the coast of Georgia in November 1910. What these bankers wanted was a bailout mechanism that would protect the financial system in the event of a speculative crash like the Panic of 1907. They knew that a new central bank would need the political backing and financial support of the federal government, but at the same time they wanted to minimize government interference, oversight, or control.[66]

However, the Aldrich plan was politically controversial; it looked like a trick to get taxpayers to finance banks and protect them from the consequences of their risky activities. Opponents argued that the problem was a cabal of big banks that were secretly running the country. This fear was likely exaggerated, but there is no doubt that Wall Street banks played a critical role in creating the industrial trusts. In

1912, the House of Representatives, then controlled by the Democratic Party, commissioned an investigation of the "money trust" and its economic influence. (The investigation was proposed by Representative Charles Lindbergh Sr., who called the Aldrich plan a "wonderfully devised plan specifically fitted for Wall Street securing control of the world."[67]) The Pujo Committee concluded that control of credit was concentrated in the hands of a small group of Wall Street bankers, who had used their central place in the financial system to amass considerable economic power.[68] The committee report provided ammunition to Louis Brandeis, a prominent lawyer and future Supreme Court justice. Beginning with a 1913 article entitled "Our Financial Oligarchy,"[69] Brandeis spoke out strongly in favor of constraining banks. He accused the powerful investment banks of using customer deposits and other money that passed through their hands in order to take control of large companies and promote the interests of those companies. The "dominant element in our financial oligarchy is the investment banker," he concluded.[70]

Brandeis served as an adviser to the new Democratic president, Woodrow Wilson, who eventually brokered the compromise that led to the Federal Reserve Act of 1913. The final bill reduced the autonomy of the central bank and gave the government a stronger hand in its operations, notably through a Federal Reserve Board appointed by the president. However, the Federal Reserve banks were (and remain) technically private entities, and private sector banks were given the power to appoint two-thirds of their directors.[71]

While the private bankers didn't get everything they wanted in the new Federal Reserve, they did get the most important thing: an institution that could bail them out with public funds when financial crises occurred. Support by the Federal Reserve can take two broad forms: liquidity loans, where the Fed gives a bank a short-term loan that can be rolled over repeatedly; and lower interest rates, which help banks by promoting economic growth and increasing the chances that bank loans will be paid back.* These steps can mitigate individual disasters.

---

*Lowering short-term interest rates can also help banks by "steepening the yield curve." Since banks typically borrow for short periods of time and lend for long periods of time, if short-term rates fall while long-term rates remain unchanged, their profit margin—the spread between long- and short-term rates—increases.

However, the existence of government insurance against a worst-case scenario creates "moral hazard"—the incentive for banks to take on more risk in order to maximize shareholder returns—thereby laying the groundwork for the next system-wide crisis. Each emergency rescue only increases banks' confidence that they will be rescued in the future, creating a cycle of repeated booms, busts, and bailouts.[72]

In principle, in exchange for providing this insurance, the Federal Reserve would supervise the banks it was protecting, preventing them from taking too much risk. But as Brandeis spotted, echoing Jefferson, this overlooked the political dimension: "We believe that no methods of regulation ever have been or can be devised to remove the menace inherent in private monopoly and overweening commercial power."[73] Although Brandeis supported the Federal Reserve Act as a means of giving the government more control over the financial system, he would have preferred to break up large concentrations of industrial or financial power. As it turned out, the original Federal Reserve lacked the modern regulatory powers necessary to constrain the banks. In addition, the first president of the powerful Federal Reserve Bank of New York was none other than Benjamin Strong, J. P. Morgan's lieutenant and the ultimate Wall Street insider. As a result, the initial "solution" to the problem revealed by the Panic of 1907 would prove to be anything but. Instead, light regulation and cheap money would encourage banks to take on enough speculative risk to threaten the entire economy.

Theodore Roosevelt was able to curtail the growth of industrial trusts and shift the mainstream consensus so that large concentrations of economic power came to be seen by most people as dangerous to society.[74] But despite this success against the trusts, the movement to constrain the power of big banks failed, even with one of its leading advocates, Louis Brandeis, as an adviser to President Wilson. The compromise of 1913 prevented private banks from directly controlling the new central banking system. However, the Federal Reserve Act did little to constrain the banks themselves, leaving them free to engage in risky lending and generate huge economic booms that would be politically difficult to rein in. The problem that was glimpsed but not fully understood in 1907 was that when a crash finally arrived, the government would face the hard choice between letting the system collapse and bailing out the banks that had been responsible for the bubble. The original Federal Reserve, with its combination of strong private sector influence and weak regulatory authority, had the power to engineer a bailout, but not to curb the risky activities that could make one necessary.

FDR AND ANDREW JACKSON

It took only sixteen years for this flaw in the system to become catastrophically apparent. Rampant speculation in the 1920s led to the Crash of 1929, which was initially followed by a generous bailout for elite New York financial firms, and then by the repeated bungling of attempts to save the rest of the financial system. Not only did the Federal Reserve's safety net encourage excessive risk-taking by bankers; the safety net, it turned out, had gaping holes that could not be fixed in the intense pressure of a crisis. The result was the Great Depression.

Speculation on its own is not necessarily a problem. Entrepreneurs' willingness to speculate on new technologies or new ways of organizing production is a key source of growth and prosperity. However, speculation combined with large amounts of borrowed money can produce dangerous financial crises. Cheap debt makes more money available to bid on assets, driving up prices, creating vast amounts of paper wealth, and attracting new investors who borrow even more heavily so they can double their bets on a rising market. When the market turns, highly leveraged investors can be wiped out quickly, forcing them to liquidate anything that can be sold and causing asset prices to plummet. This sudden collapse in the value of almost everything can trigger widespread bank failures, corporate bankruptcies, and mass unemployment.

The 1920s were a period of significant deregulation, as Republican administrations dismantled the system of state control developed in order to fight the First World War.[75] By the time the war ended and President Warren G. Harding came to power in 1921, there was a determined effort to restore laissez-faire capitalism.[76] Harding's philosophy was "The business of America is the business of everybody in America"; his successor, Calvin Coolidge, famously said, "The chief business of the American people is business."[77] But the two people who best embodied the hands-off philosophy of the decade were Andrew Mellon, treasury secretary from 1921 to 1932, and Herbert Hoover, secretary of commerce under both Harding and Coolidge and president from 1929 to 1933. Mellon's message was clear: government should just get out of the way.[78] Regulation of private business, as espoused by Brandeis and Wilson, slipped out of fashion.[79]

The antiregulatory policies of the 1920s helped make possible a period of rampant financial speculation, driven by investment banks and closely related firms that sold and traded securities in an unregulated free-for-all. Investor protection was minimal; small investors could be lured into complex financial vehicles they didn't understand, and were offered large margin loans to leverage their positions.[80] While the market rose, everyone benefited. But the result was a stock market bubble fueled by borrowing and psychological momentum.[81] Low interest rates set by the Federal Reserve also fueled an economic boom for much of the decade and encouraged increased borrowing by companies and individuals.[82] By 1929, financial assets were at all-time highs, sustained by high levels of leverage throughout the economy. The stock market crash of October 1929 not only destroyed billions of dollars of paper wealth and wiped out many small investors; it also triggered an unprecedented wave of de-leveraging as financial institutions, companies, and investors sold anything they could in an attempt to pay off their debts, sending prices spiraling downward.[83]

The Federal Reserve could have slowed down the boom and avoided the sharp crash of 1929 if it had been willing early enough to "take away the punch bowl" (in the words of later Fed chair William McChesney Martin)[84] by raising interest rates to discourage borrowing and slow down economic growth. But this is never popular with politicians concerned about the next election, banks making large profits from the boom, or ordinary people benefiting from a strong economy. Instead, the Fed was reluctant to slow down the economy; it kept interest rates low for most of the 1920s and even lowered them in 1927, citing few signs of inflation and concerns about financial fragility outside the United States. The markets responded with a strong rally in the second half of 1927, and the Fed raised rates from 3.5 percent to 5 percent in 1928.[85] But there they stopped. Higher rates, it was feared, would choke off farmers who needed capital; they would also end the bonanza of stock price gains that benefited the financial sector and investors.[86] For similar reasons, the Fed also declined to use what regulatory powers it had to rein in debt-based investment strategies and deflate the bubble by using either moral suasion or informal arm-twisting to pressure banks to cut back on loans to finance stock purchases; this too might have ended the boom and slowed down the real economy.[87] Under considerable pressure from the banking lobby, the Fed decided to stand aside.[88]

When the crash came, however, the Fed initially rushed to the rescue. Despite internal debate, the man on the spot—George Harrison, president of the New York Fed—provided liquidity to troubled institutions; "I am ready to provide all the reserve funds that may be needed," he told bankers, urging them to lend to troubled brokers.[89] By the fall of 1930, Harrison could be proud that despite a 40 percent fall in the stock market, not a single major bank had failed. The Aldrich bailout mechanism seemed to work. Instead of J. P. Morgan stepping in to stop the Panic of 1907, this time the Federal Reserve answered the call.[90] And yet the United States, and the world, still experienced the Great Depression.

For the last seventy years there has been heated debate over whether the Fed could have prevented the financial crisis of 1929 from evolving into the Great Depression, or at least limited its impact through more assertive action. A leading view, advanced by Milton Friedman and Anna Schwartz and subscribed to (in amended form) by current Fed chair Ben Bernanke, is that a spreading bank panic in the early 1930s caused a severe contraction of the money supply and credit, producing the Great Depression. If the Fed had acted assertively to expand the supply of credit, it could have stabilized the banking system and limited the damage to the real economy;[91] the Fed's mental model at the time, however, focused on "free reserves," rather than broader measures of money or credit that would have shown the need for more aggressive action. In addition, rescuing the financial system would have required printing money, which, it was feared, would have adverse consequences; generous bailouts of failing insolvent banks would have created incentive problems for the future. But instead, forced liquidation meant bankruptcy not just for companies and farmers, but also for banks.[92] Widespread bank failures encouraged people to withdraw their money from sound banks; this further dried up the credit available to businesses, causing major collateral damage to the economy, and once the financial system began contracting the process became impossible to stop.* As a result, unemployment rose above 20 percent and much of the American population suffered through a terrible decade of lost jobs, poor living standards, and severe dislocation.

Clearly, something had gone badly wrong. The problem was not that a single bank threatened to usurp political power, like the Second Bank of Jackson's day; it was that there was no effective check on the private banks as a group, whose appetite for risk had created a massive boom and a monumental bust.[94] The Federal Reserve alone lacked either the power or the will to rein in the excesses of the financial sector. The cheap money it supplied had only encouraged excessive risk-taking. When the crisis finally arrived, the government was left with the choice between bailing out banks around the country and encouraging a further speculative cycle or letting the system collapse and inviting widespread economic misery.

The only force available to constrain the banking industry was the federal government, setting up another showdown between political reformers and the financial establishment. This time, however, the magnitude and severity of the Great Depression created the opportunity for a sweeping overhaul of the relationship between government and banks. And the Pecora Commission, an investigation initiated by the Senate Banking Committee, uncovered extensive evidence of abusive practices by the banks—from pumping up questionable bonds they were selling to giving insiders stocks at below-market prices[95]—providing the political ammunition necessary to overcome the objections of the financial sector. The result was the most comprehensive attempt in American history to break up concentrated financial power and constrain banks' activities.[96]

Franklin Delano Roosevelt's favorite president was Andrew Jackson.[97] This affinity was not without its ironies. Roosevelt was a man of the

---

*An alternative explanation, advanced by Barry Eichengreen and Peter Temin, is that the Federal Reserve was constrained by its adherence to the international gold standard; expanding the money supply would have caused a severe devaluation of the dollar.[93]

Eastern establishment; while Jackson is sometimes referred to as "frontier aristocracy" and had New York allies, he had no affection for the East Coast elite. Still, both men shared an appreciation for the workings of democracy and a fear that unconstrained private interests could undermine both the economy and the political system. In a sense, they were both descendants of Jefferson, and both sought to shift the balance of power between the financial system and society at large. In January 1936, Roosevelt said, "Our enemies of today are the forces of privilege and greed within our own borders. . . . Jackson sought social justice; Jackson fought for human rights in his many battles to protect the people against autocratic or oligarchic aggression." Roosevelt also stressed that he was opposed to a "small minority of business men and financiers."[98]

Although Roosevelt faced a far more complex economic situation than did Jackson, his goals were similar: to protect society at large from the economic and political power of big banks. And he was not afraid to confront the bankers head-on; as historian Arthur Schlesinger wrote of the Roosevelt administration's first months in power, "No business group was more proud and powerful than the bankers; none was more persuaded of its own rectitude; none more accustomed to respectful consultation by government officials. To be attacked as antisocial was bewildering; to be excluded from the formation of public policy was beyond endurance."[99] The new legislation of the 1930s—primarily the Banking Act of 1933, better known as the Glass-Steagall Act—reduced the riskiness of the financial system, with a particular emphasis on protecting ordinary citizens. The regulatory framework, however, was relatively simple. Commercial banks, which handled deposits made by ordinary households and businesses, needed to be protected from failure; investment banks and brokerages, which traded securities and raised money for companies, did not. The Glass-Steagall Act separated commercial banking from investment banking to prevent commercial banks from being "infected" by the risky activities of investment banks. (One theory at the time—since largely discredited—was that this infection had weakened commercial banks and helped cause the Depression.)[100] As a result, J.P. Morgan was forced to spin off its investment banking operations, which became Morgan Stanley. Commercial banks were protected from panic-induced bank runs by the Federal Deposit Insurance Corporation (FDIC), but had to accept tight federal regulation in return. The governance of the Federal Reserve was also reformed in the 1930s, strengthening the hand of presidential appointees and weakening the relative power of banks.

The system that took form after 1933, in which banks gained government protection in exchange for accepting strict regulation, was the basis for half a century of financial stability—the longest in American history. Investment banks were also subject to new regulation and oversight by the Securities and Exchange Commission (SEC), but this regulatory regime focused primarily on disclosure and fraud prevention—making sure that banks did not abuse their customers, rather than ensuring their health and stability.

Postwar commercial banking became similar to a regulated utility, enjoying moderate profits with little risk and low competition. For example, Regulation Q, a provision of the Banking Act of 1933, allowed the Federal Reserve to set ceilings on savings account interest rates. Since savings accounts were a major source of funds for banks, the effect was to limit competition for customers' deposits while guaranteeing banks a cheap source of funds. Limits on opening branches and on expanding across state lines inhibited competition, as did the prohibition against investment banks taking deposits. As a result, banks offered a narrow range of financial products and made their money from the spread between the low (and capped) interest rate they paid depositors and the higher rate they charged borrowers. This business model was emblematized by the "3–6–3 rule": pay 3 percent, lend at 6 percent, and make it to the golf course by 3 P.M. According to one leading banking textbook, "some banks frowned on employees working in their offices after hours lest outsiders perceive lighted windows as a sign of trouble."[101]

The result was the safest banking system that America has known in its history, despite a substantial increase in leverage. The average equity-asset ratio—the share of lending financed by owners' or shareholders' capital rather than borrowed money—had already fallen from 50 percent in the 1840s to around 20 percent early in the twentieth century as informal cooperation mechanisms developed among banks. But due to the double liability principle (which made bank sharehold-

ers potentially liable for up to *twice* the money they had invested), this
meant that over 20 percent of bank assets were backed by shareholders' capital—a stunningly high cushion against loss for creditors by
modern standards. After the creation of the FDIC backstop in 1933,
the equity-asset ratio fell below 10 percent for the first time in history.[102] In other words, banks took on significantly more debt and, in
the process, generated higher returns for their shareholders.

Ordinarily, low equity levels (high debt levels) should increase a
bank's riskiness by increasing the likelihood that it will not be able to
pay off its debts in a crisis. Yet despite the increase in leverage, tighter
regulation prevented any serious banking crises. As Figure 1-1 demonstrates, the half-century following the Glass-Steagall Act saw by far
the fewest bank failures in American history.[103] But once financial
deregulation began in the 1970s, these low equity levels became
increasingly dangerous.[104]

Figure 1-1: Bank Suspensions and Failures Per Year, 1864–Present

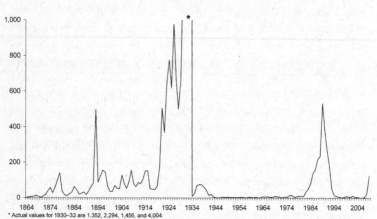

* Actual values for 1930–33 are 1,352, 2,294, 1,456, and 4,004.
Source: David Moss, "An Ounce of Prevention: Financial Regulation, Moral Hazard, and the End of 'Too Big to Fail,'" *Harvard Magazine*,
September–October 2009. Used with the permission of Mr. Moss. Updated with data from FDIC, "Failures and Assistance Transactions."

Some of the regulations in place during this period may have been
excessive. For example, it's not clear that limiting banks to a single
state—a long-standing rule in the United States that was reaffirmed in
the 1930s—makes them safer (other than by restricting competition,
which increases their profits). Even the need for the Glass-Steagall
division between investment banks and commercial banks has been

questioned,[105] and recent history has shown that pure investment banks could become systemically important (and therefore qualify for government bailouts) on their own. Still, the regulations of the 1930s were consistent with several decades of sustained growth without major financial crises. No one can conclusively prove that these reforms were essential to postwar economic development. But constraints on banking activities helped prevent the development of massive debt-fueled booms ending in spectacular crashes. The extreme boom-bust cycles of the nineteenth and early twentieth centuries faded into memory, while the financial system funneled capital effectively into productive investments.[106]

Of course, the story does not end there. The society and economy of the United States remain highly dynamic. New businesses and companies appear and old memories fade away. Political settlements hammered out in previous eras start to seem useless or quaint. Eventually the American tendency toward innovation, risk-taking, and profit-making takes over, and new economic elites arise to challenge the political order.

The laws of the 1930s were intended to protect the economy from a concentrated, powerful, lightly regulated financial sector. In the 1970s, they were beginning to look out of step with the modern world. Bright young minds were inventing new types of financial transactions; banks, particularly investment banks, were making more and more money; and the federal government, charmed by the promised miracles of the financial sector, began relaxing the rules. By the 1990s, Jefferson and Jackson, always awkward topics at any discussion of finance and economics, seemed more irrelevant than ever, and Franklin Delano Roosevelt's New Deal was under widespread attack. The financial sector was bigger, more profitable, and more complicated than it had been in decades. Productivity was rising steadily, economic growth was strong, and inflation was stable and low. Just as some political commentators thought the end of the Cold War signaled the end of history, some economic pundits believed that this "Great Moderation" heralded a turning point in economic history. Sophisticated macroeconomic theories and wise policymakers, they suggested, had learned to tame the cycle of booms and busts that had plagued capitalism for centuries.

In fact, the 1990s were a decade of financial and economic crises, but they were taking place far away, on the periphery of the developed world, in what were fashionably known as emerging markets. From Latin America to Southeast Asia to Russia, fast-growing economies were periodically imploding in financial crises that imposed widespread misery on their populations. For the economic gurus in Washington, this was an opportunity to teach the rest of the world why they should become more like the United States. We did not realize they were already more like us than we cared to admit.

2

OTHER PEOPLE'S OLIGARCHS

Financial institutions have priced risks poorly and have been willing
to finance an excessively large portion of investment plans of the corporate sector, resulting in high leveraging.

—Korea Letter of Intent to the IMF,
December 3, 1997[1]

In the mid-1990s, financial crises in less developed parts of the
world were only too common. Mexico had a major meltdown in
1994–1995 and former communist countries such as Russia, the
Czech Republic, and Ukraine struggled with severe financial shocks.
Then in 1997–1998, what seemed like the mother of all international financial crises swept from Thailand through Southeast Asia
to Korea, Brazil, and Russia. The contagion even spread to the
United States via Long-Term Capital Management (LTCM), an
enormous and terribly named hedge fund, which came to the brink
of collapse.

In the United States, economists and policymakers took two main
lessons from these crises. The first was that crises could be managed—
by pushing other countries to become more like the United States.
Through the experiences of 1997–1998, the U.S. Treasury Department and the International Monetary Fund (IMF) developed a game
plan for handling financial crises: structural weaknesses such as a failing financial sector had to be dealt with immediately, without waiting
for the economy to stabilize. Both directly and through their influence
over the IMF, the key architects of U.S. economic policy—Treasury

Secretary Robert Rubin, Deputy Treasury Secretary Larry Summers, and Federal Reserve chair Alan Greenspan—pressed crisis-stricken countries to liberalize their financial systems, increase transparency in their political systems, and model the governance of their corporations on the Anglo-American system (with a greater role for mutual funds and other institutional investors). For their pains, the Rubin-Summers-Greenspan trio was featured on the cover of *Time* magazine as the "Committee to Save the World."[2]

The second lesson was that while the U.S. economy was not completely immune to financial panics, any real damage could be contained through a few backroom deals. At the urging of the Federal Reserve, LTCM was essentially bought out and refinanced by a group of private sector banks, preventing a major crisis; a series of interest rate cuts by the Fed even kept the stock market bubble growing for another two years. The mature U.S. financial system, it seemed, could withstand any infection that might spread from the developing world, thanks to its sound financial system and macroeconomic management.

Crises were for countries with immature economies, insufficiently developed financial systems, and weak political systems, which had not yet achieved long-term prosperity and stability—countries like Thailand, Indonesia, and South Korea. These countries had three main characteristics that created the potential for serious instability in the 1990s: high levels of debt, cozy relationships between the government and powerful individuals in the private sector, and dependence on volatile inflows of capital from the rest of the world. Together, these ingredients led to economic disaster. Debt-fueled booms, collapsing bubbles, and panic-stricken financial systems were all reminiscent of the Crash of 1929, but the conventional wisdom was that the United States had put these growing pains behind it, thanks to strong corporate governance, deposit insurance, and robust financial regulation. Emerging market crises were an opportunity for the United States to teach the world how to deal with financial crises. Few people suspected that, despite the many obvious differences between emerging Asian economies and the world's largest economy, some of those lessons would become relevant to the United States only a decade later.

ANATOMY OF EMERGING MARKET CRISES

In the 1950s, South Korea was one of the most economically backward countries in the world, ravaged by war and a half-century of Japanese oppression. No outside observer would have regarded it as a candidate for rapid economic development. By 1997, however, South Korea had arrived—literally, having joined the club of rich countries, the Organization for Economic Cooperation and Development (OECD), in 1996.[3] Korea's leading companies were fast building global reputations in a wide range of technology-intensive sectors, including shipbuilding, computer chips, automobiles, and consumer electronics. Top family-owned business groups ("chaebol") such as Samsung, Daewoo, Hyundai, and LG were increasingly prominent global brands. Korea also benefited from a stable political system, with relatively open elections dating back to 1987.

However, Korea exhibited some of the classic weaknesses that produce emerging market crises. Economic activity was dominated by the giant chaebol, whose weak governance structures did little to constrain the whims of their founders. Hostile takeovers were essentially impossible due to a web of local rules. Institutional shareholders did not effectively monitor or control management.[4] The chaebol were also deeply in debt: Samsung's debt was 3.5 times its equity, Daewoo's was 4.1 times, Hyundai's was 5.6 times, and so on.[5] Leverage (the ratio of debt to equity) in the corporate sector was more than twice that of the United States.[6]

In earlier decades, the chaebol had been kept in check by state-owned banks that had carefully allocated credit, limiting the risk that the system would get out of control.[7] By the 1990s, however, the tables had turned. The chaebol had grown big enough to become a political force of their own.[8] Helped by their newfound political influence, they were in position to borrow on advantageous terms, making it possible to run up debt cheaply. Because Korea was regarded as having a sufficiently mature financial market, symbolized by membership in the OECD, its banks could easily borrow short-term money overseas and make longer-term loans to the corporate sector. Alternatively, the chaebol could borrow directly from foreign banks that were now eager to lend to Korea's booming economy.

The availability of cheap short-term debt led the chaebol to splurge on long-term capital investments. The head of Samsung decided that he needed to add an automotive wing to his already far-flung group—an expensive bet that turned out badly. The founder of Daewoo expanded aggressively into the former Soviet bloc, building manufacturing plants from Eastern Europe to Central Asia, and also placed a big bet on cars. Korean manufacturers, led by Samsung and LG, invested heavily in DRAM chip production capacity, driving down margins. These questionable investments, made possible by cheap borrowing, caused returns on capital to fall—making it harder for the chaebol to repay their ever-increasing debts.

Trouble first appeared in 1996 and early 1997 among smaller chaebol who had made risky bets with borrowed money, attempting to move up to the top tier. Hanbo Group (based on a major steel operation), the number 14 chaebol in 1995,[9] defaulted on its debts in January 1997; Kia, the carmaker that was investing heavily to break into the U.S. market, was also in serious financial trouble.[10] The government stepped in with various rescue packages, even for relatively small chaebol, typically providing subsidies or other forms of assistance so that a relatively healthy company could take over a failing company and limit job losses.[11] The largest firms enjoyed stronger implicit government guarantees—the conventional assumption that the government would not let them go under—which helped protect them from failure.[12] Still, by summer 1997, six of the thirty largest business groups had gone bankrupt.[13]

The Korean model and its high short-term-debt levels seemed sustainable as long as economic prospects looked strong and investors thought that companies could pay them back. But financing long-term investments with short-term foreign debt creates a major vulnerability: if lenders start to worry about getting repaid, they will try to pull out their money (refusing to roll over loans); but because companies put that money in long-term investments, they will not be able to pay it back on demand. In this situation, borrowing in U.S. dollars only increased the vulnerability—fears that a country is in trouble can become self-fulfilling as foreign bankers and bondholders scramble to pull their money out first, triggering the defaults that they were afraid of.

For the first nine months of 1997, the Korean economy grew at an impressive rate of around 6 percent.[14] In July, however, the "Asian financial crisis" broke out in Thailand as a crisis of confidence caused a collapse in the local currency, the baht. Overleveraged companies saw their debts double practically overnight (because their debts were in foreign currencies, the amount they owed doubled when the value of the Thai baht fell by half) and were forced to default, causing mass bankruptcies and layoffs. One month later, the crisis spread to Indonesia, where the currency collapsed and domestic companies failed.

At first investors assumed that Korea was sufficiently developed to withstand the storm, but anxiety was spreading outward from Southeast Asia. On October 23, the Hong Kong stock market declined sharply, rattling investors. Then Standard & Poor's downgraded Korean sovereign and corporate debt, stoking fears that Korea would be the next country to be hit by the crisis.* Financial markets started to think again of Korea as an emerging market subject to high economic volatility, which made its short-term debt levels seem excessive. Foreign banks became reluctant to roll over their loans and new international financing became hard to obtain. The currency depreciated sharply, falling from 886 won per dollar in July to 1,701 won per dollar in December. Everyone with dollar debts was hit hard, since now it took twice as many won to cover the same dollar debt payments.[15]

The Korean government attempted to stabilize the situation, using its foreign exchange reserves to help state-owned banks pay off their foreign debts and to slow down the depreciation. But it could not stop the downward spiral—as the currency fell, it became harder for companies to repay foreign debts, and as some fell behind on repayments, creditors became more reluctant to roll over the debts of others.[16] The stock market declined sharply and credit collapsed as banks, unable to pay their own foreign debts, reacted by cutting off loans to domestic companies—which made it harder for companies to produce the

---

*Standard & Poor's and other credit rating agencies rate bonds issued by governments and companies. The ratings are supposed to reflect the likelihood that the issuer will pay off its debts. A rating downgrade indicates that the agency is losing confidence in the issuer.

exports they needed to pay off their debts.[17] The economy declined sharply, leading to layoffs and street protests.

The International Monetary Fund, an intergovernmental organization charged with helping countries in economic distress, did provide financial support subject to some conditions. The IMF emergency lending program put limits on bailouts to the corporate sector, insisted that support to the banking system become transparent and that insolvent banks themselves be taken over, and outlined changes in the governance of chaebol to limit overinvestment. Many of these ideas were strongly supported by Korean reformers working under new president Kim Dae-jung, who wanted to take advantage of chaebol weakness to push through reforms that would make future growth more sustainable—in part by reducing what he saw as the economic and hence political clout of the chaebol.[18]

But the IMF program also contained three striking and controversial dimensions. First, consistent with the view of the U.S. Treasury, it insisted on tightening monetary policy and, despite the strength of the government's balance sheet, did not condone an increase in government spending to offset the contraction in the private sector.[19] As a result, Korea was unable to cushion its economic downturn with the type of stimulus package and low interest rates deployed by the United States and most developed countries in 2008–2009.[20]

Second, in the debt renegotiations with foreign lenders, which involved the U.S. Treasury closely,[21] there was no write-down of the amount owed by Korean banks; although the United States did help force creditors to roll over their loans, the amount they were owed did not change. So while Korean companies were left to struggle, foreign banks and bondholders were effectively bailed out of their poor lending decisions—giving them no incentive to avoid the same mistakes in the future.[22]

Third, the IMF insisted that Korea needed to become *more* open to foreign capital, quickly. Paragraph 31 of the Letter of Intent between Korea and the IMF reads as follows:

> To increase competition and efficiency in the financial system, the schedule for allowing foreign entry into the domestic financial sector will be accelerated. Foreign financial institutions will be allowed to participate in mergers and acquisitions of domestic financial institutions in a friendly manner and on equal principles. By mid-1998, foreign financial

institutions will be allowed to establish bank subsidiaries and brokerage houses. Effective immediately foreign banks will be allowed to purchase equity in domestic banks without restriction, provided that the acquisitions contribute to the efficiency and soundness of the banking sector.[23]

The premise was that the crisis had not occurred because Korea was too exposed to volatile flows of short-term foreign capital, but because it was not open enough to foreign direct investment, including in the financial sector. To many observers, it looked like the IMF and the United States were taking advantage of the crisis to push forward their program of global financial liberalization.[24]

While every crisis is unique, Korea was in many ways typical of the experiences of emerging markets in the 1990s. Large, well-connected companies expanded rapidly by taking on large amounts of cheap debt, unconstrained by the forces that should prevent irresponsible corporate behavior in a capitalist economy; outside shareholders had little influence over powerful founders, and creditors lent money freely, assuming that the leading chaebol were too important for the government to let them go bankrupt.[25] Even though state-owned banks nominally controlled the flow of capital, tight relationships between the private sector and the government meant that the chaebol felt they had little to fear. Political factors played an important role in the economic crisis.

This central role of politics is common to many emerging market crises. Political connections were even more crucial in Indonesia, where the late President Suharto could never be mistaken for Thomas Jefferson. Under no possible interpretation was Suharto interested in protecting citizens against the power of the government. Instead, his goals were some combination of maintaining order, improving the economic welfare of ordinary people, and enriching his own inner circle.

Suharto adopted neither a communist-style planned economy nor an "anything goes" free market system. Instead, he cultivated a small group of private businesspeople whose family businesses became the backbone of the economy. Aided by the president and his family, who opened doors for their friends (and shut them for their competitors), these entrepreneurs built factories, developed cities, and learned how to export raw materials, agricultural products, and simple manufactured items to the rest of the world. As in many other low-income countries in the past half-century, economic development was dominated by a small economic elite defined by their personal ties to the ruling family, which traded favors for both political support and cold, hard cash—a pattern known as "crony capitalism."[26] For example, Indofood became one of the largest conglomerates in the country, largely because of a longtime personal friendship between its founder, Liem Sioe Liong, and Suharto.[27] Suharto's wife, Siti Hartinah Suharto, known as Madame Tien, was involved in so many business deals that she was referred to by critics as "Madame Tien Percent" for her alleged fees.[28] Suharto's children also cut themselves into many major deals; his daughter was involved in the largest taxi company, one son tried to build cars, and another son was a financial entrepreneur.[29]

For a long time, the system worked reasonably well. Annual income per capita grew from $1,235 in 1970, just after Suharto came to power, to just over $4,545 by 1997.[30] Indonesia was still a poor country with pervasive poverty, but thirty years of economic growth had created higher standards of living for millions of people. The country was regarded as a development success story by the World Bank and by foreign investors, who supplied much of the capital needed to build factories, roads, and apartment buildings. Everyone knew that the flow of capital was controlled by Suharto's family and friends, but this was actually attractive to investors, who quite reasonably thought it safer to lend money to people with strong political connections. The increasing availability of foreign capital fueled economic growth.

But easy money also fueled overinvestment and increasing risk-taking, especially by well-connected businesspeople who assumed they would be bailed out by their powerful friends if things turned out badly. And over time, success in business became less a question of innovation and sound management than of using political connections to obtain government favors and subsidies. The result was an economic boom that could be sustained only by ever-increasing amounts of foreign debt, which came crashing down in 1997.

Russia provided a different example of the dangers created by a well-connected economic elite with easy access to foreign capital. With the collapse of communism after 1991, many former Soviet republics attempted to build capitalist economies with independent private sectors. In Russia, with its vast reserves of oil and gas, privatization of state enterprises provided a direct route to creating the major companies that would be the foundation of the economy. The reformers in the government of President Boris Yeltsin initially planned to create companies with a large number of relatively small shareholders. But in 1995, with Yeltsin facing a difficult reelection campaign the next year, they allowed a small group of powerful businessmen to buy large stakes in major state enterprises cheaply; in return, the businessmen provided crucial financial and media support to Yeltsin during the campaign. This was the creation of the Russian oligarchs, who dominated the economy in the 1990s.[31]

The new power of the oligarchs, however, did not translate into strong economic growth or fiscal stability for the government, whose tax revenues depended heavily on the volatile price of oil. Needing to keep social spending at a reasonable level to avoid widespread protests, the IMF (and the United States) encouraged the Russian government to open up the country to capital so that foreigners could lend enough money to bridge the government into more prosperous times—the idea being that Russia could pay back those loans with future economic growth.[32] Private capital could also help restructure the oil and gas industry, develop new fields, and fund other productive investment projects that had been neglected under communism—even if the entire enterprise had a pungent whiff of corruption.

However, Russia's fragile economy was vulnerable to the financial crisis that began in Asia in 1997. The resulting slowdown in global economic growth caused drops in the prices of the commodities that Russia exported, notably oil, hurting both company profits and government tax revenues. By mid-1998, both the government and the private sector were in serious trouble because they had large short-term debts to global banks and foreign investors—and those debts were magnified by the falling value of the ruble. Even an emergency IMF loan in July 1998 could not bail the government out of its problems, and in August Russia was forced to default on its foreign debts, causing massive capital flight out of the country.[33]

NOT ENOUGH LIFEBOATS

Financial crises, at least in emerging markets, have political roots. Although severe crises are generally preceded by a large buildup of debt, that appetite for debt is the product of political factors, most often including close relationships between the economic and political elites.

The downward spiral that occurred in Korea, Indonesia, Russia, and other countries hit by the 1997–1998 crisis was remarkably steep. When foreign credit disappears, economic paralysis ensues; the government is forced to use its own foreign currency reserves to pay for imports, service debt, and cover losses in the private sector. If the country cannot right itself before defaulting on its own government debts, it risks becoming an economic pariah.

As the currency collapses, companies default on their debts, and unemployment rises sharply, the reality on the ground becomes nasty. Leading businesspeople—often selected for their personal relationships or political skills rather than their management ability—focus on saving their most prized possessions. Facing shorter time horizons, executives care less about the long-term value of their firms and more about their friends and themselves. As George Akerlof and Paul Romer wrote in their classic paper on "looting," businesspeople will profit from bankrupting their own firms when "poor accounting, lax regulation, or low penalties for abuse give owners an incentive to pay themselves more than their firms are worth and then default on their debt obligations."[34]

In Russia, as in most emerging market crises, there was a sharp increase in "tunneling"—borderline illegal ways for managers and controlling shareholders to transfer wealth from their businesses to their personal accounts.[35] Boris Fyodorov, a former Russian minister of finance who struggled against corruption and the abuse of authority, argued that confusion only helps the powerful;[36] when there are complicated government bailout schemes, multiple exchange rates, or high inflation, it becomes difficult to monitor the real market prices of assets and protect the value of firms.[37] In the extreme confusion caused by a crisis, insiders can take the money (or other valuables) and run, leaving banks, industrial firms, and other entities to collapse. Alternatively, confusion means that government officials have extraordinary discretion to save firms or let them fail. Describing an earlier financial crisis, Carlos Diaz-Alejandro wrote,

> [T]he ad hoc actions undertaken during 1982–83 in Chile to handle the domestic and external financial crisis carry with them an enormous potential for arbitrary wealth redistribution. . . . Faith in orderly judicial proceedings to clear up debts and claims on assets appeared to be quite low; stories abounded of debtors fleeing the country, and of petty and grand financial chicanery going unpunished.[38]

From a macroeconomic perspective, the government needs to restore the confidence of foreign investors. Large government deficits (Russia) require cuts in government spending and higher taxes; large private sector debts (Korea and Indonesia) need to be rescheduled; and to attract capital, interest rates need to be higher, even though this hurts the local economy.

But responding to crises also has a political dimension. The IMF is ready to lend money, but only if it (along with its backers among the major industrial countries) believes that the government has sufficient political will to sustain the policies necessary to stabilize the situation; in the case of Indonesia, for example, this involved cutting back on the cozy relationships with economic elites that helped produce the crisis.[39] This means less use of national reserves to cover the local private sector's debts, less bailout money for the banking system, and fewer subsidies all around. Essentially, the government needs to choose whom to save; it has to squeeze at least some of the oligarchs. Of course, this is rarely the strategy of choice among emerging market rulers, whose reflex is to protect their old friends when the going gets rough—it can be tough to find new supporters in the middle of a crisis—even coming up with innovative forms of subsidies, such as guaranteeing the debts of private companies. In some instances, rulers prefer, at least in the short term, to inflict pain on the working class through layoffs, reduced government services, and higher taxes, on the assumption that big private businesses produced the original boom and can also drive the recovery.

Eventually, however, at least some within the elite have to lose out, both because there aren't enough foreign currency reserves to cover everyone's debts and because external lenders (first among them the

IMF) demand some sign that the excessive risk-taking that produced the crisis is being punished. In both Thailand and Indonesia in 1997, the real fight was over which powerful families would lose their banks. In Thailand, the issue was handled relatively smoothly; more than fifty Thai "finance houses" (lightly regulated financial intermediaries) were shut down and some of the country's largest banks were taken over by the government. In Indonesia, however, the question was whether the parliamentary government would close the banking operations belonging to one of President Suharto's sons. In the struggle that ensued, the son's bank first lost its license to operate, but then appeared to have obtained another license with the suspected aid of the presidential palace; in the end, local officials did not have sufficient political will or power to stand up to the ruling family, undermining IMF (and U.S.) support and deepening the economic crisis.[40] In Korea, the confrontation was between the government and the largest chaebol, some of which had quite blatantly broken the law. After a series of showdowns—in which Daewoo threatened to default and political forces rallied to its assistance—the government won, and the hugely powerful Daewoo group went through bankruptcy and restructuring.

It is unheard of that all the oligarchs lose out, since the government can easily claim that they are essential to the domestic economy; some typically become even more powerful by absorbing their rivals, as happened in Korea, where Hyundai acquired the failing Kia. As the oligarchs in Yeltsin's Russia found out in 1998, it's a game of musical chairs; the post-crash government has enough foreign exchange reserves to help some big companies pay their debts, but not all of them. Usually the biggest of the big—the top chaebol, Suharto's close business allies (under the protection of Bacharuddin Jusuf Habibie, who succeeded Suharto as president), and the large Russian natural resource companies (such as Gazprom)—survive and prosper thanks to generous bailouts and other forms of government support. It's their smaller competitors who are cut adrift, while ordinary people suffer through government "austerity measures." Of course, the "dispossessed" oligarchs fight back, calling in political favors or even trying subversion—including calling up their contacts in the American foreign policy establishment, as the Ukrainians did with some success in the late 1990s.[41] But the aftermath of an emerging market crisis typically leads to a shakeout of the oligarchy, with political power concentrated in a smaller number of hands.

However, another common feature of emerging market crises is that they don't last forever. Even while outside observers are still despairing over corporate governance, macroeconomic management, and crony capitalism, growth picks up again. In 1999, the Korean economy grew by 11.1 percent; the Russian recovery took slightly longer, with growth of 4.5 percent in 1999 and 11 percent in 2000; and while growth took longest to resume in Indonesia, by 2000 its economy was expanding at close to 4 percent per year.[42] A lower exchange rate boosts exports, widespread unemployment reduces the cost of labor, and companies with rescheduled debts or new companies with clean books can take advantage of both higher sales and lower costs. Surviving businesses can use their increased market shares and reaffirmed political connections to grow bigger and stronger. The oligarchs who run them can become even wealthier; Carlos Slim bought up companies on the cheap after the 1982 crisis in Mexico and used the boom-bust cycle of the early 1990s (and his strong political connections) to consolidate his dominant position in telecommunications—becoming one of the world's richest men in the process.[43]

Growth can come back without any real fundamental reforms. Foreign lenders learn exactly the wrong lessons from a crisis: they learn that when push comes to shove, the IMF will protect them against the consequences of their bad investments; and they learn that it's always best to invest in the firms with the most political power (and hence the most assurance of being bailed out in a crisis), perpetuating the pattern of crony capitalism. As a result, foreign capital flows back, and emerging markets can repeat the boom-bust-bailout cycle for a long time, perhaps indefinitely.

But long-term economic growth is unlikely to result. Although oligarchies may be consistent with episodes of growth, they are not good at supporting the development of new entrepreneurs and the commercialization of new technologies.[44] In fact, entrenched economic elites may have an interest in limiting competition from new ideas and new people. Political elites, dependent on those economic elites for support, are unlikely to adopt policies to increase competition. Without a business environment that promotes innovation and competition from new entrants—like the one enjoyed by the United States early in the nineteenth century—periodic episodes of debt-fueled expansion do not add up to sustained economic growth.

Fundamental reform requires more than rearranging the seats on the government lifeboat; it requires weakening the economic and political power of the oligarchs and creating a healthier, more competitive economic system. This is only possible for a government with an independent base of support and legitimacy strong enough for it to challenge the economic elites. These are tough conditions to achieve, but not impossible ones, as the Korean case shows.

Korea had the advantage of a serious reformer, Kim Dae-jung, winning the presidency a month after the crisis hit.[45] Kim had fought for years against the previous regime and its backers and was deeply skeptical of the chaebol and the claim that they needed special treatment. He had numerous allies, including the prominent People's Solidarity for Participatory Democracy, which lobbied hard for corporate governance reform as a way to constrain the chaebol, strengthen the economy, and protect democracy.[46] Big companies such as SK Telecom and Samsung Electronics were forced to become more transparent to protect minority shareholders against looting. The government also pushed through reforms limiting the power of the chaebol: they were no longer allowed to cross-guarantee debts within groups, investments across companies within a chaebol were curtailed, the number of affiliated companies within a chaebol was reduced, large companies were required to have outside directors, financial disclosure requirements were strengthened, chaebol control over the nonbank financial sector was restricted, and there was a push to reduce debt levels.[47]

Although the reforms did not solve all of the problems presented by economic concentration, they did lead to a solid economic recovery. The rapid expansion of 1999 and 2000 was followed by annual growth of 4–5 percent in the early 2000s—a respectable rate for a country as developed as Korea, though slower than during the pre-1997 period. There is an active debate in Korea over whether the post-crisis corporate and political reforms went far enough; the largest chaebol, including Samsung, LG, SK, and Hyundai, still dominate the economic landscape. But the reforms were a step in the right direction, because they addressed the core problem that led to the crisis—concentration of economic power in an elite with the ability to influence the political system.

Ultimately, ending the cycle of debt-fueled bubbles and wrenching crises takes more than an IMF bailout package and a new minister of finance with a Ph.D. from an American university.[48] Since emerging market crises are the result of political conditions, sustained growth requires an end to the close relationships between economic and political elites that distort the competitive environment and encourage the misallocation of capital. Making this transition successfully is one of the central challenges for all emerging market economies.

NO WORRIES

Few people, if any, thought that these crises had anything to teach the United States, the world's richest economy and flagship democracy. The differences between Indonesia or Korea and the United States are obvious: income level, financial system, political track record, and so on. Our most ingrained beliefs run directly counter to the idea that a rich, privileged oligarchy could use government relationships to enrich itself in the good times and protect itself in the bad times. Our economic system is founded on the notion of fair competition in a market free from government influence. Our society cherishes few things more than the idea that all Americans have an equal opportunity to make money or participate in government. There is no construct more important in American political discourse than the "middle class."

The United States was not untouched by the emerging markets crisis of 1997–1998. In 1998, the most prestigious hedge fund in the world was arguably Long-Term Capital Management, founded only four years before in Greenwich, Connecticut, by a legendary trader, two Nobel Prize–winning economists, and a former vice chair of the Federal Reserve, among others.[49] When the crisis broke out, LTCM had about $4 billion in capital (money contributed by investors), which it had leveraged up with over $130 billion in borrowed money.[50] It bet that money not on ordinary stocks or bonds, but on complex arbitrage trades (betting that the difference between the prices of two similar assets would vanish) and directional trades (for example, betting that volatility in a given market would decrease).

However, LTCM's models were based on data gathered under ordinary market conditions. When the financial crisis spread and various markets seized up, it began losing money on many of its major trades, and its capital fell to less than $1 billion. But the real problem was that with LTCM on the verge of becoming insolvent, the banks and hedge funds that had lent it money (either directly or through derivatives transactions) were at risk of losing billions of dollars of their own. Fearing the damage an LTCM failure could do to the financial system as a whole, the Federal Reserve Bank of New York brought together representatives from the largest New York banks and pressured them to find a solution. In September 1998, the banks put in $3.6 billion of new money in exchange for a 90 percent ownership stake in the fund, largely wiping out the existing partners; with the new money, LTCM was able to ride out the storm without causing any collateral damage.

LTCM proved that in the new, globalized world, contagion from faraway emerging markets could spread to the United States. However, it also seemed to prove that any damage could be contained through effective intervention and sound macroeconomic management, without requiring taxpayer money or slowing down the real economy. As the long boom of the 1990s continued and the stock market continued to go up, LTCM soon faded into memory.

U.S. policymakers did draw a number of important lessons from the emerging market crises, outlined by Treasury Secretary Larry Summers in a major lecture at the 2000 conference of the American Economics Association.[51] Financial crises were the result of fundamental policy weaknesses: "Bank runs or their international analogues are not driven by sunspots: their likelihood is driven and determined by the extent of fundamental weaknesses." It was more important to look at the soundness of the financial system than to simply count the total amount of debt: "When well-capitalized and supervised banks, effective corporate governance and bankruptcy codes, and credible means of contract enforcement, along with other elements of a strong financial system, are present, significant amounts of debt will be sustainable. In their absence, even very small amounts of debt can be problematic." Companies should not be allowed to expect government support in a time of crisis: "It is certain that a healthy financial system cannot be

built on the expectation of bailouts." And in a time of crisis, it was critical to take rapid action to clean up failing banks: "Prompt action needs
to be taken to maintain financial stability, by moving quickly to support
healthy institutions and by intervening in unhealthy institutions." The
best advice Summers offered was a principle famously associated with
Mexican president Ernesto Zedillo during a crisis earlier in the decade:
"markets overreact, so policy needs to overreact as well."

These were all valid conclusions. In summary, they meant that
emerging market countries should become more like the United
States, with our strong legal institutions, transparent accounting, elaborate bank regulations, and independent political system—or, more
accurately, they should become more like the conventional image that
we held of our own country.

The idea that a major financial crisis of the type that ravaged
emerging markets in the 1990s could originate in the United States
was too preposterous to even be conceived of. Two of the crucial
ingredients—tight connections between economic and political elites
and dependence on fickle short-term flows of foreign capital—seemed
completely out of the picture.[52] Despite rising debt due to growing
trade imbalances, Summers's argument implied that our superior
financial system made high debt levels sustainable. More fundamentally, political economy—the study of interactions between the political and economic systems—was only appropriate for developing and
emerging market countries. In countries that had already "emerged,"
like the United States, economic questions could be studied without
reference to politics. Instead, economic and financial policy presented
only technocratic questions, which Summers compared to regulation
of air travel:

> The jet airplane made air travel more comfortable, more efficient, and
> more safe, though the accidents were more spectacular and for a time
> more numerous after the jet was invented. In the same way, modern
> global financial markets carry with them enormous potential for bene-
> fit, even if some of the accidents are that much more spectacular. As the
> right public policy response to the jet was longer runways, better air-
> traffic control, and better training for pilots, and not the discourage-
> ment of rapid travel, so the right public policy response to financial
> innovation is to assure a safe framework so that the benefits can be real-
> ized, not to stifle the change.

_____

But in September-October 2008, when Lehman Brothers collapsed and panic seized the U.S. economy, money flooded out of the private financial system in what looked like a classic emerging market crisis.* In retrospect, it was clear that the run-up in housing prices of the 2000s was a bubble fueled by over-optimism and excess debt worthy of any emerging market. The diagnosis of the 1997 Korean Letter of Intent seemed to apply perfectly to 2008 America (substituting "household" for "corporate"): "Financial institutions have priced risks poorly and have been willing to finance an excessively large portion of investment plans of the corporate sector, resulting in high leveraging. At the same time, the dramatic decline in stock prices has cut the value of banks' equity and further reduced their net worth."[53] And when the federal government began rescuing major banks presided over by ultra-wealthy executives—while letting smaller banks fail by the dozens—it began to seem as if our government was bailing out its own, uniquely American oligarchy.

In similar situations in the 1990s, the United States had urged emerging market countries to deal with the basic economic and political factors that had created devastating crises. This advice was often perceived as arrogant (especially when the United States also insisted that crisis-stricken countries open themselves up further to American banks), but the basic logic was sound: when an existing economic elite has led a country into a deep crisis, it is time for change. And the crisis itself presents a unique, but short-lived, opportunity for change.

As in Korea a decade before, a new president came to power in the United States in the midst of the crisis. And just like Kim Dae-jung in Korea, Barack Obama had campaigned as the candidate of change. Yet far from applying the advice it had so liberally dispensed to others, the U.S. government instead organized generous financial support for its existing economic elite, leaving the captains of the financial sector in place.

What had happened?

_____

* There was one huge difference, which was that money did not leave the country; instead, it left the private sector for the safety of U.S. Treasury obligations. But the effect on the private sector financial system was the same.

3

WALL STREET RISING
1980–

In this present crisis, government is not the solution to our problem; government is the problem.

—Ronald Reagan, inaugural address,
January 20, 1981[1]

On December 9, 1985, the cover of *Business Week* featured John Gutfreund, the CEO of Salomon Brothers and "The King of Wall Street." "Merrill Lynch remains the best-known Wall Street house and Goldman Sachs the best-managed, but Salomon Bros. is the firm most feared by its competitors," wrote Anthony Bianco. "It is the prototype of the thoroughly modern investment bank—the not-so-benevolent King of the Street."[2]

Salomon was the epitome of the new breed of Wall Street investment bank, built around a swashbuckling, risk-taking bond trading operation powered by "quants" recruited from academic research institutions and filled with "financial engineers" designing new products. Its strategy was to take large risks on its own account rather than simply taking fees for providing advice or executing trades. As Bianco put it, "What sets Salomon apart is the sheer scale on which it operates in the markets, reflecting an appetite for risk unrivaled among financial middlemen." Four years later, *Liar's Poker*, Michael Lewis's memoir of his years at Salomon, would cement its status as the paradigmatic bank of the 1980s, the same decade that produced the original Oliver Stone *Wall Street* movie, with Gordon Gekko's famous "Greed is good" speech.

Looking back, however, Salomon seems so . . . small. When the *Business Week* story was written, it had $68 billion in assets and $2.8 billion in shareholders' equity. It expected to earn $1.1 billion in operating profits for all of 1985. The next year, Gutfreund earned $3.2 million.[3] At the time, those numbers seemed extravagant. Today? Not so much.

If the financial crisis of 2007–2009 produced a king of Wall Street, it would most likely be Jamie Dimon, CEO of JPMorgan Chase and the "Last Man Standing," according to the title of a recent book.[4] (Lloyd Blankfein of Goldman Sachs would be the other contender.) Compared to other megabanks, JPMorgan was less exposed to toxic securities and came through the credit crisis in better shape. In addition, it capitalized on the problems of other banks to snap up Bear Stearns and Washington Mutual, gaining strength in both investment banking and retail banking. And it took advantage of its weakened competitors to grab market share across the board, taking the top spot in investment banking revenues in the first half of 2009.[5] At his company's annual meeting in May 2009, Dimon could justifiably claim, "This might have been our finest year ever."[6] In addition, his status as a longtime Democratic donor with strong political connections, as well as the Obama administration's need to work with someone on Wall Street, gave him increased influence in Washington. Dimon, *The New York Times* wrote in July 2009, "has emerged as President Obama's favorite banker, and in turn, the envy of his Wall Street rivals."[7]

At the time, JPMorgan Chase had over $2 trillion in assets,[8] not counting positions not recorded on its balance sheet, such as derivatives exposures; it had $155 billion in balance sheet equity; and it earned $4.1 billion in operating profits in the second quarter alone. By comparison, the 1985 Salomon Brothers, even after converting to 2009 dollars to account for inflation, only had $122 billion in assets, $5 billion in equity, and $2 billion in operating profits for an entire year.[9] (Goldman Sachs, as a pure investment bank, offered perhaps a more accurate comparison to Salomon; in the second quarter of 2009, it had $890 billion in assets, $63 billion in equity, and $5 billion in operating profits.)[10]

Although Dimon voluntarily took no cash bonus for 2008, his total compensation including stock awards was still $19.7 million, more than three times Gutfreund's inflation-adjusted earnings of $5.8 million.[11] And this was in a bad year for Wall Street CEOs; in 2007, Dimon earned $34 million, Blankfein $54 million, John Thain of Merrill Lynch $84 million, and John Mack of Morgan Stanley $41 million.[12]

Something changed during the last quarter-century. One factor was a wave of mergers that created fewer and fewer, but larger and larger, financial institutions. JPMorgan Chase was the product of the mergers of Chemical Bank, Manufacturers Hanover, Chase Manhattan, J.P. Morgan, Bank One, and First Chicago—all since 1991—even before the bargain-basement acquisitions of Bear Stearns and Washington Mutual in 2008. (Salomon itself was acquired by Travelers, which then merged with Citicorp into Citigroup.)

In addition, the financial sector itself simply got bigger and bigger. When John Gutfreund became CEO of Salomon in 1978, all commercial banks together held $1.2 trillion of assets, equivalent to 53 percent of U.S. GDP. By the end of 2007, the commercial banking sector had grown to $11.8 trillion in assets, or 84 percent of U.S. GDP. But that was only a small part of the story. Securities broker-dealers (investment banks), including Salomon, grew from $33 billion in assets, or 1.4 percent of GDP, to $3.1 trillion in assets, or 22 percent of GDP. Asset-backed securities such as collateralized debt obligations (CDOs), which hardly existed in 1978, accounted for another $4.5 trillion in assets in 2007, or 32 percent of GDP.* All told, the debt held by the financial sector grew from $2.9 trillion, or 125 percent of GDP, in 1978 to over $36 trillion, or 259 percent of GDP, in 2007.[13]

Some of this growth was due to an increase in borrowing by the nonfinancial sector—the "real economy." However, the expansion of the financial sector vastly outpaced growth in households and nonfinancial companies. Instead, most of the growth in the financial sector was due to the increasing "financialization" of the economy—the transformation of one dollar of lending to the real economy into many dollars of financial transactions. In 1978, the financial sector borrowed $13 in the credit markets for every $100 borrowed by the real econ-

---

* To create asset-backed securities, a new legal entity buys and holds some assets (such as mortgages) and then issues new bonds that are backed by those assets. So the assets behind asset-backed securities are *in addition to* the assets on the balance sheets of commercial and investment banks.

omy; by 2007, that had grown to $51.[14] In other words, for the same amount of borrowing by households and nonfinancial companies, the amount of borrowing by financial institutions quadrupled.

Even these numbers do not include the derivatives positions that financial institutions were building up at the same time, because derivatives—bets on the value of other assets, such as stocks or currencies—are not conventionally accounted for on bank balance sheets. Worldwide, over-the-counter derivatives, which essentially did not exist in 1978, grew to over $33 trillion in market value—over twice U.S. GDP—by the end of 2008.[15] A large portion of these derivatives was held by U.S. financial institutions, which were among the world leaders in the business. No matter how you measure it, the size and economic influence of America's financial sector grew enormously over the past thirty years; the Salomon Brothers of 1985 would be trivial today.

As the financial sector amassed more and more assets, it became a bigger part of the national economy. Between 1978 and 2007, the financial sector grew from 3.5 percent to 5.9 percent of the economy (measured by contribution to GDP).[16] Its share of corporate profits climbed even faster, as shown in Figure 3-1. From the 1930s until around 1980, financial sector profits grew at roughly the same rate as profits in the nonfinancial sector. But from 1980 until 2005, financial sector profits grew by 800 percent, adjusted for inflation, while nonfinancial sector profits grew by only 250 percent. Financial sector profits plummeted at the peak of the financial crisis, but quickly rebounded; by the third quarter of 2009, financial sector profits were over six times their 1980 level, while nonfinancial sector profits were little more than double those of 1980.[17]

Not surprisingly, bankers' salaries and bonuses also shot upward. In 1978, average per-person compensation in the banking sector was $13,163 (in 1978 dollars)—essentially the same as in the private sector overall, which averaged $13,142. From 1955 through 1982, the average banker's compensation fluctuated between 100 percent and 110 percent of average private sector pay. Richard Fisher, chairman of Morgan Stanley in the 1990s, recalled that when he left Harvard Business School in the early 1960s, "investment banking was about the worst-paying job available to us. I started at Morgan Stanley at $5,800 a year. It was the lowest offer I had . . . I'm sure my classmates who went to Procter & Gamble started at $9,000 a year."[18] Then banking

Figure 3-1: Real Corporate Profits, Financial vs. Nonfinancial Sectors

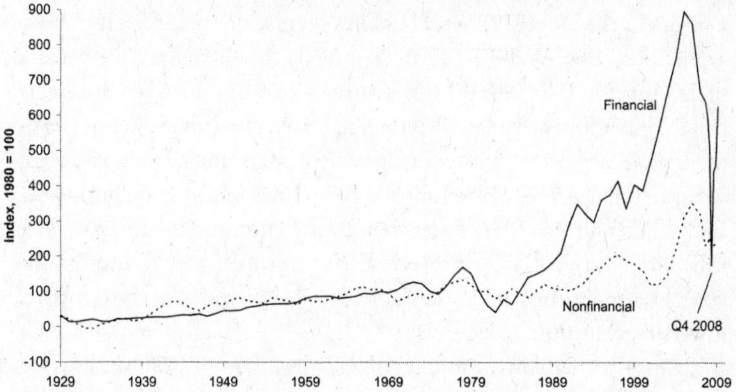

Source: Bureau of Economic Analysis, *National Income and Product Accounts*, Tables 1.1.4, 6.16; calculation by the authors. Financial sector excludes Federal Reserve banks. Annual through 2007, quarterly Q1 2008–Q3 2009.

pay took off, until by 2007, the average banker was making over twice as much as the average private sector employee.[19]

This trend was driven by stupendous growth at the top end of the income distribution. In *Liar's Poker*, $800,000 counted as a big bonus for an experienced trader.[20] In 1990, Salomon Brothers paid its top traders then shocking cash bonuses of more than $10 million.[21] In 2009, it emerged that a single executive at Citigroup—head of a commodities trading group that was loosely descended from Salomon— was due a $100 million bonus.[22] And the real money was in hedge funds; in 2007, five fund managers earned at least $1 billion each for themselves, led by John Paulson, who made $3.7 billion successfully betting against the housing market and the mortgage-backed securities built on top of it.[23]

Bigger, more profitable, and richer—the financial sector grew in every way imaginable during the last three decades. Most important, it became more powerful.

BORING BANKING

This is not what a casual observer would have expected in the 1970s, a time when the financial sector composed just over 3 percent of U.S. GDP and paid its workers little more than the private sector overall.

For the entire postwar period, finance had generally been what the authors of the Depression-era banking regulations intended it to be— safe and boring. As described in chapter 1, the regulatory framework created in the 1930s prescribed a strict separation between commercial and investment banks. Commercial banks had an explicit government guarantee in the form of federal deposit insurance, but paid for it with tight federal regulation. Boxed in by rules limiting the businesses they could engage in, the states they could enter, and the interest rates they could pay (but also protected from competition by those same rules), commercial banking became the stereotype of a conservative, low-risk profession.

Investment banking, though riskier, was a far cry from the trading floor of *Liar's Poker*, where traders routinely risked hundreds of millions of dollars and ate guacamole out of five-gallon drums.[24] Like commercial banking, investment banking had taken on the features of a cozy cartel. For example, commissions on stock trading had been fixed (since 1792) by the New York Stock Exchange, preventing price competition. Securities firms earned most of their revenues from the traditional businesses of underwriting stocks and bonds (finding buyers for new securities being issued by corporations), providing brokerage services for institutional clients and an increasingly affluent public, and advising companies on mergers and acquisitions. These businesses were built around long-term client relationships, where reputation mattered. Leading banks such as Morgan Stanley cultivated an image as genteel, "white shoe" firms that emphasized client service rather than making a buck. As Nicholas Brady, treasury secretary in the administration of George H. W. Bush and a former investment banker, said in 2009, "When I came to Wall Street in 1954, it was a profession, one that financed the building of this country's industrial capacity and infrastructure."[25]

At the time, nonfinancial corporations had relatively simple financial needs, at least compared to the plethora of products and services available today: they raised short-term money by taking out bank loans, they raised long-term money by issuing bonds, and they raised capital by issuing stock. The loans were extended and held by commercial banks; the bonds and stocks were placed by investment banks with investors for a small slice of the proceeds. Since investment banks were not making loans directly, holding large chunks of corporate debt or equity, or trading large volumes of securities on their own account, there was little need for massive investment banks; from 1946 through 1981, total financial assets of all securities broker-dealers remained under 2 percent of U.S. GDP.[26]

"Boring banking" was reflected in the nature of the work done in the financial industry, which would be largely unrecognizable to people accustomed to today's era of quantitative sophistication and perpetual innovation. Thomas Philippon and Ariell Reshef have analyzed the task complexity of the jobs done by employees in financial services firms over the last century (Figure 3-2) and found that math aptitude and decision-making were less important between 1940 and 1970 than either earlier or later in the century. By contrast, finger dexterity and routine administrative tasks were relatively more important during this period than in the earlier or later periods.[27]

This does not mean that bankers somehow became noncompetitive and lost the urge to make money after the Depression. There were plenty of attempts to skirt existing banking regulations. Large bank holding companies evaded restrictions on interstate banking by buying separate subsidiary banks in multiple states; thrifts—savings banks and savings and loan associations founded to serve households—

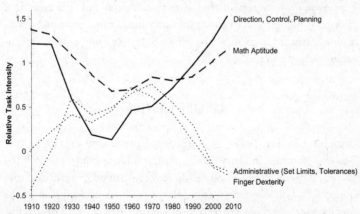

Figure 3-2: Relative Job Complexity in the Financial Sector

Direction, Control, Planning

Math Aptitude

Administrative (Set Limits, Tolerances)
Finger Dexterity

Source: Thomas Philippon and Ariell Reshef, "Wages and Human Capital in the U.S. Financial Industry: 1909–2006," Figure 3.

competed for deposits by offering interest rates above what commercial banks could pay. But during this period, the federal government took active steps to close regulatory loopholes and maintain the
basic framework created in the 1930s. The Bank Holding Company
Act of 1956 increased regulation of bank holding companies and limited their ability to buy banks in multiple states. In 1966, Congress
gave the Federal Reserve authority to regulate deposit rates paid by
thrifts. Congress even expanded the regulatory framework to include
stronger consumer protection measures, such as the Truth in Lending
Act of 1968 and the Fair Credit Reporting Act of 1970. Not only was
the government making sure that banks were safe and sound, it was
trying to make sure that banks did not abuse their customers.[28]

During most of this period, the American economy flourished.
From 1947 to 1973, real GDP (adjusted for inflation) grew at an average annual growth rate of 4.0 percent,[29] and American corporations
grew, prospered, and expanded throughout the world. This was a
period of major technological innovation in multiple capital-intensive
industries, as the middle class bought cars and household appliances,
the government spent heavily on an increasingly sophisticated defense
industry, and the revolution in computer technology began with the
development of mainframes and minicomputers. It also saw the emergence of the modern venture capital industry, which has played a crucial role in the funding of technological innovation. There were many
reasons for the success of the postwar economy, but it is clear that
"boring banking" did not constrain financing of innovation and development. Instead, it facilitated a phase of tremendous growth in economic output and prosperity.

CHANGING BANKING

Beginning in the 1970s and accelerating through the 1980s, the
financial services industry broke free from the constraints of the
Depression-era bargain. While there were banking executives who
hoped for wholesale deregulation, there was no concerted plan by the
financial sector to overthrow its regulatory constraints. Instead, like
many historical phenomena, this development emerged from a conflu-

ence of factors: exogenous events, such as the high inflation of the 1970s; the emergence of academic finance; and the broader deregulatory trend begun in the administration of Jimmy Carter but transformed into a crusade by Ronald Reagan. The eventual result was an out-of-balance financial system that still enjoyed the backing of the federal government—what president would allow the financial system to collapse on his watch?—without the regulatory oversight necessary to prevent excessive risk-taking.

Like many major trends, this one was not entirely visible to its participants at the outset. Throughout American history, regulatory change has been more about settling disputes between segments of the business community than about sweeping social transformations, and the beginnings of financial deregulation were no different.

Fixed commissions for stock trading were one of the first dominoes to fall. As David Komansky, later CEO of Merrill Lynch, recalled, "There was no discounting, no negotiating. Fixed prices meant fixed prices for the entire Street; we couldn't give you a discount even if we wanted to. It was the greatest thing in the world."[30] Most Wall Street brokerage firms were happy to profit from this cartel. But not everyone saw things this way. Large institutional investors such as mutual funds and pension funds, which had grown in importance as increasingly affluent Americans amassed savings and large corporations set up pension plans for their employees, wanted lower prices for their large orders. Donald Regan, CEO of Merrill Lynch in the early 1970s, also wanted an end to fixed commissions. Merrill, as the largest broker on Wall Street, stood to gain the most from competition, and Regan already had a vision of his company as a large, diversified financial services firm.[31] William Salomon, then head of Salomon Brothers, also supported an end to fixed commissions.[32]

Called upon to adjudicate this dispute in the early 1970s, the Securities and Exchange Commission obliged, ordering the elimination of fixed commissions in the New York Stock Exchange (NYSE).[33] The NYSE complied on May 1, 1975, which had ripple effects throughout the securities industry. Competition over brokerage commissions meant that institutional investors could make large trades much more cheaply, leading to an increase in trading volume. After enjoying comfortable, cartel-like profits for decades, securities brokers were now given a much larger market, but also a much more competitive one. One source of competition was brokers such as Charles Schwab who focused on providing discounted services to individuals. As a result, the small partnerships that had populated Wall Street for decades began to fade away, replaced by larger, more heavily capitalized firms that expanded into higher-margin businesses, searching for new sources of profits.[34]

The world of traditional commercial and savings banks was also undergoing changes that would have far-reaching implications. One precipitating factor was the high inflation of the 1970s. High inflation meant higher interest rates, since no one will lend money at 3 percent if inflation is 6 percent. Because the interest paid on traditional savings accounts was capped by Regulation Q, money flowed out of those accounts toward higher-yielding Treasury bills and other forms of short-term debt issued by corporations and governments.* Money market funds,† invented in 1971, grew from only $3 billion in assets in 1976 to $230 billion by 1982.[35] At the same time as banks were losing their easy source of cheap funds, rising interest rates meant that they were losing money on the mortgages they had made, mostly at fixed rates. Many mortgages made in the early 1970s[36] were still paying only 7 percent even as inflation spiked into double digits at the end of the decade, meaning banks were not even receiving enough interest to make up for inflation. (Homeowners, on the other hand, profited as their debts were inflated away—helping to convince a generation of Americans that houses were the best investment they could possibly make.)

These economic shifts primarily affected savings and loan associations (S&Ls), which were more exposed to mortgages than commercial banks. But at the time, the S&Ls—not the Wall Street investment

---

*Depositing money in a savings account is the same as lending money to your bank; buying short-term commercial paper is lending money to a company; buying a Treasury bill is lending money to the U.S. government. Since interest rates on savings accounts were capped but interest rates on other lending were not, people moved money out of savings accounts into other forms of lending.

†A money market fund is a mutual fund that invests in short-term, liquid debt such as Treasury bills or commercial paper. Although money markets are generally not guaranteed against losing value, they attempt to maintain a share price of $1, which makes them look and function like savings or checking accounts.

banks—and their lobbying organization, the United States League of Savings Institutions, were a powerful political force with influence on both sides of the political aisle. Although individually small, they had a favorable public image (in a country that professes to live by small-town values), they were located in virtually every congressional district, and they benefited from the disproportionate representation of rural states in the Senate. "When it came to thrift matters in Congress, the U.S. League and many of its affiliates were the de facto government," said former Federal Home Loan Bank head Edwin J. Gray in 1989.[37]

In response to S&L pressure, Congress passed the Depository Institutions Deregulation and Monetary Control Act of 1980, which phased out Regulation Q, enabling banks to compete for deposits by paying higher interest rates—in the process eliminating one pillar of the "boring banking" business model. No longer able to rely on an artificially low cost of money, banks would have to seek new sources of revenue in new businesses. The bill eased this shift by allowing S&Ls to expand from home mortgages into a range of riskier loans and investments, making it easier for them to make the mistakes that produced the S&L crisis later in the decade. The bill also overrode any state laws restricting the interest that could be charged on first mortgages—meaning that banks could charge whatever interest rates the market would bear.[38]

By 1980, the traditional business models of both investment and commercial banking were eroding in the face of macroeconomic changes and the first waves of deregulation. As historian Charles Geisst wrote of Wall Street, "A turning point had been reached on the Street. . . . The more placid days of the past were gone forever."[39] There was still no coherent program or ideology that laid out what the financial services industry should look like and what its relationship to the government should be. But that was changing.

At the time, a movement was growing in the halls of America's leading universities that would help transform the financial sector. This movement was the discipline of academic finance, pioneered by economists such as Paul Samuelson, Franco Modigliani, Merton Miller, Harry

Markowitz, William Sharpe, Eugene Fama, Fischer Black, Robert Merton, and Myron Scholes, most of whom went on to win the Nobel Prize. These scholars brought sophisticated mathematics to bear on such problems as determining the optimal capital structure of a firm (the ratio between debt and equity), pricing financial assets, and separating and hedging risks.[40]

Academic finance had a tremendous impact on the way business is done around the globe. For example, research on capital structure contributed to a significant increase in indebtedness by corporations.[41] (Debt provides leverage, and therefore increases expected returns along with risk.) It also expanded the market for advising corporations on their funding strategies—a lucrative opportunity investment bankers quickly seized. Similarly, the quantitative study of financial markets helped bankers identify a new universe of ways to make money. New methods for calculating the relative value of financial assets made possible arbitrage trading, where traders sought out small pricing discrepancies that, in theory, should not exist; by betting that the market would make these discrepancies disappear, they could make almost certain money. The Black-Scholes Model (developed by Black, Scholes, and Merton) provided a handy formula for calculating the price of a financial derivative, and in the process gave rise to the derivatives revolution.

Thus academic finance produced important tools that would create new markets and vast new sources of revenues for Wall Street. But it was perhaps even more important for the ideology it created. A central assertion of the academic finance movement in the 1960s and 1970s became known as the Efficient Market Hypothesis: precisely because traders are looking for and exploiting inefficiencies in asset prices, those inefficiencies cannot last for more than a brief period of time; as a result, prices are always "right." As outlined by Eugene Fama in 1970, the Efficient Market Hypothesis comes in a weak form, a semi-strong form, and a strong form. The weak form holds that future prices cannot be predicted from past prices; the semi-strong form holds that prices adjust quickly to all publicly available information (meaning that by the time you read the news in the newspaper, it is too late to make money on the news); and the strong form holds that *no one* has any information that can be used to predict future prices, so market prices are always right. At the time, Fama argued, with empirical evidence, that the weak and semi-strong forms were correct. He acknowledged that there are exceptions to the strong form—exchange floor traders and corporate insiders do have information they can profit from—but found no evidence that anyone else (mutual fund managers, for example) is able to "beat the market" through better information or analysis.[42]

Despite Fama's caveats, the strong form became the intellectual justification for financial deregulation. If a free market will always produce fundamentally correct asset prices, then the financial sector can be left to its own devices. This principle applies directly to securities and derivatives; for example, if a municipality buys an interest rate swap from an investment bank, it must be getting a good deal, since the price it pays is set by the "market" (even if the transaction is negotiated privately between the parties). It applies more broadly to the fees charged for financial services; if the penalty interest rate on a credit card is 30 percent, that must be the true price of the risk that the card issuer is taking on that customer. And conceptually, it even applies to compensation in the financial sector; if a trader takes home a $5 million bonus at the end of the year, that must be the true value of his labor. (Or, as Goldman Sachs CEO Lloyd Blankfein recently asserted in defense of his bankers' high pay, "If you examine our practices on compensation, you will see a complete correlation throughout our history of having remuneration match performance over the long term.")[43]

These were not mathematical consequences of the Efficient Market Hypothesis, but they flowed naturally from it. The basic belief was that if a financial transaction was taking place, it was a good thing. This belief reflects a general economic principle; given perfectly rational actors with perfect information and no externalities, all transactions should be beneficial for both parties. But few economists ever believed that these assumptions actually held in the real world. And over the next few decades, dozens of leading economists such as Joseph Stiglitz, Robert Shiller, and Larry Summers set about knocking holes in the Efficient Market Hypothesis.[44] Brad DeLong, Andrei Shleifer, Summers, and Robert Waldmann created a model showing that "noise trading can lead to a large divergence between market prices and fundamental values."[45] Even Fischer Black (of Black-Scholes fame) agreed. At the 1985 meeting of the American Finance Association, he argued that it was impossible to differentiate between noise and information, and hence impossible to determine who was a noise trader and who was an information trader. Consequently, prices could wander far away from fundamental values for indefinite periods of time.[46]

The Efficient Market Hypothesis did not develop in a vacuum; it was in the vanguard of a broad movement in economics arguing for decreased regulation and increased liberalization of markets. By the 1990s, there was also an emerging consensus that developing countries should abandon restrictions on the flow of capital and open their economies up to foreign money. The argument, as advanced by Stanley Fischer, then second-in-command at the International Monetary Fund, was that "free capital movements facilitate a more efficient global allocation of savings, and help channel resources into their most productive uses, thus increasing economic growth and welfare," providing benefits that would outweigh any risks.[47] Again, there were important skeptics. Jagdish Bhagwati argued in 1998 that trade in dollars was not the same as trade in goods, because free capital flows would generate financial crises whose potential costs needed to be taken into account.[48] But the belief in free movements of capital, like the belief in efficient markets, became strong enough in some circles to shrug off the need for empirical justification.[49]

The Efficient Market Hypothesis, like the doctrine of free capital flows, provided ready ammunition for anyone who wanted to argue that banks should be allowed to do as they pleased, that financial innovations were necessarily good, and that free financial markets would always produce optimal social outcomes. Even so, it might have remained only a cry in the academic wilderness or an esoteric Wall Street doctrine. But it had the fortune of being in the right place at the right time—of coinciding with a once-in-a-generation shift in the American political climate.

The election of Ronald Reagan marked a crucial turning point in American political history. Although Richard Nixon had already shown how to build a new Republican majority by capitalizing on resentment against Lyndon Johnson's Great Society and the culture of the 1960s, it was Reagan who gave that movement a usable political ideology. Although Jimmy Carter had overseen the beginnings of deregulation with airlines, railroads, and trucking, it was more a topic for policy wonks than for the broader electorate; drawing in part on the ideas of economist Milton Friedman, Reagan made deregulation an ideological crusade.[50] Like many successful leaders, Reagan managed to bring together many conflicting movements and beliefs in his coalition. But his central message, as he said in his first inaugural address, was that "government is not the solution to our problem; government is the problem."[51] According to Reagan, making government smaller and weaker would not only increase personal freedom, it would unleash the creativity and productivity of the private sector.

Reagan fought this battle on many fronts. He cut taxes in an unsuccessful attempt to "starve the beast"—force government to shrink by cutting its funding. He reduced funding to regulatory agencies, hoping to achieve through understaffing what he could not pass through Congress. He installed people who had no interest in regulation at the head of major regulatory agencies. Faced with a Democratic majority in the House of Representatives through his entire presidency, he was unable to fully achieve his goal of dismantling government regulation, but he set the tone for both Republican and Democratic administrations that would follow. (Reagan's ascent to power also closely followed the formation of Margaret Thatcher's first government in the United Kingdom in 1979; Thatcher's deregulatory policies helped unleash the forces of financial innovation in London, with similar results.)

For the financial sector, Reaganism meant breaking down the rules that constrained the activities of financial institutions. As his first treasury secretary (and later chief of staff), Reagan named Donald Regan, the Merrill Lynch CEO who had championed deregulation of brokerage commissions and sought to make Merrill into a diversified financial services company. It was not unusual for a treasury secretary to come from the banking industry. But it was unusual for a treasury secretary to embrace a deregulatory agenda as broad as the one Regan espoused. In an October 1981 interview, he said that his top priority was "the deregulation of financial institutions . . . trying to deregulate as quickly as possible in the field of interest rates, mandatory ceilings, things of that nature."[52]

The savings and loan industry, still struggling with high interest rates and overreliance on mortgage lending, presented an opportunity for the new administration to test out its theories. In 1982, Congress passed the Garn–St. Germain Depository Institutions Act—hailed by President Reagan as "the first step in our administration's comprehensive program of financial deregulation"[53]—which lifted many regulations on the savings and loan industry, allowing them to expand further into new businesses, such as commercial lending and investing in corporate bonds (including junk bonds), to compensate for the collapse of the "boring banking" business model.[54] In addition, the bill authorized state-chartered banks to offer mortgages with adjustable rates[55] (national banks had been able to offer adjustable rate mortgages since the previous year)[56]—a central feature of the last twenty-five years of innovation in residential lending—and relaxed other constraints on mortgage lending for national banks. The following year, acting under the authorization granted by the bill, the Office of the Comptroller of the Currency lifted all restrictions on loan-to-value ratios (the percentage of a house's appraised value that could be borrowed), maturities (fifteen years, thirty years, etc.), and amortization schedules (meaning that banks could offer mortgages where the principal balance went up over time).[57] The Garn–St. Germain Act also made it easier for banks to operate across state borders by allowing interstate mergers between banks and S&Ls.[58]

The Reagan administration's willingness to help the banking industry also extended to the new innovations that were beginning to take hold on Wall Street. Lewis Ranieri, one of the legendary traders at Salomon Brothers, worked directly with administration officials to create a new market for mortgage-backed securities.[59] In 1968, the federal agency Ginnie Mae had begun securitizing mortgages—buying mortgages from lenders, combining them in pools, and issuing securities backed by those pools to the lenders (who could then sell them to investors).* The principal on these mortgages (but not the risk that borrowers might prepay) was guaranteed by Ginnie Mae, and

---

* To create a mortgage-backed security (MBS), a large number of mortgages are pooled together; the mortgage-backed securities each have a claim on the payments made on those mortgages. The net effect is that each investor in the MBS owns a tiny piece of each mortgage, distributing each mortgage's risk of default among a large number of investors.

therefore by the U.S. government. This guarantee insulated banks from the risk of default by their borrowers and also provided a way to attract money from a wide range of investors to the housing market. In the 1970s, Salomon attempted to create its own mortgage-backed securities out of Bank of America mortgages, but ran into problems with tax laws and with state regulations.

The solution to Salomon's problem was a new bill, the Secondary Mortgage Market Enhancement Act of 1984, which Ranieri helped create and defended before Congress.[60] This bill cleared away the tax issues and state regulations that had hampered Salomon's earlier efforts, giving investment banks the ability to buy up virtually any mortgages, pool them together, and resell them in slices with varying levels of risk. Securitization was made even easier when the Tax Reform Act of 1986 created the Real Estate Mortgage Investment Conduit, or REMIC, which created tax advantages making mortgage-backed securities more attractive. These new laws were unequivocally good for the investment banks, which gained a new market from which they could earn millions of dollars in fees. In return, they were supposed to increase the flow of money into the housing sector, making it easier for people to buy houses. The new market for private mortgage-backed securities also helped commercial banks and S&Ls, which could now pass on the risk of their fixed rate mortgages (which lose value if interest rates increase) to investors in the new securities.[61]

These legislative victories showed the growing influence of Wall Street, but they also depended on Wall Street's ability to wrap itself in the ideology of homeownership—the idea that making it easier for people to buy houses is always a good thing. In contrast to the thrifts, the major commercial and investment banks did not make major gains in the 1980s, despite the friendly attitude of the Reagan administration. Major legislation to break down the Glass-Steagall barrier fell victim to Democrats in Congress. (It also faced opposition from some investment banks, which did not want commercial banks invading their turf.) The Financial Institutions Deregulation Act of 1983, which would have allowed bank holding companies to expand into securities and insurance, died in Congress.[62]

Comprehensive deregulation was also derailed by the savings and loan crisis, which worsened steadily through the 1980s. As it turned out, the Garn–St. Germain Act, by allowing S&Ls to expand into new businesses, prompted many of them to gamble on high-risk investments. S&Ls lacked experience in these businesses, as did their regulators, and over 2,000 banks failed between 1985 and 1992, with a peak of 534 in 1989. (By comparison, only seventy-nine banks failed during all of the 1970s.)[63] Ultimately, over one thousand people were indicted and thrifts suspected of fraud cost the government over $54 billion.*[64]

When Ronald Reagan left office, his program to deregulate the financial sector remained incomplete. The industry still faced significant constraints, such as limits on interstate banking and the Glass-Steagall separation of commercial and investment banks. But although his ambitions remained unfulfilled, Reagan had transformed academic theories and policy prescriptions into a potent ideology that would play a major role in political discourse for at least the next two decades. The collapse of much of the communist bloc beginning in 1989 lent further support to the idea that free market capitalism was the right answer to any question.

EXCITING BANKING

The basic principle behind any oligarchy is that economic power yields political power. The legislative failures of the Reagan administration showed that, in the 1980s, Wall Street did not yet hold sway in Washington. While academic finance provided the intellectual justification for financial nonregulation and the Reagan Revolution provided the political ideology of weak government, these would have mattered less had finance remained simply one industry among many. Instead, the banking industry went through a revolution of its own— one aided in part by academic theories and incipient deregulation, but largely driven by the creativity and competitiveness of a generation of talented bankers. Their serial innovations created the new money machines that fueled the rapid, massive growth in the size, profitability, and wealth of the financial sector over the last three decades—all

---

* The mismanagement and outright fraud that led to these failures were one of the inspirations for George Akerlof and Paul Romer's paper on "looting."

of which helped Wall Street become a dominant political force in Washington.

This process began in the 1970s, when Michael Milken, a trader at Drexel Burnham Lambert, had the insight that "junk bonds"—bonds that were rated below "investment grade" by the credit rating agencies*—were generally underpriced, either because investors had an irrational aversion to them or because they lacked a liquid market in which to trade them. He capitalized on that market inefficiency, building an operation that dominated the trading and sales of junk bonds. By creating a large, liquid market for junk bonds—which grew from $6 billion in 1970 to $210 billion in 1989[65]—he made it easier for companies to raise money and opened up vast new opportunities for investment banks to generate profits by underwriting, selling, and trading these formerly neglected bonds. By making it easy to raise large amounts of money quickly, junk bonds also made possible the leveraged buyout craze of the 1980s, in which acquirers would pay for acquisitions by issuing large amounts of new debt. Those acquisitions, in turn, generated huge fees for the investment banks that advised the companies engaged in those transactions and also underwrote and sold the necessary debt. They also left companies struggling with huge debt burdens, often requiring painful restructuring and sometimes leading to bankruptcy.

In the 1980s, the Securities and Exchange Commission and the U.S. Attorney's Office for the Southern District of New York (led by Rudy Giuliani) launched investigations of Milken and Drexel Burnham Lambert for insider trading, securities manipulation, and fraud. The investigations eventually led to convictions for both Milken and his employer for securities and reporting violations.[66] But junk bonds—rebranded as "high-yield" bonds—remained a popular form of financing, with over $600 billion in new bonds issued by U.S. cor-

*Bonds are IOUs issued by companies or governments. They are given ratings by credit rating agencies; those ratings are supposed to reflect the probability that the issuer will default on the IOU. "Investment-grade" bonds are those that are highly rated, meaning that there is a small probability of default. "Junk" bonds are any bonds that do not earn investment-grade ratings.

porations from 2003 through 2007.[67] Equally important, investor demand for higher-yield, higher-risk bonds remained strong—driving the recent boom in mortgage-backed securities, especially as returns on Treasury bonds fell to historic lows in the past decade.

The private mortgage-backed securities invented by Lewis Ranieri at Salomon Brothers, with an assist from the federal government, had even larger implications for the future than Milken's creation of the junk bond market. Without securitization, banks generally either held on to the mortgage loans that they made or sold them on the secondary market to Fannie Mae or Freddie Mac—government-sponsored enterprises that provided liquidity to the housing market. By buying mortgages, guaranteeing their principal payments, and turning them into mortgage-backed securities, Fannie and Freddie provided funding for banks to make more mortgages and absorbed some of the risk of the market. Because whole mortgages were difficult to trade (since every mortgage is unique), the number of transactions generated by each mortgage was small.

Securitization created many new ways for banks to profit. For the banks making the initial mortgages, securitization created a new market for their loans, making it easier for them to recover their cash and lend it out again to another borrower, boosting volume. Investment banks had three new ways to make money. They could take fees out of each securitization that they created; they could earn fees selling the new mortgage-backed securities to investors; and they could earn fees (or trading profits) by trading these securities. In each case, the revenues available depended on the volume of mortgage-backed securities. The total volume of private mortgage-backed securities (excluding those issued by Ginnie Mae, Fannie Mae, and Freddie Mac) grew from $11 billion in 1984 to over $200 billion in 1994 to close to $3 trillion in 2007.[68] In addition, once mortgage securitization had caught on, investment banks looked for any other financial assets they could turn into securities—credit card debt, student loans, anything that paid a more or less steady stream of cash flows—further expanding the market.

While mortgage securitization was good for the banks that originated the mortgages and turned them into securities, it was a mixed blessing for everyone else. On the one hand, by attracting additional investors to the mortgage market, it expanded the pool of money available to people who wanted to buy houses. On the other hand, it made possible the "originate to distribute" business model, in which lenders could make profits lending money to people who could not pay it back, making mortgage defaults and foreclosures more likely. Under this model, the risk of default is passed downstream to the investors buying the mortgage-backed securities, who therefore become responsible for policing the quality of the underlying loans; instead of having to make sure that borrowers were likely to pay them back over the next thirty years, lenders could be paid back immediately when they sold off the mortgages for securitization. When it turned out that investors had no idea what risks they were taking on, the result was the collapse of a housing bubble larger than any in recorded American history.

In addition to mortgage-backed securities, Salomon Brothers also pioneered arbitrage trading, which took a variety of forms. For example, traders could make certain money by finding two securities that should but did not have the same value—say, U.S. Treasury bonds maturing in August 2040 and September 2040—buying one, selling the other,* and waiting for their prices to converge. Or they could achieve the same goal by buying the interest payments and the final principal payment on a 30-year bond separately while selling the whole 30-year bond (including interest and principal) for a higher price. In general, such trades make money in one of two ways. Either there is a complex product, often involving embedded options, that other people in the market do not know how to value correctly, or there is a regulation that creates a market inefficiency that can be exploited. In any case, under ordinary market conditions, arbitrage opportunities are close to free money—at least until the number of competitors mimicking a particular strategy drives its profitability

---

*In financial markets, it is possible to sell assets that you don't actually have, known as selling "short." In a short sale, the seller borrows an asset (say, a share of stock) from Party A and then sells it to Party B; at some point in the future, the seller must buy the asset from someone in order to return it to Party A. The seller is betting that the price will have fallen in the meantime, earning it a profit.

down to zero—a far cry from the traditional business of lending money and taking the risk that it might not be paid back.

Although Salomon pioneered quantitative arbitrage trading, the practice soon spread to other investment banks, causing a huge flow of talent into Wall Street (significantly driving up the mathematical aptitude shown on the Philippon-Reshef skill curve) and leading to vast growth in banks' proprietary trading activities (trading on their own account, rather than executing trades for clients).* Its popularity also fueled the rapid growth of hedge funds (lightly regulated investment funds open only to institutions and rich individuals), which grew collectively from less than $30 billion in assets under management in 1990 to over $1.2 trillion in 2005,[69] with estimates over $2 trillion by 2008.[70] Arbitrage became a staple trading strategy of many hedge funds. And because hedge funds rely on investment banks to execute their trades, the growth of hedge funds provided another source of revenue for the banks.

But while it made the hedge funds and the investment banks plenty of money, arbitrage trading had two other effects. Because hedge funds are largely unregulated, large risk exposures were building up outside the view of the financial regulators. And because arbitrage spreads are typically very thin—pricing inefficiencies tend to vanish as traders take advantage of them—making significant profits required large amounts of borrowed money. This leverage was the reason why some proprietary trading operations lost large amounts of money during the 1997–1998 emerging markets crises when prices failed to converge as expected—leading even Salomon Brothers to largely disband its arbitrage team.[71]

The fourth money machine of modern finance—after high-yield debt, securitization, and arbitrage trading—was the modern derivatives market. While commodity futures contracts (in which, for example, a farmer commits to sell wheat in the future for a pre-specified price)

*Arbitrage trading received a tremendous boost from the rapid drop in the cost of computing power. Using computers, banks could search the markets for pricing discrepancies and profit from them, provided that they could finance their positions long enough for prices to converge.

had been around for centuries,* the market for financial derivatives remained small until the early 1980s, largely because traders—or, more accurately, the managers responsible for keeping those traders in line—had no good way of calculating what they were worth. But in the 1970s, the Black-Scholes Model gave banks a new way to calculate the value of complicated derivatives and the hedges they used to protect themselves.†

Wall Street embraced these quantitative models because they made it easier to price and trade derivatives in bulk. Nassim Taleb and Pablo Triana have argued that quantitative models are *worse* at pricing derivatives than the heuristics used by traders from the pre-quantitative era.[72] Nonetheless, the formulas gave banks the confidence to sell growing volumes of increasingly complicated trades to clients, since the models enabled them to keep track of how much money they were making on each one. Mathematical models also made it possible to break down complicated trades into simpler ones, a critical factor in the development of sophisticated financial products.

The modern derivatives revolution began with the invention of the interest rate swap (by Salomon Brothers) in 1981. In this transaction, Company A pays interest at a fixed rate to Company B and Company B pays interest at a floating rate (which can go up or down as economic conditions change) to Company A. Interest rate swaps allow companies to exchange fixed rate payments for floating rate payments, or vice versa—"swapping" interest rate risks between the two parties.‡ Similarly, currency swaps allow companies to swap currency risks by

---

*Simple options—in which the farmer pays a small amount now for the right, but not the obligation, to sell wheat in the future for a pre-specified price—were also common before the 1970s.

†In general, a derivatives dealer (a bank) attempts to hedge its positions; that is, if it sells one client an option to buy yak pelts in the future, it will try to buy an equivalent option from another counterparty so its positions cancel out. To hedge a complex trade that is customized for an individual client, the dealer may have to execute multiple trades with other counterparties, which may result in an imperfect hedge.

‡The risk of a floating rate liability, such as an adjustable rate mortgage, is that interest rates will go up and your periodic payments will go up. The risk of a fixed rate liability, such as a fixed rate mortgage, is that interest rates in general will go down and you will be stuck paying a high interest rate. Depending on the nature of their business, different parties prefer one type of risk or the other.

exchanging different currencies (or combinations of currencies). Interest rate swaps can also be combined with currency swaps. These two basic derivatives became popular ways for companies to manage financial or operational risks.

For example, a company might have issued $100 million in bonds on which it has to pay a floating interest rate (like an adjustable rate mortgage). Because it does not want to bear the risk that interest rates will go up, it can buy an interest rate swap from a derivatives dealer. The company will pay a fixed rate—say, 7 percent, or $7 million per year—to the dealer; in exchange, the dealer will pay the company the same floating rate that the company has to pay on its bonds. The net result is that the company now pays $7 million per year whether interest rates go up or down, and the dealer bears the interest rate risk. Currency swaps are similar; for example, a U.S. manufacturer with a multiyear contract in Thai baht might enter into a currency swap in order to lock in a constant future exchange rate and protect itself from the risk that the baht will fall. In either case, these derivatives allow companies to offload risks that they do not want to take onto the financial markets, where presumably some party will take on those risks in exchange for a high expected return. (Because the evolution of derivatives has run ahead of regulatory and accounting rules, derivatives can also serve other purposes, such as helping companies smooth their earnings over multiple periods or reduce their tax bills by deferring earnings into the future.)

By the middle of 2008, the market for over-the-counter (customized) interest rate swaps had grown to over $350 trillion in face value (the amount on which interest is calculated) and over $8 trillion in gross market value.*[73] The derivatives dealers—both investment banks and large commercial banks—were taking a piece of every interest rate swap in fees. Even better, the dealers would typically hedge their exposures; ideally, for every swap with one client, they would conduct an opposite swap with another client, so the two trades canceled out—leaving nothing but fees from both clients.

---

*In the interest rate swap example above, the face value, or notional value, is $100 million. However, the amount of money that changes hands is much smaller; if, at the end of a given year, the floating rate is 7.25 percent, then the dealer only pays the company 0.25 percent (the difference between the floating and fixed rates), or $250,000.

But ordinary swaps were easy for any derivatives dealer to duplicate, and competition between banks soon drove profit margins down near zero. The solution was to invent newer, more complex versions of interest rate and currency derivatives that were hard for competitors to duplicate—and hard for clients to understand. There were "inverse floaters," whose interest rates went in the opposite direction from market interest rates, souped up with leverage and embedded options. There were interest rate swaps that changed their terms based on currency exchange rates. Each of these trades was a customized combination of bonds, swaps, and options that was virtually impossible for a typical client to accurately value; the dealer would charge a large fee, break the transaction into its component parts, and hedge them individually at a much lower cost.

Derivatives expert Satyajit Das has outlined the abusive economics of these transactions. Describing the mechanics of a typical inverse floater, he wrote, "Chairman Greenspan might wax lyrical about the unbundling of risks but we spent most of our waking hours frantically rebundling the risks and stuffing them down the throats of any investor we could find."[74] Because these derivatives were zero-sum trades—one party's loss was the other's profit—one side could be badly burned. Orange County lost almost $2 billion on inverse floaters and similar trades that treasurer Robert Citron clearly did not understand; real-economy companies such as Procter & Gamble and Gibson Greetings similarly lost tens or hundreds of millions of dollars.[75] But these transactions generated large fees for the dealers; Merrill Lynch alone made $100 million on deals with Orange County.[76]

One crucial innovation in the recent history of derivatives, which played an important role in creating the latest financial crisis, was the credit default swap. A credit default swap is a form of insurance on debt; the "buyer" of the swap pays a fixed premium to the "seller," who agrees to pay off the debt if the debtor fails to do so. Typically the debt is a bond or a similar fixed income security, and the debtor is the issuer of the bond. Historically, monoline insurance companies provided insurance for municipal bonds, and Fannie Mae and Freddie Mac insured the principal payments on their mortgage-backed securities. With credit default swaps, however, now anyone could sell insurance on any fixed income security.

Credit default swaps were invented in the early 1990s by Bankers Trust, but were popularized by J.P. Morgan later in the decade as a way for banks to unload the default risk of their asset portfolios; this enabled them to lower their capital requirements, freeing up money that could be lent out again.[77] Credit default swaps also provide a way for a bond investor to hedge against the risk of default by the bond issuer. But because there is no requirement that the buyer of a credit default swap own the debt in question, these derivatives are also a handy way to gamble on the chances of *any* company defaulting on its debts (similar to buying insurance on your neighbor's house); this quality made them a new type of security that could be minted in infinite quantities and traded, providing another source of profit for derivatives dealers. And as discussed later, they would play a crucial role in greasing the wheels of the securitization machine that grew enormously in size in the last decade.

This explosion of new products created vast new profit-making possibilities for financial institutions. These opportunities were mainly available to a handful of investment banks and large commercial banks that could invest in powerful new computer technology and attract highly trained mathematicians and scientists from leading research universities. These large banks also had the scale required to build full-service derivatives operations that could assemble complex transactions and hedge their component parts. These new businesses helped blur the traditional line between commercial and investment banks, replacing it with a divide between small banks, which continued taking deposits and making loans, and big banks, which could branch out into securitization, proprietary trading, and derivatives.

BIGGER BANKING

At the same time, large banks were also growing by invading each other's territories and acquiring smaller rivals. Banks had been trying to get around the restrictions on interstate banking and the constraints of the Glass-Steagall Act for decades. Congress responded repeatedly with legislation limiting bank activities, including the Bank Holding Company Act of 1956, the Savings and Loan Holding Company Act of 1967, and the Bank Holding Company Act Amendments of 1970. Beginning in the 1970s, however, the banks became more aggressive, while Congress's resolve waned.

On the one hand, commercial banks sought to raise money for corporate clients, a traditional function of investment banks. In 1978, Bankers Trust began placing commercial paper (short-term debt) issued by corporations with investors. The Federal Reserve Board of Governors ruled that this practice did not violate the Glass-Steagall Act, opening a loophole that was ultimately (after an initial setback in the Supreme Court) upheld by the D.C. Circuit Court of Appeals in 1986.[78] In 1986, the Federal Reserve opened up another loophole, allowing commercial banks to set up affiliated companies (through a common bank holding company) to deal in specific securities that were off-limits to commercial banks, subject to limits on the revenues earned from those securities. Over the next decade, under the direction of chair Alan Greenspan, the Fed expanded the loophole, which began with municipal bonds, mortgage-backed securities, and commercial paper, to include corporate bonds and equities;[79] the Fed also raised the limit on revenues from the securities business and relaxed rules that enforced a separation between banking and securities operations within a single bank.[80] Commercial banks happily took advantage of the opportunity to plunge into new and esoteric businesses. In 1993, for example, NationsBank created a securities subsidiary, NationsSecurities, which began selling its clients mutual funds that invested heavily in inverse floaters and other complex derivatives; the next year, those funds plummeted in value when rising interest rates caused losses on many derivatives.[81]

On the other hand, investment banks sought to encroach on the territory of commercial banks. In the mid-1970s, for example, Merrill Lynch introduced the cash management account (CMA)—a brokerage product that included a money market account with check-writing privileges. This was a key element in Donald Regan's strategy to provide a full spectrum of financial services; as he said, "I wanted to get into banking, and CMA was the way to do it."[82] Cash management accounts competed directly with traditional savings and checking accounts for deposits, and enabled securities firms to sweep up a larger share of their clients' assets.

Investment banks also benefited from the general shift in financial intermediation (the movement of money from people who have it to people who need it) from banks into the capital markets. Traditionally, households and businesses would put their excess cash in deposit accounts at commercial banks or S&Ls, which would lend the cash out as mortgages and commercial loans. However, the high interest rates of the 1970s convinced investors to move their savings from bank accounts to money market funds, which invested in short-term bonds and commercial paper. Increasing affluence also fed the growth of mutual funds and pension funds, which sought out higher-yield investments. This demand for yield created the opportunity for investment banks to raise money for corporate clients by issuing commercial paper and bonds and selling them directly to large institutional investors. Money still flowed from households to corporations, but instead of passing through commercial banks, now it could pass through a money market fund or mutual fund—with a helping hand from Wall Street.

Mortgage-backed securities had a similar effect. Institutional investors bought mortgage-backed securities created by investment banks; the cash flowed to mortgage lenders, who no longer needed to be affiliated with traditional banks, because they did not rely on deposits for funding. This flow of money—from investors to special-purpose entities created by investment banks to nonbank mortgage lenders to homebuyers—bypassed the traditional banking system, escaping traditional banking regulation. Large commercial banks also got in on the action, using securitization to tap the capital markets for funds to complement the money deposited by their banking customers.

As banks created new markets and expanded into new businesses, they inevitably got bigger. But they also got bigger the old-fashioned way: by buying each other. Especially after the Riegle-Neal Interstate Banking and Branching Efficiency Act of 1994 relaxed constraints on interstate banking, a handful of large regional banks rushed to construct coast-to-coast networks. NationsBank bought Boatmen's Bancshares in 1996 and Barnett Bank in 1997 to become the biggest bank holding company in the country, passing Bank of America (which had bought Security Pacific in 1992); then NationsBank bought Bank of America in 1998, and in 2004 the new Bank of America bought Fleet-Boston (itself the merger of the three largest banks in New England). JPMorgan Chase was the product of the mergers of Chemical Bank and Manufacturers Hanover (1991), First Chicago and National Bank of Detroit (1995), Chemical and Chase Manhattan (1996), Bank One and First Chicago (1998), J.P. Morgan and Chase Manhattan (2000), and JPMorgan Chase and Bank One (2004). Wells Fargo bought First Interstate in 1996 and merged with Norwest in 1998. Wachovia was built out of the mergers of First Union, CoreStates, and Wachovia between 1998 and 2001. The largest financial services conglomerate of all (at the time) was put together by Sandy Weill, who began with Commercial Credit, bought Primerica (which owned Smith Barney) in 1988, added Travelers Insurance in 1993, bought Salomon Brothers in 1997, and finally merged his empire with Citicorp in 1998.

The major commercial banks used acquisitions not only to become bigger, but also to push their way into investment banking. Bank of America bought Robertson Stephens in 1997; NationsBank bought Montgomery Securities in 1997; and Chase Manhattan bought Hambrecht & Quist in 1999. European banks joined in, with Credit Suisse buying First Boston in 1988 and Donaldson, Lufkin & Jenrette in 2000, Swiss Bank Corporation (now part of UBS) buying Dillon, Read in 1997, and Deutsche Bank buying Bankers Trust in 1998. America remained populated with thousands of small community banks. But at the top of the pyramid, a handful of financial juggernauts were scrambling over each other to become as big and as broad as possible, as fast as possible. The goal was to create ubiquitous financial "supermarkets" that could provide the full range of financial services to both retail and corporate customers, anywhere.

In short, the financial sector was getting bigger. Between 1980 and 2000, the assets held by commercial banks, securities firms, and the securitizations they created grew from 55 percent of GDP to 95 percent.[83] Financial sector profits grew even faster, from an average of 13 percent of all domestic corporate profits from 1978 to 1987 to an average of 30 percent from 1998 to 2007.[84] The growth was faster still for the largest banks. Between 1990 and 1999, the ten largest bank holding companies' share of all bank assets grew from 26 percent to 45 percent, and their share of all deposits doubled from 17 percent to 34 percent.[85] And they continued to grow. In 1998, the merged Travelers and Citibank had $700 billion in assets;[86] at the end of 2007, Citigroup had $2.2 trillion in assets, not counting $1.1 trillion in off-balance-sheet assets,[87] even after the spinoff of the Travelers insurance businesses. Bank of America was not far behind, growing from $570 billion after the NationsBank–Bank of America merger to $1.7 trillion at the end of 2007.[88]

The transformation of the financial sector through expansion into new businesses and wave after wave of mergers changed the nature of the industry. At its peak was a handful of megabanks with hundreds of billions or trillions of dollars in assets. All of these banks, whatever their origins, were heavily involved in underwriting securities, manufacturing securities (securitization), trading securities, and trading derivatives. Some of them—the ones with roots in commercial banking, such as Citigroup, JPMorgan Chase, and Bank of America—also had wide-ranging branch operations taking hundreds of billions of dollars of deposits. Others—the traditional investment banks and brokerages such as Goldman Sachs, Morgan Stanley, and Merrill Lynch—chose to avoid the hassle and fixed cost of the deposit-taking business altogether, funding their operations through the capital markets. But these alternatives were simply different strategies to obtain the funds necessary to play in the riskier, more profitable world of modern finance. Although greater size should make banks safer, the largest banks compensated by engaging in riskier activities. In 2004, Gary Stern and Ron Feldman—president and senior vice president of the Federal Reserve Bank of Minneapolis—found that "after becoming larger, banks 'spend' their diversification benefit by taking on additional risk. For example, larger banks hold assets in riskier categories, such as commercial and industrial loans, relative to smaller banks."[89] The goal was to be big *and* to take on risk.

The main divide in the industry was no longer between commercial and investment banks; it was between the megabanks, with their portfolios of businesses that had hardly existed three decades before, and the thousands of traditional banks that still made their money taking deposits and extending loans (although now they were more likely to sell those loans off to be securitized). Federal Reserve governor Daniel Tarullo recapped the story in a 2009 speech:

> The regulatory system accommodated the growth of capital market alternatives to traditional financing by relaxing many restrictions on the type and geographic scope of bank activities, and virtually all restrictions on affiliations between banks and non-bank financial firms. The result was a financial services industry dominated by one set of very large financial holding companies centered on a large commercial bank and another set of very large financial institutions not subject to prudential regulation.[90]

These megabanks, whether based downtown, in midtown, or in North Carolina, were the new Wall Street.

4

"GREED IS GOOD"

The Takeover

Derivatives have been an extraordinarily useful vehicle to transfer risk from those who shouldn't be taking it to those who are willing to and are capable of doing so. . . . The vast increase in the size of the over-the-counter derivatives markets is the result of the market finding them a very useful vehicle.

—Alan Greenspan, chair of the Federal Reserve, July 16, 2003[1]

The 1980s came to a close with the peak of the savings and loan crisis. The failure of over 2,000 banks between 1985 and 1992 was by far the largest financial sector mass die-off since the Great Depression.[2] The government bailout of the S&L industry cost more than $100 billion, and hundreds of people were convicted of fraud.[3] In 1990, Michael Milken, the junk bond king, pleaded guilty to six felonies relating to securities transactions. In 1991, Citibank was facing severe losses on U.S. real estate and loans to Latin America and had to be bailed out by an investment from Saudi prince Al-Waleed bin Talal. In 1994, Orange County lost almost $2 billion on complicated interest rate derivatives sold by Merrill Lynch and other dealers; county treasurer Robert Citron pleaded guilty to securities fraud, although no one on the "sell side" of those transactions was convicted of anything. In 1998, Long-Term Capital Management collapsed in the wake of the Russian financial crisis and had to be rescued by a consortium of banks organized by the Federal Reserve.

Scandals are a constant refrain throughout the history of the financial services industry. Particularly severe episodes of wrongdoing often lead to the implementation of new rules that at least close the particular barn door that had been left open in the past; the most important example was the new regulatory scheme created during the Great Depression. The failures and scandals of the late 1980s and 1990s were closely linked to recent deregulatory policies or financial innovations: expansion of savings and loans into new businesses; junk bonds and leveraged buyouts; quantitative arbitrage trading; and over-the-counter derivatives. Someone familiar with the history of the financial system might have expected this record of disaster to lead to greater skepticism of financial innovation and closer oversight of the industry.

Instead, the 1990s witnessed the final dismantling of the regulatory system constructed in the 1930s. The Riegle-Neal Act of 1994 practically eliminated restrictions on interstate banking, allowing bank holding companies to acquire banks in any state and allowing banks to open branches in new states. The Gramm-Leach-Bliley Act of 1999 effectively demolished the remaining barriers separating commercial and investment banking—barriers that had already been significantly weakened during the preceding decade—by allowing holding companies to own subsidiaries engaged in both businesses (as well as insurance).

These laws only confirmed trends that had begun in the 1970s, and signified that the federal government would no longer attempt to resist the desires of the large commercial banks to become national, full-service financial supermarkets. More important, the government turned its back on the new financial products that had recently emerged, refusing to regulate over-the-counter derivatives or to police the new Wild West of mortgage lending that appeared late in the decade. Instead, leading policymakers from Alan Greenspan on down chose to rely on "self-regulation" of financial markets—the idea that market forces would be sufficient to prevent fraud and excessive risk-taking.

Despite the scandals and crises that marked the 1990s, this was the decade when Wall Street translated its growing economic power into political power and when the ideology of financial innovation and deregulation became conventional wisdom in Washington on both sides of the political aisle. The unprecedented amounts of money flowing through the financial sector, increasingly concentrated in a handful of megabanks, were the foundation of the new financial oligarchy. In the United States, however, political power on a national scale is generally not bought through simple corruption—by exchanging money under the table for political favors. Instead, Wall Street used an arsenal of other, completely legal weapons in its rise to power. The first was traditional capital: money, which wielded its influence directly via campaign contributions and lobbying expenses. The second was human capital: the Wall Street veterans who came to Washington to shape government policy and shape a new generation of civil servants. The third, and perhaps most important, was cultural capital: the spread and ultimate victory of the idea that a large, sophisticated financial sector is good for America.[4] Together, these powerful forces gave Wall Street a degree of political influence that no amount of payoffs to corrupt politicians could have bought.

CAMPAIGN MONEY

Money has long played an important role in American electoral politics. The interpretation of the First Amendment to protect the financing of political speech, along with the relative weakness of political parties (compared to other advanced democracies) in enforcing discipline among their members, has made it a requirement for individual legislators to devote considerable time and effort to raising money. The escalating cost of campaigning has increased the importance of money. Between 1974 and 1990, the cost of a seat in the House of Representatives—the average expenses of an election winner—grew from $56,500 to $410,000; from 1990 to 2006, it tripled to $1,250,000 (more than doubling even after accounting for inflation).[5]

The financial sector was a central player in this evolution. The sector was the leading contributor to political campaigns throughout the past two decades. But campaign contributions from the financial sector (including finance, insurance, and real estate) grew much faster than contributions overall, more than quadrupling, from $61 million in 1990 to $260 million in 2006. (After excluding insurance and real estate, the sector still contributed over $150 million in 2006; the second-ranking industry group, health care, contributed only $100 million in 2006.) Over the same time period, contributions from the securities and investment industry *sextupled* from $12 million to $72 million, and that $72 million omits the millions of dollars in contributions from the law firms that served the securities industry. (According to one analysis, from 1998 to 2008, the financial sector spent $1.7 billion on campaign contributions and $3.4 billion on lobbying expenses; the securities industry alone spent $500 million on campaign contributions and $600 million on lobbying.)[6] The largest commercial and investment banks, which stood to gain the most from deregulation and consolidation, were also the largest sources of campaign cash. In 1990, the companies in the banking sector that contributed the most money were Goldman Sachs, Salomon Brothers, Barnett Banks (the largest bank in Florida, bought by NationsBank in 1997), Citibank, J.P. Morgan, and Morgan Stanley; in 2006, they were Goldman, Citigroup, Bank of America, UBS, JPMorgan Chase, and Morgan Stanley.[7]

Money from the financial sector flowed precisely where it could do the most good. After becoming chair of the Senate Banking Committee in 1999, Phil Gramm raised more than twice as much money from the securities industry than from any other industry. In 1998, the securities industry's primary beneficiary in the Senate was Alfonse D'Amato, Gramm's predecessor as chair of the Senate Banking Committee; in 1996, D'Amato trailed only Gramm. More recently, the chair of the Senate Banking Committee, Christopher Dodd, received $2.9 million from the securities industry in 2007–2008—more than three times as much as any other senator who was not a major presidential candidate.[8] The securities industry was also the top donor to Barney Frank, chair of the House Financial Services Committee. And the securities industry's favorite member of Congress over the decades has been New Yorker Charles Schumer, first a member of the House Financial Services Committee and later a member of the Senate Banking Committee (and chair of the Democratic Senatorial Campaign Committee in 2006 and 2008), who has aggressively championed Wall Street over the years.[9]

There is a perpetual debate over whether politicians help their major donors because they want to make sure the money keeps flowing, or whether the donors give the money because they appreciate the politicians' positions. In any case, the 1990s, a period of increasing financial sector contributions, were also the decade when the deregulatory campaign crashed through any remaining congressional opposition. Powerful members of Congress sponsored legislation on the financial sector's wish list. Gramm put his name on the 1999 Gramm-

Leach-Bliley Act, which largely repealed the Glass-Steagall separation of commercial and investment banking. Gramm was also the major force behind the Commodity Futures Modernization Act of 2000, which prohibited federal regulation of over-the-counter derivatives. Schumer was a major proponent of Gramm-Leach-Bliley, and in 2001 he and Gramm passed legislation to cut in half fees paid by financial institutions to the SEC.[10] (Gramm left the Senate in 2002 to become a vice chair at UBS Warburg.)

Over the past twenty years, the financial services industry became an extremely powerful lobby in Washington, able to win votes in both Republican and Democratic Congresses. In April 2009, Senator Richard Durbin said, "the banks—hard to believe in a time when we're facing a banking crisis that many of the banks created—are still the most powerful lobby on Capitol Hill. And they frankly own the place."[11] No one thought he was saying anything extraordinary.

THE WALL STREET–WASHINGTON CORRIDOR

When it came to money, however, Wall Street had no particular advantage over other industries, except that it had more of it. And while campaign contributions gave Wall Street influence on Capitol Hill, important decisions elsewhere in Washington are made by appointed officials who do not depend on campaign money. Congress can pass legislation that constrains the activities of financial institutions (or not), but that legislation must be translated into regulations and those regulations must be enforced by the executive branch—either administration officials, primarily in the Treasury Department, or regulators serving in the Federal Reserve or one of an alphabet soup of agencies (SEC, CFTC, OCC, OTS, FDIC, NCUA, and so on).[12]

A second source of Wall Street's political power was its ability to place its people in key positions in Washington. As the big banks became richer, more of their executives became top-tier fund-raisers who could be tapped for administration jobs. More important, as the world of finance became more complicated and more central to the economy, the federal government became more dependent on people with modern financial expertise—which meant people from the big banks and from their most cutting-edge businesses. This constant flow of people from Wall Street to Washington and back ensured that important decisions were made by officials who had absorbed the financial sector's view of the world and its perspective on government policy, and who often saw their future careers on Wall Street, not in Washington.

The core problem in regulation is whether regulators will enforce rules that harm the interests of the industry they oversee, or whether they will be "captured" by that industry, as described in George Stigler's 1971 paper "The Theory of Economic Regulation": "as a rule, regulation is acquired by the industry and is designed and operated primarily for its benefit."[13] Capture does not imply that regulators are corrupt, or that their actions are motivated by their personal interests. By contrast, regulatory capture is most effective when regulators share the worldview and the preferences of the industry they supervise. And as banking insiders gained power and influence in Washington, the positions they held—that complex financial products, free financial markets, and large, sophisticated financial institutions were good for America—became orthodoxy inside the Beltway.

Throughout the past two decades, many senior officials moved back and forth between Wall Street and Washington. This was not a new phenomenon; after all, financial services have been an important part of the American economy for a long time. In the last two decades, however, two things changed. First, as the industry changed, the type of leaders it sent to Washington changed. Instead of people who had grown up managing large commercial banks or traditional investment banking firms, now it was people from the newer, riskier, more profitable businesses who were entering public service. Robert Rubin, President Clinton's first director of the National Economic Council (NEC) and second treasury secretary, began his Goldman Sachs career in risk arbitrage (betting on the likelihood of corporate events, such as acquisitions), branched out into relative value arbitrage (capitalizing on pricing discrepancies between similar securities), and co-headed Goldman's fixed income trading department before becoming co-chair of the firm.[14] Henry Paulson, President George W. Bush's last treasury secretary, headed Goldman Sachs from 1999 to 2006, at a time when its trading operations were the most profitable part of the firm.

Second, the increasingly complex nature of finance changed the balance of power between Wall Street insiders and other economic policy-makers. Executives from major financial institutions had always been prized in Washington for their relationships with major corporations in all industries. But as finance became more esoteric and policy questions became more technical, Wall Street experience became even more important. On many issues crucial to the financial sector—such as derivatives, securitization, or capital requirements—all the people with relevant expertise were Wall Street veterans. Financial policy took on the trappings of a branch of engineering, in which only those with hands-on experience on the cutting edge of innovation were qualified to comment. In order to stay informed about what was going on in the world of finance, the government had to borrow people from the major banks, who consequently had disproportionate influence over policy. For example, Frank Newman was CFO at Bank of America before joining Treasury in 1993 as undersecretary for domestic finance and later as deputy secretary. During the controversy triggered by the 1994 derivatives losses of Orange County, he wrote a letter urging Congress to "indefinitely postpone" legislation regulating derivatives. In 1995 he became senior vice chair of Bankers Trust, the derivatives dealer most tainted by the 1994 scandals; he was promoted to CEO in 1996.[15]

Many Wall Street bankers took on major positions in the government during the Clinton and George W. Bush administrations. Besides Rubin and Paulson, Goldman Sachs supplied treasury under-secretaries to both administrations—Gary Gensler under Clinton and Robert Steel (who went on to become CEO of Wachovia) under Bush. Other Goldman alumni included Senator Jon Corzine, a member of the Senate Banking Committee; Stephen Friedman, director of the NEC under Bush and chair of the New York Fed; William Dudley, an executive under Tim Geithner at the New York Fed and later its president; Joshua Bolten, director of the Office of Management and Budget (OMB) and chief of staff to President Bush; and a slew of Paulson advisers at Treasury, including Neel Kashkari, head of the Troubled Asset Relief Program (TARP). Other Wall Street executives in the Clinton administration included Roger Altman of Lehman Brothers and the Blackstone Group (a private equity firm) as deputy treasury secretary and Lee Sachs of Bear Stearns as a deputy assistant secretary and later as assistant secretary for financial markets.[16]

Rapid change in the financial sector put key regulators in the position to make important decisions affecting the industry, and many of those decisions were friendly to the industry. In 1993, Wendy Gramm, chair of the Commodity Futures Trading Commission (CFTC), issued an order exempting most over-the-counter derivatives from federal regulation; in the same year she was named to the board of directors of Enron, a leading trader of energy derivatives and major supporter of that order.[17] As chair of the CFTC from 1999 to 2001, William Rainer co-authored a report recommending that an existing ban on single-stock futures be lifted;[18] that recommendation was implemented by the Commodity Futures Modernization Act of 2000. In 2001, Rainer became CEO of OneChicago, a new exchange to trade single-stock futures.[19] James Gilleran, former CEO of the Bank of San Francisco, became head of the Office of Thrift Supervision in 2001. During his tenure, the agency became known for its lax regulation of thrifts; Gilleran said, "Our goal is to allow thrifts to operate with a wide breadth of freedom from regulatory intrusion."[20] In 2005, he left to become CEO of Federal Home Loan Bank of Seattle. As a Treasury official during the George H. W. Bush administration, John Dugan led a study that advocated the repeal of interstate banking restrictions and of the Glass-Steagall Act; as a lawyer advising the American Bankers Association, he helped steer the Gramm-Leach-Bliley Act through Congress. In 2005, George W. Bush named Dugan Comptroller of the Currency, in which capacity he helped shield federally chartered banks from state regulators.[21]

The close connections between the private and public sectors were also enhanced by longtime government officials who chose to move to the private financial sector. Michael Froman, a member of Rubin's NEC and then his chief of staff at Treasury, followed Rubin to become an executive at Citigroup. Gerald Corrigan worked at the Federal Reserve for over twenty years, serving as the president of the New York Fed from 1985 to 1993; in 1994 he joined Goldman Sachs, where he became a partner and senior executive in 1996. David Mullins, a former assistant secretary at Treasury and vice chair of the Federal Reserve Board of Governors, resigned from the Fed in 1994 to become a partner in Long-Term Capital Management.

The revolving door not only placed Wall Street veterans in important positions in Washington. It also ensured the development of strong personal relationships between leading bankers and government officials, giving the large banks privileged access to key policymakers, and promoted the spread of the Wall Street worldview in the corridors of political power. The prospect of landing prestigious or high-paying jobs in the financial sector may also have influenced the decisions of regulators and administration officials, who may have had an incentive not to make enemies among their potential future employers.

But banks also had a more direct means of putting pressure on their regulators—the market for regulatory fees. The Federal Reserve makes the money for its day-to-day operations from its banking activities, and the FDIC makes its money from insurance premiums levied on banks. But the other major regulators, including the Office of the Comptroller of the Currency (OCC) and the Office of Thrift Supervision (OTS), are funded by fees levied solely on the banks that they regulate. And while each regulator nominally had its own sphere of jurisdiction—bank holding companies for the Fed, national banks for the OCC, and so on—financial institutions that fell under multiple regulatory agencies were allowed to select their primary regulator. As a result, regulatory agencies had to compete for funding by convincing financial institutions to accept their regulation, which created the incentives for a "race to the bottom," in which agencies attract "customers" by offering relatively lax regulatory enforcement.

The OTS stood out in this competition. According to William Black, a law professor and former official at the Federal Home Loan Bank Board, "The reputation of the Office of Thrift Supervision was that it was the weakest, and the laxest, and it was indeed outright friendly to the worst of the non-prime lending."[22] American International Group (AIG), a massive insurance company with one of the largest derivatives trading operations in the world, opened a savings and loan—and then chose the OTS as its primary regulator, even though the agency, with its focus on mortgage lending, had no chance of monitoring the risks taken on by AIG's infamous Financial Products division. In 2005, the giant mortgage lender Countrywide, then regulated by the OCC, met with the OTS to discuss switching regulators. According to *The Washington Post*, "Senior executives at Countrywide who participated in the meetings said OTS pitched itself as a more natural, less antagonistic regulator than OCC and that [Countrywide CEO Angelo] Mozilo preferred that. Government officials outside OTS who were familiar with the negotiations provided a similar description."[23] In March 2007, the OTS approved Countrywide's application to convert itself from a bank holding company into a savings and loan holding company in order to fall under the OTS's regulation.[24]

Between the revolving door and the competition for regulatory "business," there was a confluence of perspectives and opinions between Wall Street and Washington that was far more powerful than emerging-market-style corruption. Wall Street's positions became the conventional wisdom in Washington; those who disagreed with them, such as Brooksley Born, were marginalized as people who simply did not understand the bright new world of modern finance. This group-think was a major reason why the federal government deferred to the interests of Wall Street repeatedly in the 1990s and 2000s.

One of history's curiosities is that this shift happened within a Democratic administration, headed by a president elected largely because of middle-class economic insecurity. Of all the people to migrate from Wall Street to Washington, the most important was Robert Rubin. When Rubin joined the Clinton administration in 1993—having first gained entrance to the party's inner circles through his fund-raising prowess[25]—the transformation of the financial sector into a risk-taking, moneymaking colossus was well underway. But the right of big banks to make money free from government intervention was not yet secured. There was still a major force in American politics that was skeptical about Wall Street and the unbridled pursuit of profit: the Democratic Party, which had helped block deregulatory legislation in Congress in the 1980s.

Bill Clinton was elected president in 1992 without any apparent strong opinion of the financial sector. Although his campaign theme was "the economy, stupid,"[26] as a challenger he was able to propose a broad economic platform (including health care reform, a middle-class tax cut, and education spending) without having to take a position on Wall Street. When Clinton took office, his appointments reflected a broad range of views within the Democratic Party. Lloyd Bentsen, a moderate who had spent the past twenty-two years in the Senate, was secretary of the treasury; Roger Altman, from both Wall Street and the Carter administration, was his deputy; Robert Reich, a traditional liberal (in the American sense) was secretary of labor; Laura Tyson, an advocate of industrial policy, was chair of the Council of Economic Advisers; and Rubin was director of the NEC, a new body created by Clinton to coordinate economic policymaking.

The crucial question was whether to increase spending on social programs and follow through on the campaign pledge of a middle-class tax cut, or to balance the budget in order to keep interest rates low. Rubin was a political liberal in many ways, supporting govern-ment social programs and opposing the welfare reform bill of 1996.[27] But he believed even more in fiscal responsibility and the importance of building a friendly relationship with the "bond market" in order to provide a foundation for long-term growth. The theory was that the bond market was distrustful of Democratic presidents; if it suspected Clinton of fiscal irresponsibility, it would demand higher yields on U.S. government debt, pushing up interest rates across the economy and stifling economic growth.

At a January 1993 meeting, the Clinton economic team agreed that deficit reduction should be their top priority, in order to establish credibility with Wall Street.[28] (This policy prompted Clinton adviser James Carville to say, "I used to think that if there was reincarnation, I wanted to come back as the President or the Pope or as a .400 baseball hitter. But now I would like to come back as the bond market. You can intimidate everybody.")[29] They were betting that by increasing taxes and bringing budget deficits under control, they could reduce interest rates and stimulate growth. These policy choices approximately coin-cided with the beginning of one of the longest economic booms in recent history—from 1993 to 2000, annual real GDP growth averaged 3.9 percent, while inflation averaged only 1.8 percent[30]—although other factors probably contributed to the boom, including the increas-ing use of computer technology and the impact of globalization.

In early 1995, Rubin succeeded Bentsen as treasury secretary, becoming the administration's primary economic policymaker, at a crucial moment for the White House. After its resounding defeat in the 1994 congressional elections, many insiders felt that the Democratic Party needed to turn to the left and advocate more populist economic policies. Rubin, however, favored the administration's centrist course, maintaining a pro-business stance and focusing on deficit reduction. Clinton sided with Rubin, confirming the Democrats' transformation into a market-oriented, business-friendly party that could be trusted by Wall Street.[31]

The ascendancy of the former co-chair of a premier investment bank also sent a signal that the administration would be sympathetic to Wall Street. While big business and big banks could historically count on the support of the Republicans, now they could rely on the Democrats as well. With Rubin in place, the government was unlikely to go after any of the new cash cows the financial sector had created in the last two decades, such as securitization, derivatives, or quantitative proprietary trading.

In addition to shaping the economic policies of the Clinton administration, Rubin mentored a generation of Democratic policymakers who are largely sympathetic with his views. He brought in some key Treasury officials directly from Wall Street, including Gensler from Goldman Sachs (now chair of the CFTC) and Lee Sachs from Bear Stearns (now a counselor to the treasury secretary). In contrast, Rubin's two top protégés did not come from Wall Street, but they largely adopted his perspective on economic and financial issues. Larry Summers, deputy secretary under Rubin and his successor as treasury secretary, was an academic economist and former chief economist at the World Bank. Tim Geithner, assistant secretary and then undersecretary for international affairs, was a career civil servant. But they shared Rubin's opinion that financial innovation and free markets were generally good for America. Summers opposed derivatives regulation even more strongly than Rubin; in his 2003 memoir, Rubin wrote, "Larry characterized my concerns about derivatives as a preference for playing tennis with wooden racquets—as opposed to the more powerful graphite and titanium ones used today."[32] (Summers and Geithner are now director of the NEC and treasury secretary, respectively.) Rubin was also a founder of the Hamilton Project, a centrist study group based at the Brookings Institution, which served as a way station for rising economy policy specialists such as Peter Orszag (now director of the OMB) and Jason Furman (now deputy director of the NEC). The end result was a Democratic policy establishment that no longer took its cues from unions and consumer advocates, but was now open or even friendly to the positions of Wall Street.

This political realignment was, in many ways, a huge boon to the Democratic Party. "Rubinomics" established the party's credibility in the eyes of the business and financial communities, repairing the damage done by the perceived economic mismanagement of the Carter administration and helping to balance the fund-raising scales against the Republicans. The long boom of the 1990s, whether or not it should be credited to Clinton-era policies, looked especially good when compared to the record of the George W. Bush administration, which saw slower growth (average real GDP growth of 2.2 percent, down from 3.9 percent under Clinton) and declining median income (falling from $52,500 in 2000 to $50,300 in 2008, both in 2008 dollars).[33] The shift of the Republican Party toward "cultural" issues also helped throw more investment banking and hedge fund moguls into Democratic arms.

The story of the Clinton administration demonstrates the key role that influential Wall Street insiders could play in reshaping the landscape of national politics. By 2008, the economic consensus of the Democratic establishment was based on the policies of Clinton, Rubin, and Summers.

In the 1990s, only one figure in the Washington economic elite surpassed Rubin in stature: Alan Greenspan, chair of the Federal Reserve from 1987 until 2006 and one of the most important legacies of the Reagan administration. Although Greenspan was not a Wall Street banker—he headed a New York economic consulting firm for nearly thirty years before becoming Fed chairman—there came to be no truer believer in the ideology of free markets, financial innovation, and deregulation.

Greenspan was a "lifelong libertarian Republican" and a longtime associate of Ayn Rand, the philosopher and novelist who argued for pure laissez-faire capitalism.[34] He believed in both the doctrine of effi-

cient markets and the Reagan Revolution against governmental interference in the economy. He looked forward eagerly to a world without
government regulation:

> Regulation is inherently conservative. It endeavors to maintain the sta-
> tus quo and the special interests who benefit therefrom. . . . With tech-
> nological change clearly accelerating, existing regulatory structures are
> being bypassed, freeing market forces to enhance wealth creation and
> economic growth.
>
> In finance, regulatory restraints against interstate banking and com-
> binations of investment and commercial banking are being swept away
> under the pressures of technological change. . . .
>
> As we move into a new century, the market-stabilizing private regu-
> latory forces should gradually displace many cumbersome, increasingly
> ineffective government structures. This is a likely outcome since gov-
> ernments, by their nature, cannot adjust sufficiently quickly to a chang-
> ing environment, which too often veers in unforeseen directions.
>
> The current adult generations are having difficulty adjusting to the
> acceleration of the uncertainties of today's silicon driven environment.
> Fortunately, our children appear to thrive on it. The future accordingly
> looks bright.[35]

Greenspan was naturally predisposed to be friendly toward the
financial sector and its desire to be left alone by government. As a central banker, he first made his mark injecting liquidity into the financial
system to pull the stock market out of its 23 percent fall on Black
Monday, October 19, 1987. This was the first example of what came to
be known as the "Greenspan put"—the idea that if trouble occurred in
the markets, the Fed would come to their rescue.* Greenspan cut
interest rates sharply in 1998 following the Russian crisis and in 2001
following the collapse of the Internet bubble, each time helping to
cushion the impact of the downturn and arguably pumping up the next
bubble. The underlying theory, set out in Greenspan's famous 1996
"irrational exuberance" speech, was that the Fed should not attempt to
head off bubbles, but instead should focus on helping the economy

---

*A put option gives its holder the right to sell an asset, such as a share of stock, at a predeter-
mined price. If the stock falls sharply in value, the put option allows the holder to sell it at a
higher-than-market price, and is therefore a form of protection against risk. The "Greenspan
put" was thought to be the equivalent of a put option for everyone in the market.

recover when those bubbles popped: "[H]ow do we know when irrational exuberance has unduly escalated asset values, which then become subject to unexpected and prolonged contractions as they have in Japan over the past decade? . . . We as central bankers need not be concerned if a collapsing financial asset bubble does not threaten to impair the real economy, its production, jobs, and price stability."[36] This position was an endorsement of the Efficient Markets Hypothesis and the idea that the Fed should not attempt to determine if prices are accurate, but should leave that function to the markets.

Wall Street appreciated Greenspan's monetary policy, because it meant that he would not raise interest rates preemptively to choke off a boom (unless that boom was also creating higher inflation). But it appreciated his hands-off regulatory policy even more. The Federal Reserve is one of the most important financial regulatory agencies, not only regulating bank holding companies but also enforcing consumer protection laws. But for almost two decades it was led by a man whose faith in financial innovation outweighed any interest he had in regulating the financial sector, and who had entered public life in order to "engage in efforts to advance free-market capitalism as an insider."[37]

For example, Greenspan strongly believed that financial derivatives served a valuable role in dispersing risk throughout the financial system, and that market participants were sophisticated enough to manage the risks created by derivatives. In July 2003, he told the Senate Banking Committee,

> What we have found over the years in the marketplace is that derivatives have been an extraordinarily useful vehicle to transfer risk from those who shouldn't be taking it to those who are willing to and are capable of doing so. . . . The vast increase in the size of the over-the-counter derivatives markets is the result of the market finding them a very useful vehicle. And the question is, should these be regulated? Well, indeed, for the United States, they are obviously regulated to the extent that banks, being the crucial creators of these derivatives, are regulated by the banking agencies, but not beyond that. And the reason why we think it would be a mistake to go beyond that degree of regulation is that these derivative transactions are transactions amongst professionals.[38]

For Greenspan, the rapid growth of the derivatives market was *proof* that they were socially beneficial. He believed, like many free market purists, that markets are self-regulating, and that as long as market participants have sufficient information, they will be aware of any potential dangers and protect themselves from them, and therefore outcomes in an unregulated market are necessarily good. This attitude even extended to fraud; as Brooksley Born recounted, "He explained there wasn't a need for a law against fraud because if a floor broker was committing fraud, the customer would figure it out and stop doing business with him."[39]

Greenspan dominated the Fed during his tenure, and his views became close to dogma on the Board of Governors. At an August 2005 symposium held by the Kansas City Federal Reserve Bank to honor Greenspan, Raghuram Rajan presented a paper asking in prophetic detail whether deregulation and innovation had increased rather than decreased risk in the financial system.[40] Rajan, then chief economist of the International Monetary Fund, was met with a torrent of attacks by Greenspan's defenders.[41] Fed vice chair Donald Kohn responded by restating what he called the "Greenspan doctrine." Kohn argued that self-regulation is preferable to government regulation ("the actions of private parties to protect themselves . . . are generally quite effective. Government regulation risks undermining private regulation and financial stability"); financial innovation reduces risk ("As a consequence of greater diversification of risks and of sources of funds, problems in the financial sector are less likely to intensify shocks hitting the economy and financial market"); and Greenspan's monetary policy resulted in a safer world ("To the extent that these policy strategies reduce the amplitude of fluctuations in output and prices and contain financial crises, risks are genuinely lower"). Kohn's conclusion reflected the prevailing view of Greenspan at the time: "such policies [recommended by Rajan] would result in less accurate asset pricing, reduce public welfare on balance, and definitely be at odds with the tradition of policy excellence of the person whose era we are examining at this conference."[42] Larry Summers more directly said he found "the basic, slightly lead-eyed premise of [Rajan's] paper to be misguided."[43]

Besides his considerable powers as steward of U.S. monetary policy and one of the chief regulators of the financial sector, Greenspan also mattered because of his tremendous public stature. As the U.S. economy settled into a long boom with falling unemployment and low inflation, he became probably the world's most famous and respected economist. If Greenspan said that derivatives improved the management of risk and financial innovation was always good, that provided cover for anyone in Washington who didn't know what to think about the issue.

With Greenspan at the Federal Reserve, Rubin and Summers at Treasury, a reliably friendly and compliant set of regulators, and millions of dollars flowing into Congress with each election cycle, Wall Street had friends throughout Washington in the 1990s. Little changed in the following decade under the Bush administration, which believed even more strongly in deregulation. Rarely has one industry enjoyed such unchecked power in Washington.

THE IDEOLOGY OF FINANCE

It is one thing to have important congressmen dependent on your campaign contributions, and to have your own people in key positions of power, and even to have some regulators enthralled by the prospect of lucrative jobs. Those factors alone gave Wall Street tremendous political power. But in addition to these traditional forms of political capital, the major banks amassed another form of power: cultural capital.

Politics is like sales. If you are trying to close a large deal with a major corporation, it helps to have friends on the inside, it helps to have buyers who see their fortunes aligned with yours, and it can even help to dangle the prospect of a high-paying job before the key decision-maker. But it is even better if the buyers really, independently want what you are selling. It is best of all if they believe that buying what you are selling is a symbol of their own judgment and sophistication—that buying your product marks them as part of the informed elite.

Any industry—say, Big Tobacco—can buy friends in Washington, who will work hard behind the scenes to help that industry. But over the last two decades, Wall Street's friends could work in the light of day, as the causes they championed gained an enthusiastic following among elites in Washington and New York (and major European capitals). The idea that a sophisticated, unrestrained financial sector was good for America became part of the conventional wisdom of the political and intellectual class. As a result, deregulation was no longer something to be buried in thousand-page bills—although that did happen—but was instead the focus of celebratory photo opportunities. In June 2003, representatives of three industry organizations joined the vice chair of the FDIC and the director of the OTS to kick off a project to "identify and eliminate any regulatory requirements that are outdated, unnecessary or unduly burdensome." Each of them threatened a symbolic stack of paper documents with a pair of garden shears—except for James Gilleran, director of the OTS, who brought a chainsaw.[44]

Over the past twenty years, finance changed in the public eye from a boring and slightly untrustworthy pursuit to the glistening centerpiece of the modern American economy. In much of the country, suspicion of bankers remained high or even increased with the prosecutions of people from Ivan Boesky and Michael Milken (insider trading) to Henry Blodget (talking up bad stocks). But where it mattered most—on elite academic campuses, in the business and financial media, in think tanks, and in the halls of power in Washington—banking became the latest chapter of the American Dream, the way to make vast riches by working hard and creating innovative new products that would supposedly improve life for everyone.

The positive image of Wall Street had at least three main components. The first was the idea that financial innovation, like technological innovation, was necessarily good. The second was the idea that complex financial transactions served the noble purpose of helping ordinary Americans buy houses. The third was that Wall Street was the most exciting place to be at the turn of the new millennium.

Innovation, in American English, is an unambiguously positive word. Dating back to Benjamin Franklin and Eli Whitney, we like to see ourselves as a nation of creative, resourceful inventors who solve problems through ingenuity and hard work. More recently, when we think of innovation, we think of technology: of Hewlett and Packard in their garage, or Jobs and Wozniak in theirs. And given all the material benefits that technological innovation has given us, it seems logical that financial innovation must be equally beneficial.

The language of innovation has been widely used to describe recent changes in the financial sector. In a 1995 paper, Robert Merton wrote, "Looking at financial innovations . . . one sees them as the force driving the global financial system towards its goal of greater economic efficiency. In particular, innovations involving derivatives can improve efficiency by expanding opportunities for risk sharing, by lowering transaction costs and by reducing asymmetric information and agency costs."[45] Two years later, Alan Greenspan said,

> The unbundling of financial products is now extensive throughout our financial system. Perhaps the most obvious example is the ever-expanding array of financial derivatives available to help firms manage interest rate risk, other market risks, and, increasingly, credit risks. . . . Another far-reaching innovation is the technology of securitization—a form of derivative—which has encouraged unbundling of the production processes for many credit services. . . . These and other developments facilitating the unbundling of financial products have surely improved the efficiency of our financial markets.[46]

As the financial sector became a bigger part of the U.S. economy, the celebration of financial innovation only increased. In 2006, even as he warned about potential risk management challenges generated by derivatives, Tim Geithner (then New York Fed president) said of the current wave of financial innovation,

> These developments provide substantial benefits to the financial system. Financial institutions are able to measure and manage risk much more effectively. Risks are spread more widely, across a more diverse group of financial intermediaries, within and across countries.
> These changes have contributed to a substantial improvement in the financial strength of the core financial intermediaries and in the overall flexibility and resilience of the financial system in the United States. And these improvements in the stability of the system and efficiency of the process of financial intermediation have probably contributed to the acceleration in productivity growth in the United States and in the increased stability in growth outcomes experienced over the past two decades.[47]

Even in April 2009, after the financial crisis, Greenspan's successor, Ben Bernanke, said, "Financial innovation has improved access to credit, reduced costs, and increased choice. We should not attempt to impose restrictions on credit providers so onerous that they prevent the development of new products and services in the future."[48] The fact that Bernanke, a brilliant and widely respected academic, would sing the praises of financial innovation even after the financial crisis shows the powerful hold this ideology exerted on both economists and policymakers.

Merton and Greenspan's argument about "risk sharing" and "unbundling" added intellectual heft to the ideology of innovation. According to this story, derivatives and securitization have the beneficial effect of spreading risk out among more market participants and allocating specific risks to the people who most want to hold them. Credit default swaps, for example, allow banks to divide up interest rate risk and default risk between different investors. Since all parties are negotiating freely in an open market, these transactions should be good for everyone—and they can be, if those parties know what they are doing. The rebranding of complexity as innovation, however, provided a blanket justification to any new financial products, paving the way not only for the inverse floaters sold to Orange County but for similar products sold to individual investors. Reverse convertibles, for example, are structured notes where the investor gets either a fixed interest rate *or* a share of stock, depending not only on the final stock price but on the path it takes getting there; because of their complexity, few investors are able to value them accurately, making them prey to unscrupulous brokers and banks.[49] ("I was told there was no risk with these," said one retiree who lost over $90,000 on reverse convertibles.)[50]

The ideology of innovation had its skeptics. Warren Buffett famously labeled derivatives "financial weapons of mass destruction" in the Berkshire Hathaway 2002 annual report.[51] In his 2001 book *Fooled by Randomness*, Nassim Taleb argued that modern financial technology underestimated the likelihood of extreme events, with potentially catastrophic implications.[52] Janet Tavakoli's 2003 book, *Collateralized Debt Obligations and Structured Finance*, discussed the potential problems involved in securitization, including the risk of fraud.[53] And decades before, Hyman Minsky had pointed out the role of innovation in enabling financiers to increase their profits at the risk of destabilizing the economy.[54] They could all be ignored as long as market conditions remained benign. But the Merton-Greenspan "risk unbundling" story was proven horribly wrong by the financial crisis that began in 2007—caused in part by innovative products that made it possible for financial institutions and investors to take on massive amounts of risk hidden inside AAA-rated securities that later plummeted in value. Eventually even Greenspan was forced to admit his mistake in a congressional hearing.[55]

The recent orgy of financial innovation turned out so badly because financial innovation is *not* like technological innovation. There are financial innovations that do benefit society, such as the debit card. And derivatives, as discussed earlier, can be useful tools to help companies hedge their operational risks. But there is no law of physics or economics that dictates that *all* financial innovations are beneficial, simply because someone can be convinced to buy them. The core function of finance is financial intermediation—moving money from a place where it is not currently needed to a place where it is needed. The key questions for any financial innovation are whether it increases financial intermediation and whether that is a good thing.

Much recent "innovation" in credit cards, for example, has simply made the *pricing* of credit more complex. Card issuers have lowered the "headline" price that they advertise to consumers while increasing the hidden prices that consumers are less aware of, such as late fees and penalty rates. These tactics have increased the profits of credit card issuers, but have not increased financial intermediation—except insofar as they helped consumers underestimate the cost of credit and therefore borrow excessive amounts of money.[56]

Innovation that increases the availability of credit can also be harmful. The stated-income mortgage, where loan originators explicitly did not verify borrowers' incomes, made it easier for some people to borrow more money to buy houses, but also served as an invitation to fraud (by both borrowers and mortgage brokers) and left many borrowers unable to repay their mortgages. Investments can be economically value-creating or value-destroying; when financial intermediation increases to the point where value-destroying investments are being funded, financial innovation is doing more harm than good.

But in the 1990s and 2000s, the theory of risk unbundling and diversification reigned largely unchallenged in Washington; people who didn't subscribe to it could be written off as ignoramuses who failed to understand the elegance of modern finance. Merton and his colleague Myron Scholes, after all, won the Nobel Prize in economics in 1997 (a year before the collapse of their hedge fund). It also helped that financial services were one arena where U.S. firms were in the international vanguard, inventing most of the new products and markets of the past few decades. With the trade deficit in manufactured goods widening continuously, structured securities were one of our most attractive exports, especially to European banks and investors looking for higher-yield investments. After the Internet bust, Wall Street became our most prestigious economic center, and keeping it that way became an end in itself. As Senator Schumer said in 2007 of existing financial regulations, "We are not going to rest until we change the rules, change the laws and make sure New York remains No. 1 for decades on into the future."[57]

The New American Dream was to make tens of millions on Wall Street or as a hedge fund manager in Greenwich, Connecticut. But it was also connected to the Old American Dream—to own a house of one's own. In the last thirty years, the Wall Street ideology borrowed heavily from the older, more deep-rooted American ideology of homeownership, which became widely accepted after World War II as government programs and economic prosperity made possible a homeowning middle class. Wall Street co-opted this ideology to justify the central place of modern finance in the economic and political system, especially as the homeownership rate climbed from 64 percent, where it sat from 1983 to 1994, to a high of 69 percent in the 2000s.[58]

The ideology of homeownership has its roots in two sources. The first is the idea that homeownership is intrinsically good—it encourages individual responsibility, provides financial security, promotes community attachment, encourages people to take care of property, and so on. This ethos may have something to do with the important place of independence and self-reliance in the constellation of American values. Or it may be the product of various government policies designed to encourage homeownership. There may also be an element of truth to this idea; homeownership is generally thought to create positive externalities, since homeowners are on average more likely to devote effort to improving their communities. After reviewing other empirical studies and doing their own analyses, Edward Glaeser and Jesse Shapiro conclude:

> [T]here is a limited body of evidence suggesting that homeownership creates positive spillovers for near neighbors. Homeowners do appear to be more active citizens. They vote more. They take better care of their homes. Houses that are surrounded by homeowners are worth a little more than houses that are surrounded by renters.[59]

However, much of the positive effect of homeownership is due not to ownership itself, but to other factors that differentiate owners and renters. In another paper, Glaeser and Denise DiPasquale found that "almost one-half of the effect of homeownership disappeared when we controlled for the time that the person had lived in the home."[60] William Rohe and Michael Stegman compared a sample of low-income homebuyers with similar low-income renters over time and found that the homebuyers were less likely to engage in informal neighboring, more likely to participate in block associations, and no more likely to participate in other types of community associations.[61] Alyssa Katz concludes, in *Our Lot*, "scholars found that once they set aside the various traits that tend to determine whether someone chooses to own or rent one's home, homeowners and tenants really aren't that different."[62]

The second source of the ideology of homeownership is the idea that owning a home is the best possible investment for a household. Although widely believed, this idea is questionable at best: absent government incentives, betting several times your entire net worth not only on a single type of asset, but on a single building and plot of land, is almost the worst investment you could make after accounting for risk. Many families have made money from housing price appreciation (particularly if they took out mortgages before the inflation of the 1970s), but their high returns are primarily due to the high leverage built into a typical mortgage—leverage that produces massive defaults and foreclosures in a housing downturn such as the one that began in 2006. The things that make housing attractive as an investment are favorable government policies, such as the mortgage interest tax deduction, in which the government subsidizes mortgages for homeowners.*

In any case, homeownership ranks alongside motherhood and apple pie in the firmament of American values, and helping more people buy houses is almost always seen as a good thing. Lewis Ranieri capitalized on this ideology when he created the market for private mortgage-backed securities beginning in the late 1970s. Mortgage-backed securities would enable lenders to replenish their coffers by tapping the entire world of securities investors, expanding the amount of credit available to homeowners and thereby allowing more people to buy houses at lower interest rates. At a congressional hearing, Katz recounts. "Ranieri promised that putting private bankers and their sales forces in charge of mortgage securities would save borrowers half a percent on every loan."[63] Congress agreed; in a 1983 report, the Senate Banking, Housing, and Urban Affairs Committee warned that without expanding the market for private mortgage-backed securities, "mortgages would cost more and be more costly to obtain."[64] Ranieri hitched the mortgage-backed securities market to the cause of expanding homeownership, ensuring its political success.

In the 1990s and 2000s, another financial innovation appeared on the scene with the potential to extend the dream of homeownership to millions more households: subprime mortgage lending. (Subprime lending had been around for decades, but only recently became a major source of money to buy houses, as opposed to refinancing them.)[65] During the housing boom, lenders scrambled to offer mortgages to people who would never have qualified for them before the boom. These were high-cost loans to people with no verified ability to pay them off, which made sense only assuming that continually rising housing prices would leave the lenders with valuable collateral in case of default. These practices looked a lot like predatory lending. But the mortgage lenders and the investment banks that bought and securitized their mortgages justified such activity on the grounds that it promoted homeownership. "Our innovative industry has created a great

---

*Owning a house has other advantages, such as increased freedom in deciding what to do with the house and land and increased peace of mind. However, these advantages have nothing to do with the value of the house as an investment.

way to expand homeownership by offering loans to those who can make payments, but who don't qualify for 'A' paper because of poor credit or bankruptcy," said Ron McCord, former president of the Mortgage Bankers Association, in 1997.[66]

And the story stuck. Not only did the federal government make no attempt to regulate subprime lending, but it even became a cheerleader for the subprime boom. The Clinton administration had made an expansion of homeownership a central part of its economic strategy; in 1995, Clinton set a goal of a 67.5 percent homeownership rate[67] at a time when the actual rate was 65 percent (it would peak the next decade at 69 percent).[68] In order to help meet this goal, the Department of Housing and Urban Development mandated that Fannie Mae and Freddie Mac—the giant government-sponsored enterprises that provided funding for the mortgage market—had to devote 42 percent of their money to loans to low- and moderate-income households. That target was increased to 50 percent in 2000 and then to 56 percent in 2004.[69]

Growing real household incomes helped a bit in the mid-1990s. But beginning in 1997, the growth of housing prices outstripped income growth; after 1999, real median household income *fell* for five consecutive years as housing prices soared.[70] Under these circumstances, as George W. Bush not only continued his predecessor's support for increased homeownership but even made the "ownership society" a centerpiece of his political message, the only thing that could keep the homeownership boom going was expanded availability of credit.

Alan Greenspan became an eloquent spokesman for the synergy between financial innovation and homeownership. In a 2005 speech discussing the impact of new financial technology, he said,

> Improved access to credit for consumers, and especially these more-recent developments, has had significant benefits. Unquestionably, innovation and deregulation have vastly expanded credit availability to virtually all income classes. Access to credit has enabled families to purchase homes, deal with emergencies, and obtain goods and services. Home ownership is at a record high.[71]

The only caveat that Greenspan gave was that the increase in credit availability made it more important to ensure widespread financial education.

For anyone who had doubts about the value of financial innovation and the importance of Wall Street, the ideology of homeownership provided easy assurance. The idea that complex securities could help low- and middle-income families own homes was especially attractive to Democratic congressmen and officials who might ordinarily be distrustful of mortgage lenders and investment bankers, and helped seal off Wall Street's new money machine from criticism.

The economic and political elites could agree that innovation was good, and that homeownership was good. But the ideology of finance went beyond the idea that Wall Street was good for America. Banking was not only the center of the U.S. economy—it became cool, seductive, and even sexy.

In 1987, Tom Wolfe's novel *The Bonfire of the Vanities* introduced the term "Master of the Universe" to American culture, in the form of multimillionaire investment banker Sherman McCoy, who lived in "the sort of apartment the mere thought of which ignites flames of greed and covetousness under people all over New York and, for that matter, all over the world."[72] Although the term was used sarcastically, and McCoy turns out badly in both the human and financial senses, the image of the swashbuckling, super-rich banker engaged in transactions too complex to be understood by ordinary mortals was born.

Also in 1987, Oliver Stone's movie *Wall Street* was released, with its memorable antihero, corporate raider Gordon Gekko (played by Michael Douglas). Although the movie's story shows the corruption and ultimate downfall of Gekko, it is remembered for his "Greed is good" speech, which justified the pursuit of money above all else. As screenwriter Stanley Weiser wrote recently, many people would later tell him the movie made them *want* to work on Wall Street: "A typical example would be a business executive or a younger studio development person spouting something that goes like this: 'The movie changed my life. Once I saw it I knew that I wanted to get into such and such business. I wanted to be like Gordon Gekko.'"[73]

Liar's Poker, Michael Lewis's 1989 memoir, an ironic anti-bildungsroman in which the hero is fascinated but ultimately repelled by life at Salomon Brothers, popularized life on Wall Street for a generation of college students. As Lewis wrote much later,

I hoped that some bright kid at, say, Ohio State University who really wanted to be an oceanographer would read my book, spurn the offer from Morgan Stanley, and set out to sea.

Somehow that message failed to come across. Six months after *Liar's Poker* was published, I was knee-deep in letters from students at Ohio State who wanted to know if I had any other secrets to share about Wall Street. They'd read my book as a how-to manual.[74]

Clearly, being a bond trader on Wall Street was different from being a loan officer in the era of 3–6–3 banking. The risk, the testosterone, and the sums of money at stake were all deeply seductive to over-achievers from top schools. They *wanted* to order guacamole in five-gallon drums, swear constantly, and place million-dollar bets while eating cheeseburgers.

After *Liar's Poker*, the financial sector only became more and more exciting in popular culture. From Salomon, the torch of innovation passed to Drexel Burnham Lambert and Michael Milken, who were starring characters in James Stewart's 1992 bestseller, *Den of Thieves*; the takeover binge they made possible was memorialized by Bryan Burrough and John Helyar in *Barbarians at the Gate*, their 1990 account of the leveraged buyout of RJR Nabisco. After Drexel collapsed, the cutting edge of finance shifted to derivatives desks. In his 1997 memoir, *F.I.A.S.C.O.*, former derivatives trader (and current law school professor) Frank Partnoy chronicled the derivatives culture, where people would describe a trade where they made money at the expense of a client as "ripping his face off." (The comparatively genteel phrase in *Liar's Poker* was "blowing up a customer.") But if Partnoy expected his book to slow the growth of the derivatives industry, he was no doubt disappointed. By this point, the bankers were the heroes of the story, not the villains.

No amount of cautionary tales could change the fact that Wall Street was becoming a deeply seductive place, in a way that traditional banking never was. There were the concrete-steel-and-glass towers crammed full of modern technology. There was the mathematical complexity of modern trading, a game seemingly reserved for the very smart. There was the feeling of being at the center of the financial world, whether raising billions of dollars for multinational corporations or making massive trades that moved the market prices flashing on the Bloomberg screen. There was the lifestyle—eating sushi at Nobu, riding everywhere in a Lincoln Town Car, talking on cell phones (before everyone had one), checking e-mail on BlackBerrys (before everyone had one), and globetrotting in first class (still not available to everyone). To open *Sex and the City*, the 1996 book that launched the eponymous TV show, Candace Bushnell chose an investment banker: "Tim was forty-two, an investment banker who made about $5 million a year."[75]

Figure 4-1: Real Average Annual Compensation, Banking vs. Private Sector Overall

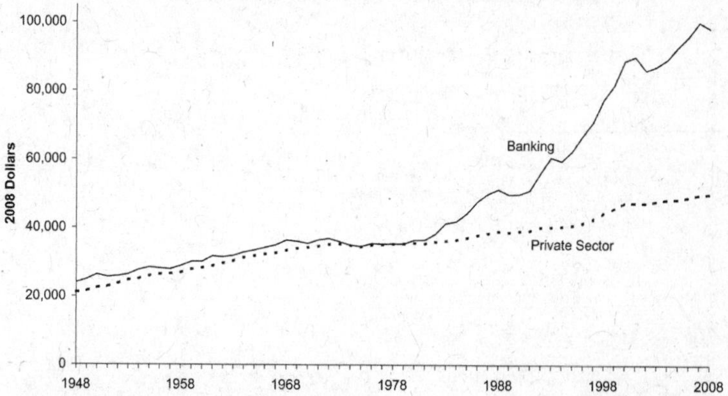

Source: Bureau of Economic Analysis, *National Income and Product Accounts*, Tables 1.1.4, 6.3, 6.5; calculation by the authors. Banking includes financial sector less insurance, real estate, and holding companies. Annual compensation is total wage and salary accruals divided by full-time equivalent employees.

And, of course, there was the money. The vast amounts of money flowing through Wall Street and the extreme free market ethos of the industry resulted in ever-larger amounts of money spinning off into the bank accounts of top traders, salesmen, and bankers. From 1948 until 1979, average compensation in the banking sector was essentially the same as in the private sector overall; then it shot upward, as shown in Figure 4-1, until in 2007 the average bank employee earned twice as much as the average private sector worker.[76] Even after taking high levels of education into account, finance still paid more than other professions. Thomas Philippon and Ariell Reshef have analyzed financial sector compensation and found that the "excess relative wage" in finance—the amount that cannot be explained by differences in education level and job security—grew from zero around 1980 to over

40 percentage points earlier this decade; 30–50 percent of excess wages in finance cannot be explained by differences in individual ability. They also found that deregulation was one factor behind the recent growth of compensation in finance. (Figure 4-2 shows the relationship between the unadjusted relative wage in the financial sector— the ratio between average wages in finance and average wages in the private sector as a whole—and the extent of financial deregulation, as calculated by Philippon and Reshef.)[77]

Figure 4-2: Relative Financial Wages and Financial Deregulation

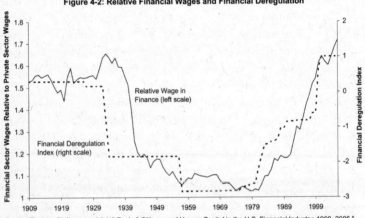

Source: Thomas Philippon and Ariell Reshef, "Wages and Human Capital in the U.S. Financial Industry: 1909–2006," Figure 6.

The rewards for success grew much, much faster as traders' potential bonuses climbed into the millions and then the tens of millions. In 2008—which was a horribly bad year for most banks—1,626 JPMorgan Chase employees received bonuses of more than $1 million; at the smaller Goldman Sachs, which had thirty thousand employees, 953 received bonuses of more than $1 million, and 212 received bonuses of more than $3 million.[78] In the 1990s, Internet start-ups were seen as the quickest route to vast wealth, for the lucky few who founded companies that successfully went public. By the 2000s, it was investment banks and hedge funds, where smart college graduates could *expect* to make millions.

Wall Street began to skim off the cream of America's top schools—

not only graduates of business schools and Ph.D. programs in math and science, but twenty-two-year-old college students with no background or expertise in anything at all. As investment banks began descending onto Ivy League campuses and tempting students with stories of client "impact," dinners at expensive restaurants, and glimpses of much greater wealth, seniors who had never even wondered what a bond was suddenly wanted to be investment bankers. Sealing the deal was the fact that Wall Street was perceived as the ultimate dooropener, a respectable way to make money and then, like Robert Rubin, go into public service. The point of the "Greed is good" speech was that by pursuing profits (both for your company and for yourself) you were contributing to the greater good. For college seniors, it was easy to think that maximizing their personal earnings coincided with maximizing societal good—making it easy to justify joining the ranks of the bankers on Wall Street.

As a result, banking and finance became more and more popular among the young and the privileged. Claudia Goldin and Lawrence Katz have examined data on Harvard undergraduates and found that while only 5 percent of men in classes around 1970 were in finance fifteen years after graduation, that figure tripled to 15 percent for classes around 1990.[79] The share of each class entering banking and finance careers grew from under 4 percent in the 1960s to 23 percent in recent years.[80] At Princeton's School of Engineering and Applied Science, "Operations Research and Financial Engineering" became the most popular undergraduate major.[81] The banks thus became major beneficiaries of the American educational system. Whether society benefited is another question. Kevin Murphy, Andrei Shleifer, and Robert Vishny have argued that society benefits more when talented people become entrepreneurs who start companies and create real innovations than when they go into rent-seeking activities that redistribute rather than increase wealth.[82] If this is true, then this diversion of talent to Wall Street constituted a real tax on economic growth over the last two decades.

Among the economic and intellectual elites, finance became a highly prestigious and desirable profession. Working on Wall Street became a widely acknowledged marker for educational pedigree, intelligence, ambition, and wealth. Outsiders may not have understood exactly what happened on a trading floor or in a hedge fund, but they knew that it was important, it was fast-moving, it was intellectually complicated, it had something to do with greasing the wheels of the global economy, and it had something to do with making it easier for ordinary people to buy houses. They also knew that it was very well paid. In America, where we like to believe that wealth is a function of hard work and contribution to society, that was all good.

THE WALL STREET–TREASURY COMPLEX

This combination of money, people, and prestige created what Jagdish Bhagwati identified in 1998 as the "Wall Street–Treasury complex."[83] Bhagwati described how the ideology of free markets "lulled many economists and policymakers into complacency about the pitfalls that certain markets inherently pose," while the revolving door placed representatives of Wall Street into influential positions in Washington. "This powerful network," he wrote, "is unable to look much beyond the interest of Wall Street, which it equates with the good of the world." Bhagwati was writing in the context of global financial liberalization, which the United States was then pushing on developing countries (both directly and through its influence at the IMF), and which had contributed to the emerging market crises of the past year.

By the time of Bhagwati's article, the power of Wall Street reached deep into Washington. The major banks, including both traditional investment banks and commercial banks that expanded into securities and derivatives, had spent the last two decades opening and exploiting vast new mines filled with money. They had funneled millions of dollars of that money to key congressmen who could make or break legislation affecting the financial sector. The treasury secretary was a former chairman of Goldman Sachs, the assistant secretary for financial markets was a former Goldman partner, and the Federal Reserve chairman was an ardent fan of Wall Street. The Clinton administration, which had tied its fortunes to keeping Wall Street bond traders happy, was deep into a multiyear campaign to boost homeownership rates and was depending on the financial sector to make it possible.

Behind these Washington power brokers was a new conventional wisdom about the importance and value of Wall Street. The previous Nobel Prize in economics had been given to two economists who had helped launch the derivatives revolution and were now partners at the hottest hedge fund in the world. The dogma of financial innovation had few doubters in Washington. Vibrant, profitable banks were assuming the status of national champions in a country that saw the transition from manufacturing to knowledge-intensive services as its destiny. And Wall Street was the most prestigious destination for graduates of America's top universities. For all intents and purposes, Wall Street had taken over.

5

THE BEST DEAL EVER

These amendments are intended to reduce regulatory costs for broker-dealers by allowing very highly capitalized firms that have developed robust internal risk management practices to use those risk management practices, such as mathematical risk measurement models, for regulatory purposes.
—Securities and Exchange Commission,
"Final Rule: Alternative Net Capital Requirements
for Broker-Dealers That Are Part of Consolidated
Supervised Entities," Effective August 20, 2004[1]

By the mid-1990s, Wall Street was a dominant force in Washington. It had survived the implosion of the savings and loan industry in the late 1980s, the election of a Democratic president in 1992, a congressional investigation of predatory subprime lending in 1993, and a wave of scandals caused by toxic derivatives deals in 1994 without facing any significant new constraints on its ability to make money.

The U.S. financial elite did not owe its rise to bribes and kickbacks or blood ties to important politicians—the usual sources of power in emerging markets plagued by "crony capitalism." But just as in many emerging markets, it constituted an oligarchy—a group that gained political power because of its economic power. With Washington firmly in its camp, the new financial oligarchy did what oligarchies do—it cashed in its political power for higher and higher profits. Instead of cashing in via preferred access to government funding or contracts, however, the major banks engineered a regulatory climate that allowed them to embark on an orgy of product innovation and risk-taking that would create the largest bubble in modern economic history and generate record-shattering profits for Wall Street.

When the entire system came crashing down in 2007 and 2008, governments around the world were forced to come to its rescue, because their economic fortunes were held hostage by the financial system. The title of Louis Brandeis's 1914 book, *Other People's Money*, referred to ordinary people's bank deposits, which could be used by investment bankers—"Our Financial Oligarchy"—to control industries and generate profits. In 2008, however, the banks found another way to tap other people's money: the taxpayer-funded bailout.

THE GOLDEN GOOSE

The boom in real estate and finance in the 2000s resulted from the explosive combination of a handful of financial "innovations" that were invented or greatly expanded in the 1990s: structured finance, credit default swaps, and subprime lending. Most financial regulators looked on the creation of this new money machine with benevolent indifference. Structured financial products were sold largely to "sophisticated" investors such as hedge funds and university endowments and therefore subject to limited oversight by the Securities and Exchange Commission; credit default swaps were insulated by regulatory inattention and then by the Commodity Futures Modernization Act; subprime lending was winked at by the Federal Reserve. That was how the financial sector wanted it, and Washington was happy to oblige.

Traditionally, investors invested in financial assets that had some direct tie to the real economy: stocks, corporate or government bonds, currencies, gold, and so on. By contrast, banks engineer structured products to have any set of properties (maturity, yield, risk, and so forth) that they want.[2] Structured products include pure derivatives, discussed in chapter 3, which are side bets on other financial assets. For example, an investor can pay $100 to a bank and get back, one year later, an amount that is calculated based on the performance of several currencies and interest rates. They can also be built by buying actual financial assets (mortgages, student loans, credit card receivables, and so on), combining them, and taking them apart in various ways to create new "asset-backed" securities. Or they can combine real assets with derivatives in increasingly complicated mixes.

Structured finance, in principle, serves two main purposes. First, it creates new assets that people can invest in. Instead of being limited to publicly traded stocks and bonds, investors can choose from a much broader menu of assets, each with unique characteristics to attract a particular investor; for example, securities can be manufactured to help investors match the timing of their assets and their liabilities.* Second, by creating assets that are more attractive to investors, structured finance should make it easier for businesses to raise money. While investors might demand a high rate of interest to invest in an airline route from Los Angeles to Shanghai, they might accept a lower rate if that route were packaged with an option to buy oil at a cheap price in the future. (If oil prices rise, hurting demand for long-distance flights, the option will increase in value.) Lower rates make it easier for businesses to raise money.

In theory, then, structured finance could increase the pie for everyone. More important, in practice it was sure to increase revenues for the banks arranging these complex transactions. The ordinary trajectory for most products and services in the business world is for profit margins to decline as competition increases. For example, the amount that a bank could make from a plain-vanilla loan to a highly rated company was minimal, because many other banks would be willing to make that loan. Like all businesses, banks needed to invent new products that were not yet commoditized and that could command high margins. Structured products were the perfect answer. They were complex products that bank customers could not arrange on their own. Moreover, because selling these products required the ability to hedge risks in multiple markets, it was difficult for new banks to break into the business, which became dominated by a small number of play-

---

*For example, pension funds with long-term liabilities should prefer to invest in long-term assets, so they are getting their money back at the same time that they need to make payouts.

ers who could charge hefty fees for their services. In his memoir, former trader Frank Partnoy described how Morgan Stanley earned $75 million on a single trade.[3]

In addition to pure derivatives such as interest rate swaps, currency swaps, and credit default swaps, asset-backed structured products were a mainstay of Wall Street derivatives desks in the early 1990s. The Repackaged Asset Vehicles that played a starring role for Morgan Stanley were structured products, in which a special-purpose vehicle (SPV, a new company that exists only on paper) bought a set of existing securities (say, bonds issued by the state electric utility of the Philippines) and paid for them by selling investors a new set of custom-designed securities.[4]

Asset-backed structured products became Wall Street's new cash cows, in the form of mortgage-backed securities (MBS) and their cousins, collateralized debt obligations (CDOs). The original mortgage-backed securities created by Ginnie Mae in the late 1960s were "pass-through" securities: mortgages were combined in a pool, and each security had an equal claim on the mortgage payments from that pool, spreading the risk evenly. Private MBS, however, are typically divided into different tranches, or classes, that have different levels of risk and pay different interest rates. Because the "senior" tranches have the first claim on all the mortgage payments, they have the least risk, and the credit rating agencies routinely stamped them with their AAA rating—the same rating given to U.S. government bonds. The "junior" tranches are riskier, but therefore pay higher interest rates to investors.*

A CDO is similar, except that instead of being built out of whole mortgages it is built out of mortgage-backed securities or securities backed by other assets (such as credit card loans, auto loans, or student loans).† By building CDOs out of junior, high-yielding MBS tranches,

---

*In a stylized example, an MBS offering might be composed of 85 percent senior MBS and 15 percent junior MBS. If 5 percent of the underlying mortgages default, the junior investors will lose one-third of their money, but the senior investors will lose nothing. The senior investors only lose if over 15 percent of the underlying mortgages default. By contrast, in a pass-through MBS, there are no tranches; if 5 percent of the mortgages default, all investors lose 5 percent of their money.

†There is not universal agreement on terminology. A mortgage-backed security with tranches is sometimes called a CDO. A CDO backed by mortgage-backed securities is sometimes classified as a mortgage-backed security (because ultimately it, too, is backed by mortgages).

banks were able to engineer new securities that offered high returns with relatively little risk—at least according to their models. It was possible to combine low-rated MBS tranches, mix them together, and create a new CDO, 60 percent or even 80 percent of which was rated AAA; even though the MBS (the inputs) had low ratings, it was unlikely that many of them would default at the same time—at least according to the models. Financial engineers even created CDO-squareds—CDOs whose raw material was other CDOs—and higher-order variants, in order to squeeze out higher yield at lower supposed risk.[5]

In the late 1990s, Wall Street became addicted to mortgage-backed securities and CDOs. As housing prices took off, it became easy to build models showing that MBS and CDOs had virtually no risk, because borrowers could always refinance their mortgages as long as prices were rising; even if they defaulted, rising prices meant that the investors would own valuable collateral. But because borrowers—especially subprime borrowers—were individually risky and paid interest rates to match, it was possible to manufacture AAA-rated securities that paid higher interest rates than other low-risk assets, such as U.S. Treasury bonds. Comforted by their AAA ratings, investors bought those CDOs without worrying about what was inside them. Most important, U.S. homeowners and homebuyers represented an enormous pool of potential borrowers that could be tapped over and over again as home prices rose and as they bought bigger houses or refinanced to turn their home equity into cash for home improvements or flat-screen televisions. Those mortgages and home equity loans were the raw material that Wall Street transformed into gleaming new CDOs for investors, taking a flat fee with each turn of the assembly line.

In comparison with MBS and CDOs, credit default swaps (insurance against default), introduced in chapter 3, are a relatively simple product, but they played a special role in the finance boom. Because the boom was based on creating, packaging, and selling debt, it depended on the assumption that borrowers would pay off their debts—or that someone else would pay in their place. Credit default swaps made it possible to insure *any* pool of mortgage loans or mortgage-backed securities, seemingly eliminating the risk of default.

In 1997, J.P. Morgan (part of today's JPMorgan Chase) pioneered the use of credit default swaps to shift the default risk of loans off of its balance sheet. In the "BISTRO" transaction, J.P. Morgan's derivatives team created a new special-purpose vehicle to insure loans the bank had made. J.P. Morgan paid insurance premiums to the SPV, and the premiums backed new bonds issued by the SPV to investors.[6] This complex piece of engineering had two benefits for the bank. First, because the risk of default on the underlying loans had been transferred from the bank to the SPV, the bank did not have to maintain capital reserves for those loans, so it could make more loans and hence more lending profits.

The other implication was more far-reaching. In effect, J.P. Morgan had created a new CDO out of thin air, without any of the raw material—loans or asset-backed securities—usually required. BISTRO was the first of what came to be known as "synthetic CDOs." If the borrowers paid off their loans, the SPV would receive a steady stream of insurance premiums from J.P. Morgan to pay off its investors; but if the borrowers defaulted, the SPV would have to make a large cash insurance payout to J.P. Morgan, and its investors would lose their money. From an economic standpoint, it was as if the SPV actually held the underlying loans. This meant that a bank could create a CDO based on the housing market without having to buy a pool of mortgages or mortgage-backed securities; instead, it only needed to find someone who would buy insurance (using credit default swaps) on securities that already existed in the market. No one, in other words, had to go to the trouble of lending new money.

In the 2000s, as demand from investors and Wall Street banks for subprime loans outstripped supply, credit default swaps were used to fill the gap. As hedge fund manager Steve Eisman said, "They weren't satisfied getting lots of unqualified borrowers to borrow money to buy a house they couldn't afford. They were creating them out of whole cloth."[7] This practice ultimately magnified the impact of mortgage defaults; as borrowers stopped paying, their defaults hurt not only the CDOs that held bits and pieces of their mortgages, but also the synthetic CDOs that mirrored them.

Credit default swaps also made possible another Wall Street business model. With a stable economy and rising housing prices, the default risk of the senior tranches of mortgage-backed securities and CDOs (the ones that got paid off first) seemed vanishingly small. Selling credit default swaps on these securities looked an awful lot like free money, and hedge funds stepped forward to take it. Notably, American International Group (AIG), the world's largest insurance company, had a Financial Products group that was willing to insure AAA-rated structured securities for almost nothing. In the late 1990s, AIG agreed to insure the "super-senior" portion of J.P. Morgan's CDOs—the part that was even safer than the AAA-rated bonds issued by the SPV[8]—for only two basis points (hundredths of a percentage point) per year. In other words, in return for insuring $100 million of loans against default, AIG would get $20,000 per year.[9] According to AIG's models, it was free money. From J.P. Morgan's perspective, because AIG was considered one of the world's safest companies—it had a AAA rating of its own at the time—it was fully insured, for a cheap price. Everyone was happy. Of course, risk never disappears, and in this case it would reappear with a vengeance in September 2008.

The third ingredient of this money machine was a wave of innovation in mortgages, often described as (but not confined to) subprime lending. Traditionally, since the 1930s, home mortgages had been relatively conventional products and mortgage lending a relatively staid business. Most mortgages were long-term, fixed-rate, "prime" mortgages, where the borrower met the lender's standards for creditworthiness, capacity (income) to repay debt, and collateral (real property sufficient to protect the lender in case of default).[10] Subprime loans, where the borrower did not meet one of these criteria,* were relatively rare. In 1993, there were only 24,000 subprime mortgages used to

*Contrary to popular belief, not all subprime loans are loans to poor people. The classification of a loan depends on the relationship between the borrower, the property, and the size of the loan. Chris Mayer and Karen Pence have found that "subprime mortgages are not only concentrated in the inner cities, where lower-income households are more prevalent, but also on the outskirts of metropolitan areas where new construction was more prominent."[11]

purchase homes and 80,000 subprime refinance mortgages. By contrast, there were 2.2 million prime home purchase mortgages and 5.2 million prime refinance mortgages; in aggregate, there were seventy prime mortgages for every subprime mortgage.[12]

The 1990s and 2000s, however, saw an explosion in all types of mortgage lending, although most attention has focused on subprime lending (and "Alt-A," a new designation for higher-end subprime loans), in which lenders lowered their standards for creditworthiness, capacity, or collateral, or all three at the same time. Before the market for private mortgage-backed securities took off in the 1990s, subprime lending was constrained by the fact that subprime lenders wanted to be paid back. Subprime loans had to conform to underwriting standards, like all loans, and were used primarily to refinance prime mortgages for borrowers who had poor credit histories but otherwise had the capacity to repay the debt. In addition, subprime loans were generally made by nonbank mortgage lenders who could not raise funds by taking deposits from customers. With the advent of securitization, however, investors and the investment banks that served them became particularly hungry for subprime loans because of the higher interest rates they paid, which were crucial to manufacturing high-yielding CDOs.

Now that loans could be resold to Wall Street, mortgage lending became a fee-driven business, where volume was the key to profits. Lenders responded by inventing new mortgage products that made it easier for borrowers to afford their monthly payments, at least for the first few years. These products went beyond the standard adjustable rate mortgage to extreme forms such as "pay option" mortgages where borrowers could choose to pay *less* than the monthly interest on the loan, causing the principal balance to go up instead of down. Lenders relaxed traditional underwriting practices, such as verifying the income and assets of the borrower; in stated-income mortgages, the lender explicitly *did not* confirm that the borrower had the income he or she claimed, and told the borrower as much. They accepted smaller down payments, resulting in higher loan-to-value (LTV) ratios, or used second mortgages to eliminate the down payment entirely; this meant that the collateral would not be sufficient to protect the lender from default unless housing prices rose.[13]

Many of these innovations applied equally to prime and subprime loans, and business in both categories boomed. In 2005, 1.0 million subprime loans were used to buy houses and 1.2 million were used for refinancing—in aggregate, a twenty-fold increase over 1993.[14] The result—whether due to mortgage brokers who pushed borrowers into inappropriate loans, or due to house "flippers" who took on as much leverage as possible to buy as many houses as possible while the market was hot—was mortgages that many borrowers would have little chance of actually paying off out of their income.

But that no longer mattered—at least not to the lenders or the investment banks—because the lending business model detached itself from the requirement that borrowers pay back their loans. Lenders made fees for originating loans; the higher the interest rate, the higher the fees. Then, when interest rates reset and borrowers became unable to make their monthly payments, lenders could earn more fees by refinancing them into new, even-higher-rate mortgages. As long as housing prices continued to rise, a single borrower could be good for multiple loans, each time increasing his debt. (This business model had been pioneered by credit card issuers, who discovered that they could make money off of borrowers even if they never fully paid off their card balances.)[15] If he finally became unable to refinance, any loss would typically be taken by a CDO investor, not by the mortgage lender, and would be confined to the junior CDO tranches. As late as 2007, according to the International Monetary Fund, "Stress tests conducted by investment banks show that, even under scenarios of nationwide house price declines that are historically unprecedented, most investors with exposure to subprime mortgages through securitized structures will not face losses." (The stress test cited by the IMF was conducted by Lehman Brothers.)[16]

As the business boomed, the large banks dived in, snapping up subprime lenders. Among the top twenty-five subprime lenders, First Franklin was bought by National City and later by Merrill Lynch; Long Beach Mortgage was bought by Washington Mutual; Household Finance was bought by HSBC; BNC Mortgage was bought by Lehman Brothers; Advanta was bought by JPMorgan Chase; Associates First Capital was bought by Citigroup; Encore Credit was bought by Bear Stearns; and American General Finance was bought by AIG.[17] Not only did buyers want the lucrative fees available from originating subprime loans, but many of them wanted a captive source of loans for their mortgage securitization machines. Large banks also expanded their subprime operations by working with independent mortgage lenders and brokers. According to the head of Quick Loan Funding, a subprime lender, Citigroup provided the money for loans to borrowers with credit scores below 450 (at the time, the national median was about 720).[18] JPMorgan Chase aggressively marketed its "no doc" and "stated-income" programs to mortgage brokers and used slogans such as "It's like money falling from the sky!"[19] If subprime lending was pioneered far from Wall Street, by the 2000s Wall Street couldn't get enough of it.

Housing was not the only bubble made possible by cheap money, aggressive risk-taking, and structured finance. The 2000s saw a parallel bubble in the commercial real estate market, where banks were willing to finance purchases at ever-increasing valuations, in part because they were able to use commercial mortgage-backed securities to unload the large, risky loans they were making. There was also an enormous boom in takeovers of companies by private equity firms, again made possible by cheap loans advanced by banks and then syndicated to groups of investors or used as raw material for new structured products. These bubbles overlapped in takeovers of real estate investment trusts (REITs), companies that invest in real estate. In February 2007, the Blackstone Group bought Equity Office Properties Trust for $39 billion in the largest leveraged buyout ever; Blackstone immediately flipped most of Equity Office's buildings to other buyers (who borrowed as much as 90 percent of the purchase price), many of whom took significant losses as the real estate market crashed.[20] In October 2007, Tishman Speyer spent $22 billion to buy Archstone-Smith Trust, much of it financed by a group of banks led by Lehman Brothers; losses on that deal would be one factor that helped lead to the downfall of Lehman less than a year later.[21]

FORCE-MOLTING

But the emblematic bubble of the decade, and the one whose implosion led directly to the financial crisis, was the housing bubble, in which prices soared to almost twice their long-term average (see Figure 5-1).[22] The increased availability of mortgage loans, with lower initial monthly payments, increased homebuyers' ability to pay, pushing prices upward. Continually rising housing prices seemed to eliminate the risk of default, since borrowers could always refinance when their mortgages became unaffordable, making mortgage-backed securities and CDOs more attractive to investors and to the investment banks that manufactured them. Higher prices also induced existing homeowners to take out home equity loans, providing more raw material for asset-backed securities and CDOs. Lower risk lowered the price of credit default swaps on mortgage-backed debt, making CDOs and synthetic CDOs easier to create. Increased Wall Street demand for mortgages (to feed the securitization pipeline) funneled cheap money to mortgage lenders, who sent their sales forces out onto the streets in search of more borrowers; by the early 2000s, many prime borrowers had already refinanced to take advantage of low rates, and so subprime lending became a larger and larger share of the market. And the cycle continued.

Figure 5-1: Real U.S. Housing Prices, 1890–2009

Source: Robert Shiller, Historical Housing Market Series. Used by permission of Mr. Shiller. Data were originally used in Robert Shiller, *Irrational Exuberance* (Princeton: Princeton University Press, 2000).

Ordinarily, the instinct for financial self-preservation should prevent lenders from making too many risky loans. The magic of securitization relieved lenders of this risk, however, leaving them free to originate as many new mortgages as they could. Because mortgages were divided up among a large array of investors, neither the mortgage lender nor the investment bank managing the securitization retained the risk of default. That risk was transferred to investors, many of whom lacked the information and the analytical skills necessary to understand what they were buying. And the investors assumed that they didn't need to worry about what they were buying, because it was blessed by the credit rating agencies' AAA rating.

Ironically, even though securitization theoretically allowed banks to pass on all the default risk to their clients, some kept some of the risk anyway. Either they really believed that the senior tranches of their CDOs were risk-free, or there was more demand for the riskier junior tranches and they couldn't find enough buyers for the senior tranches. Here again, they depended on financial innovation in the form of structured investment vehicles (SIVs)—special-purpose entities that raise money by issuing commercial paper and invest it in longer-term, higher-yielding assets. Citigroup, for example, used SIVs to buy over $80 billion in assets by July 2007.[23] These vehicles allowed banks to invest in their own structured securities without having to hold capital against them; since SIVs were technically not part of the bank in question—even though they were wholly owned by that bank, which might even have promised to bail them out if necessary[24]—their assets were not counted when determining capital requirements. The result was that SIVs enabled banks to take on more risks with the same amount of capital.

SIVs were a Wall Street variation on one form of crony capitalism. In an emerging market, when a major family-owned conglomerate sets up a new company, it can legally walk away should things go bad. Because the new company has the family name behind it, however, the family will come under pressure to prop it up in a crisis.[25] And just as in emerging markets, when things did go bad in 2007 and 2008, many banks, including Citigroup, bailed out their SIVs, incurring billions of dollars of losses in the process. But as long as housing prices were soaring, SIVs were another way to make more profits using less capital. In addition, by soaking up the senior tranches of CDOs, they helped keep the securitization machine going at full volume.

Rising housing prices created their own momentum, as bubbles do. As people saw their friends and neighbors cashing in on the housing boom, they rushed to get in on the action. The environment became so filled with stories about people making money in housing that even skeptics decided that everyone else couldn't be wrong, creating what Robert Shiller has called a "rational bubble."[26] Even investors who knew the boom could not last were betting that they could buy high and sell higher before the music stopped.

On a factory farm, when hens start laying fewer eggs, they are "force-molted"—"starved of food and water and light for several days in order to stimulate a final bout of egg laying before their life's work is done."[27] After 2004, when many qualified borrowers had already refinanced and houses were so expensive they could only be bought with exotic mortgages, the real estate and finance industries launched an all-out effort to get people into new houses and squeeze out a few last years of golden eggs. In the peak years, the bubble was sustained by brand-new mortgage products that only existed because they provided raw material for CDOs. At the height of the boom, over half of the mortgages made by Lennar, a national housing developer, were interest-only mortgages or optional-payment mortgages whose principal went *up* each month; in 2006, almost one in three had a piggyback second mortgage.[28] Between 1998 and 2005, the number of subprime loans tripled, and the number that were securitized (as measured by First American LoanPerformance) increased by 600 percent.[29] In 2005, a consortium of Wall Street banks created standard contracts for credit derivatives based on subprime mortgages, making it even easier to create synthetic subprime CDOs.[30] These developments all confirmed the predictions of economist Hyman Minsky, who had warned that "speculative finance" would eventually turn into "Ponzi finance."[31]

The end result was a gigantic housing bubble propped up by a mountain of debt—debt that could not be repaid if housing prices started to fall, since many borrowers could not make their payments out of their ordinary income. Before the crisis hit, however, the mortgage lenders and Wall Street banks fed off a giant moneymaking machine in which mortgages were originated by mortgage brokers and passed along an assembly line through lenders, investment banks, and CDOs to investors, with each intermediate entity taking out fees along the way and no one thinking he bore any of the risk.[32]

GREENSPAN TRIUMPHANT

An emerging market oligarchy uses its political power and connections to make money through such means as buying national assets at below-market prices, getting cheap loans from state-controlled banks, or selling products to the government at inflated prices. In the United States, the banking oligarchy (and its allies in the real estate industry) used its political power to protect its golden goose from interference and to clear away any remaining obstacles to its growth. The banks' objectives included both the elimination or nonenforcement of existing regulations and the prevention of new regulations that might stifle profitable innovations. Their sweeping success enabled them to take on more and more risk, increasing their profits but also increasing the potential cost of an eventual crash.

At the top of the major commercial banks' wish list was the repeal of the Glass-Steagall Act, which was finally achieved in 1999. By that point, the separation of commercial and investment banking had been severely weakened by a series of Federal Reserve actions that allowed commercial banks, through their subsidiaries, to underwrite many types of securities; in addition, the new business of derivatives fell outside Glass-Steagall altogether, and commercial banks such as Bankers Trust and J.P. Morgan were among the pioneers in that market.

In 1996, the Fed struck a major blow for deregulation, allowing bank subsidiaries to earn up to 25 percent of their revenues from securities operations, up from 10 percent.[33] That same year, the Fed overhauled its regulations to make it easier for banks to gain approval to expand into new activities. Congress also changed the rules for banks seeking to expand into new businesses, relieving banks of the need to obtain approval from the Federal Reserve and putting the onus on the Fed to actively disapprove of any new activities.[34] As long as Glass-Steagall remained on the books, however, the 25 percent revenue limit posed a barrier, and there was still the risk that Congress or the courts might overrule a friendly decision by the Fed.

When Travelers and Citicorp merged in 1998—bringing together a major commercial bank and a major insurance company that owned a major investment bank—Glass-Steagall required the new Citigroup to break itself up within two years. Citigroup's only recourse was to get the law repealed. Congress obliged in 1999 with the Gramm-Leach-Bliley Act, which created a new category of financial holding companies that are authorized to engage in any activities that are financial in nature, incidental to a financial activity, or complementary to a financial activity—including banking, insurance, and securities.[35] With this legislation, Donald Regan's dream of a true financial supermarket that could offer all financial services was not only legal, it seemed to be embodied in the new Citigroup.

The passage of Gramm-Leach-Bliley freed not only Citigroup but also Bank of America, J.P. Morgan, Chase, First Union, Wells Fargo, and the other commercial megabanks created by the ongoing merger wave to plunge headlong into the business of buying, securitizing, selling, and trading mortgages and mortgage-backed securities. Because there was no way to seal off the banks' securities operations from their ordinary banking operations, this meant that the government guarantee of the banking system, in place since the 1930s, was effectively extended to investment banking. Deposits that were insured by the Federal Deposit Insurance Corporation could be invested in risky assets, with the assurance that losses would be made up by the FDIC. The larger the bank, the stronger its government guarantee. In 1984, when Continental Illinois was bailed out, the comptroller of the currency said that the top eleven banks were too big to fail; by 2001, there were twenty banks that were as big relative to the economy as the eleventh-largest bank had been in 1984.[36] As in any capitalist system, bank employees and shareholders would enjoy the profits from their increasingly risky activities; but now the federal government was on the hook for potential losses.

A major test of Wall Street's power was regulation of derivatives. Because they did not directly involve either deposits or traditional securities, and because they defied conventional treatment on an accounting balance sheet, customized derivatives posed a new challenge to the existing regulatory framework. The first threat to this new profit center arose in 1994 because of the major derivatives losses suffered by Orange County, Procter & Gamble, and Gibson Greetings, among others.

In response, Congress took up the issue of derivatives regulation. The House Banking and Financial Services Committee conducted a major investigation, and several bills to regulate derivatives were proposed. The industry countered with a major lobbying effort coordinated by the International Swaps and Derivatives Association (ISDA), which was received sympathetically by Alan Greenspan and by the Wall Street–friendly Clinton administration. Treasury Undersecretary Frank Newman urged Congress not to regulate derivatives;[37] Treasury Secretary Lloyd Bentsen also backed the industry, saying, "Derivatives are perfectly legitimate tools to manage risk. Derivatives are not a dirty word. We need to be careful about interfering in markets in too heavy-handed a way."[38]

The Group of Thirty, an international advocacy group largely composed of private sector bank executives, central bankers, and sympathetic academics, chimed in with a study concluding that no new regulation was required and that the industry could be trusted to regulate itself.[39] The study was overseen by Dennis Weatherstone, then chair of J.P. Morgan. *The New York Times* reported at the time, "Many of those people conducting the study work at businesses that have a stake in assuring the market's continued prosperity. They were trying to head off calls for greater regulation and supervision by addressing these concerns."[40] And they were entirely successful. By the end of 1994, the lobbying effort had killed off all congressional efforts at regulation. Some customers who had been burned by derivatives were able to win settlements from their derivatives brokers, but these isolated cases did little to stem the growth of the industry.[41]

This was only one of several high-profile battles over regulation in the last two decades (but perhaps the only one that Wall Street had any chance of losing). Another struggle was precipitated by Brooksley Born's campaign as chair of the Commodity Futures Trading Commission (CFTC) to *think about* regulating over-the-counter derivatives. Born was concerned that the buildup of large derivatives positions invisible to regulatory oversight could create risks for the financial system as a whole.[42] She was opposed not only by Greenspan, Rubin, and Summers, but also by Securities and Exchange Commission chair Arthur Levitt and House Banking Committee chair Jim Leach. On May 7, 1998, the same day that Born's "concept release" was published, Rubin, Greenspan, and Levitt went public with their "grave concerns . . . about reports that the CFTC's action may increase the legal uncertainty concerning certain types of OTC derivatives."[43] In June, they proposed draft legislation imposing a moratorium on regulatory action by Born's agency.

In July 1998, before the House Banking Committee, representatives from Treasury, the SEC, and the major banking regulators lined up with Greenspan and executives from several major banks to oppose Born and testify that derivatives markets were functioning effectively without additional regulation. Greenspan said, "professional counterparties to privately negotiated contracts also have demonstrated their ability to protect themselves from losses, from fraud, and counterparty insolvencies"; he concluded, "aside from safety and soundness regulation of derivative dealers under the banking or securities laws, regulation of derivatives transactions that are privately negotiated by professionals is unnecessary. Regulation that serves no useful purpose hinders the efficiency of markets to enlarge standards of living."[44] In October, the moratorium was approved. The next year, Born decided not to seek reappointment.

From the perspective of the derivatives industry, however, winning the battle was not enough. Not satisfied that derivatives were unregulated, the industry used its influence to ensure that derivatives would never be regulated. In November 1999, the President's Working Group on Financial Markets produced a report, "Over-the-Counter Derivatives Markets and the Commodity Exchange Act," signed by Summers (then treasury secretary), Greenspan, Levitt, and new CFTC chair William Rainer. That report concluded that, in order "to promote innovation, competition, efficiency, and transparency in OTC derivatives markets, to reduce systemic risk, and to allow the United States to maintain leadership in these rapidly developing markets," those derivatives should be exempted from federal regulation.[45]

The financial sector's supporters in Congress complied by passing the Commodity Futures Modernization Act (CFMA), introduced in

May 2000 but held up in the Senate due to Senator Phil Gramm's desire for even stricter deregulatory language.[46] Ultimately, Gramm succeeded in foreclosing any possibility of regulation by the CFTC or the SEC; in the middle of December, the bill was inserted into the Consolidated Appropriations Act for Fiscal Year 2001, passed by a lame-duck Congress, and signed by a lame-duck president. The financial sector had succeeded in sealing off one of its profit-making engines from the possibility of government interference.

Another key goal of the Wall Street banks was to maximize their leverage, and structured finance was a key to their strategy. Leverage is an easy way to increase profits. If you invest $10 of your money at a 10 percent return, you will gain $1 in profits; but if you invest $10 of your money and $90 of borrowed money at a 10 percent return, your profits will be $10. Conversely, however, leverage increases the chances that you will be wiped out; a 10 percent loss on $10 of your own money is only $1, but a 10 percent loss on $10 of your money and $90 of borrowed money leaves you with nothing.

This is why regulators place limits on the amount of leverage a bank can take on, in the form of minimum capital requirements. Capital is the amount of money put up by the bank's owners (shareholders), and acts as a safety cushion in times of stress; the more capital, the more money the bank can lose before it becomes unable to return money to its depositors and repay its debts. Capital requirements are set as a percentage of the bank's assets. For every $100 in assets, a bank might have to hold $10 in capital, which means it can borrow only up to $90; this is the same as saying its leverage cannot be more than nine to one. Therefore, to maximize profits per dollar invested (capital), banks want to maximize their leverage; put another way, for the same assets, they want to hold as little capital as possible.

One motivation for securitization was to exploit a loophole in existing regulatory capital requirements. The amount of capital a bank had to hold depended on the type of assets it held; in theory, the riskier the asset, the more capital was required. The loophole was that these requirements were set somewhat arbitrarily—4 percent for home mortgages, 8 percent for unsecured commercial loans, and so on. As a result, a bank could take $100 of assets that required, say, $8 in capital; put them into a securitization pool; and, through the magic of structured finance, convert them into $100 of new securities that were treated differently by capital regulations and therefore required only $5 in capital. The true risk of the assets hadn't changed, since the probability of default hadn't changed. But because financial engineers could create securities with just the right characteristics needed to get just the right credit ratings, they could control the amount of capital that was required. So a bank could use securitization to *keep* the economic risk of its loans while reducing its capital requirements (so it could go and make more loans).

In addition to securitization, credit default swaps could be used to reduce capital requirements and increase leverage. The same J.P. Morgan team that pioneered the synthetic CDO also first lobbied federal regulators for permission to use credit default swaps to reduce their capital requirements. In 1996, the Federal Reserve Board of Governors obliged.[47] With both securitization and credit default swaps in their arsenal, Wall Street's financial engineers could concoct increasingly elaborate mechanisms for repackaging risk in ways that reduced its regulatory footprint.

Federal regulators were well aware of these practices. In 2000, for example, Federal Reserve economist David Jones published a paper with detailed examples of how banks could engage in regulatory capital arbitrage (RCA). "[R]egulatory capital standards seem destined to become increasingly distorted by financial innovation and improved methods of RCA," he wrote, "at least for those large, sophisticated banks having the resources to exploit such opportunities." Jones argued that this could actually be a good thing: "Against the backdrop of regulatory capital requirements that are often quite arbitrary, in some circumstances RCA actually may improve a bank's financial condition and the overall efficiency of the financial system. Indeed, RCA is widely perceived as a 'safety valve' for mitigating the adverse effects of regulatory capital requirements."[48]

Instead of attempting to crack down on banks' attempts to get around minimal capital requirements, federal regulators went in the other direction and loosened those requirements. In 2001, the federal bank regulators issued a new rule standardizing the capital requirements for securitizations.[49] If the bank creating the securitization retained some of the risk of the assets involved (which it often did in order to attract investors), the new rule calculated the bank's capital requirements based on ratings set by credit rating agencies (or, in some cases, the banks' own internal models). The goal of this rule was to align capital requirements with the degree of economic risk taken on by the bank, which was supposedly measured by the rating agencies. Instead, however, it meant that banks could get away with anything, so long as they could convince a rating agency to approve it.[50]

Not surprisingly, "shopping for ratings" became a standard part of securitizations. Banks would tweak their models until they got the ratings that they needed in order to sell some of the tranches to investors and keep some tranches for themselves. Rating agencies—who were being paid by the banks to rate these securities—complied, granting AAA ratings to thousands of securities at a time when only a handful of companies enjoyed AAA ratings for their bonds.*[51] According to Jim Finkel of Dynamic Credit, which created structured products, "Wall Street said, 'Hey, if you don't [give me the rating I want], the guy across the street will. And we'll get them all the business.' And they just played the rating agencies off one another." One investment banker who worked on these securitizations said, "It makes me feel really bad actually, it's very hard for me to acknowledge. . . . I knew I was doing things to get around the rules. I wasn't proud of it but I did it anyway."[52] The rating agencies were hardly passive victims. A McClatchy investigation found that even as the housing market was starting to crumble, Moody's was forcing out executives who questioned the agency's high ratings of structured products and filling its compliance department with people who had specialized in giving those ratings.[53]

By making capital requirements dependent on credit ratings, the regulators put this critical aspect of oversight in the hands of a small number of rating agencies that themselves depended on the banks for their revenues. With limited competition and little ability for investors

---

*In 2005, only eight U.S. companies had AAA bond ratings: AIG, Automatic Data Processing, Berkshire Hathaway, ExxonMobil, General Electric, Johnson & Johnson, Pfizer, and United Parcel Service.

to understand the rating process, the agencies had little incentive to give accurate ratings; by contrast, they had a lot of incentive to keep their key clients—the investment banks—happy. In 2004 and 2005, some rating agencies modified their rating models in ways that made it easier to give higher ratings to CDOs, helping extend the structured finance boom. But when the bubble finally burst, they ended up downgrading over 75 percent of asset-backed CDOs that had gotten AAA ratings in 2006 and 2007.[54]

Regulators went even further and outsourced control over minimum capital requirements to the banks they were regulating. On April 28, 2004, the Securities and Exchange Commission agreed to a request by the five large investment banks—Goldman Sachs, Morgan Stanley, Merrill Lynch, Lehman Brothers, and Bear Stearns—to use their own internal models, based on historical data, to calculate the "net capital" in their broker-dealer operations. The rule was explicitly intended to reduce the regulatory burden on the major investment banks by increasing their net capital, thereby enabling them to expand their business:

> These amendments are intended to reduce regulatory costs for broker-dealers by allowing very highly capitalized firms that have developed robust internal risk management practices to use those risk management practices, such as mathematical risk measurement models, for regulatory purposes. A broker-dealer's deductions for market and credit risk probably will be lower under the alternative method of computing net capital than under the standard net capital rule.[55]

Between 2003 and 2007, all five major investment banks increased their overall leverage, taking on larger and riskier positions that increased their expected profits while increasing their overall risk.[56] Bear Stearns's leverage reached a ratio of thirty-three to one, meaning that if its assets fell by 3 percent the bank would be insolvent; it was the first to fall in 2008 when *rumors* that it might be insolvent caused its short-term funding to dry up in a matter of days.

In exchange for being allowed to increase their leverage, the investment banks gave the SEC new powers to monitor their operations through the Consolidated Supervised Entity program. However, the SEC declined to take effective action under this program. A 2008 investigation by the SEC inspector general found that [the SEC's Division of Trading and Markets] became aware of numerous potential red flags prior to Bear Stearns' collapse, regarding its concentration of mortgage securities, high leverage, shortcomings of risk management in mortgage-backed securities and lack of compliance with the spirit of certain Basel II standards, but did not take actions to limit these risk factors.[57]

By this point, many regulators had bought into the idea that the financial markets could police themselves, so there was no need to intervene.

Securitization, credit default swaps, and more flexible capital requirements all made it possible for banks to increase their leverage, increasing both profits and risks. Historically, regulators have set limits on leverage, because it increases the likelihood of failures that may require government intervention. In the past twenty years, Wall Street banks invented new ways of getting around those limits. More important, the regulators no longer felt the need to protect the financial system by defending those limits, instead acquiescing in the general belief that markets were best left to police themselves.

Another potential threat to Wall Street's golden goose was regulation of mortgage lending, and subprime lending in particular. The mortgage lenders were not unaware of this danger. Between 2000 and 2007, the lenders that lobbied most intensively against potential legislation restricting predatory lending were precisely those lenders who originated the riskiest mortgages (measured by loan-to-income ratios), grew the fastest, and grew the proportion of mortgages that they securitized the fastest.[58] (They were also hit the hardest by the eventual financial crisis.) But the industry was fortunate to be protected by powerful figures in Washington.

In 1994, back when subprime lending was off Wall Street's radar, Congress had passed the Home Ownership and Equity Protection Act, which amended the Truth in Lending Act to read, "A creditor shall not engage in a pattern or practice of extending credit to consumers under [high-cost refinance mortgages] based on the consumers' collateral without regard to the consumers' repayment ability, including the consumers' current and expected income, current obligations and employment."[59] In other words, it banned predatory lending—loans where the lender doesn't care if the borrower can't make his or her payments, because then the lender can pick up the house cheaply. However, under the arcane structure of financial regulation, consumer protection statutes including the Truth in Lending Act were enforced by the Federal Reserve—headed throughout this entire period by Alan Greenspan, who not only opposed government regulation in general, but thought that even fraud would be deterred by the operation of a free market.

The Federal Reserve sidestepped its consumer protection responsibilities by claiming it lacked jurisdiction. Many subprime loans—52 percent of those originated in 2005, for example[60]—were made not by banks, but by nonbank consumer finance companies or mortgage lenders. By the late 1990s, however, many of these specialized lenders had been bought up by banks (through their holding companies) or had been started by banks as independent subsidiaries. Consumer groups amassed mounting evidence of abusive lending practices, particularly in low-income and minority communities, and pressed the Fed to investigate. In 1998, however, the Federal Reserve Board of Governors unanimously decided "to not conduct consumer compliance examinations of, nor to investigate consumer complaints regarding, nonbank subsidiaries of bank holding companies,"[61] claiming it could not regulate nonbank entities[62] (even though the Truth in Lending Act makes no distinction between banks and nonbanks).[63]

In 2000, a joint report issued by Treasury (then under Larry Summers) and the Department of Housing and Urban Development recommended restrictions on harmful sales practices and on abusive terms and conditions in the mortgage market.[64] The report also urged the Fed to investigate abusive lending practices, claiming it had authority to do so.[65] That same year, Edward Gramlich, a member of the Board of Governors, argued that the Fed should crack down on predatory lending by consumer finance lenders that were subsidiaries of bank holding companies. His proposal, like all the others, was shot down by Greenspan, who believed that subprime lending was an example of healthy financial innovation.[66] (Conforming to the usual practice of not airing disagreements among governors, Gramlich did not go public with his concerns while at the Fed. Shortly before he died in 2007, however, he wrote, "In the subprime market, where we badly need supervision, a majority of loans are made with very little supervision. It is like a city with a murder law, but no cops on the beat.")[67] As late as 2005, Greenspan was still celebrating the growth in subprime lending:

> Where once more-marginal applicants would simply have been denied credit, lenders are now able to quite efficiently judge the risk posed by individual applicants and to price that risk appropriately. These improvements have led to rapid growth in subprime mortgage lending; indeed, today subprime mortgages account for roughly 10 percent of the number of all mortgages outstanding, up from just 1 or 2 percent in the early 1990s.[68]

While the Federal Reserve was neglecting to protect consumers, other regulatory agencies were neglecting to ensure the soundness of the banks they supervised. At the peak of the subprime lending boom, the Office of Thrift Supervision (OTS) was allowing thrifts to *reduce* their capital levels, which fell to their lowest level in decades by 2006. Only in 2005 did the Office of the Comptroller of the Currency (OCC) initiate a proposal saying that lenders should have to make sure that borrowers could afford their monthly payments; even then, it was not actually issued until September 2006, by which point housing prices were already falling.[69] Material loss reviews conducted after many smaller banks had failed in 2009 showed that banking regulators were often aware of the risks that the banks were running, but failed to take any significant corrective action.[70]

While federal regulators were content to turn a blind eye to subprime lending—when they were not cheering it on—there remained the risk that state regulators might attempt to put an end to the party. In 1999, the North Carolina Predatory Lending Law subjected high-cost (subprime) loans to a number of constraints, such as limits on loan flipping (refinancing a borrower into a new loan after only a few years) and prepayment penalties; in 2002, the Georgia Fair Lending Act introduced similar restrictions.[71] Standard & Poor's responded by announcing that it would not allow any loans governed by the Georgia Fair Lending Act into securitizations that it rated; if similar laws had been enacted throughout the country, this would have brought the subprime mortgage securitization assembly line to a screeching halt.[72]

However, the primary federal bank regulators came to the industry's aid, ruling that state regulations are "preempted" by federal regulations.* In August 2003, the OCC ruled that state regulation of lending practices did not apply to national banks, preempting the Georgia Fair Lending Act and holding that federal regulators alone had the power to regulate lending activities by federally chartered institutions.[73] This decision followed letters by the chief counsel of the OTS concluding that federal law preempted both the Georgia Fair Lending Act and the New Jersey Home Ownership Security Act of 2002.[74] (Later in 2003, the OCC also preempted the New Jersey law; in January 2004, it exempted national banks from state mortgage regulations in general.)[75] The federal courts have usually sided with federal regulatory agencies on the issue of preemption, giving the OCC and the OTS the ultimate say on whether states may regulate banking operations.[76] During the subprime boom, the effect was to disarm state governments and give the mortgage lenders (and the investment banks securitizing their loans) free rein throughout the fifty states.

In addition to protecting the flow of subprime loans into the securitization market, the federal government also increased demand for subprime loans through its regulation of Fannie Mae and Freddie Mac. The financial crisis was not primarily due to Fannie and Freddie.[77] However, their purchases of securities that were backed by subprime loans did, at the margin, provide additional sales for the Wall Street banks manufacturing those securities.

Before 2008, Fannie Mae and Freddie Mac were government-sponsored enterprises (GSEs)—private corporations with a government mandate to provide liquidity to the housing market. They did this by buying mortgages and mortgage-backed securities on the secondary market and by creating and guaranteeing mortgage-backed securities of their own. To protect themselves, they only bought loans or guaranteed mortgage-backed securities made out of loans that conformed to their relatively strict (by industry standards) underwriting standards and size limits—so-called conforming loans. (The upper limit on con-

---

*Preemption is a legal doctrine holding that certain areas regulated by the federal government may not be regulated by the states—even if they wish to enact more stringent requirements than those prescribed by federal regulators.

forming loans for single-family houses grew from about $253,000 in 2000 to $417,000 in 2006, but still left many houses beyond its reach.)[78] Because Fannie and Freddie could borrow money cheaply, there was a ready supply of cash that could flow into mortgage lending.

The common indictment of Fannie and Freddie charges that Democrats in Congress, trying to expand homeownership among the poor and minorities, pushed the GSEs to buy more and more subprime loans, pumping up subprime lending and housing prices in the process. (The implication, of course, is that the financial crisis was caused by government intervention in the markets.) There is a grain of truth to this story. The targets set by HUD in both the Clinton and George W. Bush administrations (under a law passed in 1992) mandated that 42 percent, 50 percent, and finally 56 percent of the loans bought by Fannie and Freddie had to go to people with low or moderate incomes. In 2002, as part of the Bush administration's Blueprint for the American Dream, they committed to finance $1.1 trillion in loans to minority borrowers.[79]

The riskiest mortgages, however—the ones that pushed the housing bubble to dizzying heights—were simply off-limits to Fannie and Freddie. The GSEs could not buy many subprime mortgages (or securitize them) because they did not meet the conforming mortgage standards. As profit-maximizing private corporations, Fannie and Freddie tried to relax their underwriting standards in order to get into the party, reducing documentation requirements and lowering credit standards. But ultimately, regulatory constraints prevented them from plunging too far into subprime lending. As housing expert Doris Dungey wrote, "[T]he immovable objects of the conforming loan limits and the charter limitation of taking only loans with a maximum [loan-to-value ratio] of 80% . . . plus all their other regulatory strictures, managed fairly well against the irresistible force of 'innovation.' "[80]

As a result, in 2004–2006, as subprime lending reached its peak in both volume and innovation, Fannie and Freddie were pushed out of large parts of the market, because the loans being made violated their underwriting standards and because the Wall Street banks were so eager to get their hands on those loans. After 2003, the GSEs' share of secondary market subprime loans was cut in half, while the volume of private mortgage-backed securities (those not issued by the GSEs) soared.[81] Fannie and Freddie could not have pushed mortgage lenders into the most extreme forms of subprime lending, because those were precisely the loans they could not buy. They created demand for conforming mortgages, which were precisely what the aggressive subprime lenders were *not* selling.

Instead, however, Fannie and Freddie were able to buy the senior (AAA-rated) tranches of private mortgage-backed securities backed by subprime debt. These securities could count as money loaned to people with below-average income, and they were supposed to be safe.[82] These purchases of MBS were a mechanism by which government pressure to increase lending to low-income Americans translated into greater demand for mortgage-backed securities and therefore greater profits for Wall Street. At the end of the day, government pressure on Fannie and Freddie contributed to the housing bubble by increasing the amount of money flowing into the securitization pipeline. The two GSEs were not the primary factor stoking the subprime fire, and were consistently behind the curve as both subprime lending and securitization heated up, out-hustled by the mortgage lenders and the Wall Street banks who built, expanded, and profited from the mortgage securitization money machine. But they were yet another way that Washington provided fuel for that machine.

Finally, the Federal Reserve hooked its massive air pump to the housing bubble by keeping interest rates historically low from 2001 well into 2005. The federal funds rate (the rate at which banks borrow money from each other overnight) stood at 6.5 percent for most of 2000, before a recession and the terrorist attacks of September 11, 2001, prompted the Fed to cut it to 1.75 percent by the end of 2001.* It fell as low as 1.0 percent in 2003 and only began climbing again in June 2004, by which point real housing prices were 58 percent above their levels of January 2000. The federal funds rate didn't reach 3.0 percent—the *lowest* level of the entire 1990s—until May 2005, when real housing prices were 77 percent above their levels at the beginning of the decade.[83]

---

*The Federal Reserve controls the federal funds rate by buying and selling Treasury securities, which decreases or increases the amount of money available to banks, thereby affecting the rate at which banks lend to each other. The federal funds rate has an important though indirect influence on all interest rates in the economy.

Cheap money was important because low mortgage rates were a central ingredient in the housing and securitization boom. Low rates made it easier for people to afford larger mortgages, pushing up housing prices. Low rates also induced existing homeowners to refinance their mortgages, providing more raw material for the securitization pipeline. At any point in the decade, a sharp increase in interest rates could have punctured the housing bubble by making houses less affordable and forcing prices down. But the Federal Reserve, true to the conclusion of Greenspan's 1996 "irrational exuberance" speech—that the Fed should not attempt to identify bubbles but should simply clean up afterward—declined to act.

The irony is that the Fed's flood of cheap money did not even have the healthy effect that it should have had. Ordinarily, businesses should take advantage of low interest rates to make capital investments, which contribute to overall economic growth. In the 2000s, however, as Tim Duy notes, business investment in equipment and software grew more *slowly* than in the 1990s, despite the lower interest rates. The problem was that the cheap money was misallocated to the housing sector, resulting in anemic growth.[84] That misallocation was due to the new mortgage products that made it so easy to borrow large amounts of money, the voracious appetite of Wall Street banks and investors for securities backed by those mortgages, and a decade of government policies that encouraged the flow of money into housing. And the more money that flowed into new subdivisions in the desert, the less flowed into new factories where Americans could go to work. Ultimately, the price of the housing bubble and the financial crisis is not just trillions of dollars of losses on mortgages and mortgage-backed securities, but a decade of poor economic growth and declining real household incomes.*

Even before the financial crisis of 2007–2009, politicians and officials in Washington had opportunities to witness the potential consequences of financial innovation run riot. But they drew the wrong lessons each time, allowing the banks to take more risks and make more

---

*Average real annual growth has been lower in the 2000s (through 2008) than in any decade since the 1930s; real median household income (in 2008 dollars) has fallen from $52,587 in 1999 to $50,303 in 2008.[85]

money. The derivatives scandals of 1994 had cost clients hundreds of millions or billions of dollars, but posed no real danger to the financial system as a whole. The same could not be said of the near collapse of Long-Term Capital Management in 1998, which led to its bailout by a group of New York banks (facilitated by the Federal Reserve Bank of New York).[86]

The LTCM bailout was the right move for the Fed to make in the short term. It protected the financial system without putting public money directly at risk. However, the successful rescue sent the message that the Fed would not let private market actors suffer the consequences of their own bad decisions; while the LTCM partners lost most of their money, the banks that had blindly lent money to the fund lost none of theirs. It is impossible to say just what effect the rescue had on the behavior of Wall Street over the next decade. But it is clear that LTCM, with its $130 billion in debts and seven thousand open derivatives positions with a face value of $1.4 trillion,[87] was considered "too big to fail"—words that would become infamous almost exactly ten years later.

In addition, the ability of the Fed to avert disaster—and even to keep the stock market rising by cutting interest rates in September, October, and November 1998—undermined any incentive to do anything about the root causes of the LTCM near disaster. If this was the worst damage that unregulated financial institutions trading unregulated products could do, then perhaps regulation was unnecessary. Congress apparently agreed; it was in October 1998, only a month after LTCM had been saved, that it imposed the moratorium preventing the CFTC from regulating custom derivatives.

The collapses of Enron, WorldCom, and other high-flying companies in 2001–2002 also should have made clear that free markets did not deter fraud on their own. WorldCom committed straightforward accounting fraud that was missed by its auditors, the banks underwriting its new debt, and the credit rating agencies rating that debt.[88] Enron used special-purpose entities, derivatives, disguised loans, and aggressive accounting to shift revenues forward and backward in time, create phantom profits, and hide debts; while its intentions seemed to be fraudulent, the financial techniques it used were so novel that it was not clear which were illegal and which were merely innovative.[89] Some of its financial engineering techniques would reemerge in the financial crisis of 2007–2009, as would the banks it used—a class-action lawsuit named JPMorgan Chase, Citigroup, Credit Suisse First Boston, CIBC, Bank of America, Merrill Lynch, Barclays, Deutsche Bank, and Lehman Brothers as its enablers.[90]

Enron and WorldCom showed both the consequences of hyperactive financial innovation and the failure of "self-regulation" by the free market. Enron's creditors, who should have been lending money carefully, instead were helping it create fake transactions.[91] The credit rating agencies failed to disentangle Enron's web of special-purpose entities and maintained its investment-grade rating until well after the company's problems were front-page news. Old-fashioned regulation was also missing in action. In the wake of the Enron collapse, the Senate Governmental Affairs Committee concluded, "The Securities and Exchange Commission largely left the search for fraud to private auditors and boards of directors."[92]

Confronted with this wake-up call, Congress and the Bush administration limited themselves to bolting the particular barn door exploited by the Enron-WorldCom generation. The Sarbanes-Oxley Act of 2002 established new standards for corporate financial statements (and, by 2007, was under widespread attack from the business community for being too stringent). It did not occur to anyone in power that some of the ingredients that made Enron possible— financial innovations dreamed up by Wall Street banks hungry for large transaction fees, off-balance-sheet accounting, weak credit rating agencies, credulous investors, a largely fawning media, and ineffectual federal regulators—might already be recombining in a different form.

The SEC—the nation's chief regulator of the securities markets and investment banks—stepped up enforcement briefly after Enron, but enforcement actions declined again during the chairmanship of Christopher Cox from 2005 to 2009. Under Cox, the five-member commission that governed the agency often delayed action on opening investigations, delayed approval of settlements, or reduced penalties recommended by enforcement officials, resulting in an 84 percent decline in penalties.[93] Instead of focusing on enforcement, powerful commissioners such as Paul Atkins argued that the SEC should pare back regulations that were seen as imposing excessive costs on the free market.[94]

The SEC also failed to exercise its powers to oversee the securities industry. In the wake of the collapse of Bear Stearns, the SEC inspector general found that the agency not only took no meaningful action under the Consolidated Supervised Entity program, but also did a poor job implementing its Broker-Dealer Risk Assessment program (created in 1992 in response to the failure of Drexel Burnham Lambert). Under that program, the SEC received quarterly and annual reports from 146 broker-dealers—but generally only reviewed six of them.[95] Most famously, the SEC managed to overlook Bernie Madoff's $65 billion Ponzi scheme, despite tips and investigations going back to 1992.[96]

This failure to regulate the securities markets effectively was a consequence of the deregulatory ideology introduced by Ronald Reagan as well as the political influence of Wall Street. James Coffman, a former assistant director of the SEC's enforcement division, wrote,

> Elected deregulators appointed their own kind to head regulatory agencies and they, in turn, removed career regulators from management positions and replaced them with appointees who had worked in or represented the regulated industries. These new managers and, in many cases, the people they recruited and promoted, advanced or adhered to a regulatory scheme that, at least with respect to the most important issues, advanced the interests of the regulated.[97]

After all, the industry's mantra was that financial markets could self-regulate, so there was no need for the government. Once the government accepted this logic, it unilaterally disarmed in a sweeping abdication of its responsibility to the people it served.

THE GOLDMAN SACHS SAFETY NET

As much as the Wall Street banks wanted Washington's hands off their moneymaking businesses, they still had no stomach for doing business without the protection of the U.S. government. This attitude is consistent with the history of the business-government relationship in the United States. While occasional libertarian academics and politicians have favored deregulation in its pure form, real companies see regulatory or deregulatory policies simply as a way to improve their market position or profit-making potential. And one benefit Wall Street banks wanted was the security of knowing that the government's effectively unlimited balance sheet and borrowing power would be there for them should they need it.

Did bank executives consciously take excessive risks because they expected taxpayers to cushion their potential losses? This is not something that a Wall Street CEO is likely to admit, and it is possible that on an individual level they simply underestimated the risks involved and expected their winning streaks to continue indefinitely. But the government safety net was on at least some bankers' minds. Andrew Haldane, executive director for financial stability at the Bank of England, has told the story of a meeting (prior to the recent crisis) where government officials asked private-sector bankers why they did not conduct rigorous "stress tests" of their own portfolios; the answer, according to one participant, was that in the event of a severe shock, "the authorities would have to step in anyway to save a bank and others suffering a similar plight."[98] In any case, the behavior of major financial institutions made sense largely because of implicit government guarantees. Increasing leverage, increasing the proportion of assets held for trading purposes, buying riskier assets, and selling out-of-the-money options (such as credit default swaps) are all strategies that increase returns in good times but increase losses in bad times; therefore, they make the most sense for banks that can shift those higher losses onto someone else. (Ordinarily, banks' creditors would prevent them from pursuing these risky strategies, because their money would be on the line; if creditors expect to be bailed out by the government, however, there is no need for them to monitor the banks closely.) And they are all strategies that were pursued during the recent boom by major global financial institutions, including those in the United States.[99]

We do know that executives of at least one major bank thought about the government safety net. Since 1932, Section 13 of the Federal Reserve Act had given the Fed the power, in "unusual and exigent circumstances," to make loans to anyone—but only if the collateral provided in exchange arose "out of actual commercial transactions."[100] This requirement specifically excluded investment securities, which meant that in a crisis, investment banks might not have any valid collateral with which to borrow from the Fed.

This danger worried the remarkably prescient executives at Goldman Sachs. At their suggestion, the "actual commercial transactions" requirement was dropped in a "miscellaneous provision" of the Federal Deposit Insurance Corporation Improvement Act of 1991, ensuring that the Fed could lend against *any* collateral in a time of crisis.[101] This change gave the Fed the power to widen its protective umbrella to encompass investment banks, at the same time that those banks were increasing the riskiness of their operations by expanding their derivatives and proprietary trading businesses and taking on additional leverage. This seemingly minor change would be of crucial importance seventeen years later; when the housing bubble of the 2000s ended—and with it the seemingly unlimited supply of money flowing from novel and largely unregulated financial products—not only investment banks but a major insurance company would have to be rescued with government money.

6

TOO BIG TO FAIL

To paraphrase a great wartime leader, never in the field of financial endeavour has so much money been owed by so few to so many. And, one might add, so far with little real reform.

—Mervyn King, governor of the
Bank of England, October 20, 2009[1]

On October 13, 2008, their stock prices in tatters and the short-term viability of their firms in doubt, the heads of nine major banks—Bank of America, Bank of New York Mellon, Citigroup, Goldman Sachs, JPMorgan Chase, Merrill Lynch, Morgan Stanley, State Street, and Wells Fargo—arrived at the Treasury Department for a meeting with Treasury Secretary Henry Paulson.* Each was given a term sheet agreeing to sell shares to the government, and Paulson told them to sign it.[2]

This might seem like a government takeover of the financial sector—a seizure of ownership interests in nine major banks. And given the stakes—a near-total freeze of credit markets, a plunge in the stock market, the potential collapse of those and yet more banks—that would not have seemed too far-fetched. But the remarkable thing about this meeting was not that the government was stepping in to protect the U.S. financial system and, by extension, the global economy. What was remarkable was something that Vikram Pandit, CEO of Citigroup, noticed instantly: "This is very cheap capital!"[3] It was such a good deal

---

*All nine banks were also represented at the March 27, 2009, meeting discussed in the Introduction, except for Merrill Lynch, which was acquired by Bank of America in the interim.

that John Mack, CEO of Morgan Stanley, signed the term sheet immediately, even before consulting his board of directors.[4]

Few people at the time were arguing that the government should
sit on its hands and let the financial sector implode. But few also
expected Paulson, Federal Reserve chair Ben Bernanke, and Federal
Reserve Bank of New York president Tim Geithner to rescue the
banks on such generous terms. The October 13 deal was structured as
a purchase of preferred shares, which effectively meant that Treasury
loaned the banks money, at an initial 5 percent annual interest rate (a
rate that was not available in the market), that never had to be repaid.[5]
(Treasury also received options to buy a small amount of common
shares at a predetermined price.) The purchases theoretically meant
that the government now owned part of the banks, but Treasury
promised that it would not influence the management of the banks and
would not vote for members of their boards of directors.* It was close
to free money.

Why was this such a sweet deal? Although banks borrow most of
their money, all banks need capital—money that cannot be demanded
back by creditors. Capital serves as a buffer that prevents a bank from
failing when its assets fall in value. In good times, when capital is read-
ily available, banks prefer to borrow as much as possible in order to
maximize their profits, keeping their capital levels low; but in bad
times like October 2008, when banks most need additional capital, it is
at its most expensive—because who wants to invest in a bank that may
fail the next day?

But as Pandit recognized, the government was giving the banks capital cheaply; Warren Buffett, by contrast, had just invested in Goldman
Sachs at a 10 percent interest rate. (Buffett also received more options
than Treasury, and at a bigger discount to the then current market
price.) In short, Paulson, a former CEO of Goldman Sachs, was pushing free money at his former colleagues. Phillip Swagel, then a Treasury assistant secretary, later wrote, "This had to be the opposite of the
'Sopranos'—not a threat to intimidate banks but instead a deal so
attractive that banks would be unwise to refuse it."[6] According to

*Only if the bank failed to pay its dividends six times would the government have the right
to elect directors.

Swagel, the government had to offer attractive terms because it could not force the banks to agree to any investment, and it is true that some bankers claimed that they did not need government capital.[7] However, the government did have considerable negotiating leverage, thanks to its regulatory authority, its ability to threaten *not* to bail out banks later should they need it, and the fact that banks would be taking a risk by walking away without money that their competitors had. And the government officials involved fully appreciated the strength of their position. During the meeting, Paulson responded to an objection by saying, "Your regulator is sitting right there," referring to the director of the Office of the Comptroller of the Currency and the chair of the Federal Deposit Insurance Corporation. "And you're going to get a call tomorrow telling you you're undercapitalized and that you won't be able to raise money in the private markets."[8]

The government's largesse was not limited to capital at a bargain basement rate. At the October 13 meeting, officials also revealed that the government would begin guaranteeing debt issued by the banks, allowing them to raise money by selling bonds to private investors who now knew that the government would protect their investments. Together, these two measures constituted an extraordinary gift from the government, on behalf of taxpayers, to the financial sector.

At the time—with Lehman Brothers bankrupt, Bear Stearns and Merrill Lynch sold, and Goldman Sachs and Morgan Stanley fleeing for the safety of bank holding company status (which gave them increased access to emergency lending from the Federal Reserve)— many observers thought the financial crisis signaled the demise of Wall Street. For the onetime "masters of the universe," being forced to accept government money was a humbling blow. And even with the cushion of a large government subsidy, the banks seemed unlikely to return to the high-flying ways of the boom. America's leading business newspaper put its name on a book entitled *The Wall Street Journal Guide to the End of Wall Street as We Know It*.[9] An era, it seemed, was ending.

Today, however, it is clear that Wall Street did not end. While some fabled institutions have vanished, the survivors have emerged larger, more profitable, and even more powerful. The vague expectation that the government would bail out major financial institutions when necessary has become official policy. The connections between Wall Street and Washington have become stronger. A Democratic administration has done everything in its power to restore a private, profitable financial sector. A casual observer would be forgiven for thinking that Washington has behaved like an emerging market government in the 1990s—using public resources to protect a handful of large banks with strong political connections. Whether this was due to political capture or to unbiased economic policymaking, the result was the same: Wall Street only became stronger as a result of the financial crisis.

The story of the financial crisis of 2007–2009 has been told many times.[10] Policymakers, economists, and commentators have pointed to many causes and contributing factors, ranging from "oversaving" in China to basic human psychology.[11] However, few would deny that a U.S. financial system that inflated an asset bubble with cheap lending, manufactured colossal amounts of complex and potentially toxic securities, levered up with debt to maximize profits, and binged on short-term funding played a central role in bringing on the crisis. Even under the theory (popular among Americans) that a glut of saving in China created a flood of cheap money in the United States, leading to overborrowing and the housing bubble, that money had to flow through the American financial system, which did a phenomenally poor job of allocating it efficiently.

This system was made possible by the rise of the financial sector over the past three decades. Members of the Washington establishment bought into Wall Street's vision of free-flowing capital and unfettered innovation. Whether they were true believers or cynics out to maximize their campaign contributions or their future earning potential, policymakers helped the major banks by relaxing regulations, declining to enforce existing regulations, or neglecting to regulate new markets. This is why mortgage originators were allowed to make loans that got bigger over time, making them harder to pay off; why those mortgages could be packaged into securities that masked their intrinsic risk; why banks could stash those securities in off-balance-sheet vehicles and pretend they didn't own them; why they could use fancy risk models that said that nothing could go wrong with those securities; why trillions of dollars of side bets could be placed on those same securities; and ultimately why trillions of dollars of assets ended up precariously perched on top of a bubble of debt.

In 2006, the air began leaking out of that bubble, housing prices began to fall, and borrowers unable to refinance their mortgages started defaulting in sharply rising numbers. In 2007, the mountain of assets based on housing values began to crumble as increasing defaults torpedoed the prices of mortgage-backed securities and collateralized debt obligations (CDOs). In 2008, the resulting avalanche almost brought down the global financial system. Key government policy-makers made admirable efforts to save the financial system. But the actions they took ultimately demonstrated the importance of a partic-ular worldview in Washington—the idea that big, risk-loving banks are crucial to our economy and our way of life.

ON THE EDGE OF THE CLIFF

The financial crisis played out in a series of increasingly frightening episodes on Wall Street. Each scare prompted concern in Washington. But the three men who dominated economic policy through the end of the Bush administration—Paulson, Bernanke, and Geithner—hoped to avoid direct government intervention, preferring the approach of cushioning the downturn through increased liquidity and lower inter-est rates. Only in 2008 did they recognize that they were dealing with the kind of collapsing debt bubble common to emerging market crises in the 1990s—a scenario that required stronger measures.

Problems became widely visible in summer 2007, when Bear Stearns and then BNP Paribas revealed problems with internal hedge funds that had invested heavily in subprime mortgages. The disclo-sures made investors wonder how many other funds might contain ticking time bombs. The Federal Reserve responded with additional liquidity, lowering the discount rate and the federal funds rate* in an attempt to encourage lending and head off a credit contraction.

---

*The discount rate is the rate at which banks may borrow money directly from the Federal Reserve; the federal funds rate is the rate at which banks borrow money from each other overnight.

Fear only grew, however, as investors next became concerned about the structured investment vehicles (SIVs) that many banks had spawned in order to profit from structured securities while minimizing their capital requirements. As rumors spread that SIVs would either go bankrupt or infect the balance sheets of their sponsoring banks, the government attempted to engineer a backroom deal involving money from private banks. The theory was that the SIVs only faced a short-term liquidity crisis—given time, their assets would recover their value—and therefore deep-pocketed banks could buy them out safely. In October 2007, at the urging of the Treasury Department, several major banks announced a Master Liquidity Enhancement Conduit (MLEC) that would buy several hundred billion dollars' worth of securities from troubled SIVs. However, the idea was quietly dropped in December. Most likely the banks realized that using their own money to bail out their own SIVs—or, as some suspected, pooling the money of many banks to bail out Citigroup's SIVs—did not represent a real solution.

The failure of the MLEC implied that the major banks might be facing more than a simple liquidity crisis and might need more capital. At this point, sovereign wealth funds (investment funds owned by other countries) were still willing to supply that capital. Between October 2007 and January 2008, CITIC (China) committed to invest in Bear Stearns, the Abu Dhabi Investment Authority and the Government of Singapore Investment Group invested in Citigroup, China Investment Corporation invested in Morgan Stanley, and Temasek (Singapore), the Korean Investment Corporation, and the Kuwait Investment Authority invested in Merrill Lynch.[12] But the next time banks needed capital, it would be much harder to find.

The next firestorm erupted in March 2008 with the collapse of Bear Stearns, then considered the weakest of the big five stand-alone investment banks. Bear Stearns was brought down by a modern-day bank run.[13] On a proportional basis, it was more exposed to structured mortgage-backed securities than its rivals, and it was also highly dependent on short-term funding—cash that came from very short-term borrowing, much of it overnight.[14] This meant that its creditors could refuse to roll over their loans from one day to the next and demand their money back instead. If that happened, there was no way

Bear could pay them back, since many of its assets were illiquid; structured securities can be hard to sell on short notice, and selling them under pressure would cause their prices to collapse. If some creditors thought that this might happen, they would try to get their money out first, which would provoke other creditors to do the same, triggering a bank run as everyone scrambled to avoid being last in line.

All banks have this potential weakness, since they borrow short and lend long—they borrow money that they promise to return on short notice (deposits), and lend it out for long periods of time (mortgages). The rush by creditors to get their money out first is a classic feature of financial crises around the world, particularly in emerging markets. In the United States since the 1930s, deposit insurance has generally prevented bank runs by depositors—but that insurance did not cover the institutions lending money overnight to Bear Stearns and the hedge funds who parked their securities at Bear.

In early March, rumors surfaced that Bear Stearns was in trouble. Those rumors quickly became self-fulfilling as nervous creditors and hedge fund clients began cutting their exposure to the bank, causing Bear's cash to drain away. Treasury and the Fed faced the prospect that a major investment bank might go bankrupt, tying up its assets in bankruptcy court for months or years and leaving its creditors and counterparties without access to their money. The Fed first attempted to lend Bear money by using JPMorgan Chase as an intermediary (as an investment bank, Bear was not eligible for direct loans from the Fed). When this failed to bolster confidence, Paulson, Bernanke, and Geithner brokered the sale of Bear to JPMorgan for a paltry $2 per share. Even at that price, JPMorgan refused to go along without a government backstop, so the New York Fed agreed to assume all the losses on $30 billion of Bear's illiquid securities.

The deal was soon renegotiated to a purchase price of $10 per share, with JPMorgan now assuming the first $1 billion of losses on the $30 billion pool, which was parked in a special-purpose entity named Maiden Lane.[15] But it remained a coup for JPMorgan, which was paying for Bear Stearns approximately what its *building* was worth[16]—and for its CEO, Jamie Dimon, who happened to be on the board of directors of the New York Fed. The day the acquisition was announced, hoping to prevent the remaining stand-alone investment banks from suffering the same fate as Bear Stearns, the Federal Reserve also announced the creation of the Primary Dealer Credit Facility—a program allowing investment banks for the first time to borrow money directly from the Fed.[17] This constituted a dramatic expansion in the government's safety net for the banking system.

But the financial epidemic continued to spread as the fall in housing prices accelerated. Because of the complex way in which CDOs and other structured securities had been manufactured, falling housing prices and increasing defaults had a disproportionate impact on the prices of many such securities, which fell in value by 50 percent or more.* For example, in July 2008, Merrill Lynch sold a portfolio of CDOs with a face value of $30.6 billion to Lone Star Funds for only $6.7 billion, or 22 cents on the dollar—and even loaned Lone Star $5 billion to close the deal.[18]

No one knew how many of these toxic assets were sitting on major banks' balance sheets, or how much they would lose if they were forced to sell. Each quarter, banks were taking major write-downs—reducing the accounting value of those assets to reflect their deteriorating quality.† In 2007, Citigroup took $29 billion in write-downs, Merrill Lynch $25 billion, Lehman $13 billion, Bank of America $12 billion, and Morgan Stanley $10 billion.[19] But no one knew if the assets were being written down to their true values, or how long the write-downs would continue. In 2008, Citigroup would take another $63 billion in write-downs, Merrill $39 billion, Bank of America $29 billion, Lehman $14 billion, JPMorgan Chase $10 billion, and Morgan Stanley $10 billion. The suspicion was spreading that if they were forced to acknowledge the true decline in value of their assets, some major banks might turn out to be insolvent.

The next major institutions to come under pressure were Fannie Mae and Freddie Mac, the privately owned but government-

---

* The junior tranches of a CDO bore the first losses from the entire pool of mortgages or mortgage-backed securities that went into the CDO, so a default rate of only 6 percent could render an entire tranche of CDO securities worthless. Although securitization spread risk among many investors, it also concentrated risk into the junior tranches.

† A bank's balance sheet is supposed to record what its assets are worth; a write-down is a reduction in the recorded value of an asset. In practice, the rules on what values to use for assets can vary depending on many factors. Only some assets need to be "marked to market," meaning that their values should be adjusted to current market prices.

sponsored enterprises (GSEs) that backed up the housing market. Although Fannie and Freddie had been relatively late to the subprime party, their balance sheets were completely exposed to the housing market, and falling housing prices tore a widening hole in those balance sheets, threatening their survival. This spooked the housing market, which was unlikely to continue functioning without their guarantees. It also frightened foreign governments, China first among them, that had bought hundreds of billions of dollars of bonds from Fannie and Freddie and were counting on the U.S. government to protect them from default.

In July 2008, Paulson asked for and obtained the right to back up Fannie and Freddie with taxpayer money, betting that this alone would stem the panic; "If you've got a bazooka, and people know you've got it, you may not have to take it out," he said at the time.[20] But it was not enough. On September 7, Fannie and Freddie were taken over by the government and placed in a conservatorship—the equivalent of a managed bankruptcy.[21] The government promised to keep the GSEs in operation, and in exchange got a controlling ownership share and the right to manage them. Shareholders lost most of their money and the CEOs were replaced. In effect, the federal government took over two pillars of the financial system because they were too big to fail. Reactions were generally positive, in part because no one wanted to defend the quasi-private, quasi-public status of the GSEs. Other financial institutions had long complained about the unfair advantage that Fannie and Freddie enjoyed because of their government relationship, which made it cheaper for them to borrow money.

In the end, this was the last bailout that everyone could agree on. And it bought Paulson, Bernanke, and Geithner precisely one week.

Until September, most government support had been provided by the Federal Reserve in the form of new lending programs (the guarantee for Bear Stearns's assets was structured as a loan) and lower interest rates. By acting as a lender of last resort, the Fed hoped to engineer a "soft landing" from the boom—the goal its founders sought back in 1913. However, this strategy was about to reach its limits, leaving

Paulson, Bernanke, and Geithner with the choice between letting the free market take its course and end in financial and economic disaster, or engineering a massive government intervention in the financial system. The terms of that intervention would reveal the lasting influence and power of the Wall Street ideology—that big, private, lightly regulated financial institutions are good for America.

The precipitating factor was again the collapse of an investment bank—Lehman Brothers, now the smallest of the big four stand-alone investment banks. As with Bear Stearns, rumors emerged that Lehman was short on cash, and those rumors quickly became self-fulfilling. Over the weekend of September 13–14, the government cast about for a buyer. But this time, Paulson and Geithner made clear that they did not want to step in with taxpayer money. Paulson complained, "I'm being called Mr. Bailout. I can't do it again"; more circumspectly, Geithner observed, "There is no political will for a federal bailout."[22] On Saturday night, knowing that no federal money would be available, Jamie Dimon said to his troops at JPMorgan Chase, "We just hit the iceberg. The boat is filling with water, and the music is still playing. There aren't enough lifeboats. Someone is going to die."[23] When a plan for Barclays to acquire Lehman fell through on Sunday, the backup plan was bankruptcy early Monday morning.

Paulson, Bernanke, and Geithner declined to orchestrate a massive rescue that would have required a large loan from the Fed guaranteed by a claim on most of the bank's assets. (The principals have all insisted that they did not have the legal authority to rescue Lehman, because the bank did not have sufficient collateral to support an emergency loan from the Fed—but that argument only appeared weeks later.) They hoped that, since the Bear Stearns emergency in March, financial institutions had prepared themselves for the possibility of Lehman's collapse. As Bernanke said in congressional testimony, "[W]e judged that investors and counterparties had had time to take precautionary measures."[24] Unfortunately, those institutions had learned the opposite lesson—that the government would *not* let Lehman collapse. As Andrew Ross Sorkin wrote, describing the days before the Lehman bankruptcy, "[M]ost people on Wall Street . . . assumed that the government would intervene and prevent [Lehman's] failure."[25] The financial sector assumed it could have its cake and eat it too: the government would give it unlimited license to make money in the boom, *and* would shelter it from harm in the bust. But it turned out that the government did not have the resources to protect all of the major banks; this time, the resource in short supply was the political capital necessary to bail out another bank in the face of congressional and public criticism.

The Lehman bankruptcy triggered a chain reaction that ripped through the financial markets. American International Group, which was already struggling with the consequences of its derivatives trades, faced downgrades by all three major credit rating agencies, which would trigger collateral calls that could force it into bankruptcy.* On Tuesday, with the collateral damage caused by Lehman's failure beginning to spread, the Fed stepped in with an $85 billion credit line to keep AIG afloat, fearing that if the insurer defaulted on its hundreds of billions of dollars in credit default swaps, its counterparties would suffer devastating losses—or, at the least, fear of those losses would cause the financial markets to grind to a halt.

Also on Tuesday, the Reserve Primary Fund, one of the largest money market funds, announced that it would "break the buck"; because of losses on Lehman debt, it could not return one dollar for each dollar put in by investors. As a result, money flooded out of money market funds, forcing Treasury to create a new program to provide insurance for those funds. The flight from money market funds dried up demand for the commercial paper used by corporations to manage their cash, raising the specter that major corporations might not be able to make payroll. This forced the Fed to establish a program to buy commercial paper from issuing corporations—in effect lending money not just to banks, but directly to nonfinancial companies.

Banks that relied heavily on short-term funding saw their sources of cash dry up as investors realized that *any* financial institution could fall victim to a bank run. Washington Mutual collapsed as depositors pulled out their money, causing the largest bank failure in U.S. history,

---

*AIG's derivatives contracts gave its counterparties the right to demand collateral to protect them against the possibility that AIG might not be able to honor those contracts. The amount of collateral the counterparties could demand went up as AIG's credit rating went down.

and Wachovia, on the brink of failure, was acquired by Wells Fargo. Desperate to hold on to the cash they had, banks stopped lending. Money essentially moved in only one direction, toward U.S. Treasury bills—the presumed safest of all investments—and it stayed there. No one else could get any credit, and without credit the financial system cannot function.

On Thursday, September 18, the financial crisis burst onto the American political stage. Paulson and Bernanke went to Congress asking for $700 billion to buy toxic securities. A controversial three-page summary of their proposal gave the treasury secretary virtually unlimited power to use the money as he saw fit. Congress responded by passing the Emergency Economic Stabilization Act, but not until October 3, after its initial defeat in the House of Representatives triggered a frightening run on the stock market. That bill's central provision, the Troubled Asset Relief Program (TARP), gave Treasury $700 billion to buy "troubled assets" from financial institutions.

In the October 13 meeting at Treasury that opened this chapter, $125 billion of TARP money was committed to nine major banks. In addition to investments in smaller banks, another $40 billion was invested in Citigroup and Bank of America, two of the original nine banks, in later rescue operations; more TARP money was used to finance Federal Reserve guarantees of toxic assets held by those two banks; and $70 billion was invested in AIG to allow it to pay down its credit line from the Fed.[26] In addition, the FDIC promised to insure up to $1.5 trillion of new bank debt, and the Federal Reserve committed trillions of dollars to an ever-expanding list of liquidity programs intended to provide cheap money to the financial system: the Term Auction Facility, the Term Asset-Backed Securities Loan Facility, the Money Market Investor Funding Facility, the Asset-Backed Commercial Paper Money Market Mutual Fund Liquidity Facility, and so on.

Never before has so much taxpayer money been dedicated to save an industry from the consequences of its own mistakes. In the ultimate irony, it went to an industry that had insisted for decades that it had no use for the government and would be better off regulating itself—and it was overseen by a group of policymakers who *agreed* that government should play little role in the financial sector.

OTHER PEOPLE'S MONEY

Although the financial crisis was similar to earlier meltdowns,[27] especially in emerging markets, it was unique in its complexity and scale. A vigorous government response was necessary, particularly after the Lehman bankruptcy. Given the panic that seized financial markets, it was possible that a sudden evaporation of credit, coupled with rapid de-leveraging by financial institutions and corporations everywhere, could have led to a second Great Depression. However, at each point, the government had choices in how it responded to the crisis. To understand the nature of the government response, it is necessary to understand the options that were available.

The core problem was that various financial institutions were in trouble. The immediate threat was a panic-induced bank run, but the underlying issue was that the toxic securities held by banks had plummeted in value. If the banks had to liquidate those assets at current market prices, they would run the risk of becoming insolvent. In short, they needed more cash, or they needed insurance against those assets falling further in value. Broadly speaking, the government's choices lay on a spectrum between two main options.

The first was the "blank check" option. The government, as a source of potentially unlimited money, could keep financial institutions afloat and prevent a systemic collapse by simply giving them the money they needed (by investing new capital, overpaying for banks' assets, or insuring those assets at below-market rates). The second was the "takeover" option. The government could take over failing financial institutions and either clean them up, with the goal of ultimately returning them to private ownership, or shut them down. This is what the FDIC routinely does with smaller banks that become insolvent: it seizes their assets and then operates them in a conservatorship or sells the assets to another bank.

There has been considerable debate over whether the government had the legal authority to take over bank holding companies, as opposed to their commercial banking subsidiaries. While the takeover of holding companies was not anticipated by the regulatory scheme, the government had considerable power to dictate the terms of support to any troubled bank, both because regulators had the power to revoke the license of an insolvent bank and because the government was the only source of financing available to struggling banks.* Thomas Hoenig, president of the Federal Reserve Bank of Kansas City, argued that the government could have placed conditions on any financial support that enabled it to place failing institutions into conservatorship.[28]

Under both the blank check and the takeover scenarios, someone must take the losses. A bank is fundamentally a pile of money that is invested in a set of assets. Some of the money comes from the banks' shareholders and the rest is borrowed from depositors and other creditors. If the assets increase in value, the bank can pay back its depositors and creditors (with interest) and the shareholders keep the gains. If the assets fall in value, the shareholders take the losses, since the bank's debts do not change; if assets continue to fall after the shareholders have lost all their money, depositors (if they are uninsured) and creditors take a "haircut" because the bank cannot pay them back in full.

In the blank check scenario, the government keeps the bank afloat in its current form: managers keep their jobs, shareholders keep some value, and creditors are kept whole, so taxpayers bear most of the losses. Shareholders own all the "upside," meaning that if the bank recovers and increases in value, they will reap the benefits. In the takeover scenario, by contrast, managers lose their jobs, shareholders are wiped out, and any remaining losses are shared between taxpayers and creditors. (In a crisis, creditors' haircuts may have to be modest in order to protect those creditors from failing in turn.) Since the government now owns the bank, taxpayers can claim all the upside.

The takeover option was what the Treasury Department of Rubin and Summers (and Geithner, as treasury assistant secretary and then undersecretary for international affairs) strongly recommended for emerging market countries in the 1990s. Sick banks, they counseled, were at best a potential brake on economic recovery and at worst a serious macroeconomic risk; when investors fear a country's banks will collapse, they often abandon its other assets as well, triggering a sharp depreciation in its currency. Even if these banks happened to be run by

*In the case of General Motors, the government used its power as the only source of financing to force out CEO Rick Wagoner and to dictate "haircuts" for creditors—steps it did not take with any major commercial or investment bank.

close friends or relatives of the ruling elite, they could not be allowed to carry on in their existing form. Either they needed to be cut loose from government support, or they needed to be taken over and cleaned up, for the good of the economy.

After the Lehman bankruptcy, it became axiomatic that another major financial institution could not be allowed to fail in an uncontrolled manner that would spark panic in the markets. The question was whether the United States would follow the advice it had handed out a decade before and thousands of miles away. Ultimately, however, it was the taxpayer who would pay to rescue the financial sector—without getting very much in return.

Over the course of the financial crisis, the principal economic policymakers—first Paulson, Bernanke, and Geithner, then Geithner (as treasury secretary), Bernanke, and Summers (as director of the National Economic Council)—devised an impressive range of schemes to shore up the banking system. Their hard work and creativity cannot be doubted. But the common feature of these schemes was that they attempted to fill the gaping hole in bank balance sheets with government subsidies, more or less crudely obscured.

The original purpose of TARP was to buy toxic assets from financial institutions. This would have the salutary effect of transferring risk from banks, which were choking on it, to the federal government, which is big enough to absorb it; besides, the official government theory was that the banks only faced a liquidity crisis, and that with its long time horizon the government could simply wait until the markets recovered. But this scheme faced a fundamental problem: if Treasury offered to pay the current market price for these assets, the banks would refuse to sell, since that would lock in losses they could not afford;* if Treasury paid enough to solve the banks' problems, that would constitute a massive subsidy from the taxpayer.[29]

Instead, the government chose to recapitalize banks by giving them

*Commercial banks could record some assets on their balance sheets at high "book values" even if they could not actually sell them at those prices. So on paper, banks remained solvent—their assets exceeded their liabilities, whether or not they could actually sell the assets for enough to cover the liabilities. Selling assets would force banks to recognize their losses; not selling them allowed them to pretend that the assets had not deteriorated in value.

cash in exchange for preferred shares (exploiting an ambiguity in the TARP legislation), beginning with the October 13 meeting. They were forced to do so by the markets, which were not convinced by the plan to buy toxic assets, and by announcements from the United Kingdom and several other European countries that they would recapitalize their banks. Putting government money into some banks is standard practice in emerging market financial crises, but the money typically comes with strict conditions in order to begin the reform process. In the United States, however, those conditions were missing. The government did not insist on market prices for its investments (as set by Warren Buffett with his investment in Goldman Sachs), fearing that some banks would decline to participate. Instead, the government bent over backward to make the deal attractive for the banks, charging below-market interest and eschewing any significant ownership—so shareholders, not taxpayers, would benefit when the banks recovered. As a result, for every $100 committed by Treasury at the October 13 meeting, $22 was a subsidy to the banking sector, according to a later report by the TARP Congressional Oversight Panel.[30] (One thing that was similar to emerging markets, however, was that politically connected banks were more likely to get their hands on cheap TARP capital, according to an analysis by Jowei Chen and Connor Raso.)[31]

As opposition to taxpayer-funded bailouts increased, the subsidy mechanisms became more complex. In November 2008, with Citigroup struggling to fend off concerns about its viability, the government announced a second bailout package. In addition to another $20 billion investment, the government agreed to guarantee a $306 billion pool of Citigroup assets against falls in value (after the bank absorbed the first $29 billion in losses). The government received additional preferred stock in exchange for the guarantee, but there is no question that the guarantee was a subsidy; if Citigroup had had to buy such a guarantee on the open market, it could not have afforded the price.

A similar asset guarantee was provided to Bank of America in January, apparently in exchange for its agreeing—under government pressure—to complete the acquisition of Merrill Lynch in December.[32] This time, the government guaranteed a $118 billion pool of assets in exchange for $4 billion in preferred stock. But in a bizarre twist, even though the deal was announced—reassuring the bank's creditors and stabilizing its financial position—it never actually closed (because of technical difficulties in identifying the specific assets to be guaranteed). As a result, the government never got the $4 billion in preferred stock, and when Bank of America's outlook improved it was allowed to walk away from the deal for a fee of $425 million.[33]

The government bailout of AIG, justified as a way of preventing complete chaos in the market for credit default swaps, turned out to be another subsidy to the banking sector. AIG's counterparties for those credit default swaps were primarily large banks. By committing $180 billion to keep AIG afloat, the government ensured that those counterparties would be paid in full for their winnings on the bets they had made with AIG. In March 2009, under pressure from lawmakers, AIG finally released some details of who had been made whole by government money: Goldman Sachs received $12.9 billion from AIG, Merrill Lynch $6.8 billion, Bank of America $5.2 billion, and Citigroup $2.3 billion, along with several major foreign banks.[34] This was cash that these banks would not have received had AIG gone bankrupt, or had it been subjected to an FDIC-style conservatorship.*

The AIG bailout illustrated the ability of major banks to take advantage of the government's situation. A handful of major banks had purchased credit default swaps from AIG to insure $62 billion in CDOs. The AIG bailout included a plan for the New York Fed to finance a new entity (Maiden Lane III†) to buy the CDOs so that AIG could then settle the credit default swaps.‡ Maiden Lane III paid $30 billion (the market price) to buy the CDOs from the banks, and AIG, under instructions from the New York Fed, then paid the banks $32 billion to retire the credit default swaps. The result was that the banks received 100 cents on the dollar in what amounted to a backdoor

---

*Goldman Sachs insisted that it received no net benefit from the money it received from AIG, because it was fully hedged, primarily via credit default swaps on AIG itself; this claim has been disputed.[35]

†Maiden Lane II was the vehicle for a separate component of the AIG bailout.

‡The purpose of the transaction was to limit AIG's potential losses. With the credit default swaps outstanding, it could have been liable for the full face value of the CDOs. After the credit default swaps were retired, the remaining risk in the CDOs was held by Maiden Lane III; AIG's losses on Maiden Lane III were limited to its contribution of $5 billion, with any further losses being taken by the New York Fed.

bailout—even though AIG, prior to its bailout, had been negotiating in an attempt to get the banks to accept as little as 60 cents on the dollar.[36] The banks were confident that the government would not force AIG into bankruptcy, and simply refused requests that they accept anything less. Neil Barofsky, the special inspector general for TARP, later criticized the New York Fed, which he said "refused to use its considerable leverage" to negotiate better terms.[37]

While TARP-funded recapitalizations and the AIG conduit managed to keep calamity at bay, they did little to address the major source of fear: the toxic assets that remained on bank balance sheets. In March, Geithner announced the Public-Private Investment Program (PPIP), another attempt to relieve banks of these assets. As always, the sticking point was the gap between the price that buyers were willing to pay for these assets and the price that banks were willing to accept. The PPIP closed the gap through public subsidies. Private investors could lever up their own money with loans from the government. If the assets they bought fell in value, they could dump those assets on the government instead of paying back the loan; this limited their downside while giving them the amplified upside created by leverage.[38]

However, the PPIP failed to get off the ground. When the first transaction finally occurred in September, it was a sale by the FDIC of assets that it had inherited from a failed bank. (This made no sense, since the justification for the PPIP was to relieve *banks* of their toxic assets.) The banks themselves decided that they would be better off holding on to their toxic assets and hoping for the best, aided by an April 2 decision of the Financial Accounting Standards Board that made it even easier to set their own values for assets.

What finally turned the tide were the "stress tests" (officially the Supervisory Capital Assessment Program) that federal regulators conducted on nineteen leading banks in spring 2009, with results released on May 7.* The stated purpose of the exercise was to test whether the banks could withstand a severe economic downturn, quantify the

---

*The stress tests included eleven of the thirteen banks present at the March 27, 2009, meeting at the White House: American Express, Bank of America, Bank of New York Mellon, Citigroup, Goldman Sachs, JPMorgan Chase, Morgan Stanley, PNC, State Street, US Bank, and Wells Fargo (Freddie Mac and Northern Trust were omitted). The other eight institutions subjected to the tests were BB&T, Capital One, Fifth Third, GMAC, KeyCorp, MetLife, Regions Bank, and SunTrust.

amount of capital they would need in a worst-case scenario, and force them to raise that capital. But the more important purpose was to bolster confidence in the financial system. On one level, the exercise failed; many people doubted that the tests painted a true portrait of the banks' potential losses, especially when it came out that the Fed actually negotiated the results with the major banks, in some cases dramatically improving the banks' performance at the last minute.[39] (*Saturday Night Live*'s parody of Geithner, to some, seemed not too far from the truth: "Eventually, at the banks' suggestion, we dropped the asterisk and went with a pass/pass system. Tonight, I am proud to say that after the written tests were examined, every one of the nineteen banks scored a pass.")[40]

But on another level, the stress tests worked. For months, leading government figures had repeatedly assured the public that the banking system was secure. On April 21, Geithner testified, "Currently, the vast majority of banks have more capital than they need to be considered well capitalized by their regulators."[41] The stress tests were a way of committing the government to back those words with money. Once the government had certified the banks' balance sheets, and once the banks had raised the capital the government demanded, the government would have no excuse not to bail them out if needed. This was not entirely a good thing: once the pressure to get their houses in order was off, the banks were in no rush to unload their toxic assets.

The strengthened government guarantee was one ingredient pulling the megabanks back from the abyss. Another was reduced competition. Not only did Bear Stearns, Lehman Brothers, Merrill Lynch, Washington Mutual, and Wachovia all vanish, but an entire class of nonbank mortgage lenders evaporated with the housing bubble. With fewer competitors, the survivors could sweep up larger shares of the market and demand higher margins and fees. And a third factor was the cheap money being pumped into the economy by the Federal Reserve. Banks' primary raw material is money. Less competition and cheap money meant higher revenues and lower costs at the same time.

With low interest rates, banks could raise money from depositors virtually for free; they could borrow cheaply from each other; they could borrow cheaply at the Fed's discount window; they could sell bonds at low interest rates because of FDIC debt guarantees; they could swap their asset-backed securities for cash with the Fed; they could sell their mortgages to Fannie and Freddie, which could in turn sell debt to the

Fed; and on and on. Because so much cash was easily available to the banks, they could not suddenly run out of money. And because short-term interest rates fell further than long-term interest rates, the basic business of banking—borrowing short and lending long—became more profitable. The indefinite government lifeline gave the banks time to recapitalize themselves with profits from current operations.

Effectively, the government's strategy was to bail the banks out of their problems by helping them make large profits, juiced by reduced competition and cheap money, to plug the ever-widening hole created by their toxic assets. As part of its stress tests, the Federal Reserve concluded that the four largest banks—Bank of America, Citigroup, JPMorgan Chase, and Wells Fargo—stood to lose another $425 billion on existing assets through the end of 2010, but would fill more than half of that hole with $256 billion in profits over the same period.[42] For the stronger banks, such as JPMorgan Chase and Goldman Sachs, the result was a quick return to profitability and the appearance of health; the weaker ones, such as Citigroup and Bank of America, gained time to wait for an economic recovery to bail them out of their bad loans.

Figure 6-1: Credit Default Swap Spreads, 5-Year Senior Debt

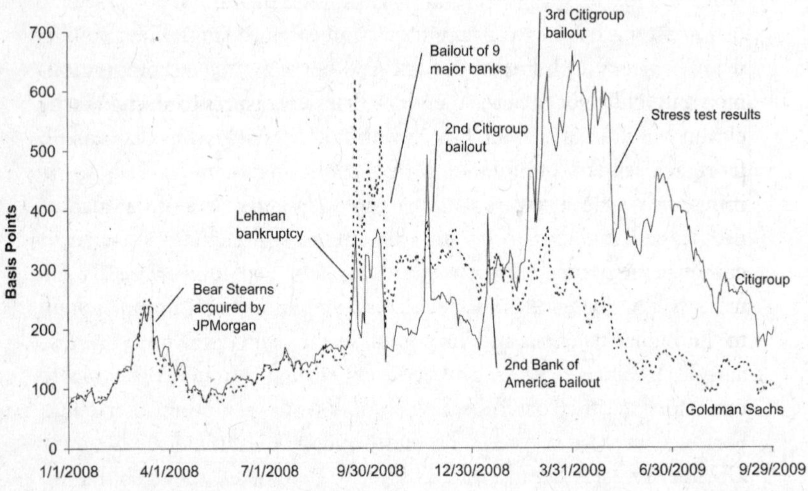

Source: Bloomberg Finance LP

Repeated public assurances, the stress test results, and the earlier emergency bailouts of Citigroup and Bank of America made it clear not only that the government would not let a major bank fail, but that the government would bail out banks in their existing form, with their existing management, and without imposing haircuts on bank creditors. Figure 6-1 shows the perceived likelihood that major banks would go bankrupt, as measured by the price of credit default swap protection on their debt; each time the government intervened, the market's fears ebbed, until finally the stress tests broke the year-long fever. That was what Wall Street needed to hear: they could go back to doing business as usual, and Washington would be there if things went wrong. A panic that began with an attempt to reduce moral hazard by letting Lehman fail only ended when everyone was convinced that the government would not let another major bank fail—magnifying moral hazard to an unprecedented degree. And as the real economy began to bottom out over the summer, it became easier and easier to make money again. But this was only true for the major banks; in the real economy, it became harder and harder to get a loan. According to the Federal Reserve's survey of bank loan officers, every type of loan became harder to get in every quarter of 2008 and through the first three quarters of 2009.[43]

In short, Paulson, Bernanke, Geithner, and Summers chose the blank check option, over and over again. They did the opposite of what the United States had pressed upon emerging market governments in the 1990s. They did not take harsh measures to shut down or clean up sick banks. They did not cut major financial institutions off from the public dole. They did not touch the channels of political influence that the banks had used so adeptly to secure decades of deregulatory policies. They did not force out a single CEO of a major commercial or investment bank, despite the fact that most of them were deeply implicated in the misjudgments that nearly brought them to catastrophe. Summers was aware of the irony, although he disagreed that the situations were exactly parallel. "I don't think I would quite accept the characterisation that we're in the position that the Russians were in in 1998," he said in a 2009 interview, because the United States did not face the problem of foreign capital flight. But, to his credit, he acknowledged,

There have been moments, certainly, when I understood better some
of the reactions of officials in crisis countries now than one was able to
from the outside at the time. It is easier to be for more radical solutions when one lives thousands of miles away than when it is one's own
country.[44]

The total cost of all those blank checks is virtually incalculable,
spread across the more or less direct subsidy programs (preferred
stock purchases, asset guarantees, and so on) and the emergency liquidity and insurance programs to unfreeze the markets for commercial
paper, asset-backed securities, or bank debt. It is incalculable because
the different types of support—lending commitments, asset guarantees, preferred stock purchases, and such—cannot simply be added
up. At the upper end of the relevant ballpark, the special inspector
general for TARP estimated a total potential support package of
$23.7 trillion, or over 150 percent of U.S. GDP.[45] This represents the
theoretical potential liabilities of the government; the net cost will be
far lower, since not all lending commitments will be used up, most
loans will be paid back, most preferred shares will be bought back,
most of the assets the government has guaranteed will not become
worthless, and so on.

In the end, the government's strategy succeeded in bringing the
financial system back from the brink of ruin, although not in restoring
that system to health and stimulating lending to the real economy.
There are three crucial steps in responding to a financial crisis: ending
the panic, preventing economic activity from collapsing, and laying
the groundwork for a sustainable recovery. The government largely
succeeded in the first step, and the stimulus package passed in early
2009 helped with the second step. But the unconditional support provided to the financial system only exacerbated the weaknesses and
incentives that had created the crisis in the first place.

Despite the tremendous cost of bailing out the financial system, the
cost of letting the system collapse would probably have been even
higher. But was bailing out Wall Street the only way to avoid disaster?
The beginning of 2009 saw a raging public debate between the

blank check option and the takeover option. The key question was not whether to intervene; virtually everyone involved acknowledged that the megabanks were too big to fail, because if any one of them collapsed the system as a whole might collapse. The question was what to do about it. The government argued that the banks' fundamental situation was not that bad—banks faced a "liquidity crisis" caused by short-term fear, not a "solvency crisis" caused by severe economic losses—and that the best way to contain that fear was to keep the banks going in their current form; anything more drastic would only cause panic.

The opposing view, put forward by many people including Nobel Prize laureates Paul Krugman and Joseph Stiglitz (and non–Nobel laureates like us), was that some major banks were deeply sick and that successive bailouts amounted to vast giveaways of taxpayer money that would do little to solve either the short-term or the long-term problems in the financial sector. As Krugman said, "Every plan we've heard from Treasury amounts to the same thing—an attempt to socialize the losses while privatizing the gains."[46] But because the government only had enough money to keep the banks afloat, it was not actually restoring them to the health necessary for them to start lending again. The problem was both political and economic. In Krugman's words:

> As long as capital injections are seen as a way to bail out the people who got us into this mess (which they are as long as the banks haven't been put into receivership), the political system won't, repeat, won't be willing to come up with enough money to make the system healthy again. At most we'll get a slow intravenous drip that's enough to keep the banks shambling along.[47]

By leaving the banks in the hands of their existing managers and going out of its way to minimize its own influence, the government was ensuring that it had no way to encourage banks to do anything other than hoard their cash, and no way to affect bank behavior in the future. Attempts by the Federal Reserve to stimulate the economy were absorbed by what Richard Fisher, president of the Federal Reserve Bank of Dallas, called "the Blob" of large, sick banks. "Those banks with the greatest toxic asset losses were the quickest to freeze or reduce their lending activity," Fisher said; in addition, "the dead weight of [the megabanks'] toxic assets diminished the capacity of markets to keep debt and equity capital flowing to businesses and scared investors away."[48] Although bank bailouts did prevent economic calamity, they would do little to ensure financial stability or economic prosperity.

Krugman, Stiglitz, and others argued that the government should take over banks, clean them up so they would function normally, and sell them back into private hands when possible, as in an FDIC intervention. In a February 2009 interview, Stiglitz said, "Nationalization is the only answer. These banks are effectively bankrupt."[49] Other prominent supporters of a government takeover included economics professors Nouriel Roubini and Matthew Richardson and Dean Baker of the Center for Economic and Policy Research.[50] While takeovers would be a form of temporary nationalization, no one ever refers to FDIC takeovers that way; instead, they are thought of as a government-managed bankruptcy process. A major bank such as Citigroup might have required government conservatorship for months or years, but the goal would have been to restore private ownership when economic conditions allowed. There were both economic and political arguments for this course of action.

The immediate economic argument was that sick banks could only be thoroughly cleaned up via a takeover. Toxic assets needed to be removed from bank balance sheets; but as long as a bank remained independent, any such transaction had to be negotiated, and the bank's managers (representing the shareholders) could simply hold up the government for a high price, knowing that if the bank failed, other people would be left holding the bag. If the government took over a bank, however, it could transfer the toxic assets to a separate government entity without negotiation, restore the bank to health by adding new capital, and return it to normal operation. Management would be replaced and shareholders wiped out, leaving the bank in the hands of taxpayers, who would get at least some of their money back when the bank could be sold into private hands. (Alternatively, the government could have simply bought a struggling bank at market value; at one point in March 2009, the market value of all of Citigroup's common stock fell below $6 billion.)[51] The toxic assets could be parked on the balance sheet of the U.S. government, which could hold them indefinitely and, if necessary, absorb the losses they entailed.

The longer-term economic argument was that a takeover was necessary to remove moral hazard—the temptation for bank executives (and shareholders) to take risky gambles, knowing that they would benefit from success but that taxpayers would bear the losses in case of failure. After the Lehman bankruptcy, the government's policy was that no major bank would be allowed to fail—and every bank CEO knew it—even while smaller banks were failing by the dozens. By contrast, major bank takeovers would send the message that there was a penalty for failure, giving executives and shareholders the incentive to avoid excessive risk, and giving creditors the incentive to be more careful with their money.

Taking over sick megabanks would also have political benefits. As in Korea a decade before, effective reform would require confronting the political roots of the crisis—the disproportionate political power of Wall Street. The right time for that confrontation was when the banks were at their weakest and most dependent on government aid. Bailing out the banks unconditionally put the government in the position of having to ask for favors later—favors that the banks would have no reason to return. By contrast, taking them over would have weakened or eliminated their ability to resist the regulatory reforms necessary to ensure long-term financial stability and economic growth.

Finally, takeover was only fair. Bankers who had run their institutions into the ground would no longer collect seven- or eight-figure bonuses made possible only by government bailouts. Shareholders who had gambled on highly leveraged banks would lose their money. Creditors who had lent blindly would lose part of their money. Taxpayers footing the largest part of the bill would at least have the possibility of making money as banks recovered. This is how capitalism is supposed to work. Failure should be punished, not rewarded. The government should be the backstop protecting society against a financial collapse, but it should exact a price for that protection. Reflecting on the emerging market crises of the 1990s in his 2000 American Economics Association lecture, Summers had emphasized, "Prompt action needs to be taken to maintain financial stability, by moving quickly to support healthy institutions and by intervening in unhealthy institutions. The loss of confidence in the financial system and episodes of bank panics were not caused by early and necessary interventions in insolvent institutions."[52] Instead, by providing serial bailouts with no meaningful conditions attached, the Bush and Obama administrations both rewarded failure and backed away from the tough medicine needed to restore a well-functioning financial sector.

As we wrote in *The Atlantic* in March 2009, "The challenges the United States faces are familiar territory to the people at the IMF. If you hid the name of the country and just showed them the numbers, there is no doubt what old IMF hands would say: nationalize troubled banks and break them up as necessary."[53] However, the administration took pains to deny that this was even a plausible option. In a February interview, when asked about "nationalization," Geithner responded, "It's not the right strategy for the country for basic practical reasons that our system will be stronger if it remains in private hands with support from the government to make sure those institutions can play their critical role going forward."[54] Then and elsewhere, Geithner carefully avoided even using the word "nationalization," as if saying it might unnerve the private sector. The administration was successful in sending the message that no major banks would be taken over on its watch, and it was a message that Wall Street heard loud and clear.

Another issue that Wall Street cared deeply about was executive compensation. By the time the Obama administration came into office, one sore point with the public was that banks receiving government assistance were subject only to weak limits on compensation (boards of directors had to ensure that senior executives' compensation packages did not motivate them to take excessive risks, bonuses based on materially inaccurate information had to be clawed back, and golden parachutes to top executives were prohibited[55]). To the public, that meant that taxpayer money could pass straight through to bankers' Ferraris and vacation homes in the Hamptons. Some administration insiders, including top political adviser David Axelrod, pressed for greater restrictions on compensation.[56] Because of a provision of the economic stimulus package passed by Congress in February, the final rule issued in June 2009 was slightly stricter—limiting the bonuses payable to certain executives, requiring that they be paid in long-term restricted stock, and requiring a nonbinding shareholder vote on executive compensation[57]—but tight restrictions and close monitoring applied only to a handful of companies receiving "exceptional assistance" from the government.[58] Even the relatively mild limits were too much for most of the megabanks, who rushed to pay back their TARP money as quickly as possible—weakening their balance sheets (by paying back cash they didn't need to pay back) so they could say they were free of government support, even as they profited from the cheap money supplied by the Federal Reserve. The main effect of the rule was to tilt the playing field against the banks that had received exceptional assistance (Citigroup and Bank of America) and therefore were subject to stricter compensation limits, making it harder for them to attract and retain key people. Any systematic attempt to curb the perverse incentives created by banking industry compensation practices was kicked down the road to a future regulatory reform bill.

The Obama administration did not uniformly support banks' interests, but what the banks could not win in the White House, they often won in Congress. On February 18, President Obama announced his "Homeowner Affordability and Stability Plan," which contained a provision allowing judges to modify the terms of home mortgages for borrowers who were in bankruptcy. The idea was that if a borrower's house was worth far less than the mortgage, a bankruptcy judge should be able to reduce the mortgage—just as the judge could reduce the amount owed to almost all other creditors. The banking lobby succeeded in killing this "cramdown" provision in the Senate, with the banks and their industry associations refusing even to negotiate with Senator Richard Durbin while the Obama administration remained on the sidelines. Instead, the bill contained a separate provision *reducing* the amount that banks had to pay the FDIC for deposit insurance.[59] This exercise in legislative muscle-flexing showed the continuing power of the big banks on Capitol Hill. Even as they depended on government investments, debt guarantees, and liquidity programs for their survival, they actually increased their lobbying expenditures to fight off potential regulatory reforms.[60]

On issue after issue, the big banks got what they wanted, and the taxpayer got the bill. The justification for these policies was that anything that threatened to weaken the banks might trigger a resurgence of the panic of September-October 2008. But the result was the same. The large banks used their political power to protect their money machines from government interference, and when those machines exploded they used their size and importance to force the government to bail them out.

BUSINESS AS USUAL

In the end, the major banks got business as usual. The shakeout of 2008 left the big banks even bigger. Bank of America absorbed Countrywide and Merrill Lynch and saw its assets grow from $1.7 trillion at the end of 2007 to $2.3 trillion in September 2009. JPMorgan Chase absorbed Bear Stearns and Washington Mutual and grew from $1.6 trillion to $2.0 trillion. Wells Fargo absorbed Wachovia and grew from under $600 billion to $1.2 trillion.[61] This growth occurred against a backdrop of falling asset values and de-leveraging, which meant that most banks were cutting their new lending and getting smaller.

Consolidation among the big banks and the collapse of the nonbank mortgage lenders meant much larger market shares for the fewer but bigger megabanks. Bank of America, JPMorgan Chase, and Wells Fargo all had to be exempted from a federal rule prohibiting any single bank from holding more than 10 percent of all deposits in the country, and from Department of Justice antitrust guidelines intended to limit monopoly power in specific metropolitan regions. By mid-2009, those three banks and Citigroup together controlled half the market for new mortgages and two-thirds of the market for new credit cards.[62] Derivatives, which had always been dominated by fewer than twenty dealers, became even more concentrated. At the end of June 2009, five banks together had over 95 percent of the market for derivatives contracts traded by U.S. banks, led by JPMorgan Chase's 27 percent share.[63]

The government's insistence that large banks would not be allowed to fail worked only too well. Large banks were able to borrow money at rates 0.78 percentage points more cheaply than smaller banks, up from an average of 0.29 percentage points from 2000 through 2007. In the banking business, where profits depend on the spread between the interest rate you receive and the interest rate you pay, 0.78 percentage points are a huge financial advantage.[64] And what were large banks doing with their newfound market power? They were boosting profits any way they could—increasing fees on deposit accounts, even while their smaller competitors were reducing fees.[65]

For JPMorgan Chase, the payoff was blowout profits fueled by both its huge footprint in consumer banking and its growing investment banking business. Bank of America and Citigroup, though still fundamentally troubled, managed to keep up the appearance of profits, in part through one-time asset sales, in part through accounting gimmicks. Most surprisingly to the casual observer, the investment banking business, which had seemed on the brink of death in September 2008, roared back to life (even if the major stand-alone investment banks were now technically bank holding companies). In the first quarter of 2009, bond trading departments took advantage of high volatility in the markets to rake in large fees and make money in proprietary trading. There was also widespread speculation (difficult to confirm, given the secretive nature of trading operations) that bank trading profits were boosted by taking advantage of the fact that AIG was trying to unwind its large positions rapidly—which meant that the banks were making money at the expense of a taxpayer-owned company.*

In the second quarter, things got even better. Goldman Sachs reported its largest quarterly profit ever—$3.4 billion—on the backs of a record performance from its bond trading division and $700 million in stock underwriting.[67] Those bond trading profits were given a helping hand by the Federal Reserve, which was buying large volumes of securities (to provide liquidity and stimulate the economy) while telegraphing its moves to Wall Street. As one asset management executive said, "You can make big money trading with the government. The government is a huge buyer and seller and Wall Street has all the pricing power."[68] And the $700 million was in part the result of federal

---

*If a trader wants to exit a large position quickly, he is at the mercy of the people he is trading with, who can essentially name their price. An e-mail from one trader, published by the blog *Zero Hedge*, included this excerpt: "During Jan/Feb AIG would call up and just ask for complete unwind prices from the credit desk in the relevant jurisdiction. These were not single deal unwinds as are typically more price transparent—these were whole portfolio unwinds. The size of these unwinds were [*sic*] enormous, the quotes I have heard were 'we have never done as big or as profitable trades—ever.' "[66]

bailouts; as the government ordered other banks to issue new stock to raise capital, they were forced to turn to the few remaining investment banks. JPMorgan Chase, Goldman Sachs, and Morgan Stanley alone accounted for 42 percent of the market for equity underwriting in the first half of 2009.[69] Finally, Goldman was making money the old-fashioned way—by taking on more risk. As the bank's president, Gary Cohn, said in August 2009, "Our risk appetite continues to grow year on year, quarter on quarter, as our balance sheet and liquidity continue to grow."[70] And Goldman's value-at-risk—a quantitative measure of the amount it stood to lose on a given day—after dipping slightly in summer 2008, continued to climb throughout the crisis to levels in 2009 five times as high as in 2002.[71]

However, the clearest indication that Wall Street was back to business as usual was the amount of money earmarked for bonuses. In the first half of 2009, Goldman Sachs set aside $11.4 billion for employee compensation—an annual rate of over $750,000 per employee and near the record levels of the boom. Even if the government's strategy was to let the banks earn their way out of their problems, that strategy was being undermined by a bonus culture that diverted the excess profits to employees rather than to capital reserves. High risk and huge payouts—nothing changed, except a strengthened government guarantee. Defending the huge bonuses in St. Paul's Cathedral in London in October 2009, Goldman Sachs executive Brian Griffiths went Gordon Gekko one better by invoking Jesus: "The injunction of Jesus to love others as ourselves is a recognition of self-interest. . . . We have to tolerate the inequality as a way to achieving greater prosperity and opportunity for all."[72] Goldman CEO Lloyd Blankfein even claimed to be "doing God's work" (because banks raise money for companies who employ people and make things).[73]

The rest of us were not so lucky. While a second Great Depression was averted, the collateral damage to the real economy was enormous. The collapse of the housing bubble tipped the economy into recession in December 2007, leading to the loss of 1.1 million jobs in the first eight months of 2008.[74] The fall of Lehman Brothers in September 2008 and the ensuing panic triggered a severe economic contraction, leading to the loss of another 5.8 million jobs over the next twelve months as the economy shrank by 4 percent.[75] The unemployment rate doubled from 4.9 percent at the beginning of the recession to 10.2 percent by October 2009; the broadest measure of unemployment, including people who gave up looking for a job and people working part-time who would prefer to work full-time, doubled from 8.7 percent to 17.5 percent—more than one in every six people in the broad workforce.[76]

As the economy declined sharply, the sudden collapse in tax revenues left government finances in disarray. State and local governments resorted to severe cutbacks in services. The federal government dedicated $800 billion in new spending and tax cuts to stimulate the economy. However, stimulus spending and lower tax revenues pushed the 2009 federal deficit up to $1.6 trillion, or 11 percent of GDP, more than doubling the previous postwar record.[77] The long-term effect of the financial crisis and recession is even greater. In January 2008, just as the economy was tipping into recession, the Congressional Budget Office (CBO) projected that, by the end of 2018, U.S. government debt would fall to $5.1 trillion, or 22.6 percent of GDP. Surveying the wreckage in August 2009, the CBO projected that debt at the end of 2018 would rise to $13.6 trillion, or 67.0 percent of GDP—a difference of $8.5 trillion.[78] This should come as no surprise; Carmen Reinhart and Kenneth Rogoff have shown that, on average, modern banking crises lead to an 86 percent increase in government debt over the three years following the crisis.[79]

The financial crisis and the government's emergency response also increased the likelihood of two bleak scenarios. First, the enormous amount of liquidity that the Federal Reserve poured into the economy created the long-term potential for high inflation; if the Fed cannot "mop up" that liquidity when the economy recovers, all that excess money could make dollars less valuable, driving up prices.

Second, the vast increase in the total national debt brought us closer to the point where it could become more difficult to raise money by issuing new government debt. Should that happen, the government will have to pay higher interest rates to borrow money, and those higher interest rates will spread throughout the entire economy, slowing economic growth. In a worst-case scenario, the government may have to raise money in foreign currencies, undermining one of our traditional advantages over much of the rest of the world. This is unlikely to occur solely as a result of the recent financial crisis; before the crisis, the United States was only moderately indebted by international standards and had the capacity to absorb one shock without seriously affecting our ability to borrow money. Whether we can absorb another such shock is another question. The United States did not look like an emerging market when the crisis began, but it has already become more like one.

J. Paul Getty is reputed to have said, "If you owe the bank $100, that's your problem. If you owe the bank $100 million, that's the bank's problem." The bank cannot afford a loss of $100 million, and therefore will do anything to help you avoid default—and that gives you power.

In 2008–2009, the tables turned. It was the major banks who were struggling with their debts, and it was the U.S. government that could not afford to let them fail, because of the damage that would inflict on the real economy and on tens or hundreds of millions of people. (Small banks, however, were like people who owed $100.) This meant that when the banks faced off with the government, they held all the cards. As Barney Frank put it, "All these years of deregulation by the Republicans and the absence of regulation as these new financial instruments have grown have allowed them to take a large chunk of the economy hostage. And we have to pay ransom, like it or not."[80]

The fact that their failure could entail the loss of millions of jobs gave the banks the power to dictate the terms of their rescue. If the government insisted on paying market prices for toxic assets, or insisted on taking majority control, the banks could simply refuse to go along, secure in the knowledge that the government would have to come back to the table. In the end, the government had more to lose from major bank failures than did the bankers themselves, who had already made their money. Citigroup CEO Vikram Pandit, for example, made $38 million in 2008[81] on top of the $165 million he made by selling his hedge fund to Citigroup in 2007.[82] At most they would suffer a reputational blow should their banks fail—which they could always blame on market conditions and the failure of the government to come to their aid. This was the problem with the strategy of negotiating with Wall Street; Wall Street held all the cards.

But that is not a complete explanation, because there is little evidence that the government attempted to force the issue. It was not only that the government had a weak hand; it was that the government negotiators came to the table largely in agreement with the bankers' view of the world. And it wasn't just a few key people. Paulson, of course, was the former head of Goldman Sachs, and his aides at Treasury included Robert Steel, Steve Shafran, and Neel Kashkari from Goldman. In summer 2008, when he realized he needed reinforcements to fight the financial crisis, he summoned Dan Jester and Ken Wilson, also Goldman veterans.[83] When faced with the potential insolvency of Fannie Mae and Freddie Mac in August 2008, Paulson hired Morgan Stanley (for a nominal fee) to analyze the two GSEs; Morgan Stanley was also hired by the Federal Reserve Bank of New York to advise on the AIG bailout.[84] Given the urgency of the situation and the technical details involved, it made sense for the government to hire outside help. But that help could only come from one place: Wall Street.

What is more remarkable is that the policies of the Bush administration were largely carried over into the Obama administration, despite the enormous policy differences between George W. Bush and Barack Obama on almost every issue. This is because by 2009, the economic policy elite of the *Democratic* Party was fully won over to the idea that finance was good.

During the Democratic primary campaign, Obama's chief economic adviser was Austan Goolsbee, an economics professor without a long track record as a party insider. But after Obama won the election, he turned to a Democratic establishment that was formed in the Clinton years, largely under the tutelage of Robert Rubin. Michael Froman, who was Rubin's chief of staff at Treasury and followed him to Citigroup, and James Rubin, Rubin's son, were both members of Obama's transition team.[85] (Froman was also an associate of Obama's from their law school days, independently of Rubin; after the transition, he became a member of both the National Economic Council and the National Security Council.) Geithner, who had built close relationships with Wall Street CEOs during his five years as president of the New York Fed,[86] became treasury secretary. Summers, most recently a managing director of the hedge fund D.E. Shaw, became director of the NEC. Peter Orszag, Clinton economic adviser and director of Rubin's Hamilton Project, became head of the Office of Management and Budget; Gary Gensler, treasury undersecretary for domestic finance under Summers (and former Goldman partner), became head of the CFTC; Mary Schapiro, first head of the CFTC under Clinton and later head of the Financial Industry Regulatory Authority, the financial industry's chief *self-regulatory* body, became head of the SEC; Neal Wolin, treasury deputy counsel and general counsel under Rubin and Summers, became deputy treasury secretary; Michael Barr, special assistant and deputy assistant secretary in the Rubin Treasury, became assistant secretary for financial institutions; Jason Furman, director of the Hamilton Project after Orszag, became deputy director of the NEC; and David Lipton, treasury undersecretary for international affairs during the Asian financial crisis and later Citigroup executive, also became one of Summers's deputies at the NEC. Even President Obama's chief of staff, Rahm Emanuel, had a similar background, having worked both as a Clinton adviser and as an investment banker at Wasserstein Perella.

Geithner's counselors as treasury secretary included Lee Sachs from the Clinton Treasury (and most recently a New York hedge fund) and Gene Sperling, Rubin's successor as director of the NEC (and most recently a highly paid adviser to a Goldman Sachs philanthropic project). The new blood that did not come from the Clinton establishment came largely from Wall Street. Mark Patterson, Goldman Sachs's chief lobbyist, became Geithner's chief of staff; Geithner's counselors also included Lewis Alexander, chief economist at Citigroup, and Matthew Kabaker from the Blackstone Group.[87] Assistant secretary for financial stability Herbert Allison was president of Merrill Lynch before heading TIAA-CREF (an asset manager) and Fannie Mae. Meanwhile, at the New York Fed, the board of directors picked William Dudley, a Goldman partner and then one of Geithner's lieutenants, to replace Geithner as president.

There is nothing sinister about the appointment of so many veterans of the Rubin Treasury; according to usual Washington practice, Obama and his lieutenants were calling on people who had gained experience in the previous Democratic administration.[88] And the fact that people worked under Rubin does not mean that they automatically sided with Wall Street on every issue. Some of them spent 2009 fighting for policies that were not friendly to Wall Street. Michael Barr, for example, was a strong advocate for a new Consumer Financial Protection Agency (CFPA), and Gary Gensler worked to plug loopholes in financial regulation bills as they worked their way through Congress.[89] But the economic brain trust was largely shaped in two complementary environments: Wall Street and the Rubin Treasury. And while the Obama administration did not close ranks with the major banks, it also does not seem to have strongly considered policies that seriously threatened the power and profits of the major banks (with the possible exception of the CFPA).

The administration also included Democratic economists from outside the Wall Street–Washington corridor, but they were outnumbered and generally (though not always) placed in less central positions. Respected academic macroeconomist Christina Romer became chair of the Council of Economic Advisers; Alan Krueger, an economics professor who served in the Labor Department under Robert Reich, became a treasury assistant secretary; Jared Bernstein became chief economic adviser to Vice President Joseph Biden; and Goolsbee became director of the President's Economic Recovery Advisory Board, a new organization that failed to gain any real influence. Even Paul Volcker, perhaps the most respected Democratic economist available, who endorsed Obama back in January 2008 when most of the establishment was backing Hillary Clinton, became chair of the Economic Recovery Advisory Board and seemed to fade from sight; in October 2009, responding to reports that his influence was fading, Volcker said, "I did not have influence to start with."[90]

Not only did key policymakers have long-standing ties to Wall Street, but during the crisis they gave tremendous access to their Wall Street contacts. In his first seven months in office, Geithner's calendar shows more than eighty contacts with Goldman CEO Lloyd Blankfein, JPMorgan CEO Jamie Dimon, Citigroup CEO Vikram Pandit, or Citigroup chairman Richard Parsons.[91] While it is necessary for the treasury secretary to talk to Wall Street executives during a financial crisis, he had more contacts with Blankfein than with Senate Banking Committee chair Christopher Dodd and more contacts with Citigroup than with House Financial Services Committee chair Barney Frank. (This was a far cry from the tone of the Roosevelt administration in 1933, of which Arthur Schlesinger wrote, "When one remembered both the premium bankers put on inside information and the chumminess they had enjoyed with past Presidents and Secretaries of the Treasury, the new chill in Washington was the cruelest of punishments.")[92] In a world where access is a prerequisite for influence, Wall Street had access to the people who mattered, when it mattered.

As a result, economic policy in 2009, just as in 2008, was set by a group of people who, despite their considerable intelligence, experience, and integrity, seemed to believe that the banks were fundamentally sound and only needed an injection of confidence; that each subsidy to the banking sector was justified because the costs of not making the subsidy would be worse; that government takeover of major banks was so anathema to the American way that it would trigger panic; that meaningful constraints on banks' activities would inhibit economic growth; and that meaningful constraints on bankers' compensation would send them fleeing to unregulated hedge funds or overseas, leaving the American economy to suffer as a result. But this is not surprising, because everybody believed all these things— everybody, that is, in the New York and Washington elite. Over thirty years, Wall Street had plied Washington with tantalizing tales of financial innovation and efficient markets while pouring rivers of money into politicians' campaign funds and lobbyists' expense accounts. In 2008 and 2009, it all paid off.

As Michael Lewis put it in 2009,

> It does feel a lot to me like the process has been queered by political influence, and it's a very curious kind of political influence. Because it isn't maybe always as simple as bribery, campaign contributions, and that kind of thing. I think that we've had twenty-five years of the Goldman Sachses of the world ruling the world, and the people like Tim Geithner, when they leave office, the way they make their living . . . is to go to work for a financial institution for huge sums of money; that people have trouble getting their mind around a world where that's not the way the world works, and there is maybe a slight quickness to believe that the world can't function without Goldman Sachs.[93]

Can it?

7

THE AMERICAN OLIGARCHY
Six Banks

What all this amounts to is an unintended and unanticipated extension of the official "safety net." . . . The obvious danger is that with the passage of time, risk-taking will be encouraged and efforts at prudential restraint will be resisted. Ultimately, the possibility of further crises—even greater crises—will increase.
—Paul Volcker, September 24, 2009[1]

If they're too big to fail, they're too big.
—Alan Greenspan, October 15, 2009[2]

Between 1985 and 1992, over 2,000 banks failed in the savings and loan crisis, a consequence of deregulation, mismanagement, and fraud. Those S&Ls had been largely overseen by the Federal Home Loan Bank Board, which had failed to shut down struggling thrifts early in the 1980s, instead hoping that they could grow into solvency by expanding into more profitable (and riskier) businesses.[3] In response, Congress passed the Financial Institutions Reform, Recovery, and Enhancement Act of 1989. Among other things, it abolished the Federal Home Loan Bank Board and replaced it with the Office of Thrift Supervision (OTS). On August 9, 1989, President George H. W. Bush signed the bill, saying, "This legislation will safeguard and stabilize America's financial system and put in place permanent reforms so these problems will never happen again."[4]

NPR correspondent Chana Joffe-Walt tells the story:

I talked to several people who worked for that predecessor agency, the Bank Board, and they describe that on that day, the day the OTS was created, they left the office, these agency employees, and they walked across the street to a hotel. They turned on the TV, and they sat and watched the first President Bush stand up at a podium and declare, "Never again will America allow any insured institution [to] operate without enough money." And then the agency employees watched as the President trashed their agency. The press conference ended, they turned off the TV, left the hotel, crossed the street, and went back to work. Pretty soon someone came by and changed the sign: The Office of Thrift Supervision.[5]

This, of course, is the same Office of Thrift Supervision that would be responsible for American International Group, Countrywide, and Washington Mutual in the 2000s.

At this crucial juncture in our history, as America emerges from a deep recession into an uncertain economic future, and in the wake of an epochal bailout of our largest banks, we must reform the financial system that made possible the financial and economic crisis that cost millions of people their jobs and added trillions of dollars to the national debt. The last few years have proven that our financial sector and its political influence are a serious risk to our economic well-being, and without significant change there is no reason to believe we will not soon experience the next boom, the next bust, and the next president explaining to the American people that he must rescue Wall Street in order to save Main Street. And significant change will require addressing the disproportionate wealth and power of a handful of large banks at the pinnacle of the financial sector.

Simply asking bankers to behave differently will not work; the solution can only come by changing the rules of the financial system, which requires government action. Five days after President Obama's election, his chief of staff, Rahm Emanuel, said, "Rule one: Never allow a crisis to go to waste. They are opportunities to do big things."[6] But more than a year after the collapse of Lehman Brothers, even relatively moderate legislation to reform the financial sector was still stuck in Congress.

The Obama administration attempted to show that it was serious about change. "The industry needs to show that they get it on the compensation issue," Obama said at the March 27, 2009, White House meeting discussed in the Introduction. "Excess is out of fashion." (According to *The New York Times*, "The bankers nodded, but made no firm commitments.")[7]

On June 17, 2009, President Obama unveiled what he called "a sweeping overhaul of the financial regulatory system, a transformation on a scale not seen since the reforms that followed the Great Depression."[8] He proposed stricter oversight of financial institutions, new regulations for securitization and over-the-counter derivatives, increased consumer protections, and new government powers to cope with a crisis.[9] Three months later, standing in the heart of the Manhattan financial district, Obama promised:

> We will not go back to the days of reckless behavior and unchecked excess that was at the heart of this crisis, where too many were motivated only by the appetite for quick kills and bloated bonuses. . . . [T]he old ways that led to this crisis cannot stand. And the extent that some have so readily returned to them underscores the need for change and change now. History cannot be allowed to repeat itself.[10]

But despite the president's lofty language, many of his proposals represented only incremental reform. They did little to address the problem at the heart of the financial system: the enormous growth of top-tier financial institutions and the corresponding increase in their economic and political power. In place of bold measures, the administration preferred technical solutions (increased capital and liquidity requirements for large banks), regulatory deck-chair-shuffling (merging the oversight functions of the OCC and the OTS in a new National Bank Supervisor), or marginally strengthened corporate governance (nonbinding shareholder votes on executive compensation packages).[11] *The New York Times*' Joe Nocera called the Obama plan "little more than an attempt to stick some new regulatory fingers into a very leaky financial dam rather than rebuild the dam itself."[12]

Nonetheless, Wall Street fought tooth and nail to block new regulation and preserve the favorable environment that emerged after the government rescue of 2008–2009, with less competition, a strengthened government guarantee, and no new restrictions on the pursuit of profits. As of October 2009, 1,537 lobbyists representing financial institutions, other businesses, and industry groups had registered to work on financial regulation proposals before Congress—outnumbering by twenty-five to one the lobbyists representing consumer groups, unions, and other supporters of stronger regulation. Even Citigroup, 34 percent owned by the government, hired forty-six lobbyists of its own. In the first nine months of 2009, the industry spent $344 million on lobbying. Senior Obama adviser David Axelrod observed, "You would hope after American taxpayers stepped in to save these companies from a disaster of their own making they would be deploying their army of lobbyists to strengthen and not thwart financial reform," but that was far from the case.[13] Instead, in the words of one congressional staffer, the industry launched "an orchestrated, well-funded effort by the banks to manipulate our legislation and leave no fingerprints."[14]

For example, the regulatory bill introduced in the House Financial Services Committee initially exempted a wide range of derivatives trades by nonfinancial companies from the new requirements proposed by the administration.[15] Michael Greenberger, a veteran of the Commodity Futures Trading Commission, claimed that the draft legislation "had to be written by someone inside the banks, because buried every few pages is a tricky and devilish 'exception.' It would greatly surprise me if these poison pills originated from anyone on Capitol Hill or the Treasury." Journalist William Greider reached the same conclusion after talking to a congressional insider.[16] Although the exemption was subsequently narrowed, this example demonstrates the ability of Wall Street to take advantage of technical complexity to advance its interests.

Wall Street also benefited from the administration's decision to defer actual reform until after the crisis had ebbed—despite Emanuel's "rule one." In part because of the debate over health insurance reform, financial regulation did not receive serious public consideration until fall 2009—after the economy had started growing again, the banking sector had returned to profitability, and months of Republican attacks had reduced Obama's approval ratings and increased skepticism about government action of any kind. By the time battle was joined, both Wall Street and Washington were back to business as usual.

DISMANTLING THE WALL STREET MODEL

For Wall Street's megabanks, business as usual now means inventing tradable, high-margin products; using their market power to capture fees based on trading volume; taking advantage of their privileged market position to place bets in their proprietary trading accounts; and borrowing as much money as possible (in part by engineering their way around capital requirements) to maximize their profits. Before 2008, they benefited from the general expectation that the government would step in if necessary to prevent a catastrophic failure. That expectation did not save Lehman Brothers. But since then, the idea that certain banks are "too big to fail" has virtually become government policy; as a result, they can take on more risk than their competitors, since creditors and counterparties know that the government will clean up after them.

Subprime lending, mortgage-backed securities, collateralized debt obligations (CDOs), and credit default swaps all flowed naturally from this business model, and absent fundamental reform, there is no reason to believe bankers will refrain from inventing new toxic products and precipitating another crisis in the future. What's more, given the growth in the size of the leading banks, the next crisis is likely to be even bigger. As *The Financial Times*' Martin Wolf wrote in September 2009, "What is emerging is a slightly better capitalised financial sector, but one even more concentrated and benefiting from explicit state guarantees. This is not progress: it has to mean still more and bigger crises in the years ahead."[17]

When the next crisis comes, either the government will ride to the rescue once again, costing taxpayers hundreds of billions of dollars, or popular revulsion at bailing out megabanks yet again will prevent Congress and the administration from saving the financial system—with potentially disastrous economic consequences.

The time for change is now. While the crisis was largely wasted in the short term, we have more than a single session of Congress or a single presidential term to fix our financial system. After the Panic of 1907, six years passed before the Federal Reserve was created, and it took another two decades (and the Great Depression) to put the financial system on a sound footing.

Public anger at Wall Street remains high. In an October 2009 poll, only 7 percent of respondents thought that major financial institutions were doing a good job at avoiding another crisis, 75 percent thought that Wall Street would "return to business as usual," 58 percent thought Wall Street had too much influence over government policy, and 59 percent favored more government regulation.[18] But that anger remains diffuse, in part because it is spread across the political spectrum, shared by progressives and conservatives who disagree on the solution. Financial regulation remains a complex topic that many people, including Washington insiders, think should be left to the experts—most of whom were formed on Wall Street or in the Wall Street–friendly climate of the past few decades. Real change will take years, and it will only happen when the conventional wisdom in Washington changes—from the idea that financial innovation and free financial markets are necessarily good, to the idea that concentrated economic and political power can have devastating effects on society.

There are many regulatory policies that could be beneficial, and some of them are included in the various proposals put forward by the Obama administration. But effective reform must address the two basic elements that created the last crisis and, absent change, will create the next one. The first is reckless borrowing and lending, which create a debt bubble that must eventually burst; the second is financial institutions that are so big or systemically important that, when the bubble bursts, they must be bailed out by the government to prevent economic disaster. The first objective should be to protect individual participants in the real economy, both households and businesses, from the potentially abusive behavior of powerful banks. But this is not sufficient to ward off a future crisis, since banks are free to load up on risky assets overseas, out of reach of U.S. protections. Therefore, the second and most important objective must be to protect the economy as a whole from the systemic risk created by enormous banks. Excess optimism, debt bubbles, and overextended banks will likely be with us forever; our goal must be a financial system where those banks can fail without being able to hold up the entire economy.

"RIPPING THE FACE OFF" THE CUSTOMER

Basic microeconomic models assume that the world is made up of rational actors who make accurate decisions, based on perfect information, to maximize their expected utility (benefits to themselves). Given these assumptions, regulation is unnecessary because parties will only engage in transactions that are good for them.

Because lawmakers have long recognized that information available in the market may not be perfect, the consumer protection regime that existed prior to the financial crisis was based on *disclosure*. The Securities Act of 1933 and the Securities Exchange Act of 1934 require companies that sell securities to the public to disclose material information in periodic reports. The Truth in Lending Act of 1968 requires lenders to disclose loan information in standardized form, such as the annual percentage rate, in order to facilitate comparison by borrowers. However, in both cases the legislation does not attempt to determine whether a given financial product is harmful to the consumer; that is left to the market. This is why, for example, there have been no interest rate caps for first mortgages since the Depository Institutions Deregulation and Monetary Control Act of 1980.

The recent financial crisis has exposed the danger of relying on markets to protect consumers. Exotic subprime loans with artificially low initial payments became a vehicle for mortgage brokers to get families into houses they had no realistic hope of affording. While some homebuyers may have consciously used these mortgages to speculate on housing prices, mortgage brokers and lenders also pushed borrowers into unnecessarily high-cost loans. The Center for Responsible Lending found that subprime borrowers ended up paying the equivalent of 1.3 percentage points of interest more for loans obtained through mortgage brokers than they would have paid borrowing directly from a retail lender.[19] The city of Baltimore sued Wells Fargo, alleging that the company systematically targeted minority borrowers through such policies as offering bonuses for steering borrowers who would have qualified for prime loans into subprime loans instead.[20] According to Shaun Donovan, secretary of housing and urban development, 33 percent of subprime mortgages in New York City went to borrowers who could have qualified for conventional loans.[21] These examples demonstrate that unscrupulous brokers and lenders, armed with dense fine print, can induce consumers to choose products that are not in their best interest.

Subprime loans are hardly the only example of the market's inability to prevent malfeasance. In 2005, the Federal Reserve ruled that overdraft "protection" is not covered by the Truth in Lending Act, allowing banks to charge overdraft fees without their customers' permission and without disclosing the effective interest rate (although the existence of the programs is typically included in fine-print disclosure statements). In 2009, banks were expected to earn $27 billion in overdraft fees—amounting, on average, to a $34 fee for a $20 transaction.[22] Credit card issuers have also become increasingly adept at maximizing revenues by adopting complex pricing structures that are hard for consumers to understand. For example, universal cross-default provisions (failing to pay one bill to a different company can count as a "default" on your credit card bill) can cause your interest rate to jump up to the "penalty" rate—even retroactively, thanks to two-cycle billing.[23] Universal cross-default and two-cycle billing policies are included in the disclosure statements that card issuers slip into monthly bills, but are often difficult to understand.

Even those who do read the fine print often fail to understand the impact it will have on them individually, due to cognitive biases that lead people to underestimate their usage of credit and the price of credit. For example, 58 percent of people say that they usually pay off their credit cards each month—but only 37–42 percent actually do.[24] The result is that people take on more debt than they intend to and pay a higher price for it than they realize. These errors are by no means confined to low-income, supposedly less sophisticated consumers. The reverse convertibles discussed in chapter 4 were largely sold to relatively affluent investors, for the simple reason that complex financial products have to be sold (few people wake up in the morning suddenly wanting to buy complex structured notes), and larger transactions translate into larger commissions. And the harm caused by deceptive pricing structures goes beyond damage to individual consumers. When it is difficult to assess the likely cost of financial products, even a competitive market does not lead to lower prices for everyone; instead, financial institutions compete by thinking of new tricks to ensnare consumers, and those that refuse to take advantage of their customers lose market share.

Ultimately, simple microeconomic models break down for a few basic reasons. First, innovation leads to financial products that are too complex for even an intelligent, financially savvy person to understand. As former Federal Reserve governor Edward Gramlich wrote of subprime lending, "[I]t is complicated and confusing for borrowers to search out all their available options, to understand all the terms of the loans, and to avoid getting misallocated into a lower credit category than may be appropriate."[25] Second, people are not rational actors, and financial institutions are more than willing to prey on this weakness. A simple cognitive fallacy such as optimism bias—the tendency to think that you won't miss a payment on your credit card or overdraw your checking account—causes people to choose financial products that are bad for them. As Shailesh Mehta, former CEO of Providian, said in an interview, "When people make the buying decision, they don't look at the penalty fees, because they never believe they'll be late. They never believe they'll be over limit."[26] Third, the negotiating table is tilted in favor of financial services providers, not consumers. Individuals have no ability to negotiate the terms of their mortgages or their credit cards. And the people that they turn to for help with these confusing products, such as mortgage brokers, do not necessarily have their best interests in mind.

These problems were exacerbated by the regulatory structure in place prior to the financial crisis. Enforcement of consumer protection statutes was entrusted to the Federal Reserve, whose priorities have historically been managing the overall economy and ensuring the soundness of bank holding companies. Banks were also subject to various federal bank regulators—the OCC, the OTS, and the Federal Deposit Insurance Corporation—but their primary mission was to prevent banks from failing, not to protect consumers. The patchwork nature of financial regulation, particularly the limited oversight of nonbank lenders, made it possible for financial institutions to engage in their most questionable practices through their least regulated subsidiaries. And with regulators competing for fees from the banks they regulated, consumers' interests were often an afterthought.

The need for stronger consumer protection in the financial arena motivated law professor Elizabeth Warren's 2007 article "Unsafe at Any Rate." Warren began:

> It is impossible to buy a toaster that has a one-in-five chance of bursting into flames and burning down your house. But it is possible to refinance an existing home with a mortgage that has the same one-in-five chance of putting the family out on the street—and the mortgage won't even carry a disclosure of that fact to the homeowner.[27]

Warren called for the creation of a Financial Product Safety Commission, modeled on the Consumer Product Safety Commission, with the power not only to establish disclosure requirements but also to study financial products, review them for safety, and require that dangerous products be modified before being made available to the public.

In 2009, Warren's idea became the Obama administration's proposed Consumer Financial Protection Agency. In its original form, the CFPA would have jurisdiction over almost any financial product sold to individuals, and would have the power to regulate "unfair, deceptive, or abusive acts or practices for all credit, savings, and payment products," including the ability to ban specific practices such as prepayment penalties or yield-spread premiums (the practice of paying mortgage originators higher commissions for generating higher-cost mortgages). The CFPA would also be able to demand that financial service providers offer "plain-vanilla" versions of products, such as a thirty-year fixed rate mortgage, alongside whatever more complicated products they chose, so that consumers could buy a product that they knew was free of hidden traps.[28]

The banking lobby and its defenders closed ranks against the CFPA. Peter Wallison of the American Enterprise Institute claimed that some consumers would be "denied the opportunity to buy products and services that are available to others," restating the textbook assumption that free choice is always good and restrictions on choice are always bad—but neglecting to ask whether meaningful choice exists when it comes to complicated products offered by a handful of oligopolists, such as credit cards.[29] Small community savings banks joined forces with Wall Street, fearful that new regulations would increase their cost of doing business.[30] The incumbent regulators also took a united stand against ceding any authority to a new agency, with Ben Bernanke of the Federal Reserve, John Dugan of the OCC, and Sheila Bair of the FDIC all taking aim at the CFPA before Congress.[31]

The full-court lobbying press had an impact. In September 2009, in order to improve the bill's chances of passage, Barney Frank, the chair of the House Financial Services Committee, eliminated the proposed "plain-vanilla" requirement.[32] (The version of the CFPA proposed in November by Christopher Dodd, chair of the Senate Banking Committee, also left out this requirement.) Small banks also won an exemption in the House from direct examination by the CFPA under most circumstances. But despite the best efforts of the financial sector, the CFPA did emerge intact from the House of Representatives in December 2009. In this case, the Obama administration was willing to confront the banking industry head-on, and Frank was willing to use enough muscle to push it through. The bill introduced by Dodd also includes an independent CFPA, but the sixty-vote threshold in the Senate (to defeat a filibuster) and the apparently unified opposition of the Republican Party's forty-one senators could mean that the banking lobby will still get its way. The large banks' grip on Congress has weakened a little, but perhaps not enough.

By consolidating regulatory authority in an agency that is dedicated to consumer protection, the CFPA would have the potential to deter some of the abusive practices that resulted in families losing their homes and fueled the debt bubble of the 2000s. Even if it does become law, however, the CFPA would still face significant obstacles. At the urging of business groups, both the House and Senate versions of the legislation exempted many businesses that provide credit to their customers, such as auto dealers, and even the administration's original proposal exempted insurance products. These gaps provide opportunities for financial institutions to dodge regulation by redefining their products to fit existing loopholes.

In addition, a consumer protection agency cannot prevent all predatory behavior by financial institutions. The unwitting losers in the financial crisis included many municipalities, pension funds, and other supposedly sophisticated investors who did not understand the products they were buying from their bankers. On the advice of their investment bank, Stifel Nicolaus, five Wisconsin school districts invested $200 million—$165 million of it borrowed from Depfa, an Irish bank—in what they (and their Stifel Nicolaus banker) thought were CDOs. In fact, their $200 million was the collateral for a synthetic CDO, meaning that the school districts were selling insurance on a portfolio of bonds. When the bonds began defaulting, the school districts ended up losing their $35 million and unable to pay off their loan from Depfa. As financial expert Janet Tavakoli said, "Selling these products to municipalities was pretty widespread. They tend to be less sophisticated. So bankers sell them products stuffed with junk."[33] While businesses, local governments, and institutional investors may not require the same protections as consumers, it is foolish to assume that they will always be able to protect themselves from toxic financial products.

Despite these reservations, a strong, motivated, independent Consumer Financial Protection Agency would serve as a powerful constraint on the ability of financial institutions to take advantage of their customers, discouraging innovations that do not benefit customers and channeling competition into innovations that reduce costs or create new services. The CFPA should also serve as a counterweight within the government to a set of regulatory agencies that have historically seen the world from the perspective of the banks they regulate rather than the customers served by those banks.

However, consumer lending is only one means by which financial institutions can mine the raw material needed for securitization and structured finance. There will always be an unregulated frontier, within our borders or outside them, where banks can place large bets with the potential to go spectacularly badly. A new agency also cannot reverse the political momentum of the last thirty years and dislodge Wall Street from its position of power in Washington. That will require stronger medicine.

TOO BIG TO EXIST

"Too big to fail" was the slogan of the financial crisis. It was the justification for bailing out Fannie Mae, Freddie Mac, AIG, Citigroup, and Bank of America (and, extended into the auto industry, General

Motors, Chrysler, and GMAC as well). It was the problem that administration officials and congressmen swore they would fix; even bank CEOs agreed, including Jamie Dimon of JPMorgan Chase, who wrote, "The term 'too big to fail' must be excised from our vocabulary."[34] The phrase has been around at least since the 1984 government rescue of Continental Illinois, and was the subject of a 2004 book by the president and vice president of the Federal Reserve Bank of Minneapolis.[35] But only in 2008 did it become a pillar of government policy.

Most observers of the financial crisis agree on the basic outlines of the "too big to fail" (TBTF) problem. Certain financial institutions are so big, or so interconnected, or otherwise so important to the financial system that they cannot be allowed to go into an uncontrolled bankruptcy; defaulting on their obligations will create significant losses for other financial institutions, at a minimum sowing chaos in the markets and potentially triggering a domino effect that causes the entire system to come crashing down. The bankruptcy of Lehman Brothers in September 2008 accelerated the collapse of American International Group, forcing it into the arms of the Federal Reserve; Lehman's failure also forced the Reserve Primary Fund to "break the buck," causing a sudden loss of confidence in all money market funds; in turn the flood of money out of money market funds caused the commercial paper market to freeze, endangering the ability of many corporations to operate on a day-to-day basis. The failure of Lehman also caused large cash outflows from the remaining stand-alone investment banks, Goldman Sachs and Morgan Stanley. The sequence of falling dominoes was only stopped by massive government rescue measures, and the panic that occurred despite the government's intervention helped transform a mild recession into the most severe recession of the postwar period.

What makes a financial institution too big to fail is the amount of collateral damage that its uncontrolled failure could cause. This damage can take several different forms. If a bank defaults on its debt, other institutions holding its debt will lose money, as happened to the Reserve Primary Fund. Although financial institutions generally attempt to avoid holding too much debt from a single issuer for precisely this reason, the problem is magnified by derivatives. Since credit default swaps allow any company to insure any amount of debt issued by any other company, a bank default can cause losses that exceed its actual debt.

Another problem is that a failing institution could have thousands of open transactions with its counterparties, which are largely other financial institutions. (At the time of its collapse, the face value of AIG's open derivatives contracts was $2.7 trillion—$1 trillion of it with only twelve financial institutions.)[36] For example, a failing bank might have sold credit default swap protection on various securities; its counterparties are assuming that they are perfectly hedged because of those swaps. But when the bank fails, suddenly those hedges vanish, and the counterparties have to take large losses on the underlying securities.* These open transactions can take an almost infinite number of forms; in the modern financial world, any financial institution's position at the end of any given day depends on its counterparties being in business the next day.

Finally, the failure of one bank can cause investors or counterparties to lose confidence in another, similar bank. Because all banks borrow short and lend long, a loss of confidence can kill even a bank that is healthy on paper. After Bear Stearns was sold to JPMorgan Chase in March 2008, all eyes turned to Lehman Brothers; after Lehman failed in September, lack of confidence in Morgan Stanley almost brought it down, and Goldman Sachs was assumed to be next in line.[37] (Merrill Lynch avoided becoming a domino only by selling itself to Bank of America as Lehman collapsed.)

For these reasons, many people have said that the real problem is not the size of a bank (conventionally measured by the total value of its assets), but its interconnectedness.[38] But whatever the term—"too big to fail," "too interconnected to fail," "systemically important" (preferred by Ben Bernanke),[39] "tier 1 financial holding company" (preferred by the Treasury Department)[40]—the fact remains that certain financial institutions cast a sufficiently large shadow over the financial system that they cannot be allowed to fail. As of early 2010, there

---

*This problem can be mitigated through collateral requirements, which mean that if a derivatives trade moves against one party, it has to give collateral to the other party to protect against its own failure. However, it is not feasible to fully collateralize a credit default swap, because when a bond defaults the value of a credit default swap on that bond suddenly jumps to almost the full face value of the bond.

are at least six banks that are too big to fail—Bank of America, Citigroup, Goldman Sachs, JPMorgan Chase, Morgan Stanley, and Wells Fargo (Figure 7-1)—even leaving aside other institutions such as insurance companies.

Figure 7-1: Growth of Six Big Banks

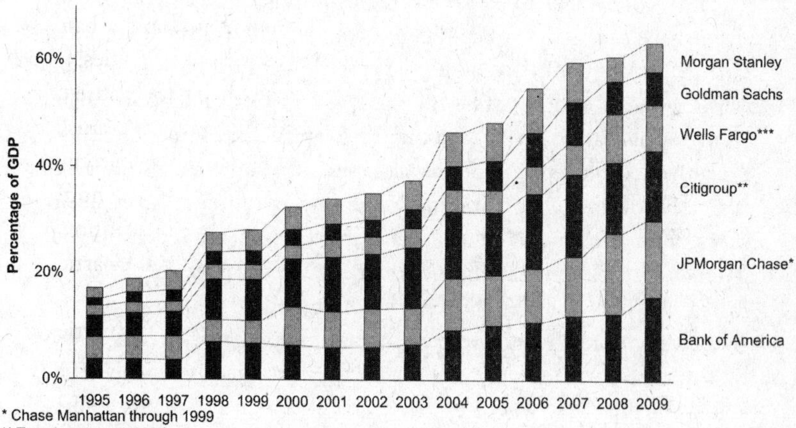

* Chase Manhattan through 1999
** Travelers through 1997
*** First Union through 2000; Wachovia 2001–2007
Source: Company annual and quarterly reports. 2009 is at end of Q3.

Not only is there widespread agreement that several financial institutions are too big to fail, but there is also widespread agreement that this is not good for the financial system or for the economy as a whole. "Too big to fail" creates three major problems for society.

The first problem is that when TBTF institutions do come to the brink of failure, they have to be bailed out, and that usually means they have to be bailed out by the government (and by taxpayers). Even if the government were to decide to wipe out shareholders and replace management, it would still have to bail out the creditors who lent money to the failing bank, since the whole point of the rescue is to limit collateral damage to other financial institutions. A TBTF bank cannot be allowed to go into an ordinary bankruptcy procedure because its creditors and counterparties would be cut off from their money for months, which could be fatal. This means that the government must keep the failing bank afloat and, without a credible threat of bankruptcy to negotiate with, must honor all of the bank's obligations; in other words, the money the bank lost has to be made up with public funds. This was the case with the AIG bailout, where the government eventually committed $180 billion in various rescue packages to keep AIG alive and pay off its counterparties. This need to protect creditors means that even a government takeover (through an FDIC-style conservatorship) will still result in significant losses to taxpayers.

The second problem is that TBTF institutions have a strong incentive to take excess risk, since the government will bail them out in an emergency. All banks are highly leveraged institutions, which means that they are betting with other people's money. There are many strategies available to banks that increase returns for shareholders (and executives) while shifting potential losses onto someone else, such as increasing leverage and holding riskier assets. Ordinarily, creditors should refuse to lend money to a bank that takes on too much risk; but if creditors believe that the government will protect them against losses, they will not play this supervisory function. (This is similar to the decision made by foreign investors in emerging markets: it's always best to lend to the oligarchs, because they are the most likely to be bailed out by the government in a crisis.) There is of course some chance that top executives would lose their jobs in a bailout, but this is more than balanced by the increased upside they gain from taking on more risk. The result is that the largest banks have the most incentive to take risks, and to take risks that would make no economic sense without the government guarantee they get because they are too big to fail. As Larry Summers said in 2000, "It is certain that a healthy financial system cannot be built on the expectation of bailouts."[41]

This problem only gets worse over time. Each time a government bails out its banks, it says, "Never again," hoping to deter the banks from repeating their past sins. But as Piergiorgio Alessandri and Andrew Haldane of the Bank of England argue, this stance becomes less and less credible: "The ex-post costs of crisis mean such a statement lacks credibility. Knowing this, the rational response by market participants is to double their bets. This adds to the cost of future crises. And the larger these costs, the lower the credibility of 'never again' announcements. This is a doom loop."[42]

The third problem is that TBTF banks are bad for competition and therefore bad for the economy. Bond investors realize that megabanks have an implicit government guarantee, and therefore they are willing to lend them money at lower interest rates than their smaller competitors. This is why large banks could pay 0.78 percentage points less for money than small banks in the wake of the financial crisis, giving them a huge competitive advantage. Dean Baker and Travis McArthur calculate that this hidden subsidy was worth up to $34 billion for eighteen large banks in 2009, accounting for roughly half of their profits.[43] This subsidy makes it harder for smaller banks to compete, deterring new entrants and only strengthening the long-term process of consolidation and concentration in the financial sector.

Where people disagree is what to do about the problem. The Obama administration initially put its faith in various technical regulatory fixes. One is to increase regulatory supervision of systemically important financial institutions. Another is to give the government "resolution authority" over holding companies that are too big to fail, similar to the power the FDIC currently has to take over and clean up insolvent banks.[44] A third proposal is to increase capital requirements for large banks in an effort to make the most systemically dangerous institutions a little safer.[45] A fourth idea floated by the administration is requiring large banks to raise "contingent capital"—debt that, in the event of a crisis, converts into equity capital at a predetermined trigger point.* The legislation introduced in the House of Representatives and the Senate in fall 2009 largely followed the administration's incrementalist approach.

These regulatory fixes make sense on paper, and it would be better to enact most of them than to do nothing. Resolution authority over holding companies would have given Treasury and the Federal Reserve another option during the financial crisis—the option to take over insolvent institutions, fire management, wipe out shareholders, and

---

*Raising equity capital makes a bank safer, since it increases the cushion of losses it can absorb before going bankrupt. However, bank shareholders do not like raising additional capital, since that reduces leverage and profits. Contingent capital is debt, so it increases leverage, but in the event of a crisis, the holders of the contingent capital can be forced to exchange it for equity capital—increasing the bank's safety cushion when it needs it most, while diluting existing shareholders' claim on profits.

impose haircuts on creditors. Some experts insist that the government could already have used its negotiating power to obtain a similar result,[46] but the proposed legislation would settle the question once and for all. The ability to impose some degree of pain on managers, shareholders, and creditors should have some deterrent effect on excessive risk-taking during a boom. (Contingent capital, however, might actually reduce the stability of the financial system, because reaching the conversion trigger point could itself cause a bank run; as *The Financial Times*' Gillian Tett has pointed out, these instruments are called "death spiral bonds" in Japan.)[47]

However, the belief that these regulatory refinements alone will solve the TBTF problem and prevent the next financial crisis reflects excessive faith in technocracy. Crises, by their nature, are difficult to predict with any degree of precision. The first problem with increased capital requirements or with contingent capital is estimating how much capital will be enough in the next crisis. Both Bear Stearns and Lehman had sufficient capital on paper—five days before its bankruptcy, Lehman had a Tier 1 capital ratio* of 11 percent[48]—yet were overwhelmed by market fears about their viability. A month after the Lehman bankruptcy, the settlement auction for Lehman credit default swaps valued Lehman debt at only 9 cents on the dollar—meaning that liquidating the firm's assets was only expected to yield 9 percent of the money needed to repay unsecured creditors.[49] How much *more* capital would have been needed to prevent panic or to keep creditors whole—and how much capital will our banks need next time? The truth is that no one knows. And it is highly likely that any increases in capital requirements will be modest. In November 2009, Morgan Stanley analysts predicted that new regulations would result in Tier 1 capital ratios of 7–11 percent for large banks—still below Lehman's pre-bankruptcy level.[50]

Resolution authority is also far from a magic bullet, especially in the global world of modern finance. Some of the most severe complications of the Lehman bankruptcy occurred not in the United States,

---

*A capital ratio is a bank's capital divided by its assets. Tier 1 capital is one common regulatory definition of capital. Eleven percent was considered a healthy amount of Tier 1 capital prior to the crisis.

but in other countries, each of which has its own laws for dealing with a failing financial institution. When a bank with assets in different countries fails, it is in each country's immediate interest to have the strictest rules on freezing assets to pay off domestic creditors. For a resolution process to have any chance of succeeding, it must be cross-border in scope; yet there are strong political reasons to believe that such an international agreement will be difficult or impossible to achieve—and that countries would be unlikely to comply with it in a serious financial crisis.

More important, solutions that depend on smarter, better regulatory supervision and corrective action ignore the political constraints on regulation and the political power of the large banks. The idea that we can simply regulate large banks more effectively assumes that regulators will have the incentive to do so, despite everything we know about regulatory capture and political constraints on regulation. It assumes that regulators will be able to identify the excess risks that banks are taking, overcome the banks' arguments that they have appropriate safety mechanisms in place, resist political pressure (from the administration and Congress) to leave the banks alone for the sake of the economy, and impose controversial corrective measures that will be too complicated to defend in public. And, of course, it assumes that important regulatory agencies will not fall into the hands of people like Alan Greenspan, who believed that government regulation was rendered largely unnecessary by the free market.

The technocratic approach assumes that political officials, up to and including the president, will have the backbone to crack down on large banks in the heat of a crisis while the banks and the administration's political opponents scream about socialism and the abuse of power. Under the administration's proposal, taking over a major bank would require a decision by the treasury secretary, consultation with the president, and the approval of two-thirds of the Federal Reserve Board of Governors,[51] which means that it would be a political decision of the first order. Even leaving aside the issue of direct pressure from bank executives who happen to be major political donors,[52] it would be politically difficult for any president to order a government takeover of an iconic American bank that was insisting through the media and its lobbyists that it was perfectly healthy. FDIC takeovers currently do not face this challenge because the banks involved are small and have little political power; the same cannot be said of JPMorgan Chase or Goldman Sachs.

Not only does the "better regulation" approach ignore the impact of politics, but it fails to solve the underlying problem—the existence of TBTF institutions. Even if the government were able to use resolution authority to take over a large bank, it is virtually certain that taxpayer funds would be necessary to finance the takeover, because of both the size of the bank and the urgency of the situation.[53] Although the government might be able to impose small haircuts on creditors and counterparties, they would have to be small, since large losses would trigger the domino effect that has to be avoided at all costs, and taxpayers would be left bearing most of the losses. In short, this approach assumes that TBTF institutions must exist, and then attempts to deal with them as well as possible—and not very well at that.

The right solution is obvious: do not allow financial institutions to be too big to fail; break up the ones that are.

This is a controversial idea. It is a virtually unquestioned assumption in the American business world that bigger is better. Banking executives have spent the last twenty years making their banks as big as possible by entering new businesses, expanding into new geographic regions, and above all acquiring other banks. The idea that the United States, as the world's largest economy, should also have its largest banks seems self-evident to most people.

Not surprisingly, the CEOs of large banks are not in favor of having their empires divided. In *The Washington Post*, Jamie Dimon wrote, "While the strategy of artificial limits may sound simple, it would undermine the goals of economic stability, job creation and consumer service that lawmakers are trying to promote."[54] In an interview, Lloyd Blankfein of Goldman Sachs said, "Most of the activities we do, and you can be confused if you read the pop press, serve a real purpose. It wouldn't be better for the world or the financial system [to change the firm's activities]."[55]

The Obama administration agreed. Diana Farrell, a member of the

National Economic Council, said in an interview, "We have created [our biggest banks], and we're sort of past that point, and I think that in some sense, the genie's out of the bottle and what we need to do is to manage them and to oversee them, as opposed to hark back to a time that we're unlikely to ever come back to or want to come back to."[56] Larry Summers said, "I don't think you can completely turn back the clock."[57]

Some economists and commentators recognized early on that breaking up the big banks was the only way to prevent a repeat of the financial crisis. Testifying before Congress in April 2009, Joseph Stiglitz said,

> We know that there will be pressures, over time, to soften any regula-
> tory regime. We know that these too-large-to-fail banks also have enor-
> mous resources to lobby Congress to deregulate. . . . Accordingly, I
> think it would be far better to break up these too-big-to-fail institutions
> and strongly restrict the activities in which they can be engaged than to
> try to control them.[58]

The Wall Street–Washington establishment at first attempted to portray this as a naive idea supported only by outsiders who didn't understand the world of modern finance (even if some of them had won the
Nobel Prize). However, cracks in the consensus began to appear in
fall 2009. In testimony before Congress, Paul Volcker, the legendary
Fed chair of the 1980s and an Obama administration adviser, said,
"I would exclude from commercial banking institutions, which are
potential beneficiaries of official (i.e., taxpayer) financial support, certain risky activities entirely suitable for our capital markets," including
internal hedge funds, internal private equity funds, and proprietary
trading.[59] In an October interview, he argued unequivocally for an
updated version of the Glass-Steagall separation of commercial and
investment banking. "People say I'm old-fashioned and banks can no
longer be separated from nonbank activity," he said. "That argument
brought us to where we are today."[60]

In October, Mervyn King, head of the Bank of England (the
world's oldest central bank), gave a speech arguing for the separation
of the "utility" aspects of banking—processing payments and trans-
forming savings into investments—which should be offered govern-

ment support, from riskier activities such as proprietary trading, which should not. A key element of his argument was that regulation would be insufficient to keep banks from taking on excessive risk: "The belief that appropriate regulation can ensure that speculative activities do not result in failures is a delusion."[61] A stronger version of King's position is *Financial Times* columnist John Kay's proposal for "narrow banking," which limits banks to taking deposits and processing payments and regulates them as utilities.[62] Similarly, economics professor Laurence Kotlikoff has argued for "limited purpose banking," a model in which banks are not allowed to borrow short and lend long, and all risky assets must be held in mutual funds.[63] In November, Richard Fisher, president of the Federal Reserve Bank of Dallas, argued for getting rid of banks that are too big to fail: "This means finding ways not to live with 'em and getting on with developing the least disruptive way to have them divest those parts of the 'franchise,' such as proprietary trading, that place the deposit and lending function at risk and otherwise present conflicts of interest."[64]

But the most surprising break with the conventional wisdom came from Alan Greenspan, who perhaps more than any other person had made the age of the megabanks possible. In an October speech, he said, "The critical problem that we have, which we've got to resolve, is the too-big-to-fail issue." Asked how to solve this problem, he responded,

> If they're too big to fail, they're too big. I—this one has got me. And the reason it's got me is that we no longer have the capability of having credible government response which says, henceforth no institution will be supported because it is too big to fail. . . .
>
> At a minimum, you've got to take care of the competitive advantage they have, because of the implicit subsidy, which makes them competitively capable of beating out their smaller competitors, who don't get the subsidy. And if you don't neutralize that, you're going to get a moribund group of obsolescent institutions, which will be a big drain on the savings of this society. . . .
>
> I don't think merely raising the fees or capital on large institutions or taxing them is enough. I think that'll—they'll absorb that; they'll work with it; and they will still be inefficient; and they'll still be using the savings.

So I mean, radical things, as you—you know, break them up, you know. In 1911, we broke up Standard Oil. So what happened? The individual parts became more valuable than the whole. Maybe that's what we need.[65]

The reasons to break up the big banks are simple. If there are no financial institutions that are too big to fail, there will be no implicit subsidies favoring some banks as opposed to others; creditors and counterparties will play their necessary role of ensuring that banks do not take on too much risk; banks will be less likely to engage in the excessive risk-taking that could cause the next financial crisis; and banks that do fail will not have to be bailed out at taxpayer expense. Additional regulations preventing banks from abusing their customers or exploiting loopholes to minimize their capital requirements are also necessary, of course; we do not want to relive the savings and loan crisis of the 1980s, when thousands of banks failed due to excessive risk-taking and inadequate supervision. But breaking up the big banks will help level the playing field and make the financial system better able to withstand the next crisis.

Opponents argue that big banks provide benefits to the economy that cannot be provided by smaller banks. A common argument, put forward by Dimon, Scott Talbott of the Financial Services Roundtable, and finance professor Charles Calomiris, is that large corporations require financial services that only large banks can provide.[66] Related to this is the idea that the global competitiveness of U.S. corporations requires that American banks be at least as big as anyone else's banks. Another argument is that large financial institutions enjoy economies of scale and scope that make them more efficient, helping the economy as a whole. Finally, supporters argue that large, global banks are necessary to provide liquidity to far-flung capital markets, making them more efficient and benefiting companies that raise money in those markets.

These arguments suffer from a shortage of empirical evidence. Large multinational corporations have large, global financing needs, but there are currently no banks that can supply those needs alone; instead, corporations rely on syndicates of banks for major offerings of equity or debt. For example, Johnson & Johnson used eleven banks to manage its most recent debt offering in 2008 (and thirteen banks for the offering before that, in 2007).[67] And even if there were a bank large enough to meet all of a large corporation's financial needs, it would defy business logic for that corporation to restrict itself to a single source of financial services, instead of selecting banks based on their expertise in particular markets or geographies. In addition, U.S. corporations already benefit from competition between U.S. and foreign banks, which can provide identical financial products; there is no reason to believe that the global competitiveness of our nonfinancial sector depends on our having the world's largest banks.

There is little evidence that large banks gain economies of scale above a very low size threshold. A review of multiple empirical studies found that economies of scale vanish at some point below $10 billion in assets.[68] The 2007 Geneva Report, "International Financial Stability," co-authored by former Federal Reserve vice chair Roger Ferguson, also found that the unprecedented consolidation in the financial sector over the previous decade had led to no significant efficiency gains, no economies of scale beyond a low threshold, and no evident economies of scope.[69] Finance professor Edward Kane has pointed out that since large banks exhibit constant returns to scale (they are no more or less efficient as they grow larger), and we know that large banks enjoy a subsidy due to being too big to fail, "offsetting diseconomies must exist in the operation of large institutions"—that is, without the TBTF subsidy, large banks would actually be less efficient than mid-size banks.[70] As evidence for economies of scope, Calomiris cited a paper by Kevin Stiroh showing that banks' productivity grew faster than the service sector average from 1991 to 1997, "during the heart of the merger wave."[71] However, the paper he cites, and other papers by Stiroh,[72] imply or argue that the main reason for increased productivity was improved use of information technology—not increasing size or scope.

There is an element of truth to the argument that large banks are necessary in certain types of trading businesses such as customized (over-the-counter) derivatives, where a corporate client may want a hedge that spans multiple markets (currencies, interest rates, and jet fuel, for example). To manufacture such a hedge cheaply, a derivatives dealer has to have significant trading volume in each of the underlying markets, which implies some minimum efficient scale. However, this alone cannot explain the enormous growth in leading investment banks over the last ten years. Goldman Sachs, for example, grew from $178 billion in assets in 1997 to over $1.1 trillion in 2007,[73] while Morgan Stanley grew from $302 billion to over $1.0 trillion.[74]

Despite the widespread assumption in both New York and Washington that big banks provide societal benefits, there is no proof that these benefits exist and no quantification of their size—certainly no quantification sufficient to show that they outweigh the very obvious costs of having banks that are too big to fail. Instead, defenders of the status quo portray our current banking system, despite its obvious failures, as a fact of nature that must be accepted, and that at best we can hope to tame through better regulation—despite the unquestioned failure of regulation in the decades leading up to the financial crisis.

It seems likely that any financial reform legislation will largely conform to the Obama administration's approach of tightening regulation of large financial institutions without tackling the underlying problem: the existence of TBTF institutions. It is possible that new legislation will empower regulators to take corrective action against such firms. In the House of Representatives, an amendment introduced by Paul Kanjorski would give the proposed Financial Services Oversight Council the power to order a TBTF institution to cut back its activities or divest some of its assets.[75] The bill introduced by Christopher Dodd in the Senate similarly allowed the new Agency for Financial Stability and the new Financial Institutions Regulatory Administration to prune back institutions that pose a risk to overall financial stability.[76] Even if some version of this provision survives into the final bill, it will be hedged in by conditions; for example, in the Kanjorski Amendment, the treasury secretary must approve any action that would result in a divestiture of $10 billion in assets, and the president effectively must approve any divestiture of more than $100 billion in assets. More important, there will be no requirement for the regulators to take action. Given the political constraints, it is unlikely that these powers would actually be used to significantly reduce the size and riskiness of megabanks.

Whatever the final form of the legislation, the problem of too big to fail will probably remain with us. But this does not mean that it cannot be solved. It only means that it may take several years, and several sessions of Congress, to solve.

The solution must be economically simple, so it can be effectively enforced; the more complex the scheme, the more susceptible it is to regulatory arbitrage, such as reshuffling where assets are parked within a financial institution's holding company structure. And the solution must change the balance of political power, so it will last.

The simplest solution is a hard cap on size: no financial institution would be allowed to control or have an ownership interest in assets worth more than a fixed percentage of U.S. GDP.* Determining the exact percentage is a technical problem that we do not claim to have solved, but the problem can be simply stated: the percentage should be low enough that banks below that threshold can be allowed to fail without entailing serious risk to the financial system. As a first proposal, this limit should be *no more than 4 percent of GDP*, or roughly $570 billion in assets today. U.S. banks could choose to operate globally or only in the United States, but in either case the size limit would be set relative to the U.S. economy, and offshore activities would count toward the limit. (U.S. subsidiaries of foreign banks would also have to comply with the size cap and with all U.S. financial regulations.) Existing megabanks would have to break themselves up in a way that maximizes value to their shareholders; the resulting smaller institutions would be free to compete fiercely for customers and profits.

Hard limits on the size of financial institutions have a precedent. Since 1994, the United States has had a rule prohibiting any single bank from holding more than 10 percent of total retail deposits—an arbitrary cap designed to prevent any one entity from becoming too central to the financial system. This rule had to be waived in 2009 for JPMorgan Chase, Bank of America, and Wells Fargo, demonstrating how recent growth and consolidation have rendered our previous safety measures obsolete.[77]

---

* The most commonly discussed alternative basis for a size cap is a fraction of total financial assets in the economy. However, this number can rise dramatically in a bubble. In addition, as financial development progresses, financial assets tend to rise relative to GDP and relative to the government's budget, which ultimately bears the brunt of any bailout.

An overall asset cap is a necessary condition for financial stability, but it is not a sufficient condition. The acute phase of the recent crisis was triggered not by mammoth commercial or savings banks, although some of them collapsed or nearly collapsed during the crisis, but by (modestly) smaller, risk-seeking investment banks; Bear Stearns had only $400 billion of assets at the end of 2007.[78] Because a financial institution could load up on $570 billion of the riskiest assets it can find, there must also be lower limits for banks that take greater risks, and these limits must take into account derivatives, off-balance-sheet positions, and other factors that increase the damage a failing institution could cause to other financial institutions. That way financial institutions that engage in riskier activities will have to be smaller than institutions that hold safer assets, in order to limit the collateral damage their failure could cause. This will require a technical formula that goes beyond the scope of this book,* but again the goal is simple: all banks, including risk-seeking ones, should be limited to a size where they do not threaten the stability of the financial system. As an initial guideline, an investment bank (such as Goldman Sachs) should be effectively limited in size to *2 percent of GDP,* or roughly $285 billion today. (If it were to choose a riskier mix of activities in the future, its effective maximum size would fall accordingly.)

Determining where to set these limits is a problem shared by all parties to this debate. Every proposed solution assumes that regulators have some way of identifying TBTF institutions so that they can take special precautions against them—which means that there must be a way of calculating the systemic importance of different institutions. If the problem is simply and clearly stated—establish limits such that no bank is too big or too important to fail—it can be solved by people with access to the right data about the financial system. These limits should not be set by regulatory agencies, which could then nudge them upward as memories of the crisis fade and faith in free markets returns. The limits should be set by Congress, with sufficient expert input, and then enforced by regulators.

---

*Risk-based size limits would require an approach similar to risk-weighting of assets. This is already a common feature of existing capital regulations, which prescribe different amounts of capital based on the riskiness of different types of assets. We propose using a similar approach to calculate the maximum allowable size for a given bank, based on its risk profile.

To be clear, size limits should not replace existing financial regulations. A world with only small banks, but small banks with minimal capital requirements and no effective oversight, would not be dangerous in the same way as today's world of megabanks, but it would be dangerous nonetheless; it was the collapse of thousands of small banks that helped bring on the Great Depression. More generally, it would be naive to assume that we can predict today all the ways that financial institutions will find to take on more risk and get into more trouble. Therefore, enhanced capital requirements and closer prudential regulation, as proposed by the Obama administration, are also necessary. Size limits, however, provide protection against both the systemic risk and the competitive distortions created by financial institutions that are too big to fail, which are not adequately addressed by existing regulations. We believe these limits should work out to no more than 4 percent of GDP for all banks and 2 percent of GDP for investment banks, but that is a debate we are willing to have.

Why 4 percent and 2 percent? The fundamental tradeoff is between safety and efficiency. A lower size limit makes the financial system safer, because it will be less vulnerable to the failure of a single bank or a handful of banks; however, draconian size limitations could introduce unintended consequences if, for example, investment banks are no longer able to maintain sufficient trading volume in global markets. Personally we would prefer even lower limits, for two main reasons. First, Bear Stearns had only $400 billion in assets—implying that, for a risk-loving investment bank, $285 billion may still be large enough to threaten the financial system. Second, lower limits would increase competition and reduce the potential political power of any single company.

However, we think that 4 percent and 2 percent present a reasonable compromise with people who believe that the real economy needs large banks. Members of the Obama administration, as described above, have said that it is impossible to "turn back the clock." A 4 percent cap would only roll back the clock to the mid-1990s. At that time, the largest commercial banks—Bank of America, Chase Manhattan, Citibank, NationsBank—each had assets roughly equivalent to 3–4 percent of U.S. GDP. On the investment banking side, Goldman Sachs and Morgan Stanley only passed the 2 percent threshold in 1997 and 1996, respectively; at the time, they were the two premier invest-ment banks in the world, and no one thought they were unable to meet their clients' needs.[79]

On the one hand, it can be argued that the world has changed since the mid-1990s. But by how much? Thomas Philippon has estimated how much of the growth of the financial sector (measured by its share of GDP) can be explained by increasing demand for corporate finan-cial services from the nonfinancial sector. His analysis shows that demand for finance around 2007, after a spike around 2000, was only 4 percent higher (as a share of GDP) than in the 1986–1995 period (while the corporate finance share of GDP had grown by 31 per-cent).[80] On the other hand, there is no reason why increased demand for finance can only be met by larger firms, rather than more firms. There is also no proof that the mid-1990s economy required commer-cial banks as large as 4 percent of GDP—which were already the prod-uct of what seemed then like blockbuster mergers—or investment banks as large as 2 percent of GDP.

Finally, these size limits would only affect *six banks*—Bank of Amer-ica (16 percent of GDP), JPMorgan Chase (14 percent), Citigroup (13 percent), Wells Fargo (9 percent), Goldman Sachs (6 percent), and Morgan Stanley (5 percent) (and none of Wells Fargo's predecessor companies was bigger than 4 percent of GDP until a few years ago).[81] Saying that we cannot break up our largest banks is saying that our economic futures depend on these six companies (some of which are in various states of ill health). That thought should frighten us into action.

Some commentators worry that smaller banks would hurt the competitiveness of our financial system; a cap on the size of U.S. banks would lead our banks to relocate overseas and do nothing to prevent the growth of megabanks based in other countries. In an interview, law professor Hal Scott said, "If we break up our banks and Europe doesn't break up theirs and the Chinese don't break up theirs, this is going to have an immense impact on who are the players in the international banking system."[82] But this does not mean that Ameri-can companies would be starved of capital. In a free market, financial intermediation is driven by real economic activity; smaller U.S. banks (and a bank with $500 billion in assets is by no means a small bank), or the U.S. subsidiaries of foreign banks, would step in to fill the gap. U.S. banks already face foreign competition in many financial markets; U.S. companies are perfectly happy buying their interest rate swaps from Deutsche Bank rather than JPMorgan, and the products work just as well.

The more serious issue is not that competition from foreign megabanks will hurt American nonfinancial companies (those foreign banks will be competing *for* the business of U.S. companies), but that foreign megabanks will continue to pose a risk to the global financial system. The ideal solution would be for all major countries to implement similar limits on bank size. One avenue for international coordination could be the World Trade Organization; any government that tolerates domestic banks that are too big to fail is subsidizing them (by allowing them to borrow money more cheaply than foreign competitors that do not have implicit government guarantees), which is a form of protectionism.

However, it is never safe to bet on international agreement, and there is no need for the United States to wait for an international solution. First, U.S. subsidiaries of foreign banks will continue to be subject to U.S. prudential regulation—which should take into account whether that subsidiary would be able to withstand a global financial crisis. If a large European bank were to fail, our financial system would be safer if it did *not* include banks that were too big to fail; the whole point of size limits is to increase the ability of the system to withstand a shock, no matter where it originates. And if European countries want to keep banks that are too big to fail, then their taxpayers will have to bail them out in case of a crisis. In effect, foreign governments would be taking on the role of insuring the global financial system against disaster—a role that the Federal Reserve and the Treasury Department played in 2008–2009.

Relying on foreign government bailouts alone would not make us invulnerable to crises originating overseas. For example, Switzerland may not be able to afford to bail out UBS should it suffer a major crisis. For this reason, our financial regulators need to evaluate the potential risks created by foreign megabanks and, if necessary, take action to limit our exposure to those banks. But in any case, we would be less exposed than we are today. And the way to start is to create a financial system that is not vulnerable to the collapse of a few towering dominoes.

A real cap on bank size will not only level the economic playing field and reduce the incentive for banks to take excess risks predicated on the government safety net, but it will also weaken the political power of the big banks and begin to undo the takeover of Washington by Wall Street that we have chronicled in this book. Without a privileged inner core of thirteen (or fewer) bankers, the financial sector will be composed of thousands of small companies and dozens or hundreds of medium-to-large companies, including hedge funds and private equity firms. The financial lobby will continue to be strong by virtue of its sheer size, and the community bankers will retain their clout in Congress. But the distortion of the playing field in favor of a small number of megabanks will come to an end.

This fragmentation of the banking industry should also help dethrone Wall Street from its privileged place in the U.S. economy. The end of "too big to fail" will reduce large banks' funding advantage, forcing them to compete on the basis of products, price, and service rather than implicit government subsidies. Increased competition will reduce the margins on fee-driven businesses such as securitization, trading, and derivatives, putting pressure on large banks' profits. A larger group of competitors will also make it harder for major banks to divert such a large proportion of their profits to employee compensation; bonuses for traders and investment bankers should fall from the historically obscene to the merely outrageous. With more competition, it will be harder for a handful of firms to dominate the cultural landscape like Salomon Brothers and Drexel Burnham Lambert in the 1980s or Goldman Sachs today, and perhaps smart college graduates will find Wall Street a little less compelling. Finance will never go back to being boring—globalization and computers have seen to that—but it should become a little less exciting.

This will create a virtuous cycle. As the major banks become a little poorer, their domination of the campaign finance system will wane, as will the allure of the revolving door. As high finance becomes less glamorous and a little more like just another business, its ideological sway over the Washington establishment will begin to fade. Fewer top administration officials will come from a handful of megabanks, and more will come from other parts of the financial industry, or from nonfinancial industries. The financial crisis has made at least some people think that everything is not right with the Wall Street view of the world; weakening the big banks will help fuel that healthy skepticism. Finance will never be just another industry. It is too big and too central to the economy, and there is something seductive about a business that deals in nothing but money. But reducing the size, profits, and power of the big banks will begin to restore balance both to our economy and to our political system.

These ideas will not be adopted overnight. In 1900, almost no reasonable person thought there was any basis for capping the size of private businesses—no well-developed economic theory supporting such a position, no common law tradition, and nothing in the U.S. Constitution (as interpreted by the Supreme Court).[83] When Theodore Roosevelt sued Northern Securities in 1902, the conventional wisdom was that the industrial trusts were a fact of nature. There was little precedent for the idea of using the Sherman Antitrust Act against a large corporation (although it was used against labor unions in the 1890s). In addition, the trusts had strong backers in Washington, including the key power brokers in Roosevelt's own Republican Party. For Roosevelt, however, any economic benefits that might be provided by the trusts did not outweigh the costs they imposed on society, both by charging monopoly prices and by stifling competition.

By 1910, the consensus view had shifted dramatically. The power of the industrial trusts and the details of their anticompetitive behavior were sufficiently obvious to provoke a political backlash. The middle class became afraid that its hard-won status and relative affluence were endangered by the rise of the super-rich, and that increasing economic inequality would undermine the dream of upward mobility. Because President Roosevelt was willing to confront the trusts, he helped change the conventional wisdom. That change was also shaped by the findings of the Pujo Committee and the writings of Louis Brandeis. And the shift in the consensus was a major reason why the antitrust movement had such lasting effect; today, few people think that unrestrained monopolies are good either for our economy or for our political system.

Our goal today is to change the conventional wisdom about enormous banks. In the long term, the most effective constraint on the financial sector is public opinion. Today, anyone proposing to end the regulation of pharmaceuticals or to suspend government supervision of nuclear power stations would not be taken seriously. Our democratic system allows the expression of all views, but we filter those views based on a collective assessment of which are sensible and which are not. The best defense against a massive financial crisis is a popular consensus that too big to fail is too big to exist.

This is at its heart a question of politics, not of economics or of regulatory technicalities. The challenge we face today is similar to the one faced by President Roosevelt a century ago; the antitrust movement was originally a *political* movement, although today antitrust law has become a field for technocratic analysis of pricing power and consumer welfare.[84] The conventional wisdom, shaped during the three decades of deregulation, innovation, and risk-taking that brought us the recent financial crisis, is that large, sophisticated banks are a critical pillar of economic prosperity. That conventional wisdom has entrenched itself in Washington, where administration officials, regulators, and legislators agree with the Wall Street line on intellectual grounds, or see their personal interests (financial or political) aligned with the interests of Wall Street, or simply do not feel qualified to question the experts in the thousand-dollar suits. Challenging this ideology is ultimately about politics. The megabanks used political power to obtain their license to gamble with other people's money; taking that license away requires confronting that power head-on. It requires a decision that the economic and political power of the new financial oligarchy is dangerous both to economic prosperity and to the democracy that is supposed to ensure that government policies serve the greater good of society.

The Obama administration and Congress have so far chosen to dance around this confrontation. It remains too early to tell if occasional outbursts of anti–Wall Street rhetoric will translate into substantive reform. It is likely that our government will use this legislative cycle to declare victory over the financial crisis, without addressing its most fundamental cause. The result will be a financial sector that is more concentrated than ever, has a more robust guarantee of government assistance than ever, and takes more risks than ever. With the same conditions in place that led to the last financial crisis, it would be folly to expect any other result. No one can predict what market will produce the next financial crisis, or when it will occur, but no one with any memory should bet against it. And when that crisis comes, the government will face the same choice it faced in 2008: to bail out a banking system that has grown even larger and more concentrated, or to let it collapse and risk an economic disaster.

But there is another choice: the choice to finish the job that Roosevelt began a century ago, and to take a stand against concentrated financial power just as he took a stand against concentrated industrial power. That is a choice that Barack Obama could make. It is a choice that the American people need to make—and sooner rather than later. The Panic of 1907 only led to the reforms of the 1930s by way of the 1929 crash and the Great Depression. We hope that a similar calamity will not be a prerequisite to action again.

Even when it goes out of fashion, Thomas Jefferson's suspicion of concentrated power remains an essential thread in the fabric of American democracy. The financial crisis of 2007–2009 has made Jefferson a little less out of fashion. It is that tradition of skepticism that, if anything, can shift the weight of public opinion against our new financial oligarchy—the most law-abiding, hardworking, eloquent, well-dressed oligarchy in the history of politics. It is to help reinvigorate that spirit of Jefferson that we have written this book.

EPILOGUE*

> The success of this landmark reform effort will ultimately depend on
> the individuals who become the regulators. The key lesson of the last
> decade is that financial regulators must use their powers, rather than
> coddle industry interests.
> —Congressman Paul Kanjorski, June 30, 2010[1]

On July 21, 2010, President Barack Obama signed the Dodd-Frank
Wall Street Reform and Consumer Protection Act—Washington's
answer to the financial crisis.[2] Standing in the Ronald Reagan Building, President Obama said,

> These reforms represent the strongest consumer financial protections
> in history. . . . Reform will also rein in the abuse and excess that nearly
> brought down our financial system. It will finally bring transparency to
> the kinds of complex and risky transactions that helped trigger the
> financial crisis. Shareholders will also have a greater say on the pay of
> CEOs and other executives, so they can reward success instead of fail-
> ure. And finally, because of this law, the American people will never
> again be asked to foot the bill for Wall Street's mistakes.[3]

The Dodd-Frank Act was the culmination of the bitter, yearlong
political battle that we described in chapter 7, ultimately passing in

---

*The manuscript of the first edition of *13 Bankers* was submitted in December 2009 and
finalized in January 2010, after a version of the financial reform bill passed the House of
Representatives but before formal debate began in the Senate. The first edition was published in the United States in March 2010, in the midst of the Senate debate.

the Senate by the thinnest of possible margins. As the bill moved through the Senate in the spring, the lobbying campaign by the financial sector only intensified as the big banks dropped any pretense of supporting reform and chose all-out war instead, hiring fifty-four lobbying firms to do their bidding.[4] In private, Wall Street executives called President Obama—whose Treasury Department had pushed for a moderate reform package to begin with—"hostile to business," "antiwealth," "anticapitalism," a "redistributionist," a "vilifier," and a "thug."[5] On the record, even Jamie Dimon, who only a year before had been the toast of both Wall Street and Washington, was reduced to complaining that banks needed *more* influence on politicians so they could give them the "right facts."[6] And a JPMorgan Chase managing director lashed out at Congress for "an unnerving ignorance of fundamental principles of market economics" and said it was "time for the grown-ups to step in."[7]

But a curious thing happened. Instead of getting weaker in the face of a full-court lobbying press, the financial reform bill actually got modestly *stronger* during the Senate debate, carried along by a cresting wave of anger and frustration aimed at the big banks that were reporting resurgent profits and compensation even as the country as a whole remained mired in high unemployment and a fitful economic recovery. That wave was fueled by the release in March of the report by the examiner in the Lehman bankruptcy documenting how the bank had used highly questionable accounting techniques to massage its financial statements in the months prior to its collapse.[8] But it became impossible to ignore the following month, when the Securities and Exchange Commission filed a civil suit against Goldman Sachs, the informal godfather of the markets, for misleading investors in a complicated subprime-backed synthetic CDO that the bank had concocted just as the subprime market was beginning to collapse.[9] The CDO in question had been designed with considerable input by John Paulson, a hedge fund manager who intended to bet *against* the CDO; the SEC alleged, in short, that Goldman had misled investors in the CDO by failing to disclose Paulson's role. (When the subprime market collapsed, Paulson's fund cleared a $1 billion profit on the deal.) The central character in the SEC's suit was Goldman vice president Fabrice Tourre, who had the misfortune to write in a January 2007 e-mail, "The whole building is about to collapse anytime now. . . . Only potential survivor, the fabulous Fab[rice Tourre] . . . standing in the middle of all these complex, highly leveraged, exotic trades he created without necessarily understanding all of the implications of those monstruosities [sic]!!!"[10]

The SEC-Goldman lawsuit followed closely on the heels of an investigative report by *ProPublica* into Magnetar, a hedge fund that made phenomenal profits by betting that the subprime mortgage market was on the verge of collapse.[11] The *ProPublica* report went national as the main story on the radio show *This American Life*.[12] Both the Magnetar story and the Goldman-Paulson story seemed to encapsulate everything that was wrong with the financial system. On the one hand, hedge funds were pushing investment banks to create highly toxic CDOs precisely so they could bet against them, thereby actually increasing the flow of capital into subprime lending and increasing the eventual costs of collapse. On the other hand, the investment banks were so eager for the up-front fees available that not only did they allegedly mislead their clients, but they sometimes held on to the toxic waste they should have known they were creating; in one transaction, JPMorgan Chase earned a fee of $20 million but ended up losing $880 million when the CDO collapsed.[13] The problem wasn't just that fund managers and bankers wanted to make a lot of money; the problem was that the banks' own internal incentive structures and risk management "systems" had allowed short-term profits to become completely unmoored from any kind of long-term economic value.

As disgust with Wall Street mounted, senators responded with amendments that were more far-reaching than anything put forward by the Treasury Department or passed by the House of Representatives, including proposals to prohibit banks from engaging in proprietary trading, to force them to spin off their derivatives trading operations, and even to break up the largest banks.[14] This placed the Obama administration and the Treasury Department in particular in the slightly awkward position of having to work, largely behind the scenes, to defeat or water down measures they feared would be too restrictive or onerous for the big banks.[15] Ultimately, however, this turned out to be ideal for the administration. The mounting pressure from reformers helped counterbalance the lobbying efforts of the banking industry, allowing the administration to claim the prized middle ground in the debate and ensuring that the final bill turned out roughly the way it wanted.

In the end, the Dodd-Frank Act was both a significant step forward and a missed opportunity. One of the bill's most important achievements was the creation of a new, nearly independent Consumer Financial Protection Bureau (CFPB), largely similar to the agency that Elizabeth Warren had envisioned in 2007 and that we argued for in chapter 7. Any regulatory agency is only as effective as the people who staff it, and there is always the possibility that a future, pro-finance president will appoint a head of the CFPB who is opposed to consumer protection. But the creation of a new agency dedicated solely to consumer protection, with broad authority to prohibit abusive practices by all financial institutions, is an undoubted benefit for the ordinary people whom existing bank regulators had largely ignored over the previous decades. Abusive practices such as prepayment penalties (locking borrowers into expensive mortgages) and yield-spread premiums (providing incentives for steering borrowers into expensive mortgages) could become a thing of the past.

In many other areas, the bill is promising, although its ultimate impact is hard to gauge. The derivatives that Brooksley Born wanted to regulate in 1998—and that were sheltered by the Commodity Futures Modernization Act of 2000—have been brought under the regulatory umbrella. Most derivatives must be centrally cleared and traded either on exchanges or swap execution facilities—steps that should increase both competition and transparency, reducing prices for market participants and risk to the financial system. Derivatives dealers will face new capital requirements and will have new duties to treat their customers fairly, particularly if those customers are municipalities or pension funds. Existing regulatory agencies and the newly formed Financial Stability Oversight Council have new powers to monitor and take action against systemic risks, for example by subjecting important nonbank financial institutions to regulatory oversight. Resolution authority—a new system for taking over and liquidating failing financial institutions (briefly discussed in chapter 7)—should make it impossible to repeat some of the more egregious bailouts of the recent financial crisis. These are all important steps, and there are many others as well.

However, whether these new laws live up to their potential depends heavily on the same regulatory agencies that performed so poorly over the past decades. The Dodd-Frank Act, like most complex legislation, leaves a dizzying number of details to regulatory discretion. Simply putting these new laws into effect requires regulators to write hundreds of new rules, many of which offer opportunities for the financial sector to weaken or pervert the intent of Congress. (The law firm Davis Polk counted 243 new rules and 67 new studies required by the bill.)[16] For example, the new requirements for trading and clearing derivatives include an exemption for "commercial end users" (nonfinancial entities) that use derivatives for hedging purposes. How big that loophole turns out to be depends largely on the wording of the rule defining exempt transactions, an issue on which Wall Street is sure to have its say; ultimately, it could depend on how the courts rule on the eventual appeals by the banks or their clients. Another rule is necessary to define what qualifies as an evasive tactic to avoid regulation. Each of these rules will be the subject of a fight that will be repeated dozens of times as the details of financial reform are hammered out.

Wall Street is gearing up for battle; or, rather, Wall Street never stopped fighting. Lobbying organizations and law firms representing the financial sector have been recruiting former regulators to press their case with their former colleagues.[17] And in this phase, the banks have two advantages. For a brief few months, financial reform was front-page news, with Goldman Sachs providing the color; rule writing, by contrast, is unlikely to command popular attention and will be relegated to the back pages of the newspaper, if it is covered at all. In addition, rule writing is inherently complicated and full of legal technicalities—the natural home turf for the battalions of lawyers employed by Wall Street. And some of the most important rules—including those determining how much capital banks are required to hold, what qualifies as capital, and how capital requirements are measured—will be set in international negotiations where the rule of the least common denominator is likely to prevail. On the other hand, many of the regulators currently in place do genuinely want to do the right thing for the country, fulfilling the potential of the Dodd-Frank Act and constraining the excesses of the financial sector. But they will be under enormous pressure from an extremely well-funded campaign to undermine regulation at every turn. As Raghuram Rajan said, "There is a great amount of ambiguity about how the bill will evolve in practice. It has tremendous promise, but also tremendous scope for disappointment."[18]

The financial reform bill itself is also far from perfect. Unfortunately, Dodd-Frank does little to address a few of the more obvious problems that helped produce the financial crisis. The main executive compensation provisions include a requirement that board compensation committees be composed entirely of independent directors and a "say on pay" rule requiring shareholder votes on executive compensation packages—but those votes are nonbinding. Despite the central role of credit rating agencies in making the credit bubble and financial crisis possible, the conference committee that crafted the final version of the legislation stripped out the most significant provision aimed at the rating agencies: Senator Al Franken's amendment, originally included in the Senate version, eliminating the ability of banks issuing new securities to decide who would rate those securities. (Instead, the final bill requires the SEC to study the issue of conflicts of interest.)[19] Finally, the bill makes virtually no mention of Fannie Mae, Freddie Mac, or the decades-old bipartisan policy of promoting homeownership and propping up housing prices.

The missed opportunity is that the financial reform bill does too little to weaken the dominant economic and political power of the largest banks. The SAFE Banking Amendment, proposed by Senators Sherrod Brown and Ted Kaufman, would have imposed strict size limits on banks similar to those we argued for in chapter 7. Despite having no support from the congressional leadership or the Obama administration, it improbably made it to a vote on the Senate floor, losing 61–33. "If enacted, Brown-Kaufman would have broken up the six biggest banks in America," a senior Treasury official said to journalist John Heilemann. "If we'd been for it, it probably would have happened. But we weren't, so it didn't."[20]

Instead of breaking up the largest banks, the administration and its congressional allies settled for a version of the "Volcker Rule," named after former Federal Reserve chair and Obama administration adviser Paul Volcker, which aimed at preventing banks from engaging in proprietary trading or sponsoring hedge funds or private equity funds.

However, the version that was finally written into the bill contains enough exceptions that even Volcker himself was reportedly disappointed with it.[21] A stronger version proposed by Senators Jeff Merkley and Carl Levin (and supported by Volcker)[22] was kept off the floor in a last-minute procedural maneuver.[23]

Instead of preventing banks from being too big to fail, Dodd-Frank gave regulators new resolution authority to protect the financial system from a collapsing financial institution in a crisis, hoping that fear of being "resolved" would be enough to deter financial institutions from taking excessive risks in the first place. While this is better than nothing, it is highly improbable that authority granted to U.S. regulators over U.S. institutions will be sufficient if a major global bank with subsidiaries in many countries is about to fail. The bill also gives regulators new weapons they can use against big banks, if they so choose. These include the ability to set higher capital requirements for the largest, most important financial institutions, as well as the Kanjorski Amendment (discussed in chapter 7), allowing regulators to force banks to shrink if they pose a risk to the financial system. But whether those weapons will ever be used remains a big question mark.

Just as it had a year earlier when it summoned thirteen bankers to Washington, the Obama administration decided to stick with the banks and the bankers it knew. This decision was not born of corruption, influence peddling, or even any love for the banks. By the middle of 2010, both Barack Obama and Tim Geithner were fed up with an industry that repaid all their efforts to save the major banks—and the bankers' jobs—with all-out attacks in the back rooms of Capitol Hill.[24]

But that decision was born of a belief that America needed the financial system it had, with an oligarchy of megabanks at its pinnacle. Ultimately, the administration agreed with Jamie Dimon that big banks were crucial to the health of the economy and decided it could not live without them. Instead of changing the financial system, the Dodd-Frank Act places its faith in the idea that regulators, armed with additional, sorely needed powers, could constrain its excesses and prevent it from once again torpedoing the global economy.

As we said above, the financial reform bill was a step forward. Doing nothing would have left us with the same financial system that gave us the recent crisis, now even more concentrated and even more emboldened by its ability to call on government support to survive. But Dodd-Frank is not enough. At its core it is a bet on smarter, better regulation—yet it does too little to change the balance of power between Wall Street bankers and Washington officials that was the dominant factor in recent U.S. financial history. The financial sector still has the power to unleash torrential floods of money into the political process. The debate over financial issues is still dominated by people who come from or are going to Wall Street. And the ideology of finance—the idea that behemoth banks peddling increasingly incomprehensible products are somehow good for ordinary people—though shaken, remains dominant in Washington.

On the one hand, it is hard to escape the feeling that we will return to business as usual. In July 2010, only a few days before President Obama signed the Dodd-Frank Act into law, the SEC dropped its charges against Goldman Sachs as part of a settlement agreement. Goldman acknowledged that its marketing materials "contained incomplete information" and that not disclosing Paulson's role in designing the synthetic CDO was a "mistake,"[25] yet insisted that it was not admitting the SEC's allegations.[26] Goldman also agreed to pay a fine of $550 million—the largest penalty ever paid by a Wall Street firm, yet only a fraction of the $3.5 billion in profits the bank had earned in just the first three months of 2010.

And while the job of financial reform remains unfinished, it is not clear who will finish it. Not only do bankers have the incentive to seek short-term profits and ignore long-term risks; politicians also have the incentive to pretend that all is well in the short term and hope the next financial crisis will happen on someone else's watch. The Republican line is that Dodd-Frank is excessive government intrusion into the private sector; the mainstream Democratic line is that Dodd-Frank is the best possible solution. There is no powerful constituency for far-reaching structural reform of the financial system.

But on the other hand, the fight is far from over. The Dodd-Frank Act, though imperfect, marked the end of over three decades of deregulation and nonregulation of the financial sector. As with the Sherman Antitrust Act of 1890, legislation can play a significant role in changing the mainstream consensus. Wall Street's apologists still sing the praises of free market fundamentalism and unfettered financial innovation, but their accustomed air of inevitability and triumphalism is gone. The American public has become deeply skeptical of financial machinations they cannot understand, and many of them have invested untold hours in learning how the financial system works and whom it benefits.

We are perhaps at a pivotal moment in the battle between Jefferson and Hamilton. Hamilton remains ascendant, but his perch appears shaky and his view of finance has been discredited. What happens next will depend, improbably enough, on people like you. We can sigh with relief that the financial crisis is over and go back to our uncomprehending admiration for the fabulously rich men and women of Wall Street. Or we can continue to demand a financial sector that serves the interests of ordinary people and the real economy. In our democratic system, the political establishment, though slowly and very imperfectly, reflects the will of the people. It is there that the rest of this story will play out.

—Simon Johnson and James Kwak,
September 2010

Notes

EPIGRAPH

1. F. Scott Fitzgerald, *The Great Gatsby* (New York: Scribner, 2004), 179. This quotation was used by Bill Moyers to introduce his program on September 19, 2008, the week that Lehman Brothers filed for bankruptcy and AIG was bailed out by the Federal Reserve. *Bill Moyers Journal*, September 19, 2008, transcript available at http://www.pbs.org/moyers/journal/09192008/transcript4.html. It was recommended to us by Graham Smith.

INTRODUCTION

1. Quoted in Eamon Javers, "Inside Obama's Bank CEOs Meeting," *Politico*, April 3, 2009, available at http://www.politico.com/news/stories/0409/20871.html. Also confirmed by ABC News. Rick Klein, "Obama to Bankers: I'm Standing 'Between You and the Pitchforks,' " The Note Blog, available at http://blogs.abcnews.com/thenote/2009/04/obama-to-banker.html.
2. Stock market data are based on the S&P 500 index. Job losses are from Bureau of Labor Statistics, *Current Employment Statistics*, available at http://www.bls.gov/ces/.
3. World output was 2.7 percent lower in Q1 2009 than in Q1 2008; this was the lowest year-over-year figure during the recent global recession. International Monetary Fund, *World Economic Outlook, October 2009: Sustaining the Recovery* (Washington: International Monetary Fund, 2009), 2, available at http://www.imf.org/external/pubs/ft/weo/2009/02/.
4. "List of Bank CEOs Meeting with Obama at the White House," Real Time Economics Blog, *The Wall Street Journal*, March 27, 2009, available at http://blogs.wsj.com/economics/2009/03/27/list-of-bank-ceos-meeting-with-obama-at-the-white-house/.
5. Obama, Gibbs, and Pandit were quoted in Eric Dash, "Bankers Pledge Cooperation with Obama," *The New York Times*, March 27, 2009, available at http://www.nytimes.com/2009/03/28/business/economy/28bank.html. Stumpf was quoted in Jonathan Weisman, Damian Paletta, and Dan Fitzpatrick, "Bankers, Obama in Uneasy Truce," *The Wall Street Journal*, March

28, 2009, available at http://online.wsj.com/article/SB123816459546857301 .html.

6. Javers, "Inside Obama's Bank CEOs Meeting," *supra* note 1.

7. Elizabeth Williamson and Damian Paletta, "Obama Urges Bankers to Back Financial Overhaul," *The Wall Street Journal*, September 15, 2009, available at http://online.wsj.com/article/SB125292937349508441.html.

8. Alan Greenspan, "Current Monetary Policy" (lecture, Haskins Partners Dinner of the Stern School of Business, New York University, New York, May 8, 1997), available at http://www.federalreserve.gov/BoardDocs/Speeches/1997/ 19970508.htm.

9. On Brooksley Born, see Rick Schmitt, "Prophet and Loss," *Stanford Magazine*, March–April 2009, available at http://www.stanfordalumni.org/news/magazine/ 2009/marapr/features/born.html; Manuel Roig-Franzia, "Credit Crisis Cassandra: Brooksley Born's Unheeded Warning Is a Rueful Echo 10 Years On," *The Washington Post*, May 26, 2009, available at http://www.washingtonpost .com/wp-dyn/content/article/2009/05/25/AR2009052502108.html; and "The Warning," *Frontline* (PBS television broadcast October 20, 2009), available at http://www.pbs.org/wgbh/pages/frontline/warning/.

10. Frank Partnoy, *F.I.A.S.C.O.: Blood in the Water on Wall Street* (New York: W. W. Norton, 2009), 59. For another account of the derivatives industry, see Satyajit Das, *Traders, Guns and Money: Knowns and Unknowns in the Dazzling World of Derivatives* (Harlow, England: Prentice Hall, 2006).

11. Bank for International Settlements, *Semi-Annual OTC Derivatives Statistics*, available at http://www.bis.org/statistics/derstats.htm.

12. Quoted in Frank Partnoy, *Infectious Greed: How Deceit and Risk Corrupted the Financial Markets* (New York: Henry Holt, 2004), 163.

13. Alan Greenspan, "Government Regulation and Derivative Contracts" (lecture, Financial Markets Conference of the Federal Reserve Bank of Atlanta, Coral Gables, FL, February 21, 1997), available at http://www.federalreserve .gov/BoardDocs/Speeches/1997/19970221.htm.

14. Quoted in Roig-Franzia, "Credit Crisis Cassandra," *supra* note 9. Summers declined to comment for the Roig-Franzia article. See also interview with Michael Greenberger, *Frontline*, July 14, 2009, transcript available at http:// www.pbs.org/wgbh/pages/frontline/warning/interviews/greenberger.html. Born declined to provide details of her conversations with other government officials. Interview with Brooksley Born, *Frontline*, August 28, 2009, transcript available at http://www.pbs.org/wgbh/pages/frontline/warning/interviews/born.html.

15. *Commodity Futures Modernization Act of 2000*, 106th Cong., 2nd sess., Senate Rep. 106-390, available at http://thomas.loc.gov/cgi-bin/cpquery/?&sid= cp106s5nKF&refer=&r_n=sr390.106&db_id=106&item=&sel=TOC_42836&.

16. Derivatives statistics are from Bank for International Settlements, *Semi-Annual OTC Derivatives Statistics*, *supra* note 11. On the growth and importance of credit default swaps, see Gillian Tett, *Fool's Gold: How the Bold Dream of a Small Tribe at J.P. Morgan Was Corrupted by Wall Street Greed and Unleashed a Catastrophe* (New York: Free Press, 2009).

17. U.S. real GDP declined by 4 percent from Q2 2008 to Q2 2009; Bureau of Economic Analysis, *National Income and Product Accounts*, Table 1.1.6, available at http://bea.gov/national/nipaweb/SelectTable.asp. Actual and projected write-downs are from International Monetary Fund, *Global Financial Stability Report: Responding to the Financial Crisis and Measuring Systemic Risks, April 2009* (Washington: International Monetary Fund, 2009), 32–34, available at http://www.imf.org/External/Pubs/FT/GFSR/2009/01/index.htm.

18. David Cho, "Banks 'Too Big to Fail' Have Grown Even Bigger: Behemoths Born of the Bailout Reduce Consumer Choice, Tempt Corporate Moral Hazard," *The Washington Post*, August 28, 2009, available at http://www.washingtonpost.com/wp-dyn/content/article/2009/08/27/AR2009082704193.html; Elizabeth Hester and Elisa Martinuzzi, "JPMorgan Tightens Grip on Equity Sales by Selling Own Shares," Bloomberg, June 28, 2009, available at http://www.bloomberg.com/apps/news?pid=20601087&sid=aYlWNEyLQzPk.

19. Press Release, Goldman Sachs, "Goldman Sachs Reports Third Quarter Earnings per Common Share of $5.25," October 15, 2009, available at http://www2.goldmansachs.com/our-firm/press/press-releases/current/pdfs/2009-q3-earnings.pdf.

20. John Gapper, "Master of Risk Who Did God's Work for Goldman Sachs but Won It Little Love," *Financial Times*, December 23, 2009, available at http://www.ft.com/cms/s/0/479ac4ba-eb32-11de-bc99-00144feab49a.html.

21. In 2007, 3.2 percent of U.S. GDP was $450 billion. Bureau of Economic Analysis, *supra* note 17, at Table 1.1.5. Data for 1983 are from Gary H. Stern and Ron J. Feldman, *Too Big to Fail: The Hazards of Bank Bailouts* (Washington: Brookings Institution Press, 2009), 65. Data for 2007 are from *Federal Reserve Statistical Release, Large Commercial Banks*, December 31, 2007, available at http://www.federalreserve.gov/releases/lbr/20071231/default.htm, and from the annual reports of Goldman Sachs, Morgan Stanley, Merrill Lynch, and Lehman Brothers.

22. Annualized GDP in Q1 2009 was $14.178 trillion. Bureau of Economic Analysis, *supra* note 17, at Table 1.1.5. Asset data are from company quarterly reports.

CHAPTER 1: THOMAS JEFFERSON AND THE FINANCIAL ARISTOCRACY

1. Theodore Roosevelt, "State of the Union Message," December 3, 1901, in John T. Woolley and Gerhard Peters, *The American Presidency Project*, available at http://www.presidency.ucsb.edu/ws/index.php?pid=29542.

2. Jefferson thought and wrote extensively about economic issues. See, e.g., Herbert E. Sloan, *Principle and Interest: Thomas Jefferson and the Problem of Debt* (Charlottesville: University Press of Virginia, 2001). For the broader context, see Drew McCoy, *The Elusive Republic: Political Economy in Jeffersonian America* (Chapel Hill: University of North Carolina Press, 1980).

3. From a letter to John Taylor, in Albert Ellery Bergh, ed., *The Writings of Thomas Jefferson*, Volume XV (Washington: Thomas Jefferson Memorial Association, 1907), 23.

4. Ron Chernow, *Alexander Hamilton* (New York: Penguin, 2004), 352.

5. Jerry W. Markham, *A Financial History of the United States, Volume I: From Christopher Columbus to the Robber Barons (1492–1900)* (Armonk, NY: M. E. Sharpe, 2002), 89–90.

6. Thomas Jefferson, "Jefferson's Opinion on the Constitutionality of a National Bank," in Paul Leicester Ford, ed., *The Federalist: A Commentary on the Constitution of the United States by Alexander Hamilton, James Madison and John Jay* (New York: Henry Holt, 1898), available at http://avalon.law.yale.edu/18th_century/bank-tj.asp; Alexander Hamilton, "Hamilton's Opinion as to the Constitutionality of the Bank of the United States," in Ford, *supra*, available at http://avalon.law.yale.edu/18th_century/bank-ah.asp.

7. Chernow, *Alexander Hamilton, supra* note 4, at 353–54.

8. Richard Scott Carnell, Jonathan R. Macey, and Geoffrey P. Miller, *The Law of Banking and Financial Institutions*, fourth edition (Austin: Wolters Kluwer Law & Business, 2009), 2–5.

9. Richard Sylla, "Financial Systems and Economic Modernization," *Journal of Economic History* 62 (2002): 277–92; Peter L. Rousseau, "Historical Perspectives on Financial Development and Economic Growth," *Federal Reserve Bank of St. Louis Review* (July–August 2003): 81–106; and Peter L. Rousseau and Richard Sylla, "Emerging Financial Markets and Early U.S. Growth," *Explorations in Economic History* 42 (2005): 1–26. As the need for large amounts of capital increased (e.g., for canals and railroads), new corporate forms evolved. Jonathan Barron Baskin and Paul J. Miranti, Jr., *A History of Corporate Finance* (Cambridge: Cambridge University Press, 1997). This does not imply that all necessary institutions were in place and functioning smoothly in the United States by 1800; see Bruce Mann, *Republic of Debtors: Bankruptcy in the Age of American Independence* (Cambridge: Harvard University Press, 2002).

10. Rousseau and Sylla, "Emerging Financial Markets," *supra* note 9, at 3. Rousseau and Sylla stress that the United States developed the first truly competitive banking system. Stephen Haber explores how this system emerged from the political logic of competition between states. Stephen Haber, "Political Institutions and Financial Development: Evidence from the Political Economy of Bank Regulation in the United States and Mexico," in Stephen Haber, Douglass C. North, and Barry R. Weingast, eds., *Political Institutions and Financial Development* (Palo Alto: Stanford University Press, 2008): 10–59. For more on the political origins of the American corporate legal environment, see Lawrence E. Mitchell, *The Speculation Economy: How Finance Triumphed over Industry* (San Francisco: Berrett-Koehler, 2007).

11. Markham, *Financial History*, Volume I, *supra* note 5, at 83, 90. His reports to Congress included one on the subject of manufactures and two on public credit. See Chernow, *Alexander Hamilton, supra* note 4.

12. The national debt argument and its outcome are covered in Robert E. Wright, *One Nation Under Debt: Hamilton, Jefferson, and the History of What We Owe* (New York: McGraw-Hill, 2008). See also Albert Jay Nock, *Mr. Jefferson* (New York: Harcourt, Brace, 1926), chapter 5; and Willard Sterne Randall, *Thomas Jefferson: A Life* (New York: Harper Perennial, 1994), chapter 19.

13. Chernow, *Alexander Hamilton*, *supra* note 4, at 345. More generally, Chernow argues that Hamilton interpreted and applied the Constitution in ways that were intended to help commerce develop.

14. Rousseau and Sylla, "Emerging Financial Markets," *supra* note 9, at 5.

15. "The state-chartered banks, like the federally chartered [Bank of the United States], were corporations with limited liability, which is a major reason why they were able to attract so much capital." Ibid.

16. Richard Sylla, "U.S. Securities Markets and the Banking System, 1790–1840," *Federal Reserve Bank of St. Louis Review* (May–June 1998): 83–98, at 93. His comparison is based on converting U.K. bank capital into dollars at the then prevailing market exchange rate.

17. Richard Sylla, Jack W. Wilson, and Robert E. Wright, "America's First Securities Markets: Emergence, Development, and Integration" (working paper presented at the Cliometric Society Meetings, Toronto, and the NBER Summer Institute, 1997).

18. Rousseau and Sylla, "Emerging Financial Markets," *supra* note 9, at 8–9.

19. On the importance of personal relationships in early U.S. banking, see Naomi Lamoreaux, *Insider Lending: Banks, Personal Connections, and Economic Development in Industrial New England* (Cambridge: Cambridge University Press, 1996).

20. Richard Hofstadter, *The American Political Tradition and the Men Who Made It* (New York: Alfred A. Knopf, 1948).

21. Calvin Coolidge, "The Press Under a Free Government" (lecture, American Society of Newspaper Editors, Washington, D.C., January 17, 1925), in Calvin Coolidge, *Foundations of the Republic: Speeches and Addresses* (Freeport, NY: Books for Libraries Press, 1968), 183–90, at 187.

22. Bray Hammond argues that some of Jackson's strongest supporters were actually New York bankers who opposed the Second Bank because it was based in Philadelphia; they wanted some of its more lucrative functions for themselves. Bray Hammond, *Banks and Politics in America from the Revolution to the Civil War* (Princeton: Princeton University Press, 1957).

23. Carnell et al., *Law of Banking*, *supra* note 8, at 5.

24. The Second Bank was not a central bank in the modern sense. Peter Temin, *The Jacksonian Economy* (New York: W. W. Norton, 1969), 53.

25. Richard H. Timberlake, *Monetary Policy in the United States: An Intellectual and Institutional History* (Chicago: University of Chicago Press, 1993), chapter 3. See also Temin, *Jacksonian Economy*, *supra* note 24.

26. Arthur Schlesinger, *The Age of Jackson* (New York: Book Find Club, 1945), chapter 7.

27. Quoted in ibid. at 102. Emphasis in original.

28. On the Bank War in general, see Markham, *Financial History*, Volume I, *supra* note 5, at 141–46.

29. Ibid. at 145.

30. Andrew Jackson, "Veto Message," July 10, 1832, in James D. Richardson, ed., *Messages and Papers of the Presidents (Volume II, Part 3: Andrew Jackson, March 4, 1829, to March 4, 1833)*, available at http://onlinebooks.library.upenn.edu/webbin/gutbook/lookup?num=10858.

31. Quoted in Jon Meacham, *American Lion: Andrew Jackson in the White House* (New York: Random House, 2008), 201. Emphasis in original.

32. Markham, *Financial History*, Volume I, *supra* note 5, at 145. The actual economic power of Biddle should not be exaggerated; the ensuing recession was small despite the strong rhetoric on all sides. Temin, *Jacksonian Economy*, *supra* note 24.

33. The Bank of England began as a powerful commercial bank and, during the nineteenth century, became in part a central bank. *Report of the Committee on Finance and Industry, British Parliamentary Reports on International Finance, The Cunliffe Committee and the Macmillan Committee Reports* (New York: Arno, 1978), chapter 4. On the origins of the Bank of England, see Steve Pincus, *1688: The First Modern Revolution* (New Haven: Yale University Press, 2009).

34. Robert V. Remini, *The Life of Andrew Jackson* (New York: Harper Perennial, 2001); Meacham, *American Lion, supra* note 31.

35. Quoted in Schlesinger, *Age of Jackson, supra* note 26, at 84 (emphasis in original). Webster received a retainer as one of the Bank's lawyers. Still, in Schlesinger's assessment, "Webster fought for [the Bank] in great part because it was a dependable source of private revenue." Schlesinger also points out that both opponents and supporters of the Bank were in its debt. Ibid. at 86, n. 22.

36. Meacham, *American Lion, supra* note 31; Robert V. Remini, *Andrew Jackson and the Bank War* (New York: W. W. Norton, 1967).

37. Carnell et al., *Law of Banking, supra* note 8, at 4–5.

38. Nelson W. Aldrich, "The Work of the National Monetary Commission" (lecture, Economic Club of New York, November 29, 1909), available at http://books.google.com/books?id=vDcuAAAAYAAJ. For Aldrich's assessment, see Nathaniel Wright Stephenson, *Nelson W. Aldrich: A Leader in American Politics* (New York: Charles Scribner's Sons, 1930).

39. Stephen Haber, "Financial Markets and Industrial Development: A Comparative Study of Governmental Regulation, Financial Innovation, and Industrial Structure in Brazil and Mexico, 1840–1930," in Stephen Haber, ed., *How Latin America Fell Behind: Essays on the Economic Histories of Brazil and Mexico, 1800–1914* (Palo Alto: Stanford University Press, 1997); Stephen Haber, "Politics, Banking, and Economic Development: Evidence from New World Economies," in Jared Diamond and James Robinson, eds., *Natural Experiments of History* (Cambridge: Harvard University Press, 2009): 88–119. On emerging markets, see chapter 2 of this book. On the general problem of elites blocking economic development, see Daron Acemoglu, James Robinson, and Simon Johnson, "Institutions as the Fundamental Cause of Long-Run Growth," in Philippe Aghion and Steve Durlauf, eds., *Handbook of Economic Growth* (Amsterdam: North-Holland, 2005).

40. The United States had strong institutions—tending to control the power of elites—due to its colonial experience, in contrast to those of Latin America. Acemoglu et al., "Institutions as the Fundamental Cause of Long-Run Growth," *supra* note 39. Jefferson's ideas and Jackson's success at opposing concentrated power in part reflected those strong institutions.

41. The latest historical work suggests that the United States moved away from agriculture and adopted industrial technologies and new forms of commercial organization earlier than previously believed. See Charles Sellers, *The Market Revolution: Jacksonian America, 1815–1846* (Oxford: Oxford University Press, 1991); David Reynolds, *America, Empire of Liberty* (New York: Basic Books, 2009); and Daniel Walker Howe, *What Hath God Wrought: The Transformation of America, 1815–1848* (Oxford: Oxford University Press, 2007).

42. Lamoreaux, *Insider Lending, supra* note 19; Robert E. Wright, *The Wealth of Nations Rediscovered: Integration and Expansion in American Financial Markets, 1780–1850* (Cambridge: Cambridge University Press, 2002). This point has been emphasized by IMF first deputy managing director John Lipsky. John Lipsky, "Finance and Economic Growth" (lecture, Bank of Mexico Conference, "Challenges and Strategies for Promoting Economic Growth," Mexico City, Mexico, October 19, 2009), available at http://www.imf.org/external/np/speeches/2009/101909.htm.

43. Rousseau and Sylla, "Emerging Financial Markets," *supra* note 9.

44. Hofstadter, *American Political Tradition, supra* note 20, at chapter 7; Matthew Josephson, *The Robber Barons* (San Diego: Harcourt Brace, 1934).

45. Kevin Phillips, *Wealth and Democracy: A Political History of the American Rich* (New York: Broadway Books, 2003), 239–40; Hofstadter, *American Political Tradition, supra* note 20, at chapter 7; Nathaniel Wright Stephenson, *Nelson W. Aldrich, supra* note 38; Edmund Morris, *Theodore Rex* (New York: Random House, 2001).

46. Daron Acemoglu and James A. Robinson, "Economic Backwardness in Political Perspective," *American Political Science Review* 100 (2006): 115–31.

47. On income levels, see Daron Acemoglu, Simon Johnson, and James A. Robinson, "The Colonial Origins of Comparative Development: An Empirical Investigation," *American Economic Review* 91 (2001): 1369–1401; and Daron Acemoglu, Simon Johnson, and James A. Robinson, "Reversal of Fortune: Geography and Institutions in the Making of the Modern World Income Distribution," *Quarterly Journal of Economics* 118 (2002): 1231–94. On Mexican finance, see Haber, "Political Institutions and Financial Development," *supra* note 10; Stephen Haber and Noel Maurer, "Related Lending and Economic Performance: Evidence from Mexico," *The Journal of Economic History* 67 (2007): 551–81; and Noel Maurer, *The Power and the Profits: The Mexican Financial System, 1876–1932* (Palo Alto: Stanford University Press, 2002). The Haber and Maurer paper argues that, in the Mexican case, concentration in the banking sector was compatible with effective corporate governance, but did lead to concentration in nonfinancial industries. On financial development and growth in other countries, see Peter L. Rousseau and Richard Sylla, "Financial Revolutions and Economic Growth: Introducing This EEH Symposium," *Explorations in Economic History* 43 (2006): 1–12; and Michael D. Bordo and Peter L. Rousseau, "Legal-Political Factors and the Historical Evolution of the Finance-Growth Link," *European Review of Economic History* 10 (2006): 421–44.

48. Hofstadter, *American Political Tradition, supra* note 20, at chapter 7.

49. Alfred Chandler, *The Visible Hand: The Managerial Revolution in American Business* (Cambridge, MA: Belknap Press, 1976).

50. Thomas K. McCraw, *Prophets of Regulation* (Cambridge, MA: Belknap Press, 1984), 98.

51. Charles R. Morris, *The Tycoons: How Andrew Carnegie, John D. Rockefeller, Jay Gould, and J. P. Morgan Invented the American Supereconomy* (New York: Henry Holt, 2005), chapter 8.

52. Ibid. at 235; this estimate is for the "liquid industrial, commercial, and financial capital of the United States" that was guided by Morgan directly or indirectly. Brad DeLong finds that "in 1911–12 the presence on one's board of directors of a partner in J.P. Morgan and Co. added about 30 percent to common stock equity value, and about 15 percent to the total market value of the firm." J. Bradford DeLong, "Did J. P. Morgan's Men Add Value? An Economist's Perspective on Financial Capitalism," in Peter Temin, ed., *Inside the Business Enterprise: Historical Perspectives on the Use of Information* (Chicago: University of Chicago Press, 1991): 205–36. See also Ron Chernow, *The House of Morgan: An American Banking Dynasty and the Rise of Modern Finance* (New York: Grove, 2001); Jean Strouse, *Morgan: American Financier* (New York: Random House, 1999); and David M. Kotz, *Bank Control of Large Corporations in the United States* (Berkeley and Los Angeles: University of California Press, 1978).

53. Roosevelt, "State of the Union Message," *supra* note 1.

54. The origins of the Sherman Antitrust Act remain somewhat shrouded in mystery. It appears to have been part of a broader political deal that allowed the Republicans to increase the tariff. There is no indication that it was intended to be used against big business; nor was it used in that manner for the first decade after it passed. See Thomas W. Hazlett, "The Legislative History of the Sherman Act Re-examined," *Economic Inquiry* 30 (1992): 263–76.

55. *Northern Securities Co. v. United States*, 193 U.S. 197 (1904). For the development of Roosevelt's antitrust approach, see Morris, *Theodore Rex, supra* note 45.

56. Morris, *Theodore Rex, supra* note 45, at 91. The conversation took place on the morning of February 22, 1902.

57. On Roosevelt's intellectual antecedents, how he saw his place in the American tradition, and his political objections to concentrated commercial power, see Hofstadter, *American Political Tradition, supra* note 20, at chapter 9. Roosevelt's earlier thinking and interaction with the Republican Party machine and industrial interests are covered in Edmund Morris, *The Rise of Theodore Roosevelt* (New York: Modern Library, 2001).

58. George J. Stigler, "The Economists and the Problem of Monopoly," *American Economic Review* 72 (1982): 1–12.

59. The mergers were a way to remove "excess capacity" in some industries, but did not create more efficient operations. There was no systematic antitrust policy in the face of this merger wave; see Naomi R. Lamoreaux, *The Great Merger Movement in American Business, 1895–1904* (Cambridge: Cambridge University Press, 2008).

60. On the crisis of 1907, see Morris, *Theodore Rex, supra* note 45; Chernow, *House of Morgan, supra* note 52; Robert F. Bruner and Sean D. Carr, *The Panic of 1907: Lessons Learned from the Market's Perfect Storm* (Hoboken, NJ: John Wiley & Sons, 2007).

61. On financial crises in general, see Charles P. Kindleberger, *Manias, Panics, and Crashes: A History of Financial Crises,* fourth edition (Hoboken, NJ: Wiley, 2000). On the role of credit in booms and busts, see also Wesley C. Mitchell, *Business Cycles* (Berkeley: University of California Press, 1913). On the banking panics between the National Bank Act of 1863 and the creation of the Fed, see Elmus Wicker, *Banking Panics of the Gilded Age* (Cambridge: Cambridge University Press, 2000).

62. On the "financial accelerator," see Ben S. Bernanke, "The Financial Accelerator and the Credit Channel" (lecture, The Credit Channel of Monetary Policy in the Twenty-first Century Conference, Federal Reserve Bank of Atlanta, Atlanta, Georgia, June 15, 2007), available at http://www.federalreserve.gov/newsevents/speech/Bernanke20070615a.htm; Ben S. Bernanke, "Non-Monetary Effects of the Financial Crisis in the Propagation of the Great Depression," *American Economic Review* 73 (1983): 257–76; and Ben S. Bernanke and Mark Gertler, "Agency Costs, Net Worth, and Business Fluctuations," *American Economic Review* 79 (1989): 14–31.

63. Chernow, *House of Morgan, supra* note 52, at 123–24.

64. For a detailed history of the formation of the Fed and a discussion of the roles of Aldrich and others, see Elmus Wicker, *The Great Debate on Banking Reform: Nelson Aldrich and the Origins of the Fed* (Columbus: Ohio State University Press, 2005). Wicker traces the origins of the Fed back to the banking panic of 1893–1894.

65. Aldrich, "The Work of the National Monetary Commission," *supra* note 38.

66. Chernow, *House of Morgan, supra* note 52; Stephenson, *Nelson W. Aldrich, supra* note 38; and Melvin Urofsky, *Louis Brandeis: A Life* (New York: Pantheon, 2009).

67. Quoted in "The 'Money Trust,'" *The New York Times,* July 24, 1911, available at http://query.nytimes.com/gst/abstract.html?res=9F05E4DD1131E233A25757C2A9619C946096D6CF.

68. For the reports of the Pujo Committee, see Federal Reserve Archival System for Economic Research, *Money Trust Investigation. Investigation of Financial and Monetary Conditions in the United States Under House Resolutions Nos. 429 and 504,* available at http://fraser.stlouisfed.org/publications/montru/.

69. Louis Brandeis, "Our Financial Oligarchy," *Harper's Weekly,* November 1913.

70. Louis Brandeis, *Other People's Money, and How the Bankers Use It* (New York: F. A. Stokes, 1914), 4. *Other People's Money* republished a series of articles that originally appeared in *Harper's Weekly.* See also Alexander D. Noyes, "The Money Trust," *The Atlantic Monthly,* May 1913, 653–67.

71. For the history of the Fed, see Milton Friedman and Anna Jacobson Schwartz, *A Monetary History of the United States, 1867–1960* (Princeton: Princeton University Press, 1963); and Alan H. Meltzer, *A History of the Federal Reserve, Vol-*

ume 1, 1913–1951 (Chicago: University of Chicago Press, 2003). For the political compromise that created the Federal Reserve, see David Wessel, *In Fed We Trust: Ben Bernanke's War on the Great Panic* (New York: Crown Business, 2009), 36–38.

72. A version of this idea is central to the historical account in Kindleberger, *Manias, Panics, and Crashes, supra* note 61.

73. Quoted in Urofsky, *Louis Brandeis, supra* note 66, at 346.

74. This was not a new view, but it had previously been held only by "populists" or "progressives" who were not generally part of the mainstream consensus. See, e.g., Michael McGerr, *A Fierce Discontent: The Rise and Fall of the Progressive Movement in America, 1870–1920* (Oxford: Oxford University Press, 2005).

75. David M. Kennedy, *Over Here: The First World War and American Society* (Oxford: Oxford University Press, 2004), chapter 2.

76. Ironically, the origins of the "laissez-faire" philosophy lay in opposition to big business and monopoly power based on state charters and other restrictions on free entry. From the late nineteenth century there was an active debate in the United States about the extent to which this doctrine was still relevant; see Lawrence E. Mitchell, *The Speculation Economy: How Finance Triumphed over Industry* (San Francisco: Berrett-Koehler, 2008). By 1920 "laissez faire" rhetoric was a mainstay of big business, for example as represented by Andrew Mellon and Herbert Hoover, as part of its resistance to regulation (as represented by Brandeis). See David Cannadine, *Mellon: An American Life* (New York: Vintage, 2008); McCraw, *Prophets of Regulation, supra* note 50; and Urofsky, *Louis Brandeis, supra* note 66.

77. Calvin Coolidge, "The Press Under a Free Government," *supra* note 21.

78. Cannadine, *Mellon, supra* note 76; Hofstadter, *American Political Tradition, supra* note 20, at chapter 11. Harding is quoted in Cannadine, *Mellon,* at 277.

79. McCraw, *Prophets of Regulation, supra* note 50, at chapters 4 and 5.

80. Jerry W. Markham, *A Financial History of the United States, Volume II: From J. P. Morgan to the Institutional Investor (1900–1970)* (Armonk, NY: M. E. Sharpe, 2002), chapter 4. Deposit-taking commercial banks were allowed to promote securities; Charles E. Mitchell rose to prominence at National City Bank doing just that—on a salary of $25,000 a year, Mitchell's bonuses pushed his total compensation to $3.5 million between 1927 and 1929. Ibid. at 117. The McFadden Act of 1926 "codified the existing practice of buying and selling 'investment' securities by national banks." Ibid. at 113.

81. J. K. Galbraith, *The Great Crash, 1929* (New York: Mariner, 2009); Charles R. Geisst, *Wall Street: A History from Its Beginnings to the Fall of Enron* (Oxford: Oxford University Press, 2004).

82. The operation of the gold standard meant that the Fed adjusted interest rates to reflect flows of gold in and out of the country; monetary policy was affected more by developments in major European trading nations than by concerns about speculative bubbles. The broader economic philosophy was: stay on gold, let the private sector sort out its own problems, and all will be well. For more details, see Barry Eichengreen, *Golden Fetters: The Gold Standard and the*

Great Depression, 1919–1939 (New York: Oxford University Press, 1992); Lester V. Chandler, *Benjamin Strong: Central Banker* (Washington: Brookings Institution Press, 1958); and Liaquat Ahamed, *Lords of Finance: The Bankers Who Broke the World* (New York: Penguin, 2009).

83. Galbraith, *The Great Crash, supra* note 81; Kindleberger, *Manias, Panics, and Crashes, supra* note 61.

84. Quoted in William Greider, *Secrets of the Temple: How the Federal Reserve Runs the Country* (New York: Simon & Schuster, 1987), 65.

85. The definitive source for interest rates is Sidney Homer and Richard Sylla, *A History of Interest Rates,* fourth edition (Hoboken, NJ: Wiley, 2005). Friedman and Schwartz argue that even the tightening in 1928 was a mistake. Friedman and Schwartz, *Monetary History, supra* note 71. See also Ben S. Bernanke, "Money, Gold, and the Great Depression" (H. Parker Willis Lecture in Economic Policy, Washington and Lee University, Lexington, VA, March 2, 2004), available at http://www.federalreserve.gov/boarddocs/speeches/2004/200403022/default.htm.

86. Ahamed, *Lords of Finance, supra* note 82; Chandler, *Benjamin Strong, supra* note 82.

87. The Fed was weak by modern standards, but it was not without some power—see William L. Silber, *When Washington Shut Down Wall Street: The Great Financial Crisis of 1914 and the Origins of America's Monetary Supremacy* (Princeton: Princeton University Press, 2007).

88. There was an active debate within the Federal Reserve system, with the New York Fed (which had more autonomy than today) favoring tighter conditions for credit, while the board in Washington preferred to keep the boom going. Meltzer, *History of the Federal Reserve, supra* note 71; Friedman and Schwartz, *Monetary History, supra* note 71; Ahamed, *Lords of Finance, supra* note 82; Cannadine, *Mellon, supra* note 76.

89. Quoted in Ahamed, *Lords of Finance, supra* note 82, at 360; Harrison was at odds with the Federal Reserve Board, but still lent over $100 million into the market. Ibid. at 358–59. He also persuaded the board to cut interest rates from November, but other members of the Fed Board were reluctant to go further. Ibid. at 365, 369.

90. Ibid. at chapter 20.

91. Friedman and Schwartz stressed the importance of a decline in the money supply. Friedman and Schwartz, *Monetary History, supra* note 71. Bernanke argued that the real problem was the failure of banks, as these had local information about borrowers that disappeared when they collapsed. Bernanke, "Non-Monetary Effects," *supra* note 62. See also Alan H. Meltzer, *History of the Federal Reserve, supra* note 71, at chapter 5. The major bank failures began in late 1930 with the Bank of the United States (no relation to the U.S. government). For the full dynamics of the bank failures, see Elmus Wicker, *The Banking Panics of the Great Depression* (Cambridge: Cambridge University Press, 1996).

92. Within New York, the largest banks (e.g., J.P. Morgan, Chase, National City) rescued other large banks (e.g., Kidder Peabody) but declined to save the less

prominent Bank of the United States at the end of 1930; this helped trigger wider runs on banks. Ahamed, *Lords of Finance, supra* note 82, at 387–88.

93. Eichengreen, *Golden Fetters, supra* note 82; Peter Temin, *Lessons from the Great Depression* (Cambridge: MIT Press, 1989). Chang-Tai Hsieh and Christina D. Romer are skeptical, at least with regard to the monetary expansion in 1932. Chang-Tai Hsieh and Christina Romer, "Was the Federal Reserve Constrained by the Gold Standard During the Great Depression? Evidence from the 1932 Open Market Purchase Program," *Journal of Economic History* 66 (2006): 140–76, at 172. On the debate over the cause of the Great Depression, see also Peter Temin, *Did Monetary Forces Cause the Great Depression?* (New York: W. W. Norton, 1976); Charles H. Feinstein, Peter Temin, and Gianni Toniolo, *The World Economy Between the World Wars* (Oxford: Oxford University Press, 2008); and Christina D. Romer, "Great Depression," in *Encyclopedia Britannica* (2003), available at http://elsa.berkeley.edu/~cromer/great_depression.pdf. Besides the theories that the Depression resulted from mistakes by the Federal Reserve and that it was caused by the international gold standard, another explanation is that the international community was unable to deal with shocks in Europe. Ahamed, *Lords of Finance, supra* note 82. Alternatively, the federal government may have simply lacked the capacity to counteract the contraction in the private sector, since federal government spending was only 2.5 percent of GDP before the 1929 crash.

94. National City Bank, for example, paid high bonuses tied to selling risky stock. More generally, the prudential standards in banking were lax; Markham, *Financial History,* Volume II, *supra* note 80.

95. Geisst, *Wall Street, supra* note 81, at 214–15, 224–25.

96. On the relationship between private sector banks and the Federal Reserve and regulation more generally, see John T. Woolley, *Monetary Politics: The Federal Reserve and the Politics of Monetary Policy* (Cambridge: Cambridge University Press, 1984), chapter 4. On the history of Federal Reserve politics, see Greider, *Secrets of the Temple, supra* note 84.

97. H. W. Brands, *Traitor to His Class: The Privileged Life and Radical Presidency of Franklin Delano Roosevelt* (New York: Anchor, 2008), 431.

98. Quotations in this paragraph are from ibid. at 450; a slightly later but similar statement is quoted in David M. Kennedy, *Freedom from Fear: The American People in Depression and War, 1929–1945* (Oxford: Oxford University Press, 1999), 282. Roosevelt did not mention Jackson's mistreatment of American Indians. See, e.g., H. W. Brands, *Andrew Jackson: His Life and Times* (New York: Anchor, 2005); Remini, *Life of Andrew Jackson, supra* note 34.

99. Arthur M. Schlesinger, Jr., *The Coming of the New Deal: 1933–1935* (Boston: Mariner, 2003), 444.

100. Carnell et al., *Law of Banking, supra* note 8, at 17.

101. Ibid. at 20.

102. Allen N. Berger, Richard J. Herring, and Giorgio P. Szego, "The Role of Capital in Financial Institutions," *Journal of Banking and Finance* 19 (1995): 393–430. Double liability existed in some states, and for nationally chartered banks

from the National Banking Act of 1863, and only ended with the Banking Acts of 1933 and 1935. Anthony Saunders and Berry Wilson, "Contingent Liability in Banking: Useful Policy for Developing Countries?" (Policy Research Working Paper 1538, World Bank, November 1995). Comparable data are not available prior to 1850.

103. The figure is from David Moss, "An Ounce of Prevention: Financial Regulation, Moral Hazard, and the End of 'Too Big to Fail,'" *Harvard Magazine*, September–October 2009, available at http://harvardmagazine.com/2009/09/financial-risk-management-plan. Data are from Bureau of the Census, *Historical Statistics of the United States: Colonial Times to 1970, Part 2* (Washington: U.S. Government Printing Office, 1975), Series X-741; Federal Deposit Insurance Corporation, "Failures and Assistance Transactions," *Historical Statistics on Banking*, available at http://www2.fdic.gov/hsob/SelectRpt.asp?EntryTyp=30.

104. Leading independent students of central banking argue that thin equity layers make sense only when there is tight regulation. See, e.g., Charles Goodhart, "Financial Crisis and the Future of the Financial System" (paper presented at the 100th BRE Bank–CASE Seminar, Warsaw, Poland, January 22, 2009).

105. See G. J. Bentson, *The Separation of Commercial and Investment Banking* (London: Macmillan, 1990); and Alexander Tabarrok, "The Separation of Commercial and Investment Banking: The Morgans vs. the Rockefellers," *The Quarterly Journal of Austrian Economics* 1 (1998): 1–18.

106. Thomas Philippon, "The Evolution of the U.S. Financial Industry from 1860 to 2007: Theory and Evidence" (working paper, New York University, NBER, CEPR, November 2008), available at http://pages.stern.nyu.edu/~tphilipp/papers/finsize.pdf.

CHAPTER 2: OTHER PEOPLE'S OLIGARCHS

1. Republic of Korea, "Korea Letter of Intent to the IMF," December 3, 1997, available at http://www.imf.org/external/np/loi/120397.htm.

2. *Time*, February 15, 1999, available at http://www.time.com/time/covers/0,16641,19990215,00.html.

3. Korea was a leading example of what the World Bank famously and perhaps prematurely termed "The East Asian Miracle." *The East Asian Miracle: Economic Growth and Public Policy*, World Bank Policy Research Report (Oxford: Oxford University Press, 1993).

4. Sung Wook Joh, "Corporate Governance and Firm Profitability: Evidence from Korea Before the Economic Crisis," *Journal of Financial Economics* 68 (2003): 287–322, available at http://ideas.repec.org/a/eee/jfinec/v68y2003i2p287-322.html.

5. These ratios are calculated by aggregating total debt and equity up to the chaebol level. Calculated from National Information Credit Evaluation data, as used in Todd Gormley, Simon Johnson, and Changyong Rhee, " 'Too Big to Fail': Government Policy vs. Investor Perceptions" (working paper, November

2009). Figures are for the end of calendar year 1997, and may be affected by currency depreciation if the companies borrowed in foreign currency. But the debt-equity ratios at the end of 1996 were also high: Daewoo's ratio was 3.3, Samsung's was 2.6, and Hyundai's was 4.1.

6. In 1997, the average debt-equity ratio of Korean firms far exceeded that of other countries (Korea, 396 percent; United States, 154 percent; Japan, 193 percent; and Taiwan, 86 percent). Joh, "Corporate Governance and Firm Profitability," *supra* note 4. Se-Jik Kim has slightly different data and puts the debt-equity ratio of Korean firms at 350 percent in 1996, with most of the debt being bank loans. Se-Jik Kim, "Bailout and Conglomeration," *Journal of Financial Economics* 71 (2004): 315–47, at 317. There is no disagreement that the Korean corporate sector was one of the most highly indebted in the world.

7. Anne O. Krueger and Jungho Yoo, "Falling Profitability, Higher Borrowing Costs, and Chaebol Finances During the Korean Crisis," in David T. Coe and Se-Jik Kim, eds., *Korean Crisis and Recovery* (Washington: International Monetary Fund and Korea Institute for International Economic Policy, 2002). For more background on chaebol development, see Eun Mee Kim, *Big Business, Strong State: Collusion and Conflict in South Korean Development, 1960–1990* (Albany: State University of New York Press, 1997).

8. For example, the founder of Hyundai, Chung Ju Yong, formed a political party and ran in the presidential election of 1992.

9. Joh reports chaebol rankings for each year from 1993 through 1997 from the Korea Fair Trade Commission. Joh, "Corporate Governance and Firm Profitability," *supra* note 4, at Table 10. Based on total assets belonging to firms in the same chaebol, Hanbo was number 14 in 1995, up from number 28 in 1994.

10. See Donald Kirk, *Korean Crisis: Unraveling of the Miracle in the IMF Era* (New York: Palgrave, 2001), chapter 8.

11. See Stephan Haggard, *The Political Economy of the Asian Financial Crisis* (Washington: Peterson Institute for International Economics, 2000), 56–57.

12. Sung Wook Joh, "Korean Corporate Governance and Firm Performance" (working paper, 12th NBER seminar on East Asian Economics, 2001).

13. Joh, "Corporate Governance and Firm Profitability," *supra* note 4. See also Jae-Seung Baek, Jun-Koo Kang, and Kyung Suh Park, "Corporate Governance and Firm Value: Evidence from the Korean Financial Crisis," *Journal of Financial Economics* 71 (2004): 265–313.

14. Details of Korea's economic performance immediately prior to the crisis are in "Korea Letter of Intent to the IMF," *supra* note 1.

15. For a timeline of events, see Congressional Research Service Report for Congress, *The 1997–98 Asian Financial Crisis*, February 6, 1998, available at http://www.fas.org/man/crs/crs-asia2.htm. For more detail on the banking dynamics, see Philippe F. Delhaise, *Asia in Crisis: The Implosion of the Banking and Finance Systems* (Singapore: John Wiley & Sons [Asia], 1998).

16. "By the end of 1997, 6.7% of all loans were nonperforming loans, totaling 64.7 trillion won (over $45.6 billion). . . . By June 1998, over 10% of all loans were nonperforming loans. These nonperforming loans severely weakened many

banks and eventually provoked the liquidity crisis." Joh, "Corporate Governance and Firm Profitability," *supra* note 4, at 292.

17. "Korea Letter of Intent to the IMF," *supra* note 1. Further reforms affecting the financial sector were included in a second Letter of Intent on December 24, 1997, which allowed Korea to access further IMF funding. Republic of Korea, "[Second] Korea Letter of Intent to the IMF," December 24, 1997, available at http://www.imf.org/external/np/loi/122497.htm. See James M. Boughton, *Tearing Down the Walls: The International Monetary Fund, 1990–1999* (Washington: International Monetary Fund, 2010) (forthcoming), chapter 11. Paul Blustein explains the U.S. role in arranging this additional support (which included official loans and an agreement that foreign banks would not demand immediate repayment of their loans to Korea). Paul Blustein, *The Chastening: Inside the Crisis That Rocked the Global Financial System and Humbled the IMF*, revised edition (New York: PublicAffairs, 2001), chapter 7.

18. The IMF agreement was negotiated in the run-up to the presidential election, but the incoming president clearly expressed his support at critical moments and his team implemented the reforms. Blustein, *The Chastening*, *supra* note 17, at chapter 7.

19. In such situations it is hard to determine where U.S. suggestions leave off and IMF advice begins. The first deputy managing director of the IMF at the time, Stanley Fischer, was appointed at the behest of the Clinton administration. Fischer, a leading academic authority on macroeconomics, was in charge of economic strategy at the IMF and in that capacity consulted on a frequent basis with Larry Summers of the U.S. Treasury Department. On this relationship and other connections between Treasury and the IMF, see ibid.

20. The IMF program was insufficiently expansionary at first because the depth of the collapse was not initially understood; fiscal conditions set by the IMF were relaxed later as the crisis deepened.

21. Blustein, *The Chastening*, *supra* note 17, at chapter 7.

22. See, e.g., Louis Uchitelle, "Crisis in South Korea: The Lenders; A Bad Side of Bailouts: Some Go Unpenalized," *The New York Times*, December 4, 1997, available at http://www.nytimes.com/1997/12/04/business/crisis-in-south-korea-the -lenders-a-bad-side-of-bailouts-some-go-unpenalized.html.

23. "Korea Letter of Intent to the IMF," *supra* note 1.

24. Jagdish Bhagwati argues that a Wall Street–Treasury complex pushed countries into liberalizing their capital inflows in a way that created excessive risks. Jagdish Bhagwati, "The Capital Myth," *Foreign Affairs*, May–June 1998. Rawi E. Abdelal argues that leading European politicians and bureaucrats also pushed this line—including Michel Camdessus, managing director of the IMF at the time of the Korean crisis. Rawi E. Abdelal, *Capital Rules: The Construction of Global Finance* (Cambridge: Harvard University Press, 2006). Paul Blustein, based on extensive interviews with the protagonists, concludes that the United States pushed Korea directly and through the IMF to open up to direct investment by foreign investors in financial services. Blustein, *The Chastening*, *supra* note 17.

25. Specific ways in which chaebol faced fewer financing constraints are explored in Hyun-Han Shin and Young S. Park, "Financing Constraints and Internal Capital Markets: Evidence from Korean Chaebols," *Journal of Corporate Finance* 5 (1999): 169–91.

26. The extent to which families run businesses around the world is documented by Rafael La Porta, Florencio Lopez-de-Silanes, and Andrei Shleifer, "Corporate Ownership Around the World," *Journal of Finance* 54 (1999): 471–517. For Asia, see Stijn Claessens, Simeon Djankov, and Larry H. P. Lang, "The Separation of Ownership and Control in East Asian Corporations," *Journal of Financial Economics* 58 (2000): 81–112. For the prevalence of political connections between powerful businesspeople and government, see Mara Faccio, "Politically Connected Firms," *American Economic Review* 96 (2006): 369–86. Specific countries for which we have detailed data on the role of powerful business interests and their political clout include Thailand (Marianne Bertrand, Simon Johnson, Antoinette Schoar, and Krislert Samphantharak, "Mixing Family with Business: A Study of Thai Business Groups," *Journal of Financial Economics* 88 [2008]: 466–98); Malaysia (Simon Johnson and Todd Mitton, "Cronyism and Capital Controls: Evidence from Malaysia," *Journal of Financial Economics* 67 [2003]: 351–82; Edmund Terence Gomez and Jomo K. S., *Malaysia's Political Economy: Politics, Patronage, and Profits* [Cambridge: Cambridge University Press, 1997]); and Pakistan (Asim I. Khwaja and Atif Mian, "Do Lenders Favor Politically Connected Firms? Rent Provision in an Emerging Financial Market," *Quarterly Journal of Economics* 120 [2005]: 1371–1411).

27. Liem headed the Salim Group. Bob Hasan, head of the Numsamba group, was another longtime Suharto friend and business ally. George J. Aditjondro, "Suharto and Sons (And Daughters, In-Laws, and Cronies)," *The Washington Post*, January 25, 1998, C1, available at http://www.washingtonpost.com/wp-srv/business/longterm/asiaecon/stories/sons012598.htm.

28. Marilyn Berger, "Suharto Dies at 86; Indonesian Dictator Brought Order and Bloodshed," *The New York Times*, January 28, 2008, available at: http://www.nytimes.com/2008/01/28/world/asia/28suharto.html.

29. On the nature and value of political connections in Indonesia, see Ray Fisman, "Estimating the Value of Political Connections," *American Economic Review* 91 (2001): 1095–1102. See also Michael Backman, *Asian Eclipse: Exposing the Dark Side of Business in Asia* (Singapore: John Wiley & Sons [Asia], 2001); chapter 14 has details on how the Suharto regime interacted with the private sector. On how subsidies were provided, see Andrew McIntyre, "Funny Money: Fiscal Policy, Rent-Seeking and Economic Performance in Indonesia," in Mustaq H. Khan and Jomo Kwame Sundaram, eds., *Rents, Rent-Seeking and Economic Development* (Cambridge: Cambridge University Press, 2000). See also Adam Schwarz, *A Nation in Waiting: Indonesia in the 1990s* (Boulder, CO: Westview, 1994), chapter 6.

30. Real GDP per capita (constant prices: chain series), from Alan Heston, Robert Summers, and Bettina Aten, *Penn World Table Version 6.3*, Center for International Comparisons of Production, Income and Prices at the University of

Pennsylvania, August 2009. This measure adjusts incomes for their purchasing power, a method that has limitations but is reasonably accurate for assessments over long periods of time; see Simon Johnson, William Larson, Chris Papageorgiou, and Arvind Subramanian, "Is Newer Better? Penn World Table Revisions and Their Impact on Growth Estimates" (working paper, NBER, October 2009).

31. On Russian reform and the oligarchs, see Anders Aslund, *Russia's Capitalist Revolution: Why Market Reform Succeeded and Democracy Failed* (Washington: Peterson Institute for International Economics, 2007); Chrystia Freeland, *Sale of the Century: Russia's Wild Ride from Communism to Capitalism* (New York: Crown Business, 2000); and David Hoffman, *The Oligarchs: Wealth and Power in the New Russia* (New York: PublicAffairs, 2002). For early accounts of privatization and other reforms before the rise of the oligarchs, see Joseph R. Blasi, Maya Kroumova, and Douglas Kruse, *Kremlin Capitalism: Privatizing the Russian Economy* (Ithaca, NY: Cornell University Press, 1997); and Thane Gustafson, *Capitalism Russian-Style* (Cambridge: Cambridge University Press, 1999). For a broader assessment of Russian reform, emphasizing that there were no good alternatives, see Andrei Shleifer and Daniel Treisman, *Without a Map: Political Tactics and Economic Reform in Russia* (Cambridge: MIT Press, 2000). On powerful groups controlling the state in the former Soviet Union, see Joel S. Hellman, Geraint Jones, and Daniel Kaufmann, "Seize the State, Seize the Day: State Capture and Influence in Transition Economies," *Journal of Comparative Economics* 31 (2003): 751–73.

32. It is difficult to separate the influence of the IMF and the U.S. Treasury Department. The senior IMF staff member responsible for Russia makes it clear that the G7 (the group of seven large industrial nations, within which the United States has a leading voice) agreed with the IMF's overall direction; if anything, the G7 preferred a bigger budget deficit and, by implication, more capital inflows to the short-term government debt market. See John Odling-Smee, "The IMF and Russia in the 1990s" (IMF working paper WP/04/155, August 2004), available at http://www.imf.org/external/pubs/ft/wp/2004/wp04155.pdf. The general U.S. preference for capital account liberalization is clear in its subsequent free trade agreements with Singapore and with Chile, as well as in its negotiations over China's accession to the World Trade Organization.

33. Aslund, *Russia's Capitalist Revolution, supra* note 31, at chapter 5.

34. George A. Akerlof, Paul M. Romer, Robert E. Hall, and N. Gregory Mankiw, "Looting: The Economic Underworld of Bankruptcy for Profit," *Brookings Papers on Economic Activity* 24 (1993): 1–73.

35. The classic techniques involve managers transferring assets (below market price) to, or buying inputs (above market price) from, companies they control. See, for example, the discussion of Gazprom in Vladimir A. Atansov, Bernard S. Black, and Conrad S. Conticello, "Unbundling and Measuring Tunneling" (working paper, January 2008), available at http://papers.ssrn.com/sol3/papers.cfm?abstract_id=1030529. These phenomena are also seen in high-income countries. Simon Johnson, Rafael La Porta, Florencio Lopez-de-Silanes, and

Andrei Shleifer, "Tunneling," *American Economic Review Papers and Proceedings* 90 (2000): 22–27.

36. Peter Boone and Boris Fyodorov, "The Ups and Downs of Russian Economic Reforms," in Wing Thye Woo, Stephen Parker, and Jeffrey Sachs, eds., *Economies in Transition: Comparing Asia and Europe* (Cambridge: MIT Press, 1996). There is more evidence of tunneling during the 1997–1998 emerging markets crises in Simon Johnson, Peter Boone, Alasdair Breach, and Eric Friedman, "Corporate Governance in the Asian Financial Crisis," *Journal of Financial Economics* 58 (2000): 141–86.

37. On the appropriation of state property at the fall of the Soviet Union, see Simon Johnson and Heidi Kroll, "Managerial Strategies for Spontaneous Privatization," *Soviet Economy* 7 (1991): 281–316. There was a great deal more theft under the smoke screen created by very high inflation. Anders Aslund, Peter Boone, Simon Johnson, Stanley Fischer, and Barry W. Ickes, "How to Stabilize: Lessons from Post-Communist Countries," *Brookings Papers on Economic Activity* 1996: 217–313.

38. Carlos Diaz-Alejandro, "Good-Bye Financial Repression, Hello Financial Crash," *Journal of Development Economics* 19 (1985): 1–24.

39. The IMF's voting structure is determined by countries' quotas (their potential financial commitments to the IMF), which imperfectly reflect their economic and financial power. The G7 and its close allies control a majority of the votes at the IMF and the United States has an effective veto over any major policy decision.

40. The Indonesia Letter of Intent, dated October 31, 1997, promised to clean up the banking system. Republic of Indonesia, "Indonesia Letter of Intent," October 31, 1997, available at http://www.imf.org/external/np/loi/103197.htm. In its retrospective study, the IMF's Independent Evaluation Office stressed that closing sixteen banks in November 1997 was supposed to "imply a new way of doing business. However, several factors undermined the credibility of this policy. Most important, the President's family challenged the closures. His son arranged for the business operations of Bank Andromeda to be shifted to another bank in which he had acquired an interest. The President's half-brother initiated a legal challenge to the closure of his bank. The public also saw some inconsistency in the closure of the 16 banks when it was widely—and correctly—believed that many other banks were in similar condition. . . . Under pressure from the President, the Minister of Finance soon reversed his previously announced tough position, saying there would be no more bank closures." IMF Independent Evaluation Office, *The IMF and Recent Capital Account Crises: Indonesia, Korea, Brazil* (Washington: International Monetary Fund, 2003), 75. See also Haggard, *Asian Financial Crisis, supra* note 11, at 66–67. In January 1998, the Indonesian government was supposed to pass a budget that had a surplus equal to 1 percent of GDP. Instead they proposed a budget that appeared to be balanced (with no surplus), which was interpreted as a further sign that Suharto was not willing to take resources away from his family and associated patronage networks. The initial critical

reaction from the IMF and the United States helped trigger a further depreciation of the Indonesian rupiah. Eva Reisenhuber, *The International Monetary
Fund Under Constraint: Legitimacy of Its Crisis Management* (New York:
Springer, 2001), 207. More companies struggled to pay their debts and had to
cut costs, contributing to social unrest.

41. See International Monetary Fund, *Ukraine: 2005 Article IV Consultation and Ex
Post Assessment of Longer-Term Program Engagement*, November 2005, available
at http://imf.org/external/pubs/ft/scr/2005/cr05415.pdf.

42. Growth rate of real GDP per capita from Heston, Summers, and Aten, *Penn
World Table Version 6.3, supra* note 30.

43. See David Luhnow, "The Secrets of the World's Richest Man: Mexico's Carlos
Slim Makes His Money the Old-Fashioned Way: Monopolies," *The Wall
Street Journal*, August 4, 2007, available at http://online.wsj.com/article/
SB118615255900587380.html.

44. Daron Acemoglu, "Oligarchic vs. Democratic Societies," *Journal of the European Economic Association* 6 (2008): 1–44. Societies with highly unequal power
structures did not industrialize early in the nineteenth century and generally
did not catch up to the income levels of the more prosperous countries in the
twentieth century. Daron Acemoglu, Simon Johnson, James Robinson, and
Pierre Yared, "Income and Democracy," *American Economic Review* 98 (2008):
808–42; Daron Acemoglu, Simon Johnson, and James Robinson, "Institutions
as the Fundamental Cause of Long-Run Growth," in Philippe Aghion and
Steve Durlauf, eds., *Handbook of Economic Growth* (Amsterdam: North-
Holland, 2005).

45. Kim came to power between the first and second IMF programs in December
1997.

46. See "Jang Ha Sung, Shareholder Activist, South Korea," *Business Week*, June 14,
1999, available at http://www.businessweek.com/1999/99_24/b3633089.htm.

47. See Ajai Chopra, Kenneth Kang, Meral Karasulu, Hong Liang, Henry Ma,
and Anthony Richards, "From Crisis to Recovery in Korea: Strategy, Achievements, and Lessons," in Coe and Kim, eds., *Korean Crisis and Recovery, supra*
note 7; Haggard, *Asian Financial Crisis, supra* note 11, at chapter 4; Isao Yana-
gimachi, "Chaebol Reform and Corporate Governance in Korea" (Policy
and Governance Working Paper Series No. 18, Graduate School of Media
and Governance, Keio University, Japan), available at http://coe21-policy
.sfc.keio.ac.jp/ja/wp/WP18.pdf; and Frederic Mishkin, *The Next Great Globalization: How Disadvantaged Nations Can Harness Their Financial Systems to Get
Rich* (Princeton: Princeton University Press, 2006), 99–103. Mishkin, a governor of the Federal Reserve from 2006 to 2008, argues that further capital market liberalization is the key to growth in emerging markets.

48. In the 1990s, Argentina tried a version of the Russian strategy—capital inflows
that supported a budget deficit and allowed a boom in private sector investment. This was the brainchild of Domingo Cavallo, a distinguished economist
with a Ph.D. from Harvard, and received strong support from the IMF (and
the United States) even as the approach ran into trouble. Failing to deal with

underlying political issues, including the inability to effectively tax powerful business elites, ended in a collapse of the currency, a banking crisis, and defaults on Argentina's public and private debt in 2001–2002. See Paul Blustein, *And the Money Kept Rolling In (and Out)* (New York: PublicAffairs, 2005); and Michael Mussa, *Argentina and the Fund: From Triumph to Tragedy* (Washington: Peterson Institute for International Economics, 2002).

49. On the LTCM crisis, see Roger Lowenstein, *When Genius Failed: The Rise and Fall of Long-Term Capital Management* (New York: Random House, 2000).

50. Ibid. at 159, 179–80.

51. Larry Summers, "International Financial Crises: Causes, Prevention, and Cures," *The American Economic Review Papers and Proceedings* 90 (2000): 1–16.

52. Some analysts have long worried about the sustainability of the U.S. current account deficit; see, e.g., C. Fred Bergsten, "The Dollar and the Deficits: How Washington Can Prevent the Next Crisis," *Foreign Affairs*, November–December 2009, available at http://www.foreignaffairs.com/articles/65475/c-fred -bergsten/the-dollar-and-the-deficits. But these worries are more about the growth of U.S. net foreign debt (and government borrowing) than they are about unstable capital inflows. The United States borrows only in U.S. dollars, thus removing the foreign exchange rate risk that contributed to downfall in Korea, Indonesia, and Russia. And the United States remains the ultimate safe haven, at least for now. When the world becomes more unstable, the ensuing "flight to quality" means that investors buy U.S. government debt; no emerging market country has this advantage.

53. "Korea Letter of Intent to the IMF," *supra* note 1.

CHAPTER 3: WALL STREET RISING

1. Ronald Reagan, Inaugural Address, January 20, 1981, available at http://www.reaganlibrary.com/pdf/Inaugural_Address_012081.pdf.

2. Anthony Bianco, "The King of Wall Street," *Business Week*, December 9, 1985.

3. "Gutfreund's Pay Is Cut," *The New York Times*, December 23, 1987, available at http://www.nytimes.com/1987/12/23/business/gutfreund-s-pay-is-cut.html.

4. Duff McDonald, *Last Man Standing: The Ascent of Jamie Dimon and JPMorgan Chase* (New York: Simon & Schuster, 2009).

5. Colin Barr, "JPMorgan Is the New King of Wall Street," *Fortune*, June 26, 2009, available at http://money.cnn.com/2009/06/26/news/companies/jpmorgan .underwriting.fortune/index.htm.

6. Quoted in Matthias Rieker, "J.P. Morgan's Meeting Is Noteworthy for Its Calm," *The Wall Street Journal*, May 21, 2009, available at http://online .wsj.com/article/SB124275791780135573.html.

7. Jackie Calmes and Louise Story, "In Washington, One Bank Chief Still Holds Sway," *The New York Times*, July 18, 2009, available at http://www.nytimes .com/2009/07/19/business/19dimon.html.

8. Annualized GDP in Q2 2009 was $14.2 trillion. Bureau of Economic Analysis, *National Income and Product Accounts*, Table 1.1.5, available at http://www.bea .gov/national/nipaweb/SelectTable.asp.

9. Conversion done using GDP price indexes. Ibid. at Table 1.1.4.

10. JPMorgan Chase and Goldman Sachs financial data are from company annual and quarterly reports.

11. "JPMorgan CEO Dimon's 2008 Compensation Falls," Reuters, March 18, 2009, available at http://www.reuters.com/article/ousiv/idUSTRE52H7ZL20090318.

12. The figure for Dimon comes from ibid.; the others are from "Executive Pay: The Bottom Line for Those at the Top," *The New York Times*, April 5, 2008, available at http://www.nytimes.com/interactive/2008/04/05/business/20080405_EXECCOMP_GRAPHIC.html.

13. Financial sector data are from the *Federal Reserve Flow of Funds*, Tables L.1, L.109, L.126, and L.129, available at http://www.federalreserve.gov/releases/z1/Current/. Nominal GDP is from the Bureau of Economic Analysis, *supra* note 8, at Table 1.1.5. We used the end of 2007 rather than the end of 2008 because there was a major shift in assets from investment banks to commercial banks in 2008—because three major investment banks were bought by commercial banks (most of Lehman's assets were bought by Barclays) and the other two major investment banks became bank holding companies.

14. *Federal Reserve Flow of Funds, supra* note 13, at Table L.1.

15. Data are from Bank for International Settlements, *Semiannual OTC Derivatives Statistics*, available at http://www.bis.org/statistics/derstats.htm.

16. Bureau of Economic Analysis, *supra* note 8, at Table 1.5.5.

17. Ibid. at Table 6.16. We use corporate profits with inventory valuation adjustment, and exclude Federal Reserve banks from the financial sector. Profits are deflated using the GDP price index. Ibid. at Table 1.1.4.

18. Quoted in Eric J. Weiner, *What Goes Up: The Uncensored History of Wall Street as Told by the Bankers, Brokers, CEOs, and Scoundrels Who Made It Happen* (New York: Little, Brown, 2005), 31.

19. Bureau of Economic Analysis, *supra* note 8, at Tables 1.1.4, 6.3, 6.5; calculation by the authors. Banking includes financial sector less insurance, real estate, and holding companies. Annual compensation is total wage and salary accruals divided by full-time equivalent employees. See Figure 4-1 of this book.

20. Michael Lewis, *Liar's Poker: Rising Through the Wreckage on Wall Street* (New York: Penguin, 1990), 203.

21. Frank Partnoy, *Infectious Greed: How Deceit and Risk Corrupted the Financial Markets* (New York: Henry Holt, 2004), 85.

22. David Segal, "$100 Million Payday Poses Problem for Pay Czar," *The New York Times*, August 1, 2009, available at http://www.nytimes.com/2009/08/02/business/02bonus.html.

23. Poppy Trowbridge, "Paulson's $3.7 Billion Pay Tops Hedge Fund Managers, Alpha Says," Bloomberg, April 16, 2008, available at http://www.bloomberg.com/apps/news?pid ewsarchive&sid=axHxRPBdtun8. See also Gregory Zuckerman, *The Greatest Trade Ever: The Behind-the-Scenes Story of How John Paulson Defied Wall Street and Made Financial History* (New York: Broadway Business, 2009).

24. Lewis, *Liar's Poker, supra* note 20, at 119.

25. Nicholas Brady (lecture, Institute of International Finance, Washington, D.C., April 25, 2009).

26. *Federal Reserve Flow of Funds, supra* note 13, at Table L.129.

27. Thomas Philippon and Ariell Reshef, "Wages and Human Capital in the U.S. Financial Industry: 1909–2006" (working paper, December 2008), Figure 3, available at http://pages.stern.nyu.edu/~tphilipp/research.htm.

28. On attempts to skirt regulation and government responses, see Richard Scott Carnell, Jonathan R. Macey, and Geoffrey P. Miller, *The Law of Banking and Financial Institutions*, fourth edition (Austin: Wolters Kluwer Law & Business, 2009), 20–23.

29. Bureau of Economic Analysis, *supra* note 8, at Table 1.1.6.

30. Quoted in Weiner, *What Goes Up, supra* note 18, at 162.

31. Brett Duval Fromson, "Merrill Lynch: The Stumbling Herd," *Fortune*, June 20, 1988, available at http://money.cnn.com/magazines/fortune/fortune_archive/1988/06/20/70693/index.htm.

32. Weiner, *What Goes Up, supra* note 18, at 166.

33. Charles R. Geisst, *Wall Street: A History: From Its Beginnings to the Fall of Enron* (Oxford: Oxford University Press, 2004), 306.

34. Ibid. at 315, 327.

35. Jerry W. Markham, *A Financial History of the United States, Volume III: From the Age of Derivatives into the New Millennium (1970–2001)* (Armonk, NY: M. E. Sharpe, 2002), 6–7.

36. Freddie Mac, *Primary Mortgage Market Survey Archives*, available at http://www.freddiemac.com/pmms/pmms30.htm.

37. Gretchen Morgenson and Andrew Martin, "Citigroup Hires Mr. Inside," *The New York Times*, October 10, 2009, available at http://www.nytimes.com/2009/10/11/business/11hohlt.html.

38. Pub. L. 96-221. Interest ceilings on deposit accounts were phased out in Title II. State usury laws were preempted in Title V.

39. Geisst, *Wall Street, supra* note 33, at 327.

40. On academic finance, see Justin Fox, *The Myth of the Rational Market: A History of Risk, Reward, and Delusion on Wall Street* (New York: Harper Business, 2009); John Cassidy, *How Markets Fail: The Logic of Economic Calamities* (New York: Farrar, Straus & Giroux, 2009), chapter 7; Peter Bernstein, *Capital Ideas: The Improbable Origins of Modern Wall Street* (New York: Free Press, 1992); and Peter Bernstein, *Capital Ideas Evolving* (Hoboken, NJ: Wiley, 2007).

41. Liabilities of the nonfinancial business sector in the United States grew from 68 percent of GDP in 1970 to 129 percent of GDP in 2007. *Federal Reserve Flow of Funds, supra* note 13, at Table L.101.

42. Eugene F. Fama, "Efficient Capital Markets: A Review of Theory and Empirical Work," *The Journal of Finance* 25 (1970): 383–417. See also Bernstein, *Capital Ideas: Improbable Origins, supra* note 40, at 132–39.

43. John Arlidge, " 'I'm Doing God's Work.' Meet Mr. Goldman Sachs," *The Sunday Times* (London), November 8, 2009, available at http://www.timesonline.co.uk/tol/news/world/us_and_americas/article6907681.ece.

44. See Cassidy, *How Markets Fail*, *supra* note 40, at 93–94; Fox, *Myth of the Rational Market*, *supra* note 40, at 196–200.

45. Bradford DeLong, Andrei Shleifer, Lawrence H. Summers, and Robert J. Waldmann, "Noise Trader Risk in Financial Markets," *The Journal of Political Economy* 98 (1990): 703–38. The concept of noise traders was first posited in Albert S. Kyle, "Continuous Auctions and Insider Trading," *Econometrica* 53 (1985): 1315–35.

46. Fischer Black, "Noise," *The Journal of Finance* 41 (1986): 529–43. See also Fox, *Myth of the Rational Market*, *supra* note 40, at 201–2.

47. Stanley Fischer, "Capital Account Liberalization and the Role of the IMF" (lecture, IMF Annual Meetings, September 19, 1997), available at http://www.imf.org/external/np/speeches/1997/091997.htm.

48. Jagdish Bhagwati, "The Capital Myth: The Difference Between Trade in Widgets and Trade in Dollars," *Foreign Affairs*, May–June 1998.

49. On the strength of this belief and the lack of empirical support at the time, see Dani Rodrik and Arvind Subramanian, "Why Did Financial Globalization Disappoint?" *IMF Staff Papers* 56 (2009), available at http://www.piie.com/publications/papers/subramanian0308.pdf.

50. For a summary of Friedman's views, see Cassidy, *How Markets Fail*, *supra* note 40, at chapter 6.

51. Reagan, Inaugural Address, *supra* note 1.

52. Edward Cowan, "How Regan Sees the Budget," *The New York Times*, October 18, 1981.

53. Ronald Reagan, *Remarks on Signing the Garn–St. Germain Depository Institutions Act of 1982*, October 15, 1982, available at http://www.reagan.utexas.edu/archives/speeches/1982/101582b.htm.

54. The Garn–St. Germain Depository Institutions Act of 1982, Pub. L. 97-320.

55. Ibid., at Title VIII.

56. OCC regulation 46 F.R. 18932-01.

57. OCC regulation 48 F.R. 40698-01, taking effect September 9, 1983.

58. Markham, *Financial History*, Volume III, *supra* note 35, at 132.

59. See Alyssa Katz, *Our Lot: How Real Estate Came to Own Us* (New York: Bloomsbury, 2009), 15–21.

60. Pub. L. 98-440.

61. Richard K. Green and Susan M. Wachter, "The American Mortgage in Historical and International Context," *Journal of Economic Perspectives* 19 (2005): 93–114, at 98–99.

62. Charles R. Geisst, *Undue Influence: How the Wall Street Elite Put the Financial System at Risk* (Hoboken, NJ: Wiley, 2005), 222–23; William S. Haraf, "Bank and Thrift Regulation," *Regulation: The Cato Review of Business and Government*, available at http://www.cato.org/pubs/regulation/regv12n3/reg12n3-haraf.html.

63. Federal Deposit Insurance Corporation, "Bank Failures and Assistance Transactions," *Historical Statistics on Banking*, at http://www2.fdic.gov/hsob/SelectRpt.asp?EntryTyp=30.

64. Markham, *Financial History*, Volume III, *supra* note 35, at 171. The $54 billion

estimate does not include the resolution costs for some institutions where those costs were not available. George A. Akerlof, Paul M. Romer, Robert E. Hall, and N. Gregory Mankiw, "Looting: The Economic Underworld of Bankruptcy for Profit," *Brookings Papers on Economic Activity* 24 (1993): 1–73.

65. Markham, *Financial History*, Volume III, *supra* note 35, at 111.

66. On the investigation of Milken and Drexel Burnham Lambert, see James B. Stewart, *Den of Thieves* (New York: Simon & Schuster, 1992).

67. Securities Industry and Financial Markets Association Research and Statistics, *U.S. Corporate Bond Issuance—Investment Grade and High Yield*, available at http://www.sifma.org/research/research.aspx?ID=10806.

68. Mortgage assets held by issuers of asset-backed securities. *Federal Reserve Flow of Funds*, *supra* note 13, at Table L.126.

69. Center for International Securities and Derivatives Markets, "The Benefits of Hedge Funds: 2006 Update," May 2006, available at http://cisdm.som.umass .edu/research/hedge.shtml.

70. Alternative Investment Management Association, "AIMA's Roadmap to Hedge Funds," November 2008, available at http://www.aima.org/en/knowledge _centre/education/aimas-roadmap-to-hedge-funds.cfm.

71. Monica Langley, *Tearing Down the Walls: How Sandy Weill Fought His Way to the Top of the Financial World . . . and Then Nearly Lost It All* (New York: Wall Street Journal Books, 2004), 270. Losses on mergers and acquisitions arbitrage also contributed to the decision to downsize the proprietary trading operation.

72. Nassim Taleb, Foreword to Pablo Triana, *Lecturing Birds on Flying: Can Mathematical Theories Destroy the Financial Markets?* (Hoboken, NJ: Wiley, 2009), xiii.

73. *Semiannual OTC Derivatives Statistics*, *supra* note 15, at Table 19.

74. Satyajit Das, *Traders, Guns and Money: Knowns and Unknowns in the Dazzling World of Derivatives* (Harlow, England: Prentice Hall, 2006), 47. For an explanation of a leveraged inverse floater, see ibid. at 45–50.

75. On the transactions that created these losses, see Frank Partnoy, *F.I.A.S.C.O.: Blood in the Water on Wall Street* (New York: W. W. Norton, 2009), 90–93, 155–69; and Das, *Traders, Guns and Money*, *supra* note 74, at 101–4.

76. Partnoy, *Infectious Greed*, *supra* note 21, at 117.

77. See Gillian Tett, *Fool's Gold: How the Bold Dream of a Small Tribe at J.P. Morgan Was Corrupted by Wall Street Greed and Unleashed a Catastrophe* (New York: Free Press, 2009), 41–56.

78. *Securities Industry Association v. Board of Governors of the Federal Reserve System*, 468 U.S. 137 (1984); *Securities Industry Association v. Board of Governors of the Federal Reserve System*, 807 F.2d 1052 (D.C. Cir. 1986). See Carnell et al., *Law of Banking*, *supra* note 28, at 142–51.

79. Geisst, *Undue Influence*, *supra* note 62, at 223, 245, 249.

80. Simon Kwan, "Cracking the Glass-Steagall Barriers," *Federal Reserve Bank of San Francisco Economic Letter* 97-08 (March 21, 1997), available at http:// www.frbsf.org/econrsrch/wklyltr/el97-08.html.

81. Partnoy, *Infectious Greed*, *supra* note 21, at 132–33.

82. Quoted in Weiner, *What Goes Up, supra* note 18, at 176.

83. Asset data from *Federal Reserve Flow of Funds, supra* note 13, at Tables L.109, L.126, and L.129; GDP data from Bureau of Economic Analysis, *supra* note 8, at Table 1.1.5.

84. Bureau of Economic Analysis, *supra* note 8 at Table 6.16.

85. Kevin J. Stiroh and Jennifer P. Poole, "Explaining the Rising Concentration of Banking Assets in the 1990s," *Federal Reserve Bank of New York Current Issues in Economics and Finance* 6, no. 9 (August 2000), available at http://papers.ssrn.com/sol3/papers.cfm?abstract_id=722526.

86. Mitchell Martin, "Citicorp and Travelers Plan to Merge in Record $70 Billion Deal: A New No. 1: Financial Giants Unite," *The New York Times*, April 7, 1998, available at http://www.nytimes.com/1998/04/07/news/07iht-citi.t.html.

87. Bradley Keoun, "Citigroup's $1.1 Trillion of Mysterious Assets Shadows Earnings," Bloomberg, July 13, 2008, available at http://www.bloomberg.com/apps/news?pid=20601109&sid=a1liVM3tG3aI.

88. Laura M. Holson, "Upheaval in Banking: The New BankAmerica; Hands in a Lot of Markets and a Foot on Each Coast," *The New York Times*, April 14, 1998.

89. Gary H. Stern and Ron J. Feldman, *Too Big to Fail: The Hazards of Bank Bailouts* (Washington: Brookings Institution Press, 2009), 64–65.

90. Daniel K. Tarullo, "Confronting Too Big to Fail" (lecture, Exchequer Club, Washington, D.C., October 21, 2009), available at http://www.federalreserve.gov/newsevents/speech/tarullo20091021a.htm.

CHAPTER 4: "GREED IS GOOD"

1. Reported in Thomas B. Edsall, "Alan Greenspan: The Oracle or the Master of Disaster?" *The Huffington Post*, February 19, 2009, available at http://www.huffingtonpost.com/2009/02/19/alan-greenspan-the-oracle_n_168168.html. A shorter version of the quotation was reported in Peter S. Goodman, "Taking Hard New Look at a Greenspan Legacy," *The New York Times*, October 8, 2008, available at http://www.nytimes.com/2008/10/09/business/economy/09greenspan.html.

2. Federal Deposit Insurance Corporation, "Bank Failures and Assistance Transactions," *Historical Statistics on Banking*, available at http://www2.fdic.gov/hsob/SelectRpt.asp?EntryTyp=30.

3. Council of Economic Advisers, *Economic Report of the President*, February 1991, 173; Timothy Curry and Lynn Shibut, "The Cost of the Savings and Loan Crisis: Truth and Consequences," *FDIC Banking Review* (December 2000): 26–35, available at http://www.fdic.gov/bank/analytical/banking/2000dec/brv13n2_2.pdf.

4. The term "cultural capital" is from the French sociologist Pierre Bourdieu, but is used slightly differently here. For Bourdieu, cultural capital denoted (to simplify greatly) a set of understandings and judgments of the world that are accumulated by members of the upper class and that are used to distinguish them from other classes. See, e.g., Pierre Bourdieu, *Distinction: A Social Critique of the*

Judgment of Taste, trans. Richard Nice (Cambridge: Harvard University Press, 1984).

5. Figure for 1974 is from Robert G. Kaiser, *So Much Damn Money: The Triumph of Lobbying and the Corrosion of American Government* (New York: Alfred A. Knopf, 2009), inside jacket flap. All other aggregate campaign contribution statistics, unless otherwise cited, are from OpenSecrets.org, a project of the Center for Responsive Politics.

6. Essential Information and Consumer Education Foundation, *Sold Out: How Wall Street and Washington Betrayed America*, March 2009, available at http://www.wallstreetwatch.org.

7. Company rankings include contributions by individual employees and by political action committees.

8. Dodd was a minor candidate for the Democratic presidential nomination. The only senators who received more from the industry were the much more significant presidential candidates Barack Obama, John McCain, and Hillary Clinton.

9. Eric Lipton and Raymond Hernandez, "A Champion of Wall Street Reaps Benefits," *The New York Times*, December 13, 2008, available at http://www.nytimes.com/2008/12/14/business/14schumer.html.

10. Ibid.

11. Interview with Ray Hanania, *Radio Chicagoland*, April 27, 2009, available at http://rayhanania.libsyn.com/index.php?post_id=464814; quotation transcribed by Adam Doster, "Durbin on Congress: The Banks 'Own the Place,' " *Progress Illinois*, April 29, 2009, available at http://progressillinois.com/2009/4/29/durbin-banks-own-the-place.

12. Securities and Exchange Commission, Commodity Futures Trading Commission, Office of the Comptroller of the Currency, Office of Thrift Supervision, Federal Deposit Insurance Corporation, and National Credit Union Administration.

13. George Stigler, "The Theory of Economic Regulation," *The Bell Journal of Economics and Management Science* 2 (1971): 3–21, at 3, available at http://www.jstor.org/stable/3003160.

14. Robert E. Rubin and Jacob Weisberg, *In an Uncertain World: Tough Choices from Wall Street to Washington* (New York: Random House, 2003), 39–103.

15. Frank Partnoy, *Infectious Greed: How Deceit and Risk Corrupted the Financial Markets* (New York: Henry Holt, 2004), 153–54; Saul Hansell, "Bankers Trust Hires Former Treasury Deputy," *The New York Times*, September 22, 1995, available at http://www.nytimes.com/1995/09/22/business/bankers-trust-hires-former-treasury-deputy.html; Andy Serwer, "Frank Newman Feels the Heat," *Fortune*, October 26, 1998, available at http://money.cnn.com/magazines/fortune/fortune_archive/1998/10/26/249977/index.htm.

16. Who Runs Gov, "Lee Sachs," available at http://www.whorunsgov.com/Profiles/Lee_Sachs.

17. Partnoy, *Infectious Greed*, *supra* note 15, at 147.

18. "Over-the-Counter Derivatives Markets and the Commodity Exchange Act,"

Report of the President's Working Group on Financial Markets, November 1999, available at http://www.ustreas.gov/press/releases/reports/otcact.pdf.

19. Press Release, Chicago Board Options Exchange, Chicago Mercantile Exchange, and Chicago Board of Trade, "CBOE, CME, CBOT, Name William Rainer to Head Joint Venture on Single Stock Futures," August 29, 2001, available at http://www.onechicago.com/?p=438.

20. Binyamin Appelbaum and Ellen Nakashima, "Banking Regulator Played Advocate over Enforcer: Agency Let Lenders Grow Out of Control, Then Fail," *The Washington Post*, November 23, 2008, available at http://www.washingtonpost.com/wp-dyn/content/article/2008/11/22/AR2008112202213.html.

21. Zach Carter, "A Master of Disaster," *The Nation*, December 16, 2009, available at http://www.thenation.com/doc/20100104/carter/.

22. Quoted in "The Watchmen," *This American Life*, originally broadcast June 5, 2009, audio and transcript available at http://thislife.org/Radio_Episode.aspx?sched=1301.

23. Appelbaum and Nakashima, "Banking Regulator Played Advocate," *supra* note 20.

24. Press Release, Office of Thrift Supervision, "OTS Approves Countrywide Application," March 5, 2007, available at http://files.ots.treas.gov/777014.html.

25. Rubin and Weisberg, *In an Uncertain World*, *supra* note 14, at 93–96.

26. The phrase was actually only the second of three points written on a sign in Clinton's campaign headquarters. *The War Room* (Cyclone Films, 1993).

27. Rubin and Weisberg, *In an Uncertain World*, *supra* note 14, at 198–201.

28. Ibid. at 118–26.

29. Louis Uchitelle, "The Bondholders Are Winning; Why America Won't Boom," *The New York Times*, June 12, 1994, available at http://www.nytimes.com/1994/06/12/weekinreview/ideas-trends-the-bondholders-are-winning-why-america-won-t-boom.html.

30. GDP data from Bureau of Economic Analysis, *National Income and Product Accounts*, Table 1.1.6, available at http://www.bea.gov/national/nipaweb/SelectTable.asp. Inflation based on GDP price indexes. Ibid. at Table 1.1.4.

31. Rubin and Weisberg, *In an Uncertain World*, *supra* note 14, at 160–64.

32. Ibid. at 197–98.

33. GDP data from Bureau of Economic Analysis, *supra* note 30, at Table 1.1.6; median income from U.S. Census Bureau, *Income, Poverty, and Health Insurance Coverage in the United States: 2008*, Table A-1, available at http://www.census.gov/prod/2009pubs/p60–236.pdf.

34. Alan Greenspan, *The Age of Turbulence: Adventures in a New World* (New York: Penguin, 2007), 51–53, 208.

35. Alan Greenspan (lecture, Annual Conference of the Association of Private Enterprise Education, April 12, 1997), available at http://www.federalreserve.gov/boarddocs/speeches/1997/19970412.htm.

36. Alan Greenspan (lecture, American Enterprise Institute, December 5, 1996), available at http://www.federalreserve.gov/boarddocs/speeches/1996/19961205.htm.

37. Alan Greenspan, *Age of Turbulence, supra* note 34, at 52.

38. Reported in Edsall, "Alan Greenspan," *supra* note 1. See also Goodman, "Taking Hard New Look at a Greenspan Legacy," *supra* note 1.

39. Quoted in Manuel Roig-Franzia, "Credit Crisis Cassandra: Brooksley Born's Unheeded Warning Is a Rueful Echo 10 Years On," *The Washington Post*, May 26, 2009, available at http://www.washingtonpost.com/wp-dyn/content/article/2009/05/25/AR2009052502108.html.

40. Raghuram G. Rajan, "Has Financial Development Made the World Riskier?" (paper presented at a symposium sponsored by the Federal Reserve Bank of Kansas City, Jackson Hole, WY, August 27, 2005), available at www.kc.frb.org/publicat/SYMPOS/2005/PDF/Rajan2005.pdf.

41. Justin Lahart, "Mr. Rajan Was Unpopular (But Prescient) at Greenspan Party," *The Wall Street Journal*, January 2, 2009, available at http://online.wsj.com/article/SB123086154114948151.html.

42. Donald Kohn (lecture, symposium sponsored by the Federal Reserve Bank of Kansas City, Jackson Hole, WY, August 27, 2005), available at http://www.federalreserve.gov/boarddocs/speeches/2005/20050827/default.htm.

43. Quoted in Lahart, "Mr. Rajan Was Unpopular (But Prescient) at Greenspan Party," *supra* note 41.

44. Federal Deposit Insurance Corporation, *2003 Annual Report*, available at http://www.fdic.gov/about/strategic/report/2003annualreport/intro_insurance.html. Thanks to Robert Waldmann (http://rjwaldmann.blogspot.com/2008/03/banking-regulation-illustrated-paul.html) and *Economics of Contempt* (http://economicsofcontempt.blogspot.com/2008/03/cutting-through-red-tape-with-chainsaw.html) for tracking down the photograph.

45. Robert Merton, "Financial Innovation and the Management and Regulation of Financial Institutions," *Journal of Banking and Finance* 19 (1995): 461–81.

46. Alan Greenspan, "Technological Change and the Design of Bank Supervisory Policies" (lecture, Conference on Bank Structure and Competition of the Federal Reserve Bank of Chicago, May 1, 1997), available at http://www.federalreserve.gov/boarddocs/speeches/1997/19970501.htm.

47. Timothy F. Geithner, "Risk Management Challenges in the U.S. Financial System" (lecture, Global Association of Risk Professionals 7th Annual Risk Management Convention and Exhibition, New York), February 26, 2008, available at http://www.ny.frb.org/newsevents/speeches/2006/gei060228.html.

48. Ben S. Bernanke, "Financial Innovation and Consumer Protection" (lecture, Federal Reserve System's Sixth Biennial Community Affairs Research Conference, Washington, D.C., April 17, 2009), available at http://www.federalreserve.gov/newsevents/speech/bernanke20090417a.htm.

49. See Larry Light, "Reverse Converts: A Nest-Egg Slasher?" *The Wall Street Journal*, June 16, 2009, available at http://online.wsj.com/article/SB124511060085417057.html; Mike Konczal, "Consumer Protection: Reverse Convertibles," *Rortybomb*, June 18, 2009, available at http://rortybomb.wordpress.com/2009/06/18/consumer-protection-reverse-convertibles/.

50. Quoted in Light, "Reverse Converts," *supra* note 49.

51. Warren Buffett, "Chairman's Letter," *Berkshire Hathaway 2002 Annual Report*, available at http://www.berkshirehathaway.com/letters/2002pdf.pdf.

52. Nassim Nicholas Taleb, *Fooled by Randomness: The Hidden Role of Chance in the Markets and in Life* (New York: Texere, 2001).

53. Janet Tavakoli, *Structured Finance and Collateralized Debt Obligations: New Developments in Cash & Synthetic Securitization*, second edition (Hoboken, NJ: Wiley, 2008); originally published as *Collateralized Debt Obligations and Structured Finance* in 2003.

54. See John Cassidy, *How Markets Fail: The Logic of Economic Calamities* (New York: Farrar, Straus and Giroux, 2009), 212.

55. Brian Naylor, "Greenspan Admits Free Market Ideology Flawed," NPR, October 24, 2008, available at http://www.npr.org/templates/story/story.php?storyId=96070766.

56. See Adam Levitin, "Complex Pricing of Credit Cards Should Be Simplified," *Chicago Tribune*, December 27, 2007, available at http://archives.chicagotribune.com/2007/dec/27/opinion/chi-oped1227creditdec27; Adam Levitin, "New Credit Card Tricks, Traps, and 79.9% APRs," *Credit Slips*, December 18, 2009, available at http://www.creditslips.org/creditslips/2009/12/new-credit-card-tricks-traps-and-799-aprs.html.

57. Quoted in Eric Lipton and Raymond Hernandez, "A Champion of Wall Street Reaps Benefits," *The New York Times*, December 13, 2008, available at http://www.nytimes.com/2008/12/14/business/14schumer.html.

58. U.S. Census Bureau, *Housing Vacancies and Homeownership*, Table 14, available at http://www.census.gov/hhes/www/housing/hvs/historic/index.html.

59. Edward L. Glaeser and Jesse M. Shapiro, "The Benefits of the Home Mortgage Interest Deduction," *Tax Policy and the Economy* 17 (2003): 37–82, available at http://www.jstor.org/stable/20140504.

60. Edward L. Glaeser, "Attack of the Home Buyers' Tax Credit," Economix Blog, *The New York Times*, November 10, 2009, available at http://economix.blogs.nytimes.com/2009/11/10/attack-of-the-home-buyers-tax-credit/. The paper he cites is Denise DiPasquale and Edward L. Glaeser, "Incentives and Social Capital: Are Homeowners Better Citizens?" (NBER Working Paper 6363, January 1998), available at http://www.nber.org/papers/w6363.pdf; compare Tables 2 and 4.

61. William M. Rohe and Michael A. Stegman, "The Impact of Home Ownership on the Social and Political Involvement of Low-Income People," *Urban Affairs Review* 30 (1994): 152–72.

62. Alyssa Katz, *Our Lot: How Real Estate Came to Own Us* (New York: Bloomsbury, 2009), 40.

63. Ibid. at 19. Ranieri testified before the Subcommittee on Housing and Urban Affairs of the Committee on Banking, Housing, and Urban Affairs, September 21 and 22, 1983.

64. Senate Rep. No. 98–293, November 2, 1983.

65. Doris "Tanta" Dungey, "What Is Subprime?" *Calculated Risk*, November 25, 2007, available at http://www.calculatedriskblog.com/2007/11/what-is-subprime.html.

66. Quoted in Katz, *Our Lot, supra* note 62, at 65.

67. Ibid. at 29.

68. Actual homeownership rates are from U.S. Census Bureau, *Housing Vacancies and Homeownership, supra* note 58, at Table 14.

69. Wayne Barrett, "Andrew Cuomo and Fannie and Freddie: How the Youngest Housing and Urban Development Secretary in History Gave Birth to the Mortgage Crisis," *The Village Voice*, August 5, 2008, available at http://www.villagevoice.com/2008–08–05/news/how-andrew-cuomo-gave-birth-to-the-crisis-at-fannie-mae-and-freddie-mac/.

70. Housing prices are from the S&P/Case-Shiller Composite-10 Home Price Index, deflated by the CPI–All Urban Consumers; Bureau of Labor Statistics, *Consumer Price Index*, available at http://www.bls.gov/cpi/data.htm. Household income data are from U.S. Census Bureau, *Income, Poverty, and Health Insurance Coverage, supra* note 33, at Table A-1.

71. Alan Greenspan, "Consumer Finance" (lecture, Federal Reserve System's Fourth Annual Community Affairs Research Conference, Washington, D.C., April 8, 2005), available at http://www.federalreserve.gov/BoardDocs/speeches/2005/20050408/default.htm.

72. Tom Wolfe, *The Bonfire of the Vanities* (New York: Farrar, Straus & Giroux, 1987), 9.

73. Stanley Weiser, "Repeat After Me: Greed Is Not Good," *Los Angeles Times*, October 5, 2008, available at http://articles.latimes.com/2008/oct/05/entertainment/ca-wallstreet5.

74. Michael Lewis, "The End," *Portfolio*, December 2008, available at http://www.portfolio.com/news-markets/national-news/portfolio/2008/11/11/The-End-of-Wall-Streets-Boom.

75. Candace Bushnell, *Sex and the City* (New York: Grand Central, 2006), 1.

76. Data are from Bureau of Economic Analysis, *supra* note 30, at Tables 1.1.4, 6.3, and 6.5. We begin with the finance, insurance, and real estate sector and exclude insurance, real estate, and holding companies. Figures are converted to 2008 dollars using the GDP price index.

77. Thomas Philippon and Ariell Reshef, "Wages and Human Capital in the U.S. Financial Industry: 1909–2006" (working paper, December 2008), Sections 3.4 and 3.5, available at http://pages.stern.nyu.edu/~tphilipp/research.htm. Note that the relative wage in Figure 4-2, which exceeds 1.7 at its peak, is *not* corrected for differences in education. The excess relative wage—the difference between average finance wages and what one would predict based on educational differences—reaches a peak of around 40 percentage points in the 2000s. See Figure 11 in ibid.

78. Andrew Cuomo, "No Rhyme or Reason: The 'Heads I Win, Tails You Lose' Bank Bonus Culture," July 2009, available at "Cuomo Report Details Wall St. Bonuses," DealBook Blog, *The New York Times*, available at http://dealbook.blogs.nytimes.com/2009/07/30/cuomo-report-blasts-wall-street-bonus-culture/.

79. Claudia Goldin and Lawrence F. Katz, "Transitions: Career and Family Life Cycles of the Educational Elite," *American Economic Review: Papers and Proceedings* 98 (2008): 363–69.

80. Steve Lohr, "Wall St. Pay Is Cyclical. Guess Where We Are Now," *The New York Times*, February 4, 2009, available at http://www.nytimes.com/2009/02/05/business/05bonus.html.

81. "The ORFE Department is currently the largest of the six undergraduate concentrations within Princeton's School of Engineering and Applied Science (SEAS), accounting for approximately 30% of all undergraduate engineers." Operations Research and Financial Engineering, Princeton University, "Undergraduate Program," available at http://orfe.princeton.edu/undergraduate (as of November 2009).

82. Kevin M. Murphy, Andrei Shleifer, and Robert W. Vishny, "The Allocation of Talent: Implications for Growth," *The Quarterly Journal of Economics* 106 (1991): 503–30.

83. Jagdish Bhagwati, "The Capital Myth: The Difference Between Trade in Widgets and Trade in Dollars," *Foreign Affairs*, May–June 1998, 7–12.

CHAPTER 5: THE BEST DEAL EVER

1. U.S. Securities and Exchange Commission, *Final Rule: Alternative Net Capital Requirements for Broker-Dealers That Are Part of Consolidated Supervised Entities*, available at http://www.sec.gov/rules/final/34-49830.htm.

2. For a more detailed discussion of structured finance, see Janet Tavakoli, *Structured Finance and Collateralized Debt Obligations: New Developments in Cash & Synthetic Securitization*, second edition (Hoboken, NJ: Wiley, 2008).

3. Frank Partnoy, *F.I.A.S.C.O.: Blood in the Water on Wall Street* (New York: W. W. Norton, 2009), 215–31.

4. Ibid., especially at 107–38.

5. For more on CDOs and structured finance, see Joshua D. Coval, Jakub Jurek, and Erik Stafford, "The Economics of Structured Finance" (Harvard Business School Working Paper 09–060), available at http://www.hbs.edu/research/pdf/09-060.pdf.

6. Gillian Tett, *Fool's Gold: How the Bold Dream of a Small Tribe at J. P. Morgan Was Corrupted by Wall Street Greed and Unleashed a Catastrophe* (New York: Free Press, 2009), 51–56.

7. Quoted in Michael Lewis, "The End," *Portfolio*, November 11, 2008, available at http://www.portfolio.com/news-markets/national-news/portfolio/2008/11/11/The-End-of-Wall-Streets-Boom/.

8. For an explanation of super-senior tranches, see Felix Salmon, "What's a Super-Senior Tranche?" Market Movers Blog, *Portfolio*, December 1, 2008, available at http://www.portfolio.com/views/blogs/market-movers/2008/12/01/whats-a-super-senior-tranche/.

9. Tett, *Fool's Gold, supra* note 6, at 62–63.

10. On the "Three Cs" of mortgage lending, see several articles by Doris "Tanta" Dungey on *Calculated Risk*, such as Doris "Tanta" Dungey, "What Is 'Subprime?,' " *Calculated Risk*, November 25, 2007, available at http://www.calculatedriskblog.com/2007/11/what-is-subprime.html.

11. Chris Mayer and Karen Pence, "Subprime Mortgages: What, Where, and to Whom?" Finance and Economics Discussion Series 2008–29, Divisions of Research and Statistics and Monetary Affairs, Federal Reserve Board, Washington, D.C., available at http://www.federalreserve.gov/pubs/feds/2008/200829/200829pap.pdf.

12. Based on HMDA data gathered by the Federal Financial Institutions Examination Council, matched with the HUD list of subprime lenders; cited in Kenneth Temkin, "Subprime Lending: Current Trends and Policy Issues," *The Neighbor-Works Journal*, Spring–Summer 2000, available at http://www.knowledgeplex.org/kp/text_document_summary/article/relfiles/partner_content/nrc/ht_nrc_temkin.pdf.

13. On the increase in subprime mortgages and the deterioration of lending standards, see Jesse M. Abraham, Andrey Pavlov, and Susan Wachter, "Explaining the United States' Uniquely Bad Housing Market," Institute for Law and Economics Research Paper No. 08–34, University of Pennsylvania Law School, available at http://papers.ssrn.com/sol3/papers.cfm?abstract_id=1320197.

14. HMDA data matched with the HUD list of subprime lenders; in Mayer and Pence, "Subprime Mortgages," *supra* note 11.

15. Ronald J. Mann, "Bankruptcy Reform and the 'Sweat Box' of Credit Card Debt," *University of Illinois Law Review*, 2007: 375–404; Felix Salmon, "Adam Levitin on Credit Card Minimum Payments," Market Movers Blog, *Portfolio*, December 17, 2008, available at http://www.portfolio.com/views/blogs/market-movers/2008/12/17/adam-levitin-on-credit-card-minimum-payments/.

16. International Monetary Fund, *Global Financial Stability Report: Market Developments and Issues, April 2007* (Washington: International Monetary Fund, 2009), 7, available at http://www.imf.org/External/Pubs/FT/GFSR/2007/01/index.htm.

17. Alyssa Katz, *Our Lot: How Real Estate Came to Own Us* (New York: Bloomsbury, 2009), 70; Center for Public Integrity, *Who's Behind the Financial Meltdown? The Top 25 Subprime Lenders and Their Wall Street Backers*, available at http://www.publicintegrity.org/investigations/economic_meltdown/the_subprime_25/.

18. Bob Ivry, " 'Deal with Devil' Funded Carrera Crash Before Bust," Bloomberg, December 18, 2007, available at http://www.bloomberg.com/apps/news?pid=20601170&refer=home&sid=alNDZa.Hm6O0.

19. JPMorgan Chase marketing flyer, available at http://graphics8.nytimes.com/images/blogs/executivesuite/ChaseFlyer.pdf; reported by Joe Nocera, "Subprime and the Banks: Guilty as Charged," Executive Suite Blog, *The New York Times*, October 14, 2009, available at http://executivesuite.blogs.nytimes.com/2009/10/14/subprime-and-the-banks-guilty-as-charged/.

20. Charles V. Bagli, "Sam Zell's Empire, Underwater in a Big Way," *The New York Times*, February 6, 2009, available at http://www.nytimes.com/2009/02/07/business/07properties.html.

21. Terry Pristin, "Risky Real Estate Deals Helped Doom Lehman," *The New York Times*, September 16, 2008, available at http://www.nytimes.com/2008/09/17/realestate/commercial/17real.html.

22. See Robert J. Shiller, *The Subprime Solution: How Today's Global Financial Crisis Happened, and What to Do About It* (Princeton: Princeton University Press,

2008), 30–34. Data for Figure 5-1 are from Robert Shiller, available at http://www.econ.yale.edu/~shiller/data.htm and used with his permission. Shiller's historical housing data series was first used in Robert Shiller, *Irrational Exuberance* (Princeton: Princeton University Press, 2000) and later in Shiller, *The Subprime Solution, supra*.

23. Press Release, Citigroup, "Citi Finalizes SIV Wind-down by Agreeing to Purchase All Remaining Assets," November 19, 2008, available at http://www.citibank.com/citi/press/2008/081119a.htm.

24. On the forms of recourse that banks provided to investors in their SIVs, see David Jones, "Emerging Problems with the Basel Capital Accord: Regulatory Capital Arbitrage and Related Issues," *Journal of Banking and Finance* 24 (2000): 35–58. This paper was brought to our attention by Arnold Kling.

25. Eric Friedman, Simon Johnson, and Todd Mitton, "Propping and Tunneling," *Journal of Comparative Economics* 31 (2003): 732–50.

26. Shiller, *Subprime Solution, supra* note 22, at 45–47.

27. Michael Pollan, "An Animal's Place," *The New York Times Magazine*, November 10, 2002, available at http://www.michaelpollan.com/article.php?id=55.

28. Katz, *Our Lot, supra* note 17, at 116, 126–27.

29. Mayer and Pence, "Subprime Mortgages," *supra* note 11.

30. Mark Pittman, "Subprime Securities Market Began as 'Group of 5' Over Chinese," Bloomberg, December 17, 2007, available at http://www.bloomberg.com/apps/news?pid ewsarchive&sid=aA6YC1xKUoek.

31. Hyman P. Minsky, *Stabilizing an Unstable Economy* (New York: McGraw-Hill, 2008), chapter 9 (originally published in 1986).

32. On the day-to-day workings of this chain, see "The Giant Pool of Money," *This American Life*, originally broadcast on May 9, 2008, available at http://www.thisamericanlife.org/Radio_Episode.aspx?episode=355.

33. Charles R. Geisst, *Undue Influence: How the Wall Street Elite Put the Financial System at Risk* (Hoboken, NJ: John Wiley & Sons, 2005), 256.

34. Richard Scott Carnell, Jonathan R. Macey, and Geoffrey P. Miller, *The Law of Banking and Financial Institutions*, fourth edition (Austin: Wolters Kluwer Law & Business, 2009), 466–67.

35. 12 U.S.C. § 1843(k). See Carnell et al., *Law of Banking, supra* note 34, at 465–70.

36. Gary H. Stern and Ron J. Feldman, *Too Big to Fail: The Hazards of Bank Bailouts* (Washington: Brookings Institution Press, 2009), 30–31, 63–65.

37. Frank Partnoy, *Infectious Greed: How Deceit and Risk Corrupted the Financial Markets* (New York: Henry Holt, 2004), 153–54.

38. Cited in Tett, *Fool's Gold, supra* note 6, at 39.

39. Ibid. at 34–35.

40. Saul Hansell, "Group Approves Use of Derivatives," *The New York Times*, July 22, 1993, available at http://www.nytimes.com/1993/07/22/business/market-place-group-approves-use-of-derivatives.html.

41. Jerry W. Markham, *A Financial History of the United States, Volume III: From the Age of Derivatives into the New Millennium (1970–2001)* (Armonk, NY: M. E. Sharpe, 2002), 202–4.

42. See interview with Brooksley Born, *Frontline*, August 28, 2009, transcript

available at http://www.pbs.org/wgbh/pages/frontline/warning/interviews/born .html.

43. Press Release, U.S. Treasury Department, "Joint Statement by Treasury Secretary Robert E. Rubin, Federal Reserve Board Chairman Alan Greenspan and Securities and Exchange Commission Chairman Arthur Levitt," May 7, 1998, available at http://www.treas.gov/press/releases/rr2426.htm.

44. Hearings of the House Committee on Banking and Financial Services, July 17 and July 24, 1998, available at http://commdocs.house.gov/committees/bank/hba50076.000/hba50076_0f.htm.

45. "Over-the-Counter Derivatives Markets and the Commodity Exchange Act," Report of the President's Working Group on Financial Markets, November 1999, available at http://www.ustreas.gov/press/releases/reports/otcact.pdf.

46. On the passage of the CFMA, see Paul Blumenthal, "Read the Bill: The Commodity Futures Modernization Act," *The Sunlight Foundation Blog*, April 1, 2009, available at http://blog.sunlightfoundation.com/2009/04/01/read-the -bill-the-commodity-futures-modernization-act/.

47. Tett, *Fool's Gold, supra* note 6, at 48–49. The Federal Reserve decision is Federal Reserve Board Supervisory Letter SR 96–17 (GEN), August 12, 1996, available at http://www.federalreserve.gov/boarddocs/SRLetters/1996/sr9617.htm.

48. Jones, "Emerging Problems," *supra* note 24. The views expressed in the paper were those of the author, not necessarily the Federal Reserve. See also Arnold Kling, "Not What They Had in Mind: A History of Policies That Produced the Financial Crisis of 2008," Mercatus Center at George Washington University, September 2009, available at http://papers.ssrn.com/sol3/papers.cfm ?abstract_id=1474430.

49. The rule was issued by the OCC, the OTS, the FDIC, and the Federal Reserve. Published in the Federal Register, November 29, 2001, available at http://files.ots.treas.gov/73135.pdf.

50. Reported by Corine Hegland, "Why It Collapsed," *National Journal*, April 11, 2009. On the impact of relaxed capital requirements, see Kling, "Not What They Had in Mind," *supra* note 48.

51. See, e.g., Standard & Poor's, "Structured Finance Rating Transition and Default Update as of Feb. 27, 2009," available at http://www2.standardandpoors .com/spf/pdf/media/Transition_Report_022709.pdf. Matt Krantz, "As Company Priorities Shift, Fewer Get AAA Debt Rating," *USA Today*, March 15, 2005, available at http://www.usatoday.com/money/companies/management/2005–03–15-aaa-usat_x.htm.

52. Quoted in "The Watchmen," *This American Life*, originally broadcast on June 5, 2009; transcript available at http://thislife.org/extras/radio/382 _transcript.pdf.

53. Kevin G. Hall, "How Moody's Sold Its Ratings—and Sold Out Investors," McClatchy, October 18, 2009, available at http://www.mcclatchydc.com/227/story/77244.html.

54. Elliot Blair Smith, " 'Race to Bottom' at Moody's, S&P Secured Subprime's

Boom, Bust," Bloomberg, September 25, 2008, available at http://www .bloomberg.com/apps/news?pid=20601109&sid=ax3vfya_Vtdo. Gary Witt has contested the accuracy of this article, at least as far as Moody's is concerned. See James Kwak, "Moody's, Rating Models, and CDOs," 13 Bankers Blog, April 28, 2010, available at http://13bankers.com/2010/04/28/moodys-rating -models-and-cdos/.

55. U.S. Securities and Exchange Commission, *Alternative Net Capital Requirements*, *supra* note 1.

56. Reported by Stephen Labaton, "Agency's '04 Rule Let Banks Pile Up New Debt," *The New York Times*, October 2, 2008, available at http://www.nytimes .com/2008/10/03/business/03sec.html.

57. U.S. Securities and Exchange Commission Office of Inspector General, *SEC's Oversight of Bear Stearns and Related Entities: The Consolidated Supervised Entity Program*, September 25, 2008, available at http://www.sec-oig.gov/Reports/ AuditsInspections/2008/446-a.pdf, ix.

58. Deniz Igan, Prachi Mishra, and Thierry Tressel, "A Fistful of Dollars: Lobbying and the Financial Crisis" (paper presented at the 10th Jacques Polak Annual Research Conference, hosted by the International Monetary Fund, Washington, D.C., November 5–6, 2009), available at http://www.imf.org/ external/np/res/seminars/2009/arc/pdf/igan.pdf.

59. P.L. 103–325 § 152(d); codified as 15 U.S.C. § 1639(h).

60. Greg Ip, "Did Greenspan Add to Subprime Woes? Gramlich Says Ex-Colleague Blocked Crackdown on Predatory Lenders Despite Growing Concerns," *The Wall Street Journal*, June 9, 2007, available at http://online.wsj .com/article/SB118134111823129555.html.

61. Quoted in Binyamin Appelbaum, "As Subprime Lending Crisis Unfolded, Watchdog Fed Didn't Bother Barking," *The Washington Post*, September 27, 2009, available at http://www.washingtonpost.com/wp-dyn/content/article/ 2009/09/26/AR2009092602706.html.

62. On Fed nonregulation of subprime mortgage lenders, see ibid., and Mike Konczal, "Consumer Protection at the Fed: July, 2000," *Rortybomb*, September 27, 2009, available at http://rortybomb.wordpress.com/2009/09/27/consumer -protection-at-the-fed-july-2000/.

63. 15 U.S.C. § 1602.

64. Press Release, U.S. Department of Housing and Urban Development, "HUD, Treasury Release Joint Report Recommending Actions to Curb Predatory Lending," available at http://www.hud.gov/library/bookshelf12/pressrel/ pr00–142.html.

65. Appelbaum, "Watchdog Fed Didn't Bother Barking," *supra* note 61.

66. Ip, "Did Greenspan Add to Subprime Woes?" *supra* note 60.

67. Edward M. Gramlich, "Booms and Busts: The Case of Subprime Mortgages," *Federal Reserve Bank of Kansas City Economic Review* (Fourth Quarter 2007): 105–13, available at http://www.kc.frb.org/PUBLICAT/ECONREV/PDF/ 4q07Gramlich.pdf.

68. Alan Greenspan (lecture, Federal Reserve System's 4th Annual Community Affairs

Research Conference, April 8, 2005), available at http://www.federalreserve
.gov/BoardDocs/speeches/2005/20050408/default.htm.

69. Binyamin Appelbaum and Ellen Nakashima, "Banking Regulator Played Advocate over Enforcer: Agency Let Lenders Grow Out of Control, Then Fail," *The
Washington Post*, November 23, 2008, available at http://www.washingtonpost
.com/wp-dyn/content/article/2008/11/22/AR2008112202213.html.

70. Eric Dash, "Post-Mortems Reveal Obvious Risk at Banks," *The New York
Times*, November 18, 2009, available at http://www.nytimes.com/2009/11/19/
business/19risk.html.

71. 1999 N.C. SB 1149; Ga. Code Ann., § 7–6A.

72. Press Release, Standard & Poor's, "Standard & Poor's to Disallow Georgia Fair
Lending Act Loans," January 16, 2003, available at http://www.mortgagebankers
.org/NewsandMedia/PressCenter/32153.htm.

73. Office of the Comptroller of the Currency, Department of the Treasury, *Preemption Determination and Order*, August 5, 2003, 68 F.R. 46264.

74. Cited in Christopher R. Childs, "So You've Been Preempted—What Are You
Going to Do Now?: Solutions for States Following Federal Preemption of
State Predatory Lending Statutes," *Brigham Young University Law Review*,
2004: 701–37.

75. "Except where made applicable by Federal law, state laws that obstruct, impair,
or condition a national bank's ability to fully exercise its powers to conduct
activities authorized under Federal law do not apply to national banks." 12
C.F.R. 7.009. This regulation was created by a rule of the OCC issued on January 13, 2004: 69 F.R. 1904.

76. See *Barnett Bank of Marion County v. Nelson*, 517 U.S. 25 (1996); and *Watters v.
Wachovia Bank*, 550 U.S. 1 (2007).

77. For an opposite perspective, see Charles W. Calomiris and Peter J. Wallison,
"Blame Fannie Mae and Congress for the Credit Mess," *The Wall Street
Journal*, September 23, 2008, available at http://online.wsj.com/article/
SB122212948811465427.html.

78. Fannie Mae Historical Conventional Loan Limits, updated July 30, 2009,
available at http://www.fanniemae.com/aboutfm/pdf/historicalloanlimits.pdf.

79. Katz, *Our Lot*, *supra* note 17, at 71–72; Department of Housing and Urban
Development, *Blueprint for the American Dream*, 2002, available at http://www
.hud.gov/news/releasedocs/blueprint.pdf; Wayne Barrett, "Andrew Cuomo
and Fannie and Freddie: How the Youngest Housing and Urban Development
Secretary in History Gave Birth to the Mortgage Crisis," *The Village Voice*,
August 5, 2008, available at http://www.villagevoice.com/2008–08–05/news/
how-andrew-cuomo-gave-birth-to-the-crisis-at-fannie-mae-and-freddie-mac/.

80. Doris "Tanta" Dungey, "Krugman on the GSEs," *Calculated Risk*, July 14,
2008, available at http://www.calculatedriskblog.com/2008/07/krugman-on
-gses.html.

81. James Hamilton, "Did Fannie and Freddie Cause the Mortgage Crisis?," *Econbrowser*, July 15, 2008, available at http://www.econbrowser.com/archives/
2008/07/did_fannie_and.html; David Goldstein and Kevin G. Hall, "Private

Sector Loans, Not Fannie or Freddie, Triggered Crisis," McClatchy, October 12, 2008, available at http://www.mcclatchydc.com/251/story/53802.html; Menzie Chinn, "CRA and Fannie and Freddie as Bêtes Noire," *Econbrowser*, October 21, 2008, available at http://www.econbrowser.com/archives/2008/10/cra_fannie_and.html.

82. Katz, *supra* note 17, at 71–73; Michael Carliner, "Fannie Mae and Freddie Mac—Androgynous Financiers," *Musings on Housing and the Economy*, July 12, 2008, available at http://michaelcarliner.com/blog/2008/07/12/fannie-mae-and-freddie-mac-androgynous-financiers/.

83. For the federal funds rate, see Federal Reserve Board of Governors, *Open Market Operations*, available at http://www.federalreserve.gov/fomc/fundsrate.htm. Housing prices are from the S&P/Case-Shiller Composite-10 House Price Index, adjusted using the CPI–All Urban Consumers.

84. Tim Duy, "Hawkishness Dominates," *Tim Duy's Fed Watch*, October 1, 2009, available at http://economistsview.typepad.com/timduy/2009/10/hawkishness-dominates.html.

85. Bureau of Economic Analysis, *National Income and Product Accounts*, Table 1.1.6, available at http://www.bea.gov/national/nipaweb/Index.asp; U.S. Census Bureau, *Income, Poverty, and Health Insurance Coverage in the United States: 2008*, Table A-1, available at http://www.census.gov/prod/2009pubs/p60-236.pdf.

86. On the LTCM crisis, see Roger Lowenstein, *When Genius Failed: The Rise and Fall of Long-Term Capital Management* (New York: Random House, 2000).

87. Ibid. at 159, 179–80.

88. Partnoy, *Infectious Greed, supra* note 37, at 368–70.

89. Bethany McLean and Peter Elkind, *The Smartest Guys in the Room: The Amazing Rise and Scandalous Fall of Enron* (New York: Portfolio, 2003).

90. Press Release, University of California Office of the President, "Banks, Law Firms Were Pivotal in Executing Enron Securities Fraud," April 8, 2002, available at http://www.ucop.edu/news/enron/art408.htm. The University of California was the lead plaintiff in the lawsuit.

91. For example, Enron borrowed $500 million from Citigroup, used the money to buy Treasury bills, sold the Treasury bills, and repaid Citigroup—and booked the $500 million as operating revenues. Floyd Norris, "Bankrupt Thinking: How the Banks Aided Enron's Deception," *The New York Times*, August 1, 2003, available at http://www.nytimes.com/2003/08/01/business/bankrupt-thinking-how-the-banks-aided-enron-s-deception.html.

92. Press Release, Senate Committee on Governmental Affairs, "Report Reveals 'Systemic and Catastrophic Failure' of Financial Oversight in Enron Case: Governmental Affairs Committee Recommends Reform for SEC, Wall Street Analysts, Credit Raters," October 7, 2002, available at http://hsgac.senate.gov/public/index.cfm?FuseAction=Press.MinorityNews&ContentRecord_id=2efc364b-8472-43b4-9ad1-16b9b1b96f24&Region_id=&Issue_id=2ed9adc5-1c1e-4035-90b5-62bd98bdff7f.

93. Reported in Zachary A. Goldfarb, "In Cox Years at the SEC, Policies Undercut

Action: Red Tape Halted Cases, Drove Down Penalties," *The Washington Post*, June 1, 2009, available at http://www.washingtonpost.com/wp-dyn/content/article/2009/05/31/AR2009053102254.html.

94. David Reilly, "Wall Street Fox Beds Down in Taxpayer Henhouse," Bloomberg, August 25, 2009, available at http://www.bloomberg.com/apps/news?pid=20601039&sid=aP7ePs7AR.SE; Paul S. Atkins, "Is Excessive Regulation and Litigation Eroding U.S. Financial Competitiveness?" (lecture, conference co-sponsored by the American Enterprise Institute and the Brookings Institution, Washington, D.C., April 20, 2007), available at http://www.sec.gov/news/speech/2007/spch042007psa.htm.

95. U.S. Securities and Exchange Commission Office of Inspector General, *SEC's Oversight of Bear Stearns and Related Entities: Broker-Dealer Risk Assessment Program*, September 25, 2008, available at http://www.sec-oig.gov/Reports/AuditsInspections/2008/446-b.pdf.

96. U.S. Securities and Exchange Commission, Office of Investigations, *Investigation of Failure of the SEC to Uncover Bernard Madoff's Ponzi Scheme—Public Version*, August 31, 2009, available at http://graphics8.nytimes.com/packages/pdf/business/20090904secmadoff.pdf. The total amount missing from client accounts was approximately $65 billion, including fake investment returns; the actual amount invested by and not returned to clients was closer to $20 billion.

97. James Coffman, "An Inside Perspective on Regulatory Capture," *The Baseline Scenario*, August 14, 2009, available at http://baselinescenario.com/2009/08/14/an-inside-perspective-on-regulatory-capture/.

98. Andrew G. Haldane, "Why Banks Failed the Stress Test" (lecture at the Marcus Evans Conference on Stress-Testing, February 9–10, 2009), available at http://www.bankofengland.co.uk/publications/speeches/2009/speech374.pdf.

99. Piergiorgio Alessandri and Andrew G. Haldane, "Banking on the State," *BIS Review* 139/2009, available at http://www.bis.org/review/r091111e.pdf.

100. The original Federal Reserve Act, passed in 1913, is 38 Stat. 251. The "unusual and exigent circumstances" paragraph was added to Section 13 as part of the Emergency Relief and Construction Act of 1932, 47 Stat. 709. The relevant provisions are codified as 12 U.S.C. § 343.

101. See David Wessel, *In Fed We Trust: Ben Bernanke's War on the Great Panic* (New York: Crown Business, 2009), 161. The 1991 amendment was Pub. L. 102–242, Title IV, § 473.

CHAPTER 6: TOO BIG TO FAIL

1. Mervyn King (lecture to Scottish business organizations, Edinburgh, Scotland, October 20, 2009), available at http://www.bankofengland.co.uk/publications/speeches/2009/speech406.pdf.

2. For accounts of the meeting, see Mark Landler and Eric Dash, "Drama Behind a $250 Billion Banking Deal," *The New York Times*, October 14, 2008, available at http://www.nytimes.com/2008/10/15/business/economy/15bailout.html;

and Andrew Ross Sorkin, *Too Big to Fail: The Inside Story of How Wall Street and Washington Fought to Save the Financial System from Crisis—and Themselves* (New York: Viking, 2009), chapter 20.

3. Quoted in David Wessel, *In Fed We Trust: Ben Bernanke's War on the Great Panic* (New York: Crown Business, 2009), 239.

4. Sorkin, *Too Big to Fail, supra* note 2, at chapter 20.

5. Fact Sheet, U.S. Treasury Department, TARP Capital Purchase Program: Senior Preferred Stock and Warrants: Summary of Senior Preferred Terms, available at http://www.treas.gov/press/releases/reports/document5hp1207.pdf. The preferred shares had a perpetual term, meaning they did not have to be paid back until the banks wanted to. The 5 percent interest rate increased to 9 percent after five years.

6. Phillip Swagel, "The Financial Crisis: An Inside View," Brookings Papers on Economic Activity, Spring 2009, available at http://www.brookings.edu/economics/bpea/~/media/Files/Programs/ES/BPEA/2009_spring_bpea_papers/2009_spring_bpea_swagel.pdf, 39.

7. Such as Richard Kovacevich of Wells Fargo. Landler and Dash, "Drama Behind a $250 Billion Banking Deal," *supra* note 2.

8. Sorkin, *Too Big to Fail, supra* note 2, at 525.

9. Dave Kansas, *The Wall Street Journal Guide to the End of Wall Street as We Know It: What You Need to Know About the Greatest Financial Crisis of Our Time—and How to Survive It* (New York: HarperCollins, 2009).

10. See, e.g., Gillian Tett, *Fool's Gold: How the Bold Dream of a Small Tribe at J.P. Morgan Was Corrupted by Wall Street Greed and Unleashed a Catastrophe* (New York: Free Press, 2009); Wessel, *In Fed We Trust, supra* note 3; and Sorkin, *Too Big to Fail, supra* note 2.

11. On the psychological propensity for bubbles, see Virginia Postrel, "Pop Psychology," *The Atlantic*, December 2008, available at http://www.theatlantic.com/doc/200812/financial-bubbles. On the idea that Chinese oversaving (caused by an artificially high currency) caused the crisis, see Sebastian Mallaby, "What OPEC Teaches China," *The Washington Post*, January 25, 2009, available at http://www.washingtonpost.com/wp-dyn/content/article/2009/01/23/AR2009012303291.html.

12. Sameera Anand, "Citic's Close Call with Bear Stearns," *Business Week*, March 19, 2008, available at http://www.businessweek.com/globalbiz/content/mar2008/gb20080319_886607.htm. CITIC is technically a conglomerate owned by the Chinese government, not a sovereign wealth fund. CITIC was able to back out of its deal with Bear Stearns.

13. For more on the fall of Bear Stearns, see Kate Kelly, *Street Fighters: The Last 72 Hours of Bear Stearns, the Toughest Firm on Wall Street* (New York: Portfolio, 2009); and William D. Cohan, *House of Cards: A Tale of Hubris and Wretched Excess on Wall Street* (New York: Doubleday, 2009).

14. Heidi N. Moore, "Can What Happened to Bear Happen to Other Banks?" Deal Journal Blog, *The Wall Street Journal*, March 18, 2008, available at http://blogs.wsj.com/deals/2008/03/18/repos-just-where-do-the-other-banks-stand/.

15. Kate Kelly, "Bear Stearns Neared Collapse Twice in Frenzied Last Days," *The Wall Street Journal*, May 29, 2008, available at http://online.wsj.com/article/SB121202057232127889.html.

16. On the value of the building, see Yalman Onaran, "JPMorgan Chase to Buy Bear Stearns for $240 Million," Bloomberg, March 17, 2008, available at http://www.bloomberg.com/apps/news?pid=20601087&sid=aWbXzzlzNAnw; $240 million was the total price when the deal was at $2 a share.

17. Press Release, Federal Reserve Bank of New York, "Federal Reserve Announces Establishment of Primary Dealer Credit Facility," March 16, 2008, available at http://newyorkfed.org/newsevents/news/markets/2008/rp080316.html.

18. "Merrill's Bitter Pill May Be a Sweet Deal for Lone Star," DealBook Blog, *The New York Times*, July 29, 2008, available at http://dealbook.blogs.nytimes.com/2008/07/29/merills-bitter-pill-may-be-a-sweet-deal-for-lone-star/.

19. "Factbox—U.S., European Bank Writedowns, Credit Losses," Reuters, September 24, 2009, available at http://www.reuters.com/article/fundsFundsNews/idUSLO12760820090924.

20. Quoted in Suddep Reddy, "Paulson's Bazooka: A Weapon to Be Remembered?" *The Wall Street Journal*, September 24, 2008, available at http://blogs.wsj.com/economics/2008/09/24/paulsons-bazooka-a-weapon-to-be-remembered/.

21. On Paulson's role, see Sheryl Gay Stolberg, "Paulson's Influence Displayed in Fannie and Freddie Rescue," *The New York Times*, September 9, 2008.

22. Quoted in Wessel, *In Fed We Trust*, *supra* note 3, at 14, 16.

23. Quoted in Sorkin, *Too Big to Fail*, *supra* note 2, at 336.

24. Quoted in Wessel, *In Fed We Trust*, *supra* note 3, at 23.

25. Sorkin, *Too Big to Fail*, *supra* note 2, at 2.

26. Troubled Asset Relief Program Office of the Special Inspector General, *Quarterly Report to Congress*, April 21, 2009.

27. See Carmen M. Reinhart and Kenneth S. Rogoff, "Is the 2007 U.S. Subprime Crisis So Different? An International Historical Comparison," *American Economic Review* 98 (2008): 339–44; and Carmen M. Reinhart and Kenneth S. Rogoff, "The Aftermath of Financial Crises" (paper presented at the meetings of the American Economic Association, January 3, 2009), available at http://www.aeaweb.org/annual_mtg_papers/2009/retrieve.php?pdfid=140.

28. Thomas Hoenig, "Troubled Banks Must Be Allowed a Way to Fail," *Financial Times*, May 3, 2009, available at http://www.ft.com/cms/s/0/46e2f784-380b-11de-9211-00144feabdc0.html. See also Thomas Hoenig, "Too Big Has Failed" (lecture, Omaha, NE, March 6, 2009), available at http://www.kc.frb.org/speechbio/hoenigPDF/Omaha.03.06.09.pdf.

29. See, e.g., Simon Johnson and James Kwak, "The Price of Salvation," Economists' Forum, *Financial Times*, September 24, 2008, available at http://blogs.ft.com/economistsforum/2008/09/the-price-of-salvation/; John P. Hussman, "You Can't Rescue the Financial System if You Can't Read a Balance Sheet," *Hussman Funds Weekly Market Comment*, September 29, 2008, available at http://www.hussmanfunds.com/wmc/wmc080929.htm; Luigi Zingales, "Why Paulson Is Wrong," *VOX*, September 21, 2008, available at http://voxeu.org/index.php?q-node/1670.

30. TARP Congressional Oversight Panel, *February Oversight Report: Valuing Treasury's Acquisitions*, February 6, 2009, available at http://cop.senate.gov/documents/cop-020609-report.pdf. The Congressional Budget Office separately valued the subsidy at $18 per $100 invested. Congressional Budget Office, *The Troubled Asset Relief Program: Report on Transactions Through December 31, 2008*, January 2009, available at http://www.cbo.gov/ftpdocs/99xx/doc9961/01–16-TARP.pdf.

31. Jowei Chen and Connor Raso, "Do TARP Bank Bailouts Favor Politically Connected Firms?" (working paper, October 15, 2009).

32. Dan Fitzpatrick, Damian Paletta, and Susanne Craig, "Bank of America to Get Billions in U.S. Aid: Sides Finalizing Terms for Fresh Bailout Cash; Lender Told Treasury That Without Funds, It Couldn't Close Deal for Ailing Merrill," *The Wall Street Journal*, January 15, 2009, available at http://online.wsj.com/article/SB123197132814683053.html.

33. See James Kwak, "More on Bank of America," *The Baseline Scenario*, September 28, 2009, available at http://baselinescenario.com/2009/09/28/more-on-bank-of-america/.

34. Mary Williams Walsh, "A.I.G. Lists Banks It Paid with U.S. Bailout Funds," *The New York Times*, March 15, 2009, available at http://www.nytimes.com/2009/03/16/business/16rescue.html.

35. See Gretchen Morgenson, "Revisiting a Fed Waltz with A.I.G.," *The New York Times*, November 21, 2009, available at http://www.nytimes.com/2009/11/22/business/22gret.html. For Goldman Sachs's rebuttal, see "Goldman's Response to Questions About A.I.G.," DealBook Blog, *The New York Times*, November 23, 2009, available at http://dealbook.blogs.nytimes.com/2009/11/23/goldmans-response-to-questions-about-aig/.

36. Richard Teitelbaum and Hugh Son, "New York Fed's Secret Choice to Pay for Swaps Hits Taxpayers," Bloomberg, October 27, 2009, available at http://bloomberg.com/apps/news?pid=20601109&sid=a7T5HaOgYHpE.

37. Mary Williams Walsh, "Audit Faults New York Fed in A.I.G. Bailout," *The New York Times*, November 16, 2009, available at http://www.nytimes.com/2009/11/17/business/17aig.html. UBS offered to take 98 cents on the dollar, but the New York Fed insisted on treating all banks equally, so the offer was refused.

38. In the first PPIP transaction, private investors paid about 70 cents on the dollar for a portfolio of loans, while they would only have been willing to pay 50 cents without the government financing. Edmund Andrews, "F.D.I.C. Sells Failed Bank's Troubled Mortgages to Private Investor," *The New York Times*, September 16, 2009, available at http://www.nytimes.com/2009/09/17/business/17loans.html. See also Mike Konczal, "PPIP Gets Its Debut," *Rortybomb*, September 18, 2009, available at http://rortybomb.wordpress.com/2009/09/18/ppip-debut/.

39. David Enrich, Dan Fitzpatrick, and Marshall Eckblad, "Banks Won Concessions on Tests: Fed Cut Billions off Some Initial Capital-Shortfall Estimates; Tempers Flare at Wells," *The Wall Street Journal*, May 9, 2009, available at http://online.wsj.com/article/SB124182311010302297.html.

40. *Saturday Night Live* (NBC television broadcast May 11, 2009), available at

http://www.nbc.com/Saturday_Night_Live/video/clips/geithner-cold-open/1099562/.

41. Tim Geithner, "Written Testimony: Congressional Oversight Panel," April 21, 2009, available at http://www.treas.gov/press/releases/tg94.htm.

42. Board of Governors of the Federal Reserve System, *The Supervisory Capital Assessment Program: Overview of Results*, May 7, 2009, available at http://www.federalreserve.gov/newsevents/bcreg20090507a1.pdf. Profits are "Resources Other than Capital to Absorb Losses in the More Adverse Scenario." Estimates are from the "More Adverse" scenario; however, detailed estimates were only provided for that scenario.

43. Federal Reserve, *Senior Loan Officer Opinion Survey on Bank Lending Practices*, October 2009, available at http://www.federalreserve.gov/boarddocs/snloansurvey/200911/. Data after Q3 2009 were not available at time of writing. Loan types include commercial and industrial loans (for large and small companies), commercial real estate loans, residential mortgage loans, and consumer loans.

44. Chrystia Freeland, "Lunch with the FT: Larry Summers," *Financial Times*, July 10, 2009, available at http://www.ft.com/cms/s/2/6ac06592-6ce0-11de-af56-00144feabdc0.html.

45. Office of the Special Inspector General for the Troubled Asset Relief Program, *Quarterly Report to Congress*, July 21, 2009, available at http://www.sigtarp.gov/reports/congress/2009/July2009_Quarterly_Report_to_Congress.pdf.

46. Paul Krugman, "Zombie Financial Ideas," The Conscience of a Liberal Blog, *The New York Times*, March 3, 2009, available at http://krugman.blogs.nytimes.com/2009/03/03/zombie-financial-ideas/.

47. Paul Krugman, "All the President's Zombies," The Conscience of a Liberal Blog, *The New York Times*, February 25, 2009, available at http://krugman.blogs.nytimes.com/2009/02/25/all-the-presidents-zombies/.

48. Richard W. Fisher, "Paradise Lost: Addressing 'Too Big to Fail' (With Reference to John Milton and Irving Kristol)" (lecture, Cato Institute's 27th Annual Monetary Conference, Washington, D.C., November 19, 2009).

49. "Nationalized Banks Are 'Only Answer,' Economist Stiglitz Says," *Deutsche Welle*, February 6, 2009, available at http://www.dw-world.de/dw/article/0,,4005355,00.html.

50. Nouriel Roubini, "Nationalize Insolvent Banks," *Forbes*, February 12, 2009, available at http://www.forbes.com/2009/02/11/geithner-banks-nationalization-opinions-columnists_0212_nouriel_roubini.html; Matthew Richardson and Nouriel Roubini, "Nationalize the Banks! We're All Swedes Now," *The Washington Post*, February 15, 2009, available at http://www.washingtonpost.com/wp-dyn/content/article/2009/02/12/AR2009021201602.html; Dean Baker, "The Banks Have Stolen Enough; It's Time to Take Them Over," *The Huffington Post*, January 25, 2009, available at http://www.huffingtonpost.com/dean-baker/the-banks-have-stolen-eno_b_160677.html.

51. Christine Harper and Jeff Kearns, "Citigroup Falls Below $1 as Investor Faith Erodes," Bloomberg, March 5, 2009, available at http://www.bloomberg.com/apps/news?pid=20601087&sid=aKLJO8S5nFaU.

52. Larry Summers, "International Financial Crises: Causes, Prevention, and Cures," *The American Economic Review Papers and Proceedings* 90 (2000): 1–16.

53. Simon Johnson with James Kwak, "The Quiet Coup," *The Atlantic*, May 2009 (published online on March 26, 2009), available at http://www.theatlantic.com/doc/200905/imf-advice.

54. "Hear: Geithner's Stress Test" (podcast), *Planet Money*, February 25, 2009, audio available at http://www.npr.org/blogs/money/2009/02/hear_geithners_stress_test.html.

55. Department of the Treasury, *TARP Standards for Compensation and Corporate Governance*, June 10, 2009, available at http://www.treas.gov/press/releases/reports/ec%20ifr%20fr%20web%206.9.09tg164.pdf.

56. Stephen Labaton and Edmund L. Andrews, "Geithner Said to Have Prevailed on the Bailout," *The New York Times*, February 9, 2009, available at http://www.nytimes.com/2009/02/10/business/economy/10bailout.html.

57. Department of the Treasury, *TARP Standards for Compensation and Corporate Governance*, *supra* note 55.

58. Stephen Labaton, "Treasury to Set Executives' Pay at 7 Ailing Firms," *The New York Times*, June 10, 2009, available at http://www.nytimes.com/2009/06/11/business/11pay.html.

59. Stephen Labaton, "Ailing, Banks Still Field Strong Lobby at Capitol," *The New York Times*, June 4, 2009, available at http://www.nytimes.com/2009/06/05/business/economy/05bankrupt.html.

60. Ibid.

61. Company annual and quarterly reports.

62. David Cho, "Banks 'Too Big to Fail' Have Grown Even Bigger: Behemoths Born of the Bailout Reduce Consumer Choice, Tempt Corporate Moral Hazard," *The Washington Post*, August 28, 2009, available at http://www.washingtonpost.com/wp-dyn/content/article/2009/08/27/AR2009082704193.html.

63. Office of the Comptroller of the Currency, *Quarterly Report on Bank Trading and Derivatives Activities, Second Quarter 2009*, Table 2, available at http://www.occ.treas.gov/deriv/deriv.htm. Market share is the top five bank holding companies' share of all derivatives contracts held by all U.S. bank holding companies, by notional value.

64. From Federal Deposit Insurance Corporation data, cited in Dean Baker and Travis McArthur, "The Value of the 'Too Big to Fail' Big Bank Subsidy," Center for Economic and Policy Research Issue Brief, September 2009, available at http://www.cepr.net/documents/publications/too-big-to-fail-2009-09.pdf.

65. Cho, "Banks 'Too Big to Fail' Have Grown Even Bigger," *supra* note 62.

66. Tyler Durden, "Exclusive: AIG Was Responsible for the Banks' January & February Profitability," *Zero Hedge*, March 29, 2009, available at http://zerohedge.blogspot.com/2009/03/exclusive-aig-was-responsible-for-banks.html.

67. Press Release, Goldman Sachs, "Goldman Sachs Reports Second Quarter Earnings per Common Share of $4.93," July 14, 2009, available at http://www2.goldmansachs.com/our-firm/press/press-releases/current/pdfs/2009-q2-earnings.pdf.

68. Quoted in Henny Sender, "Wall Street Profits from Trades with Fed," *Financial*

Times, August 2, 2009, available at http://www.ft.com/cms/s/0/e84383dc-7f8c -11de-85dc-00144feabdc0.html.

69. Elizabeth Hester and Elisa Martinuzzi, "JPMorgan Tightens Grip on Equity Sales by Selling Own Shares," Bloomberg, June 28, 2009, available at http:// www.bloomberg.com/apps/news?pid=20601087&sid=aYlWNEyLQzPk.

70. Quoted in Jenny Anderson, "Despite Bailouts, Business as Usual at Goldman," *The New York Times*, August 5, 2009, available at http://www.nytimes.com/ 2009/08/06/business/06goldman.html.

71. Felix Salmon, "Chart of the Day: Goldman VaR," Reuters, July 15, 2009, available at http://blogs.reuters.com/felix-salmon/2009/07/15/chart-of-the-day -goldman-var/. See also Andrew Ross Sorkin, "Taking a Chance on Risk, Again," DealBook Blog, *The New York Times*, September 17, 2009, available at http://dealbook.blogs.nytimes.com/2009/09/17/taking-a-chance-on-risk-again/. While VaR—value-at-risk—is a poor way of estimating potential losses under extreme market conditions, it does measure the change in the riskiness of a portfolio relative to historical data.

72. Quoted in Simon Clark and Caroline Binham, "Profit 'Is Not Satanic,' Barclays CEO Varley Says," Bloomberg, November 3, 2009, available at http:// www.bloomberg.com/apps/news?pid ewsarchive&sid=aGR1F_bjSIZw.

73. Quoted in John Arlidge, "I'm Doing 'God's Work.' Meet Mr Goldman Sachs," *The Sunday Times* (London), November 8, 2009, available at http://www .timesonline.co.uk/tol/news/world/us_and_americas/article6907681.ece.

74. Job losses are seasonally adjusted nonfarm employment data from the Bureau of Labor Statistics, *Current Employment Statistics*, available at http://www.bls .gov/ces/.

75. GDP data are from Bureau of Economic Analysis, *National Income and Product Accounts*, Table 1.1.6, available at http://bea.gov/national/nipaweb/ SelectTable.asp.

76. Unemployment statistics are from Bureau of Labor Statistics, *Current Population Survey*, available at http://www.bls.gov/webapps/legacy/cpsatab12.htm (U-3 and U-6).

77. Deficit for 2009 is from Congressional Budget Office, *Budget Projections*, available at http://cbo.gov/budget/budproj.shtml; historical deficit figures are from Office of Management and Budget, *Historical Tables*, available at http://www .whitehouse.gov/omb/budget/Historicals/.

78. Congressional Budget Office, *The Budget and Economic Outlook: Fiscal Years 2008 to 2018*, January 2008, available at http://cbo.gov/ftpdocs/89xx/ doc8917/01–23–2008_BudgetOutlook.pdf; Congressional Budget Office, *The Budget and Economic Outlook: An Update*, August 2009, available at http:// cbo.gov/ftpdocs/105xx/doc10521/08–25-BudgetUpdate.pdf.

79. Carmen M. Reinhart and Kenneth S. Rogoff, *This Time Is Different: Eight Centuries of Financial Folly* (Princeton: Princeton University Press, 2009), 231–32.

80. Maura Reynolds and Janet Hook, "Critics Say Bush Is Not Doing Enough," *Los Angeles Times*, March 18, 2008, available at http://articles.latimes.com/ 2008/mar/18/nation/na-bush18; cited in Sorkin, *Too Big to Fail*, *supra* note 2, at 38.

81. "Executive Compensation: Vikram S. Pandit," *Equilar*, available at http://www.equilar.com/CEO_Compensation/Citigroup_Vikram_S._Pandit.php.

82. David Enrich, "Old Lane Managers Look for Exit from Citi," *The Wall Street Journal*, December 24, 2008, available at http://online.wsj.com/article/SB123008418545132173.html.

83. Sorkin, *Too Big to Fail, supra* note 2, at 201–2.

84. Ibid., at 210–11, 221–22, 382.

85. Jackie Calmes, "Obama's Economic Team Shows Influence of Robert Rubin—With a Difference," *The New York Times*, November 24, 2008.

86. Jo Becker and Gretchen Morgenson, "Geithner, Member and Overseer of Finance Club," *The New York Times*, April 26, 2009, available at http://www.nytimes.com/2009/04/27/business/27geithner.html.

87. Robert Schmidt, "Geithner Aides Reaped Millions Working for Banks, Hedge Funds," Bloomberg, October 14, 2009, available at http://www.bloomberg.com/apps/news?pid=20601087&sid=abo3Zo0ifzJg.

88. For a less positive interpretation, see Matt Taibbi, "Obama's Big Sellout," *Rolling Stone*, December 9, 2009, available at http://www.rollingstone.com/politics/story/31234647/obamas_big_sellout.

89. Michael Barr, Written Testimony Before the Senate Committee on Banking, Housing and Urban Affairs, July 14, 2009, available at http://www.treas.gov/press/releases/tg208.htm; Noam Scheiber, "Could Wall Street Actually Lose in Congress?," *The New Republic*, November 23, 2009, available at http://www.tnr.com/blog/the-stash/could-wall-street-actually-lose-congress.

90. Louis Uchitelle, "Volcker Fails to Sell a Bank Strategy," *The New York Times*, October 20, 2009, available at http://www.nytimes.com/2009/10/21/business/21volcker.html.

91. Information on Geithner's calendar was reported in Matt Apuzzo and Daniel Wagner, "Mr. Geithner, Wall Street Is on Line 1 (Again): When These Men Call, the Treasury Boss Listens," Associated Press, October 8, 2009, available at http://finance.yahoo.com/news/Mr-Geithner-Wall-Street-is-on-apf-3283001415.html?x=0.

92. Arthur M. Schlesinger, Jr., *The Coming of the New Deal, 1933–1935* (Boston: Mariner, 2003), 444.

93. Michael Lewis (lecture, Hudson Union Society, New York, NY, June 1, 2009), video available at http://www.huffingtonpost.com/2009/06/18/michael-lewis-attacks-gol_n_217542.html.

CHAPTER 7: THE AMERICAN OLIGARCHY

1. Paul Volcker, Statement Before the Committee on Banking and Financial Services of the House of Representatives, September 24, 2009, available at http://www.house.gov/apps/list/hearing/financialsvcs_dem/volcker.pdf.

2. Alan Greenspan, "The Global Financial Crisis: Causes and Consequences" (lecture, C. Peter McColough Series on International Economics, Council on Foreign Relations, October 15, 2009), available at http://www.cfr.org/publication/20417/.

3. Richard Scott Carnell, Jonathan R. Macey, and Geoffrey P. Miller, *The Law of Banking and Financial Institutions*, fourth edition (Austin: Wolters Kluwer Law & Business, 2009), 29.

4. Robert D. Hershey, Jr., "Bush Signs Savings Legislation; Remaking of Industry Starts Fast," *The New York Times*, August 10, 1989, available at http://www.nytimes.com/1989/08/10/business/bush-signs-savings-legislation-remaking-of-industry-starts-fast.html.

5. "The Watchmen," *This American Life*, first broadcast on June 5, 2009, transcript available at http://www.thisamericanlife.org/extras/radio/382_transcript.pdf.

6. Quoted in Jeff Zeleny, "Obama Weighs Quick Undoing of Bush Policy," *The New York Times*, November 9, 2009, available at http://www.nytimes.com/2008/11/10/us/politics/10obama.html.

7. Eric Dash, "Bankers Pledge Cooperation with Obama," *The New York Times*, March 27, 2009, available at http://www.nytimes.com/2009/03/28/business/economy/28bank.html.

8. Barack Obama, "Remarks by the President on 21st Century Financial Regulatory Reform," June 17, 2009, available at http://www.whitehouse.gov/the_press_office/Remarks-of-the-President-on-Regulatory-Reform.

9. For an overview of the administration's proposals, see Department of the Treasury, *Financial Regulatory Reform: A New Foundation: Rebuilding Financial Supervision and Regulation*, June 17, 2009, available at http://www.financialstability.gov/docs/regs/FinalReport_web.pdf.

10. Barack Obama, "Remarks by the President on Financial Rescue and Reform," Federal Hall, New York, NY, September 14, 2009, available at http://www.whitehouse.gov/the_press_office/Remarks-by-the-President-on-Financial-Rescue-and-Reform-at-Federal-Hall.

11. Proposals to strengthen shareholder governance may help a little, but they overlook the fact that shareholders themselves benefit from increased risk-taking and government guarantees just like bank executives. See, e.g., Lucian A. Bebchuk and Holger Spamann, "Regulating Bankers' Pay," Harvard Law and Economics Discussion Paper No. 641, June 2009, available at http://papers.ssrn.com/sol3/papers.cfm?abstract_id=1410072.

12. Joe Nocera, "Only a Hint of Roosevelt in Financial Overhaul," *The New York Times*, June 17, 2009, available at http://www.nytimes.com/2009/06/18/business/18nocera.html.

13. Jonathan D. Salant and Lizzie O'Leary, "Citigroup Taxpayer Ownership Doesn't Prevent Lobbying," Bloomberg, October 23, 2009, available at http://www.bloomberg.com/apps/news?pid=20601103&sid=axiOjGkS2zYY; Michael Hirsh, "Why Is Barney Frank So Effing Mad?," *Newsweek*, December 5, 2009, available at http://www.newsweek.com/id/225781.

14. Quoted in Hirsh, "Barney Frank," *supra* note 13.

15. Stephen Labaton, "Bill Shields Most Banks from Review," *The New York Times*, October 15, 2009, available at http://www.nytimes.com/2009/10/16/business/16regulate.html; Hirsh, "Barney Frank," *supra* note 13.

16. William Greider, "The Money Man's Best Friend," *The Nation*, November 11, 2009, available at http://www.thenation.com/doc/20091130/greider.

17. Martin Wolf, "Why Narrow Banking Alone Is Not the Finance Solution," *Financial Times*, September 29, 2009, available at http://www.ft.com/cms/s/0/34cbca0c-ad28-11de-9caf-00144feabdc0.html.

18. *Time* Magazine/ABT SRBI Survey, conducted October 26–27, 2009; results available at http://www.srbi.com/Wall%20Street%20Questionnaire%20and%20Poll%20Results.pdf.

19. Keith Ernst, Debbie Bocian, and Wei Li, "Steered Wrong: Brokers, Borrowers, and Subprime Loans," Center for Responsible Lending, April 8, 2008, available at http://www.responsiblelending.org/mortgage-lending/research-analysis/steered-wrong-brokers-borrowers-and-subprime-loans.pdf.

20. Michael Powell, "Bank Accused of Pushing Mortgage Deals on Blacks," *The New York Times*, June 6, 2009, available at http://www.nytimes.com/2009/06/07/us/07baltimore.html.

21. Cited in Michael Powell and Janet Roberts, "Minorities Affected Most as New York Foreclosures Rise," *The New York Times*, May 15, 2009, available at http://www.nytimes.com/2009/05/16/nyregion/16foreclose.html.

22. Ron Lieber and Andrew Martin, "The Card Game: Overspending on Debit Cards Is a Boon for Banks," *The New York Times*, September 8, 2009, available at http://www.nytimes.com/2009/09/09/your-money/credit-and-debit-cards/09debit.html; Center for Responsible Lending, "Quick Facts on Overdraft Loans," available at http://www.responsiblelending.org/overdraft-loans/research-analysis/quick-facts-on-overdraft-loans.html.

23. See Adam Levitin, "Complex Pricing of Credit Cards Should Be Simplified," *Chicago Tribune*, December 27, 2007, available at http://archives.chicagotribune.com/2007/dec/27/opinion/chi-oped1227creditdec27.

24. Adam Levitin, "Priceless? The Social Costs of Credit Card Merchant Restraints," *Harvard Journal on Legislation* 45 (2008): 1–58. See also Felix Salmon, "How Banks Give Up Trust for Money," Reuters, August 11, 2009, available at http://blogs.reuters.com/felix-salmon/2009/08/11/how-banks-give-up-trust-for-money/.

25. Edward M. Gramlich, *Subprime Mortgages: America's Latest Boom and Bust* (Washington: Urban Institute Press, 2007), 19.

26. Interview with Shailesh Mehta, *Frontline*, July 7, 2009, available at http://www.pbs.org/wgbh/pages/frontline/creditcards/interviews/mehta.html.

27. Elizabeth Warren, "Unsafe at Any Rate," *Democracy: A Journal of Ideas*, Summer 2007, available at http://www.democracyjournal.org/article.php?ID=6528.

28. Department of the Treasury, *Financial Regulatory Reform*, *supra* note 9, at 67–68.

29. Peter J. Wallison, "Elitist Protection Consumers Don't Need," *The Washington Post*, July 13, 2009, available at http://www.washingtonpost.com/wp-dyn/content/article/2009/07/12/AR2009071201663.html. See also James Kwak, "The AEI Versus the Real World," *The Baseline Scenario*, July 15, 2009, available at http://baselinescenario.com/2009/07/15/consumer-financial-protection-peter-wallison/.

30. See, e.g., R. Michael S. Menzies, Sr., "Testimony on Behalf of the Independent Community Bankers of America Before the House Financial Services Committee," July 15, 2009, available at http://www.icba.org/files/ICBASites/PDFs/test071509.pdf.

31. Stephen Labaton, "Regulators Spar for Turf in Financial Overhaul," *The New York Times*, July 24, 2009, available at http://www.nytimes.com/2009/07/25/business/economy/25regulate.html.

32. Kevin Drawbaugh, "Rep. Frank Extracts Vanilla from Consumer Agency," Reuters, September 22, 2009, available at http://www.reuters.com/article/wtUSInvestingNews/idUSTRE58L6YR20090922.

33. Charles Duhigg and Carter Dougherty, "From Midwest to M.T.A., Pain from Global Gamble," *The New York Times*, November 1, 2008, available at http://www.nytimes.com/2008/11/02/business/02global.html; Tavakoli was quoted in the article.

34. Jamie Dimon, "No More 'Too Big to Fail,' " *The Washington Post*, November 13, 2009, available at http://www.washingtonpost.com/wp-dyn/content/article/2009/11/12/AR2009111209924.html.

35. Gary H. Stern and Ron J. Feldman, *Too Big to Fail: The Hazards of Bank Bailouts* (Washington: Brookings Institution Press, 2009).

36. Andrew Ross Sorkin, *Too Big to Fail: The Inside Story of How Wall Street and Washington Fought to Save the Financial System—and Themselves* (New York: Viking, 2009), 236.

37. On the race to save Morgan Stanley and Goldman Sachs, see ibid. at 409–83.

38. See, e.g., Paul Krugman, "Too Big to Fail FAIL," The Conscience of a Liberal Blog, *The New York Times*, June 18, 2009, available at http://krugman.blogs.nytimes.com/2009/06/18/too-big-to-fail-fail/.

39. See, e.g., Ben Bernanke, "Financial Regulation and Supervision After the Crisis: The Role of the Federal Reserve" (lecture, Federal Reserve Bank of Boston 54th Economic Conference, Chatham, MA, October 23, 2009), available at http://www.federalreserve.gov/newsevents/speech/bernanke20091023a.htm.

40. See, e.g., Department of the Treasury, *Financial Regulatory Reform, supra* note 9.

41. Larry Summers, "International Financial Crises: Causes, Prevention, and Cures," *The American Economic Review Papers and Proceedings* 90 (2000): 1–16.

42. Piergiorgio Alessandri and Andrew G. Haldane, "Banking on the State," *BIS Review* 139/2009, available at http://www.bis.org/review/r091111e.pdf.

43. Dean Baker and Travis McArthur, "The Value of the 'Too Big to Fail' Big Bank Subsidy," Center for Economic and Policy Research Issue Brief, September 2009, available at http://www.cepr.net/documents/publications/too-big-to-fail-2009-09.pdf.

44. See Department of the Treasury, *Financial Regulatory Reform, supra* note 9, at Part IV.A.

45. Department of the Treasury, *Principles for Reforming the U.S. and International Regulatory Capital Framework for Banking Firms*, September 3, 2009, available at http://www.treas.gov/press/releases/docs/capital-statement_090309.pdf.

46. See, e.g., Thomas Hoenig, "Troubled Banks Must Be Allowed a Way to Fail," *Financial Times*, May 3, 2009, available at http://www.ft.com/cms/s/0/

46e2f784–380b–11de–9211–00144feabdc0.html.

47. Gillian Tett, "The Sweet Fix of CoCos?," *Financial Times*, November 12, 2009, available at http://www.ft.com/cms/s/0/797f2cb6-cfb5–11de-a36d -00144feabdc0.html; Gillian Tett, *Saving the Sun: How Wall Street Mavericks Shook Up Japan's Financial World and Made Billions* (New York: HarperCollins, 2003).

48. Lehman Brothers, "Q3 2008 Guidance Call," September 10, 2008, transcript available at http://www.scribd.com/doc/13231363/Lehman-Transcript.

49. Shannon D. Harrington and Neil Unmack, "Lehman Credit-Swap Auction Sets Payout of 91.38 Cents," Bloomberg, October 10, 2008, available at http:// www.bloomberg.com/apps/news?pid=20601087&sid=aLkOZnNcDmSQ.

50. Research Report, Morgan Stanley, "Banking—Large and Midcap Banks: Bid for Growth Caps Capital Ask," November 17, 2009.

51. According to the proposal of the Treasury Department. Department of the Treasury, *Financial Regulatory Reform, supra* note 9, at Part IV.A.

52. See, e.g., Aaron Kiersch, "JPMorgan CEO Jamie Dimon Donates Serious Cash to Democrats," *OpenSecrets.org*, July 21, 2009, available at http://www .opensecrets.org/news/2009/07/jpmorgan-ceo-jamie-dimon-donat.html.

53. See Adam Levitin, "Too-Big-to-Fail Resolution: Why One Size Can't Fit All," *Credit Slips*, October 25, 2009, available at http://www.creditslips.org/creditslips/ 2009/10/toobigtofail-resolution-why-one-size-cant-fit-all.html.

54. Dimon, "No More 'Too Big to Fail,' " *supra* note 34.

55. Quoted in Christine Harper, "Blankfein Defends Goldman Sachs Against Breakup," Bloomberg, November 10, 2009, available at http://www.bloomberg .com/apps/news?pid=20601087&sid=ap5t.QjB.veg.

56. Quoted in Alex Blumberg, "Rewriting the Rules of the Financial System," NPR, October 9, 2009, available at http://www.npr.org/templates/story/ story.php?storyId=113650178.

57. Quoted in Eric Dash, "If It's Too Big to Fail, Is It Too Big to Exist?," *The New York Times*, June 20, 2009, available at http://www.nytimes.com/2009/06/ 21/weekinreview/21dash.html.

58. Joseph Stiglitz, "Too Big to Fail or Too Big to Save? Examining the Systemic Threats of Large Financial Institutions," Statement Before the Joint Economic Committee, April 21, 2009, available at http://jec.senate.gov/index.cfm ?FuseAction=Hearings.HearingsCalendar&ContentRecord_id=c89b185b-5056 –8059–7670–0ce56df64713&Region_id=&Issue_id=. At the same hearing, Simon Johnson said, "[T]he advice from those with experience in severe banking crises would be just as simple: break the oligarchy. In the U.S., this means breaking up the oversized institutions that have a disproportionate influence on public policy." Simon Johnson, "Too Big to Fail or Too Big to Save? Examining the Systemic Threats of Large Financial Institutions," Statement Before the Joint Economic Committee, April 21, 2009, available at the same URL.

59. Paul Volcker, Statement Before the Committee on Banking and Financial Services, *supra* note 1.

60. Louis Uchitelle, "Volcker Fails to Sell a Bank Strategy," *The New York Times*,

October 20, 2009, available at http://www.nytimes.com/2009/10/21/business/21volcker.html.

61. Mervyn King (lecture to Scottish business organizations, Edinburgh, Scotland, October 20, 2009), available at http://www.bankofengland.co.uk/publications/speeches/2009/speech406.pdf.

62. John Kay, *Narrow Banking: The Reform of Banking Regulation* (London: Centre for the Study of Financial Innovation, 2009).

63. Laurence J. Kotlikoff, *Jimmy Stewart Is Dead: Ending the World's Financial Plague Before It Strikes Again* (Hoboken, NJ: Wiley, 2010).

64. Richard W. Fisher, "Paradise Lost: Addressing 'Too Big to Fail' (With Reference to John Milton and Irving Kristol)" (lecture, Cato Institute's 27th Annual Monetary Conference, Washington, D.C., November 19, 2009).

65. Alan Greenspan, "The Global Financial Crisis: Causes and Consequences" (lecture, C. Peter McColough Series on International Economics, Council on Foreign Relations, October 15, 2009), available at http://www.cfr.org/publication/20417/.

66. Dimon, "No More 'Too Big to Fail,'" *supra* note 34; Scott Talbott of the Financial Services Roundtable, recorded during a panel discussion of the Pew Charitable Trusts, "Planet Money Live," *Planet Money*, September 14, 2009, available at http://www.npr.org/blogs/money/2009/09/podcast_planet_money_live.html; Charles Calomiris, "In the World of Banks, Bigger Can Be Better," *The Wall Street Journal*, October 19, 2009, available at http://online.wsj.com/article/SB10001424052748704500604574483222678425130.html.

67. From 424(b)(5) filings with the SEC, dated June 18, 2008, available at http://sec.gov/Archives/edgar/data/200406/000095012308007069/y60660b5e424b5.htm, and October 30, 2007, available at http://sec.gov/Archives/edgar/data/200406/000095012307014699/y41496b5e424b5.htm.

68. Dean Amel, Colleen Barnes, Fabio Panetta, and Carmelo Salleo, "Consolidation and Efficiency in the Financial Sector: A Review of the International Evidence," *Journal of Banking and Finance* 28 (2004): 2493–2519. See also Stephen A. Rhoades, "A Summary of Merger Performance Studies in Banking, 1980–93, and an Assessment of the 'Operating Performance' and 'Event Study' Methodologies," Federal Reserve Board Staff Studies 167, summarized in *Federal Reserve Bulletin*, July 1994, complete paper available at http://www.federalreserve.gov/Pubs/staffstudies/1990–99/ss167.pdf: "In general, despite substantial diversity among the nineteen operating performance studies, the findings point strongly to a lack of improvement in efficiency or profitability as a result of bank mergers, and these findings are robust both within and across studies and over time." See also Allen N. Berger and David B. Humphrey, "Bank Scale Economies, Mergers, Concentration, and Efficiency: The U.S. Experience," Wharton Financial Institutions Center Working Paper 94–24, 1994, available at http://fic.wharton.upenn.edu/fic/papers/94/9425.pdf.

69. Roger W. Ferguson, Jr., Philipp Hartmann, Fabio Panetta, and Richard Portes, *International Financial Stability* (London: Centre for Economic Policy Research, 2007), 93–94. However, the jury remains out on whether there are significant economies of scale in U.S. banking. See David C. Wheelock and

Paul W. Wilson, "Are U.S. Banks Too Large?" (Federal Reserve Bank of St. Louis Working Paper 2009–054A, October 2009), available at http://research .stlouisfed.org/wp/more/2009–054/.

70. Edward J. Kane, "Extracting Nontransparent Safety Net Subsidies by Strategically Expanding and Contracting a Financial Institution's Accounting Balance Sheet," *Journal of Financial Services Research* 36 (2009): 161–68.

71. Kevin J. Stiroh, "How Did Bank Holding Companies Prosper in the 1990s?," *Journal of Banking and Finance* 24 (2000): 1703–45.

72. See, e.g., Kevin J. Stiroh, "Information Technology and the U.S. Productivity Revival: What Do the Industry Data Say?," *American Economic Review* 92 (2002): 1559–76.

73. Goldman Sachs, 1999 Annual Report, available at http://www2.goldmansachs .com/our-firm/investors/financials/archived/annual-reports/attachments/1999 -annual-report.pdf; Goldman Sachs, 2008 Annual Report, available at http:// www2.goldmansachs.com/our-firm/investors/financials/current/annual-reports/ 2008-annual-report.html.

74. Morgan Stanley Dean Witter, 1998 Annual Report, available at http:// www.morganstanley.com/about/ir/annual/1998/html/index.html; Morgan Stanley, 2008 Annual Report (Form 10-K), available at http://www.morganstanley .com/about/ir/shareholder/10k2007/10k11302007.pdf.

75. "Amendment to the Committee Print of October 29, 2009 Offered by Mr. Kanjorski of Pennsylvania," available at http://www.house.gov/apps/list/speech/ financialsvcs_dem/kanjorski_amendment_002_xml.pdf.

76. Committee Print of the Restoring American Financial Stability Act, available at http://banking.senate.gov/public/index.cfm?FuseAction=Files.View&FileStore _id=943242e1-ca66–411c-89e2–8954eb3fc085.

77. David Cho, "Banks 'Too Big to Fail' Have Grown Even Bigger: Behemoths Born of the Bailout Reduce Consumer Choice, Tempt Corporate Moral Hazard," *The Washington Post*, August 28, 2009, available at http://www.washingtonpost .com/wp-dyn/content/article/2009/08/27/AR2009082704193.html.

78. Bear Stearns, 2007 Annual Report (Form 10-K), available at http://www .bearstearns.com/includes/pdfs/investor_relations/proxy/10k2007.pdf.

79. Company annual reports. See also Figure 7-1 in this book.

80. Thomas Philippon, "The Evolution of the U.S. Financial Industry from 1860 to 2007: Theory and Evidence" (working paper, November 2008), Table 3, available at http://pages.stern.nyu.edu/~tphilipp/papers/finsize.pdf.

81. Company annual and quarterly reports; GDP data from Bureau of Economic Analysis, *National Income and Product Accounts*, Table 1.1.5, available at http:// www.bea.gov/national/nipaweb/Index.asp. Figures are as of September 2009.

82. "Officials Fear Systemic Risks of Bailout," *Marketplace*, October 21, 2009, available at http://marketplace.publicradio.org/display/web/2009/10/21/ pm-systemtic-risk/.

83. The origins of the Sherman Act of 1890 are unclear and remain controversial. See Robert H. Bork, "Legislative Intent and the Policy of the Sherman Act," *Journal of Law and Economics* 9 (1966): 7–48; and George J. Stigler, "The Origins of the Sherman Act," *Journal of Legal Studies* 14 (1985): 1–12. Thomas

Hazlett argues it was a political compromise designed to provide Republican legislators "with a cosmetic defense on the trust question, in anticipation of the upcoming consumer-to-industry transfers in the McKinley Tariff," and "it was not thought to do more than codify and federalize the common law." Thomas W. Hazlett, "The Legislative History of the Sherman Act Re-examined," *Economic Inquiry* 30 (1992): 263–76.

84. Richard Hofstadter, "What Happened to the Antitrust Movement?" in Richard Hofstadter, *The Paranoid Style in American Politics and Other Essays* (New York: Vintage, 2008), 188–237.

EPILOGUE

1. Paul E. Kanjorski, "Explanation of Vote on the Conference Report for the Dodd-Frank Wall Street Reform and Consumer Protection Act (H.R. 4173)," June 30, 2010.

2. The Dodd-Frank Act is Public Law 111-203, available at http://thomas.loc.gov/cgi-bin/query/z?c111:H.R.4173:.

3. Barack Obama, "Remarks by the President at Signing of Dodd-Frank Wall Street Reform and Consumer Protection Act," July 21, 2010, available at http://www.whitehouse.gov/the-press-office/remarks-president-signing-dodd-frank-wall-street-reform-and-consumer-protection-act.

4. John Cassidy, "The Volcker Rule," *The New Yorker*, July 26, 2010.

5. John Heilemann, "Obama Is from Mars, Wall Street Is from Venus," *New York*, May 22, 2010, available at http://nymag.com/news/politics/66188/.

6. "JPMorgan Chief Warns of Overregulation—Report," Reuters, April 18, 2010, available at http://www.reuters.com/article/idUSLDE63H0E420100418.

7. Shahien Nasiripour, "JPMorgan Chase Memo Sneers at 'Ignorant' Senators, 'Time for the Grown-ups to Step In,'" *The Huffington Post*, May 4, 2010, available at http://www.huffingtonpost.com/2010/05/04/jpmorgan-chase-memo-goldman_n_562459.html.

8. "Lehman Brothers Holdings Inc. Chapter 11 Proceedings Examiner's Report," available at http://lehmanreport.jenner.com/.

9. Press Release, SEC, "SEC Charges Goldman Sachs with Fraud in Structuring and Marketing of CDO Tied to Subprime Mortgages," April 16, 2010, available at http://www.sec.gov/news/press/2010/2010-59.htm. Synthetic CDOs are discussed in chapter 5 of this book.

10. Complaint, *Securities and Exchange Commission v. Goldman Sachs & Co. and Fabrice Tourre*, available at http://www.sec.gov/litigation/complaints/2010/comp-pr2010-59.pdf.

11. Jesse Eisinger and Jake Bernstein, "The Magnetar Trade: How One Hedge Fund Helped Keep the Bubble Going," *ProPublica*, April 9, 2010, available at http://www.propublica.org/article/the-magnetar-trade-how-one-hedge-fund-helped-keep-the-housing-bubble-going. Magnetar was also discussed in Yves Smith, *ECONned: How Unenlightened Self Interest Undermined Democracy and Corrupted Capitalism* (New York: Palgrave Macmillan, 2010).

12. "Inside Job," *This American Life*, first broadcast on April 9, 2010.

13. Eisinger and Bernstein, "The Magnetar Trade," *supra* note 11.

14. David M. Herszenhorn, "Senate Liberals Push for Strict Financial Rules," *The New York Times*, May 5, 2010, available at http://www.nytimes.com/2010/05/06/business/economy/06dems.html.

15. See, for example, Shahien Nasiripour and Ryan Grim, "Obama's Treasury Dept. Working to Defeat Derivatives Proposal 'Of Utmost Importance' to Reforming Wall Street," *The Huffington Post*, June 14, 2010, available at http://www.huffingtonpost.com/2010/06/14/obamas-treasury-dept-work_n_611205.html.

16. Davis Polk, "Summary of the Dodd-Frank Wall Street Reform and Consumer Protection Act, Enacted into Law on July 21, 2010," July 21, 2010, available at http://www.davispolk.com/files/Publication/efb94428-9911-4472-b5dd-006e9c6185bb/Presentation/PublicationAttachment/efd835f6-2014-4a48-832d-00aa2a4e3fdd/070910_Financial_Reform_Summary.pdf.

17. Eric Lichtblau, "Ex-Regulators Get Set to Lobby on New Financial Rules," *The New York Times*, July 27, 2010, available at http://www.nytimes.com/2010/07/28/business/28lobby.html.

18. Cassidy, "The Volcker Rule," *supra* note 4.

19. David M. Herszenhorn, "House-Senate Talks Drop New Credit-Rating Rules," *The New York Times*, June 15, 2010, available at http://www.nytimes.com/2010/06/16/business/16regulate.html.

20. Heilemann, "Obama Is from Mars, Wall Street Is from Venus," *supra* note 5.

21. Yalman Onaran, "Volcker Said to Be Disappointed with Final Version of His Rule," Bloomberg, June 30, 2010, available at http://www.bloomberg.com/news/2010-06-30/volcker-said-to-be-disappointed-with-final-version-of-rule-named-after-him.html.

22. Volcker wrote, "I am fully in support of the Merkley-Levin amendment," in a letter obtained by *The Huffington Post*, available at http://big.assets.huffingtonpost.com/VolckerMay192010.pdf.

23. Cassidy, "The Volcker Rule," *supra* note 4.

24. See Heilemann, "Obama Is from Mars, Wall Street Is from Venus," *supra* note 5.

25. Press Release, SEC, "Goldman Sachs to Pay Record $550 Million to Settle SEC Charges Related to Subprime Mortgage CDO," July 15, 2010, available at http://www.sec.gov/news/press/2010/2010-123.htm.

26. Press Release, Goldman Sachs, "Goldman, Sachs & Co. Agrees to Settlement with SEC," July 15, 2010, available at http://www2.goldmansachs.com/our-firm/press/press-releases/current/settlement.html.

Further Reading

Tens of millions of words have been written about the recent global financial crisis, its causes, and the lessons one might draw from it. We are probably responsible for a few hundred thousand of them on our blog, *The Baseline Scenario* (http://baselinescenario.com). The specific sources we drew on are detailed in the Notes to this book. This section is intended only to provide a starting point for readers who would like to learn more about the financial crisis and the issues discussed in this book; we have chosen to include only books and blogs (not academic papers), as they are most likely to be useful for a general audience. The lists below are necessarily incomplete and arbitrary, but we hope that at least some readers will find them useful.

BOOKS

Detailed Accounts of the Financial Crisis

Cohan, William D. *House of Cards: A Tale of Hubris and Wretched Excess on Wall Street*. New York: Doubleday, 2009.

Kelly, Kate. *Street Fighters: The Last 72 Hours of Bear Stearns, the Toughest Firm on Wall Street*. New York: Portfolio, 2009.

Lewis, Michael. *The Big Short: Inside the Doomsday Machine*. New York: W. W. Norton, 2010.

McDonald, Lawrence G., and Patrick Robinson. *A Colossal Failure of Common Sense: The Inside Story of the Collapse of Lehman Brothers*. New York: Crown Business, 2009.

Sorkin, Andrew Ross. *Too Big to Fail: The Inside Story of How Wall Street and Washington Fought to Save the Financial System—and Themselves*. New York: Viking, 2009.

Tett, Gillian. *Fool's Gold: How the Bold Dream of a Small Tribe at J.P. Morgan Was Corrupted by Wall Street Greed and Unleashed a Catastrophe*. New York: Free Press, 2009.

Wessel, David. *In Fed We Trust: Ben Bernanke's War on the Great Panic*. New York: Crown Business, 2009.

Zuckerman, Gregory. *The Greatest Trade Ever: The Behind-the-Scenes Story of How John Paulson Defied Wall Street and Made Financial History*. New York: Broadway Business, 2009.

Academic Economics and the Financial Crisis

Cassidy, John. *How Markets Fail: The Logic of Economic Calamities*. New York: Farrar, Straus & Giroux, 2009.

Fox, Justin. *The Myth of the Rational Market: A History of Risk, Reward, and Delusion on Wall Street*. New York: Harper Business, 2009.

Economic and Policy Analyses

Goodman, Peter S. *Past Due: The End of Easy Money and the Renewal of the American Economy*. New York: Henry Holt, 2009.

Hacker, Jacob S., and Paul Pierson. *Winner-Take-All Politics: How Washington Made the Rich Richer—And Turned Its Back on the Middle Class*. New York: Simon & Schuster, 2010.

Huffington, Arianna. *Third World America: How Our Politicians Are Abandoning the Middle Class and Betraying the American Dream*. New York: Crown, 2010.

Jarsulic, Marc. *Anatomy of a Financial Crisis: A Real Estate Bubble, Runaway Credit Markets, and Regulatory Failure*. New York: Palgrave Macmillan, 2010.

Krugman, Paul. *The Return of Depression Economics and the Crisis of 2008*. New York: W. W. Norton, 2009.

Pozen, Robert. *Too Big to Save? How to Fix the U.S. Financial System*. Hoboken, NJ: Wiley, 2009.

Rajan, Raghuram G. *Fault Lines: How Hidden Fractures Still Threaten the World Economy*. Princeton: Princeton University Press, 2010.

Reich, Robert B. *Aftershock: The Next Economy and America's Future*. New York: Knopf, 2010.

Ritholtz, Barry, with Aaron Task. *Bailout Nation: How Greed and Easy Money Corrupted Wall Street and Shook the World Economy*. Hoboken, NJ: Wiley, 2009.

Roubini, Nouriel, and Stephen Mihm. *Crisis Economics: A Crash Course in the Future of Finance*. New York: Penguin Press, 2010.

Smith, Yves. *ECONned: How Unenlightened Self Interest Undermined Democracy and Corrupted Capitalism*. New York: Palgrave Macmillan, 2010.

Stiglitz, Joseph E. *Freefall: America, Free Markets, and the Sinking of the World Economy*. New York: W. W. Norton, 2010.

Subprime Lending and the Housing Bubble

Gramlich, Edward M. *Subprime Mortgages: America's Latest Boom and Bust*. Washington: Urban Institute Press, 2007.

Katz, Alyssa. *Our Lot: How Real Estate Came to Own Us*. New York: Bloomsbury, 2009.

Shiller, Robert J. *The Subprime Solution: How Today's Global Financial Crisis Happened, and What to Do About It*. Princeton: Princeton University Press, 2008.

History

Ferguson, Niall. *The Ascent of Money: A Financial History of the World.* New York: Penguin, 2008.

Frieden, Jeffry A. *Global Capitalism: Its Fall and Rise in the Twentieth Century.* New York: W. W. Norton, 2006.

Kindleberger, Charles P., and Robert Aliber. *Manias, Panics, and Crashes: A History of Financial Crises,* fifth edition. Hoboken, NJ: Wiley, 2005.

Phillips, Kevin. *Wealth and Democracy: A Political History of the American Rich.* New York: Broadway Books, 2003.

Reinhart, Carmen M., and Kenneth S. Rogoff. *This Time Is Different: Eight Centuries of Financial Folly.* Princeton: Princeton University Press, 2009.

Trading, Derivatives, and the Culture of Wall Street

Das, Satyajit. *Traders, Guns and Money: Knowns and Unknowns in the Dazzling World of Derivatives.* Harlow, England: Prentice Hall, 2006.

Lewis, Michael. *Liar's Poker: Rising Through the Wreckage on Wall Street.* New York: Penguin, 1990.

Partnoy, Frank. *F.I.A.S.C.O.: Blood in the Water on Wall Street.* New York: W. W. Norton, 2009.

———. *Infectious Greed: How Deceit and Risk Corrupted the Financial Markets.* New York: Henry Holt, 2004.

Taleb, Nassim Nicholas. *Fooled by Randomness: The Hidden Role of Chance in Life and in the Markets,* second edition. New York: Random House, 2005.

BLOGS

The financial crisis significantly increased the popularity and importance of many blogs focusing on economics, finance, and public policy. Blogs enabled commentators to offer almost immediate reactions to breaking news stories or policy announcements, and policymakers began paying attention to bloggers as an important audience. There are hundreds of worthwhile blogs that cover economics and economic policy. These are some of the ones that we read, with apologies to those that we are sure to have overlooked.

The Balance Sheet (James Surowiecki):
    http://www.newyorker.com/online/blogs/jamessurowiecki/
Beat the Press (Dean Baker):
    http://www.prospect.org/csnc/blogs/beat_the_press
Calculated Risk: http://calculatedriskblog.com
The Conscience of a Liberal (Paul Krugman):
    http://krugman.blogs.nytimes.com/
J. Bradford DeLong's Grasping Reality with Opposable Thumbs:
    http://delong.typepad.com/
Econbrowser (Menzie Chinn and James Hamilton):
    http://www.econbrowser.com/

Econlog (Arnold Kling, Bryan Caplan, and David Henderson):
  http://econlog.econlib.org/
Economists' Forum (Martin Wolf and guests):
  http://blogs.ft.com/economistsforum/
Economist's View (Mark Thoma):
  http://economistsview.typepad.com/
Economix (*New York Times* reporters and guest economists):
  http://economix.blogs.nytimes.com/
Executive Suite (Joe Nocera):
  http://executivesuite.blogs.nytimes.com/
Free Exchange (*The Economist*):
  http://www.economist.com/blogs/freeexchange/
Interfluidity (Steve Randy Waldman):
  http://www.interfluidity.com/
Ezra Klein: http://voices.washingtonpost.com/ezra-klein/
Making Sense (Paul Solman):
  http://www.pbs.org/newshour/economy/makingsense/
Greg Mankiw: http://gregmankiw.blogspot.com/
Marginal Revolution (Tyler Cowen and Alex Tabarrok):
  http://www.marginalrevolution.com/
Naked Capitalism (Yves Smith and others):
  http://www.nakedcapitalism.com/
Planet Money: http://www.npr.org/blogs/money/
Real Time Economics (*Wall Street Journal*):
  http://blogs.wsj.com/economics/
Rortybomb (Mike Konczal): http://rortybomb.wordpress.com/
Felix Salmon: http://blogs.reuters.com/felix-salmon/

Acknowledgments

This book is the product of a friendship that began twenty years ago and a collaboration that began at the peak of the financial crisis in 2008. Along the way, many people have contributed in many ways to making this book possible.

After Simon discussed the "American oligarchs" on *Bill Moyers Journal* in February 2009, Don Peck of *The Atlantic* invited us to write an article about the relationship between emerging market crises and the 2008–2009 financial crisis; that article, "The Quiet Coup," presented some of the initial ideas that developed into this book. Our agent, Rafe Sagalyn, helped us frame our ideas in book form and guided us through the world of publishing. This book would not exist without the support and assistance of our editor, Erroll McDonald, and the many other professionals at Pantheon, Knopf Doubleday, and Random House who transformed words on a computer screen into a book that you can hold in your hands—Jeff Alexander, Peter Andersen, Paul Bogaards, Fred Chase, Molly Erman, Lily Evans, Angela Hayes, Altie Karper, Dan Ozzi, Kate Runde, Sonya Safro, and no doubt others we have overlooked.

Many other friends and colleagues provided valuable assistance as we were writing this book. David Moss, Thomas Philippon, Ariell Reshef, and Robert Shiller graciously shared data or charts. Daron Acemoglu, Anders Aslund, Fred Bergsten, Jim Boughton, Ron Feldman, Peter Fox-Penner, Jeff Frieden, Joe Gagnon, Dan Geldon, Larry Glickman, Todd Gormley, Michael Greenberger, Steve Haber, Alyssa Katz, Amir Kermani, Se-Jik Kim, Mike Konczal, Pradeep Kumar, Nosup Kwak, Subir Lall, Lawrence Lessig, Richard Locke, Jonathan Macey, Bruce Mann, Matt Matera, Brad Miller, Todd Mitton, Don Peck, Mahmood Pradhan, Jim Robinson, Jeff Rosen, Marcus Ryu, Felix Salmon, Paul Solman, Alex Stricker, Arvind Subramanian, Janet Tavakoli, Zephyr Teachout, Peter Temin, Poul Thomsen, Elizabeth Warren, Steve Weisman, and Gary Witt provided feedback on specific ideas or portions of the manuscript. Rachael Brown, Hilary McClellan, Jessica Murphy, and Eleanor Smith checked thousands of the facts contained in this book. Matt Matera edited the citations in our endnotes. Matt Matera, Maggie Wittlin, and Daniel Winik pitched in with proofreading. Jonathan Macey helped James find the time for this book while a full-time student at law school.

Our work over the last year and a half has benefited from the input of editors and journalists in other media. Besides Don Peck and Bill Moyers, they include Catherine Rampell of Economix at *The New York Times;* Frank Foer, Richard Just, and Ben Eisler of *The New Republic;* Clay Risen and Ethan Porter of *Democracy: A Journal of Ideas;* and Adam Davidson and Alex Blumberg of NPR and *This American Life.*

Simon has enjoyed the constant support of many people at both MIT Sloan School of Management and the Peterson Institute for International Economics, beginning with the unflappable Deborah Cohen. He benefited from his presentations at MIT, including a joint session with Larry Fish, and from the participants in his Global Markets and Global Entrepreneurship Lab classes. Dave Schmittlein, Rob Freund, and JoAnne Yates allowed Simon to teach (on very short notice) a course on the global financial crisis, which aided in developing our ideas. Along with Steve Eppinger, S. P. Kothari, and Richard Locke, they have been consistently supportive in all regards. Simon's co-teachers—Jonathan Lehrich, Richard Locke, and Anjali Sastry—have helped make the past eighteen months possible. Fred Bergsten, head of the Peterson Institute, provided a unique environment for constructive debate. Generous funding from the Smith-Richardson Foundation and from Lynn Rothschild was a great help. Among Simon's many colleagues at Peterson, Arvind Subramanian and Steve Weisman deserve special thanks for their availability and feedback.

Many of our ideas were first presented on our blog, *The Baseline Scenario,* where they received the benefit of scrutiny from hundreds of thousands of readers and constructive criticism from thousands of commenters. Without the readers who make it worthwhile, the blog would not exist; and without the blog, this book would almost certainly not exist. Graham Smith, one of our readers, suggested the quotation from *The Great Gatsby* that is the epigraph to this book. We have also learned and benefited tremendously from interactions over the Internet with the large, vibrant, and growing community of economics, finance, and public policy bloggers; for a small selection, see the Further Reading section. In addition, even a brief glance at the Notes will demonstrate that we could not have researched this book without the tremendous work done by many journalists to investigate the causes and the course of the financial crisis.

Peter Boone worked closely with us on several major articles for our blog and for other publications, including "The Next Financial Crisis: It's Coming—and We Just Made It Worse," in *The New Republic.* Peter's unparalleled insights into financial markets and the global economy helped us develop and hone many of the ideas presented here.

We owe a deep debt of gratitude to our families. James would like to thank his parents, Nosup Kwak and Inkyung Liu, for so many things, including giving him the interest in public affairs that eventually led to this book; his sister, Mary Kwak, for her encouragement over many years; his wife, Sylvia Brandt, for her constant support and understanding; Ed and Faydine Brandt for their invaluable help over the past several years; and his daughter, Willow, for being the happiest little girl in the world. Simon thanks his parents, Ian and Cedar Johnson, for favoring education above all else; his wife, Mary Kwak, for being the best through thick and thin; and his daughters, Celia and Lucie, for putting everything in its proper perspective and (they now remind him) for giving him the time that made this book possible. We both thank Mary for reading and editing the entire manuscript; no one else could have done what she did.

Index

Page numbers in *italics* refer to figures.

Randall, Willard Sterne, 236*n*
Ranieri, Lewis, 72, 73, 76, 111, 261*n*
Raso, Connor, 168, 273*n*
rational bubbles, 132
Reagan, Ronald, 57, 252*n*, 255*n*
  deregulation as crusade of, 65, 70–1,
    74, 150
Reagan administration, 72–3, 100
real economy, U.S., 173
  financial reform and, 194
  financial sector vs., 59–60, *61*,
    121–2, 182
  2007–9 financial crisis and, 182–4
real estate
  commercial, 129
  housing, *see* housing sector
real estate investment trusts (REITs),
  129
Real Estate Mortgage Investment
  Conduit (REMIC), 73
recession of 2007–9, *see* financial crisis
  of 2007–9
Reddy, Suddep, 272*n*
Regan, Donald, 65, 71, 83, 134
Regions Bank, 170*fn*
regulation, *see* financial regulation
Regulation Q, 35, 66, 67
regulatory capital arbitrage (RCA),
  138
Reich, Robert, 98, 187
Reilly, David, 270*n*
Reinhart, Carmen M., 183, 272*n*, 276*n*
Reisenhuber, Eva, 251*n*
Remini, Robert V., 238*n*, 244*n*
Repackaged Asset Vehicles, 123
Republican administrations, 23
  deregulation and, 30–1
Republican Party, 99
  economic elites and, 22, 23
Reserve Primary Fund, 163, 201
Reshef, Ariell, 63, 78, 115–16, 254*n*,
  262*n*
resolution authority, 205–7
return on equity, of derivatives trades,
  8*fn*
reverse convertibles, 107, 196

revolving door, *see* Wall
  Street–Washington corridor
Reynolds, David, 239*n*
Reynolds, Maura, 276*n*
Rhee, Changyong, 245*n*
Rhoades, Stephen A., 282*n*
Richards, Anthony, 251*n*
Richardson, James D., 237*n*
Richardson, Matthew, 176, 274*n*
Riegle-Neal Interstate Banking and
  Branching Efficiency Act (1994),
    84, 89
Rieker, Matthias, 252*n*
risk, risk-taking, 29, 30, 33, 37, 46, 65,
    211, 219, 221
  financial innovation and, 103–4, 106
  by investment banks, 34, 57, 62, 152,
    157, 215, 216
  by megabanks, 11, 86, 133, 147–8,
    151, 177, 182, 193, 194, 204, 207,
    213, 222
  moral hazard and, 29, 30, 173, 177,
    189
  regulatory oversight and, 65, 103,
    120–1, 206, 210
  shifting of, 30, 88, 102, 106, 107–8,
    130–1, 132
  structured financial products and,
    123–4, 126, 130–1, 138
  unbundling of, 106–9
  see also speculation
RJR Nabisco, 114
Roberts, Janet, 279*n*
Robertson Stephens, 85
Robinson, James A., 238*n*, 239*n*, 251*n*
Rodrik, Dani, 255*n*
Rogoff, Kenneth S., 183, 272*n*, 276*n*
Rohe, William M., 110, 261*n*
Rohr, James, 4*fn*
Roig-Franzia, Manuel, 234*n*, 260*n*
Romer, Christina A., 187, 244*n*
Romer, Paul M., 48, 74*fn*, 249*n*, 256*n*
Roosevelt, Franklin D., 18, 33–4, 37,
  244*n*
Roosevelt, Theodore, 6, 14, 18, 23, 25,
  29, 220, 221, 222, 235*n*, 240*n*